Core Exam

Core Exam

Accelerated A+ Certification Study Guide

Total Seminars, LLC

McGraw-Hill
New York • San Francisco • Washington, D.C. • Auckland
Bogotá • Caracas • Lisbon • London • Madrid • Mexico City
Milan • Montreal • New Delhi • San Juan • Singapore
Sydney • Tokyo • Toronto

Library of Congress Cataloging-in-Publication Data

Core exam / Total Seminars LLC.
p. cm.—(Accelerated A+ certification study guide)
Includes index.
ISBN 0-07-044466-8
1. Electronic data processing personnel—Certification—Study guides 2. Computer technicians—Certification—Study guides.
I. Total Seminars LLC. II. Series.
QA76.3.C67 1998
621.39'16'076—dc21 98-33237
CIP

McGraw-Hill

A Division of The ***McGraw-Hill*** *Companies*

1 2 3 4 5 6 7 8 9 0 AGM/AGM 9 0 3 2 1 0 9 8

ISBN 0-07-044466-8

The sponsoring editor for this book was Michael Sprague and the production supervisor was Clare Stanley. It was set by D & G Limited, LLC.

Printed and bound by Quebecor/Martinsburg.

This book is printed on recycled, acid-free paper containing a minimum of 50% recycled de-inked fiber.

Contents

1 The Visible PC **1**

The Visible PC 1

Get Thee to a Screwdriver! 1

2 Microprocessors **45**

Understanding Microprocessors 45

External Data Bus 47

The 486 CPU Family 75

The Pentium CPU—the Early Years 90

Early Pentium Competitors 97

The Pentium Pro (P6) 102

Later Pentiums 104

Pentium II 106

3 Power Supplies **111**

The One Truly Standard Piece of Equipment in Your PC 111

Motherboard Connections 113

Connections to Peripherals 115

When Power Supplies Die 120

Switches 123

When Power Supplies Die Hard 125

Danger, Will Robinson, Danger!! 125

4 RAM **127**

What is RAM? 127

DRAM 128

RAM Packaging: Part I 136

Banking 143

RAM Packaging: Part 2 148

Improvements on DRAM 154

Troubleshooting RAM 161

5 Motherboards and BIOS **163**
Motherboards & BIOS 163
The Communications Gap 163
BIOS 164
POST—Power on Self Test 185
Motherboard Layouts 194
Motherboard Installation and Replacement 198

6 Expansion Bus **203**
It's The Crystals, Dammit! 204
History of PC Expansion Busses — Part 1 206
I/O Addresses 208
Interrupts 216
COM and LPT Ports 219
Back to the 8259 222
DMA 226
History of Expansion Busses — Part 2 231

7 Floppy Drives **241**
History 241
Care and Feeding of Floppy Drives 246
Repairing Floppy Drives 246

8 Hard Drives **249**
Inside the Drive 249
Why Geometry? 256
IDE/EIDE 257
The Old Stuff 284
ST506 284
ESDI 286

9 SCSI **289**
What is SCSI? 289
SCSI Flavors 297
SCSI-1 298
SCSI-2 299
Beyond SCSI-2 301
Bus Mastering 303
SCSI Cabling & Connectors 305
Cable/Bus Lengths 306

ASPI 307
ASPI 308
SCSI Performance 309
Compatibility among Flavors of SCSI 310
Compatibility with IDE and Other Standards 310
Repair/Troubleshooting 311
Cost/Benefit 313
RAID 315
Other Storage Options 316
Additional Facts from Adaptec Technical Support Line 316

10 Video 319

Video—Complex Choices 319
Video Monitor Components 320
Troubleshooting Monitors 334
Video Cards 338
Resolution, Color Depth and Memory Requirements 343
Video Memory 345

11 Printers 349

Impact Printers 349
Ink Jet Printers 352
Laser Printers 353
Parallel Communication 374

12 Portable PCs 383

History 386
Laptops 388
Batteries 394
LCD Displays 398
PC Cards 399
Power Management 403

INTRODUCTION

The A+ Certification

In this introduction, we will learn about the following concepts:

- Understanding the importance of A+ Certification.
- Discovering the structure and goals of the exam.
- Receiving the *where's, when's,* and *how much* for the exams.

The Path to A+ Certification

Since the inception of microcomputers in the late '70s, there has been no common way for a PC technician to show clients or employers they know what they are doing under the hood of a personal computer. Sure, there have been vendor-specific certifications, but the only way to receive them was to get a job at an authorized warranty or repair facility first, and then earn the certification. There is nothing wrong with vendor-specific training, but no one manufacturer has taken enough market share to make that IBM or Compaq training something that works for any job. Then, there is always that little detail of getting the job first before you can become certified.

Until recently, there also has been no nationally recognized certification for PC technicians to show a certain level of competence.

Techs have not had a piece of paper to put on their wall or a pin to stick on their chest to show they know their stuff—until now. Welcome to A+ Certification.

What is A+ Certification?

A+ Certification is an industry-wide, vendor-neutral program developed and sponsored by the *Computing Technology Industry Association* (CompTIA). Receiving an A+ Certification shows that you have a basic competence in supporting microcomputers. The goal is to test what is generally assumed to be the knowledge of a technician with six months of full-time PC support experience. You achieve this certification by taking two computer-based multiple-choice examinations. This certification is widely recognized throughout the computer industry and significantly improves a technician's ability to secure and keep employment.

What is CompTIA?

CompTIA is a non-profit, industry trade association based in Lombard, IL. It consists of more than 7,500 computer resellers, *value-added-resellers* (VARs), distributors, manufacturers, and training companies throughout the United States and Canada. Only companies and organizations are members of CompTIA—there are no individual memberships.

The goal of CompTIA is to provide a forum for networking (as in meeting people), to represent the interests of its members in government and to provide certifications for many different aspects of the computer industry. Currently, their only significant certification is A+. Check out the CompTIA Web site at `http://www.comptia.org` for details on the other certifications you can obtain from CompTIA.

How Do I Become A+ Certified?

You pass two computer-based multiple-choice exams. That is it. There are no prerequisites for A+ Certification. You pay the testing fee and take the two exams. You will immediately know whether you have passed or failed. If you pass both exams, you are an *A+ Certified Service Technician*. There are no requirements for professional experience. You do not have to go through an authorized training center. There are no annual dues. There are no continuing education requirements. You pass, and you are in. That is it. Now, here are the details.

The two exams are called the *A+ Core* and the *A+ DOS/Windows* examinations. The Core exam concentrates on the aspects of the PC that are not operating system-specific. This test is primarily a hardware identification and configuration exam. The DOS/Windows exam concentrates on the organization, operation, function, and troubleshooting of DOS, Windows 3.X, and Windows 95. This exam also includes basic network and Internet configuration questions.

What Are the Tests Like, and How Are They Structured?

Both of the exams are extremely practical, with little or no questions relating to theory. All questions are multiple-choice. You should schedule to take both exams at the same time.

Core Exam

The Core exam consists of 69 multiple-choice questions. You need about 65 percent correct to pass (you will be told the exact score needed to pass when you take the exam, because it is a function of which questions are on the exam you are taking). All of the Core exam questions fit into one of eight areas, called *domains*. The number of questions for each domain is based on the percentages.

1. Installation, Configuration and Upgrading	30%
2. Diagnosing and Troubleshooting	20%
3. Safety and Preventive Maintenance	10%
4. Motherboard/Processors/Memory	10%
5. Printers	10%
6. Portable Systems	5%
7. Basic Networking	5%
8. Customer Satisfaction	10%

NOTE

Since customer satisfaction is a key aspect of providing microcomputer hardware service, this exam will include questions that measure your knowledge of effective behaviors that contribute to customer satisfaction. The customer satisfaction questions will be scored but will not impact your final pass/fail score on the exam. It will be important, however, to

respond to these questions, because customer satisfaction scores will be reported on your final score report. An employer also may ask to see these details, besides knowing that you passed the A+ exam.

The core exam tests your understanding of hardware at a fairly deep level. You should be able to recognize, clean, handle, install, diagnose, understand the function of, and know the different types of each of these components:

CPUs

RAM

Motherboards

Power supplies

ROM/CMOS

Expansion busses

Floppy drives

IDE drives

SCSI devices

CD-ROMs

Video cards

Monitors

Modems

Printers

Cables and connectors

Laptops

Network hubs and cabling

You should be able to install physically any device into a PC and completely assemble a standard PC. You should recognize every cable, every connector, and every plug used in a PC. The Core exam assumes that you are comfortable with basic troubleshooting. You should be able to pick an obvious *first step* for a broad cross-section of symptoms linked to the mentioned hardware and software. You also should be comfortable with the tools used for PC assembly and disassembly.

You should be quite comfortable with I/O addressing, IRQs, and DMAs. You will be tested on your knowledge of I/O addresses and IRQs assigned to COM and LPT ports. You should know the default functions for all IRQs and DMAs, as well as for the most common I/O addresses. You must be able to look at a diagram for jumpers or switches and be able to set them properly for all possible I/O addresses, IRQs or DMAs. A good knowledge of basic binary is assumed, because many switches and jumpers use binary.

The network section is very basic. Make sure that you can recognize the different types of network cabling and their capacities and limits. You should be able to recognize the different topologies and understand their benefits and weaknesses. You will be tested on the different protocols used, and you should know when to use one protocol instead of another. Finally, you should be able to diagnose basic network problems.

You should be comfortable with basic electrical components and the proper use of *Volt-Ohm-Meters* (VOMs) to test them. You should be able to identify basic electrical components and their electronic symbols. The A+ Core exam also requires you to be comfortable with the control of *electro-static discharge* (ESD) and *electro-magnetic interference* (EMI).

Last, the Core exam assumes that you are comfortable with both binary and hexadecimal in the context of practical use in PC configuration.

The Customer Satisfaction questions are graded, but are not added to the total score for determining whether you pass or fail the A+ Core exam. You can miss every Customer Satisfaction question, and it will not affect your grade. These questions have been added as a service to CompTIA members who wish to test their employee's Customer Satisfaction skills. It is a good idea to do your best on these questions, because your employer (present or future) may ask to see your exam score report to see how you did on those questions. This book does not cover Customer Satisfaction, because these questions do not affect the A+ exams final score.

The following is an example of the types of questions you will see on the exam:

A dot-matrix printer is printing blank pages. The first item to check is:

A. The printer drivers

B. The platen

C. The printhead

D. The ribbon

The correct answer is D— the ribbon. You can make an argument for any of the others, but common sense tells you to check the simplest possibility first.

DOS/WINDOWS EXAM

The DOS/Windows exam consists of 70 questions. You need about 66 percent to pass. The DOS/Windows exam follows the ideas of the Core exam, assuming all of the same hardware and software knowledge that you need to pass the Core. The DOS/Windows exam, however, takes a strong slant toward understanding DOS, Windows 3.X, and Windows 95. All of the DOS/Windows exam questions fit into one of five domains. The number of questions for each domain is based on the percentages.

1. Function, Structure, Operation, and File Management	30%
2. Memory Management	10%
3. Installation, Configuration, and Upgrading	25%
4. Troubleshooting	25%
5. Networks and the Internet	10%

From a hardware standpoint, you will be expected to know how to install and configure all the hardware devices mentioned in the Core exam in a DOS or Windows PC. Make sure you are comfortable with the concept of device drivers and how to edit any settings in DOS (using the `CONFIG.SYS` file), Windows 3.X (using the `CONFIG.SYS` and `SYSTEM.INI` files), or Windows 95 (using the `CONFIG.SYS` and `SYSTEM.INI` files and Device Manager).

This exam is extremely concerned with drive access. Be sure to understand disk caching and swapping files and ramdrives in DOS, Windows 3.X, and Windows 95. Also, know how to defragment and scan a drive for errors, using standard DOS and Windows tools. Last, make sure you can completely install a drive, from plugging it in to running Windows.

The DOS/Windows exam aggressively tests your knowledge of DOS. If it is a file in the \DOS directory, know it. You should be comfortable with the proper configuration of the boot files `AUTOEXEC.BAT` and `CONFIG.SYS`. Another area that catches many of people off-guard is that the test assumes you can easily work from the DOS prompt. You must understand DOS filename conventions. You need to be able to copy, move, and delete files from the DOS prompt. You also need to be able to create and delete directories. Be sure to know how to use the ATTRIB command and understand the different types of attributes.

The DOS/Windows exam asks a number of questions regarding system optimization. This includes DOS memory management, caching, and power management. You will be tested on your ability to configure hardware, CMOS, boot files, and TSRs to optimize a system properly.

The DOS/Windows exam covers Windows 3.X and Windows 95 in a similar fashion. First, you must know the structure, organization and critical files of both Windows 3.X (Win3) and Windows 95 (Win95). Be sure to know the important .INI files and the main sections of the Registry—and how to edit them.

Last, the DOS/Windows exam will challenge your knowledge of boot options. Verify that you know how to boot Windows 95 into Safe Mode—and know why you can or should do it.

HOW DO I TAKE THE TESTS?

The tests are administered by Sylvan Prometric. There are thousands of Sylvan Prometric testing centers across the United States and Canada, as well as in 75 other countries around the world. You may take the exam at any testing center. In the U.S. and Canada, call Sylvan Prometric at (800) 77-MICRO to schedule the exams and to locate the nearest testing center. Internationally, CompTIA works in conjunction with *The Association for Services Management International* (AFSMI). To register, go to CompTIA's Web site at `www.comptia.org` and go to *How to Register* on the A+ Certification page. The contacts for each country are listed by region. You must pay for the exam when you call to schedule. Be prepared to sit on hold for a while. Have your social security number and a credit card ready when you call. Sylvan Prometric will be glad to issue an invoice, but you will not be able to take the test until it receives full payment.

How Much Does it Cost?

The cost of the exam depends on whether you work for a CompTIA member or not. Also, there are discounts for taking both exams at once. At the time I am writing this, the cost for non-CompTIA members is $120 for one exam or $215 for two exams together. There are also discounts for CompTIA members. These prices are subject to change.

You must pass both exams within 90 days to be A+ Certified. You do not have to pass the Core exam before you can take the DOS/Windows exam. If you pass one exam and fail another, you must repay and retake the other exam within 90 days. You must pay for every test you take, whether you pass or fail. If you fail to pass both exams within 90 days, you will have to pay for and retake BOTH exams.

How to Pass the A+ Exam

The single most important aspect to remember about A+ Certification is that the exams are designed to test the knowledge of a new technician with only six months' experience, so keep it simple. The tests are not interested in your ability to set DRAM timings in the CMOS manually or your ability to explain the differences between the Intel 430TX and 430VX chipset. Do not bother with a lot of theory. The fact that you can do hex-to-binary conversions in your head will not help a bit. Think in terms of practical knowledge. Read the book, seriously review any topics you do not know, and you will pass with no problem.

If you have any problems or questions, or if you just want to argue about something, feel free to send an e-mail to the author: michaelm@totalsem.com.

Computing Technology Industry Association (CompTIA)

450 E. 22nd Street
Suite 230
Lombard, IL 60148-6158
Contact: Kelle Veverka, public relations manager
Internet Address:

http://www.comptia.org

Telephone:
(630)268-1818
Fax:
(630) 268-1384
E-mail:
General information: info@comptia.org

CHAPTER 1

The Visible PC

The Visible PC

In this chapter, we will

- See the major components of a PC
- Understand the different connectors in the PC
- Recognize the most common cards in a PC
- Learn how to set jumpers and switches

Get Thee to a Screwdriver!

Sometimes, in order to understand the details, you first need to understand the big picture. This chapter's job is to allow you to understand the function and to be able to recognize the main components of the CPU. Also, we will see all of the major connectors, the plugs and sockets, and be able to recognize a particular part by simply seeing what type of connectors that are attached to that part. Even if you are an expert, don't skip this chapter! It introduces a large amount of terms that will be used throughout the rest of the book. Many of these terms you will know and some you won't, so take some time and read it!

If you have a PC, it is handy, although certainly not required, to take the lid off and inspect as we progress. So get thee to a screwdriver, grab a PC, take off the lid, and see if you can recognize the various components on your PC as they are discussed.

If you want to get to techs into a fight, strip them down to their underwear, throw them into a padded cell, and just before you lock them in, yell "A good PC tech toolkit contains . . . " and then quickly close the door! There's a lot of room for argument about what tools you should carry. Here's a quick list of my tools:

Large Phillips screwdriver

Small Phillips screwdriver

Large regular screwdriver

Small regular screwdriver

3/16" Nut driver

7/32" Nut driver

1/4" Nut driver

Torx® wrench set: T-10 and T-15 sizes only (Torx® are star-shaped screws that are relatively popular among PC makers. They require special Torx® screwdrivers)

Curved hemostats

Retractable claw pickup tool

1 or 2 storage tubes for loose screws

Anti-static wrist strap

Small notepad and pen

Can of pressurized air

Feel free to add or subtract as you become more comfortable with the tools you need. Also, remember that the more tools you add, the more tools you carry.

CPU

The *Central Processing Unit* (CPU, also called the microprocessor) is where all the calculations take place in the PC. CPUs come in a variety of shapes and sizes (see Figure 1.1). The most common shapes in today's PC will be either *Pin Grid Array* (PGA) or *Single Edge Cartridge* (SEC).

Figure 1.1 Typical CPUs.

NOTE

Modern CPUs generate a lot of heat. To cool the CPU, a cooling fan or a heatsink is attached to the CPU (see Figure 1.2). The cooling device is usually removable, although some CPU manufacturers sell the CPU with a fan permanently attached.

Figure 1.2 Installed CPU under a fan.

CPUs have a *make* and a *model*, just like an automobile. When talking about a particular car, we say terms such as *Ford Taurus*. When we talk about a CPU, we say terms like *Intel 486* or *AMD K6* (see Figure 1.3). Some of the more common makes are AMD, Cyrix, and Intel. Some of the more common models are 8088, 286, 386, 486, Pentium, Pentium Pro, K5, K6, and 6x86. In the early years of CPUs, makers would sometime make the exact same models. You could get an AMD 486 or an Intel 486. This is no longer true, although some models are very similar, like the Intel Pentium and the Cyrix 6x86.

Figure 1.3 One AMD 486 and one Intel 486.

CPUs have a top speed that is determined at the factory. This is called the *clock speed,* and is measured in a unit called a *Megahertz* (MHz). The first CPU used in PCs had a clock speed in the range of 4.77 MHz. Today's CPUs have clock speeds approaching 500 MHz. When we are talking about a CPU, we say the make, the model, and the clock speed. For example, we would say "Intel Pentium Pro, 180 MHz." CPUs of the same make and model are produced with many different clock speeds. For example, the Intel Pentium Pro comes in three different speeds: 166, 180, and 200 MHz. The main reason for picking one speed over another is primarily the thickness of your wallet.

RAM

Random Access Memory (RAM) is where the CPU stores programs and data that it is currently using. RAM is measured in units called *bytes.* Modern PCs have many millions of bytes of RAM, so for convenience, RAM is measured in units called *Megabytes.* An average PC will usually have anywhere from 8 Megabytes up to 64 Megabytes of RAM, although it can easily have more or less. There are many different ways that RAM has been packaged over the years. The two most current packages are called *Single In-line Memory Modules* (SIMMs) and *Dual In-line Memory Modules* (DIMMs); see Figure 1.4.

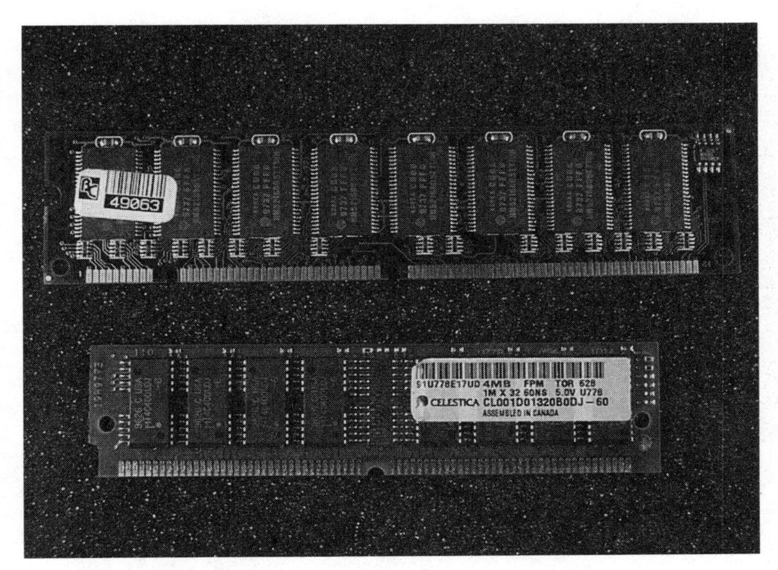

Figure 1.4 SIMM and DIMM RAM packages.

There are many different sizes of SIMMs and DIMMs. The two most common sizes of SIMMs are 30-pin and 72-pin (see Figure 1.5). It's easy to tell the difference between them because the 72-pin SIMM is much larger than the 30-pin SIMM. 72-pin SIMMs are more modern, and are designed to hold more Megabytes than 30-pin SIMMs. 72-pin SIMMs can also transfer information to and from the CPU faster than 30-pin SIMMs.

There are also two different sizes of DIMMs used by PCs. These are called the *168-pin DIMM* and the *72-pin SO DIMM.* The SO DIMM is very small and its small size makes it very popular in laptops. Only the 168-pin DIMMs are commonly used in desktop PCs (see Figure 1.6).

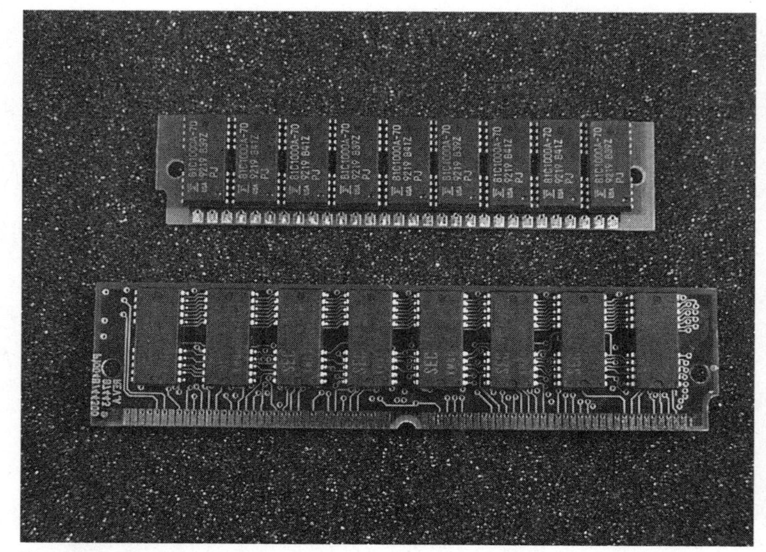

Figure 1.5 30 and 72-pin SIMM.

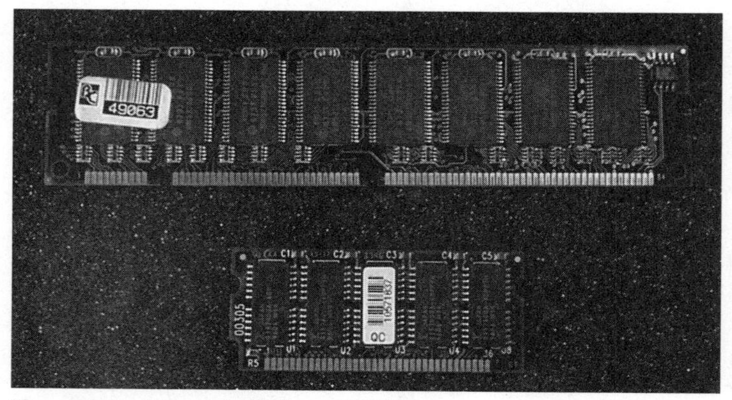

Figure 1.6 168-pin DIMM and SO-DIMM.

MOTHERBOARD

The motherboard is like a car chassis. In a car, everything is connected to the chassis, either directly or indirectly. In a PC, everything is connected to the motherboard, either directly or indirectly. A motherboard is a thin, flat piece of circuit board, usually of green or gold color, and typically slightly larger than a piece of paper (see Figure 1.7).

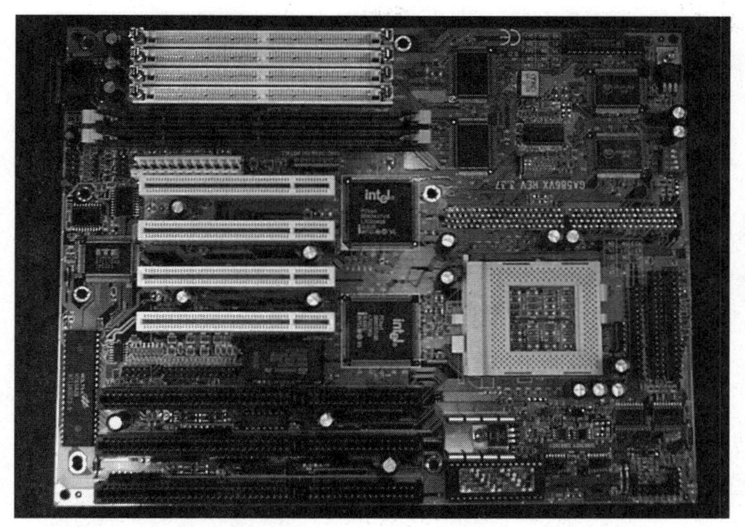

Figure 1.7 Photo of bare motherboard.

A motherboard has a number of special sockets that accept the various PC components. There are sockets for the microprocessor... (see Figure 1.8).

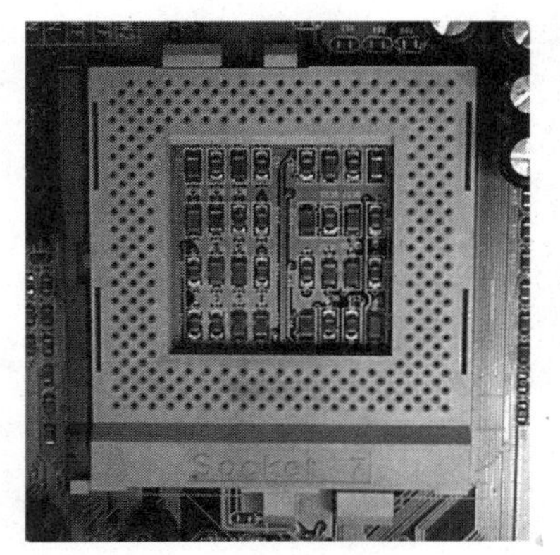

Figure 1.8 Socket for CPU.

Sockets for RAM... (see Figure 1.9).

Figure 1.9 Sockets for RAM.

Sockets to provide power... (see Figure 1.10).

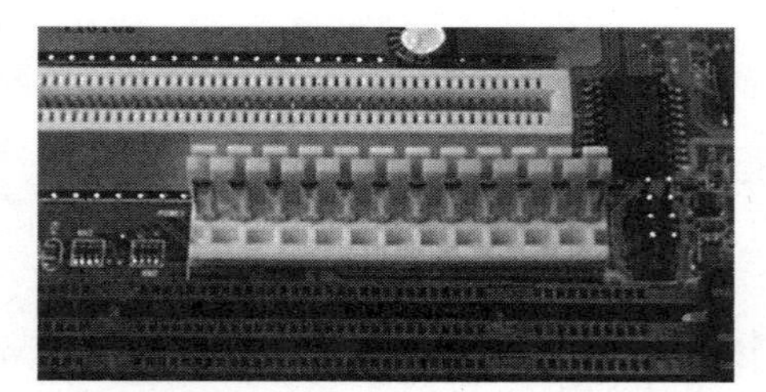

Figure 1.10 Sockets for power plugs.

Connectors for floppy drives and hard drives...(see Figure 1.11).

Figure 1.11 Floppy and hard drive connectors.

As well as connectors for external devices such as mice, printers, joysticks and keyboards (see Figure 1.12).

Figure 1.12 Various external connectors.

A few components are soldered directly to the motherboard (see Figure 1.13).

Figure 1.13 Soldered components.

Between the various devices, the motherboard is filled with tiny wires, called *traces*, which electrically link the various components of the PC together (see Figure 1.14).

Figure 1.14 Traces.

All motherboards also have multi-purpose *expansion slots* that allow the addition of optional components. There are thousands of different types of optional devices that can be added to a PC. These devices include scanners, modems, network cards, sound cards, tape backups, etc. The expansion slots are the connections that allow optional devices to communicate with the PC. The device used to connect to the expansion slots is generically called an *expansion card* or just a *card* (see Figure 1.15). There are different types of expansion slots for different types of cards.

Figure 1.15 Expansion slots—one slot has a card inserted.

The positions of the expansion slots and external components are very standardized. They have to be. The motherboard is mounted to the box or case, which is the part of the PC that you actually see (see Figure 1.16).

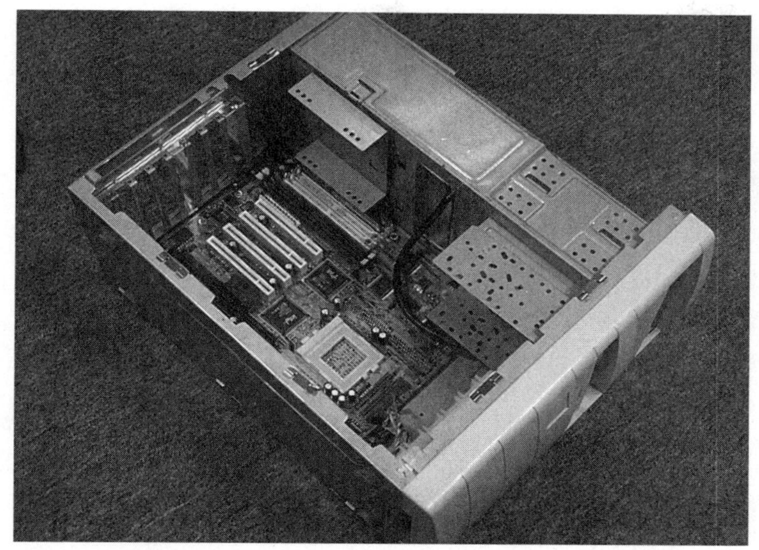

Figure 1.16 Motherboard in box.

The box needs to have holes that allow devices to be able to access the external connectors (see Figure 1.17). For example, if the motherboard has a connector for a keyboard, there has to be a hole in the box through which the keyboard plug is inserted!

Figure 1.17 Keyboard socket visible through hole in box.

Equally important, if the expansion slots allow us to add cards to the PC, then there also must be holes that allow different devices to connect to their cards (see Figure 1.18).

Figure 1.18 Inserted card from back of PC.

Clearly, there must be a certain type of box to go with a certain type, or layout, of motherboard. Fortunately, there are very few different layouts of motherboard, requiring only a few different types of boxes. We'll visit this in more detail later.

POWER SUPPLY

The power supply, as its name implies, provides the necessary electrical power to make the PC operate. The power supply takes standard 110 volt AC power and converts it into 12, 5 and sometimes 3.3 volt DC power. The vast majority of power supplies are about the size of a shoebox cut in half and are usually gray or metal colored (see Figure 1.19).

Leading out of the power supply are several connectors. There is one set of connectors for the motherboard...(see Figure 1.20).

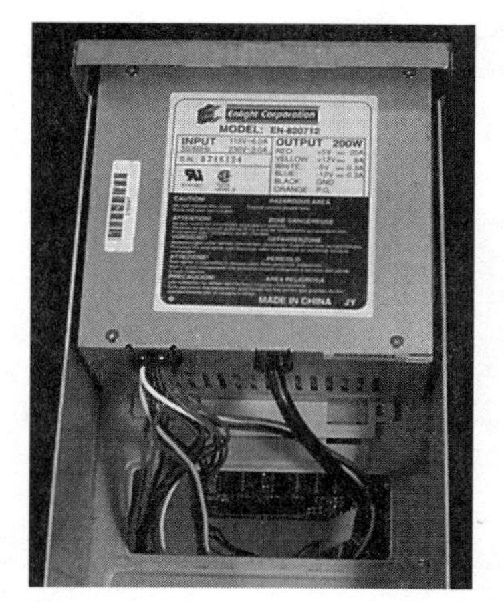

Figure 1.19 Typical power supply.

Figure 1.20 Power connectors for motherboard.

And a number of other *general use* connectors that are used to provide power to any device that needs electricity (see Figure 1.21).

On most PCs, the back of the power supply is visible, with a connection for the power plug. There is always a fan that is used to keep the interior of the PC cool (see Figure 1.22).

Figure 1.21 General use power connectors.

Figure 1.22 Power supply fan.

FLOPPY DRIVE

The floppy drive allows you to access floppy diskettes. There are two types of floppy drives, a 3 1/2" and a 5 1/2" (see Figure 1.23). The 5 1/2" drive is completely obsolete but is still encountered on older PCs.

The floppy drive is connected to the computer via a 34-pin ribbon cable, which in turn is connected to the floppy controller. In early PCs, the floppy controller was a special card that was inserted into an expansion slot. Today's PCs all have the floppy controller built into the motherboard (see Figure 1.24).

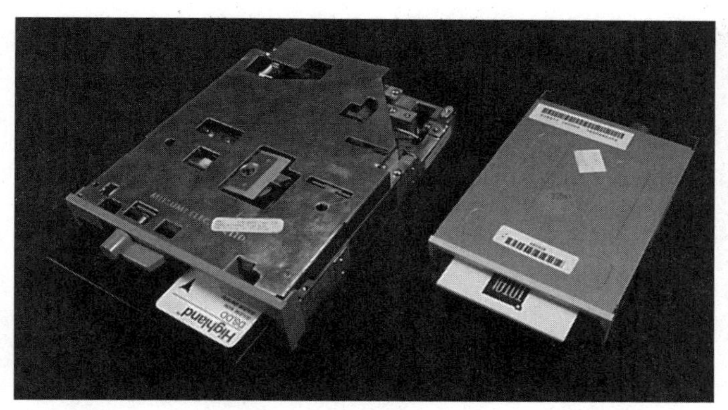

Figure 1.23 3 1/2" and 5 1/2" floppy drives.

Figure 1.24 On-board floppy controller.

Floppy ribbon cables are different from any other type of cable in two ways. First, they are the narrowest ribbon cable, only slightly more than 1" wide. Second, there is a twist in the cable, usually close to where the floppy cable is connected to the floppy drive (see Figure 1.25).

A PC can support up to two floppy drives. If a PC has two floppy drives, they will be connected to the same ribbon cable (see Figure 1.26).

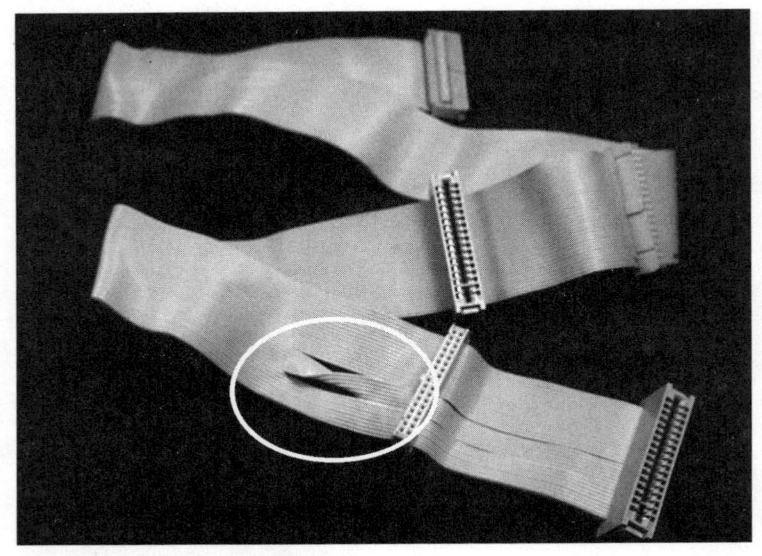

Figure 1.25 Floppy drive cable.

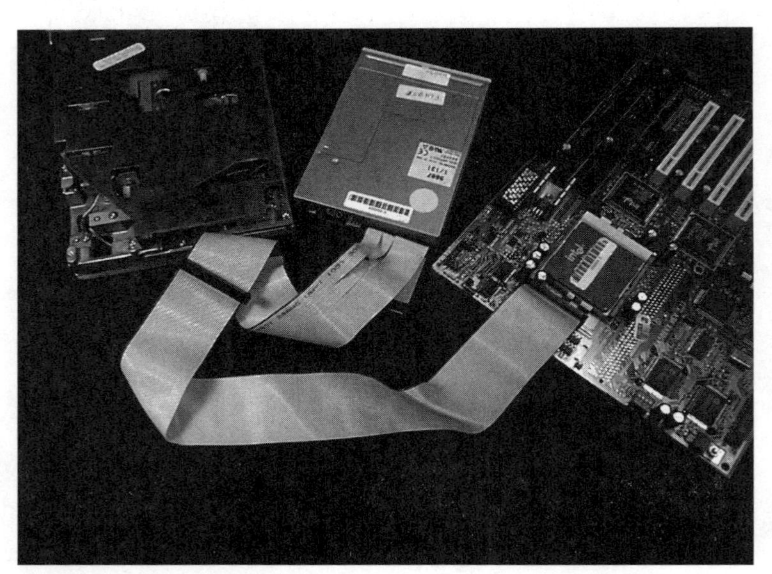

Figure 1.26 Two floppy drives.

Last, floppy drives need power and must have one of the power connectors attached to supply power to them (see Figure 1.27).

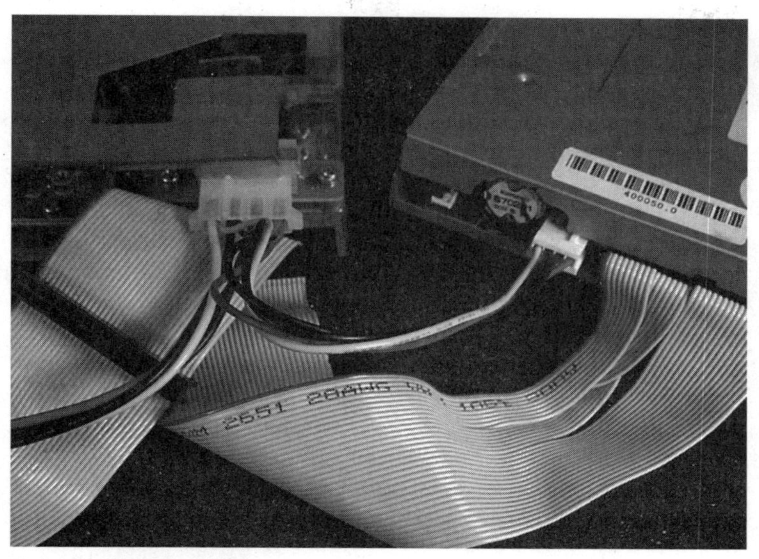

Figure 1.27 Floppy drive power connectors.

HARD DRIVE

Hard drives store programs and data that are not currently being used by the CPU. Like RAM, a hard drive capacity is measured in Megabytes. Unlike RAM, however, a hard drive capacity will be measured in the hundreds or thousands of Megabytes. Because most hard drives have capacities of over 1000 Megabytes, most hard drives capacities are measured in *Gigabytes*—roughly 1000 Megabytes. An average PC will have at least one hard drive (see Figure 1.28). The capacity of a single hard drive can vary from as low as 10 Megabytes (very old systems) up to 4 Gigabytes. The average size hard drive for new systems today is slightly over 2 Gigabytes.

There are two common types of hard drives: IDE and SCSI. IDE drives are far more common in the average PC. SCSI drives tend to be more common in high-end PCs such as network servers or graphics workstations. Any PC might have IDE, SCSI, or both installed. SCSI and IDE drives look quite similar (see Figure 1.29). They are both sized the same, about the same size as a floppy drive, but will use a wider ribbon cables. These cables will have no twist.

IDE drives use a roughly 1 1/2" wide, 40-pin ribbon cable, while SCSI drives will use a roughly 2" wide, 50-pin cable.

Figure 1.28 Typical hard drive.

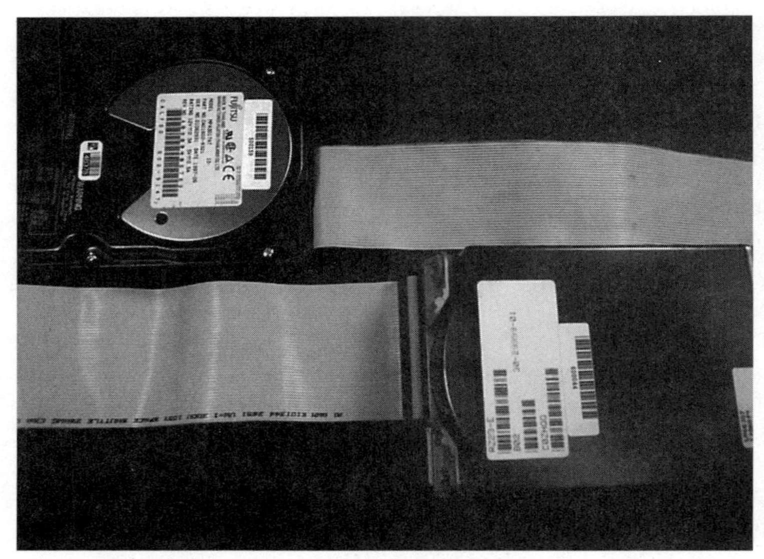

Figure 1.29 IDE and SCSI hard drives with cables.

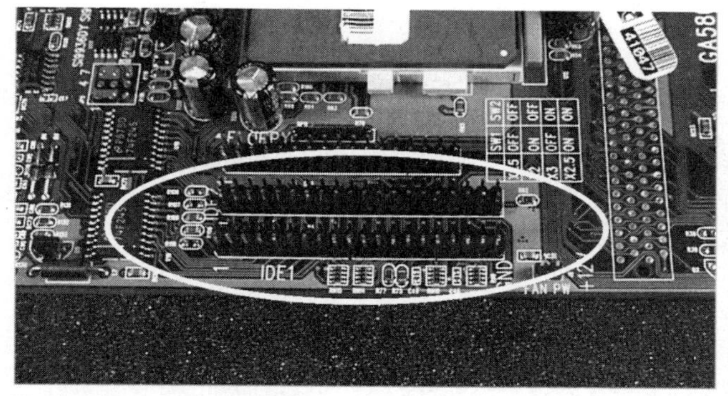

Figure 1.30 On-board IDE controllers.

Because IDE drives are so common, they will usually have the controller built into the motherboard. Years ago, there was only one controller, although today motherboards have two controllers. Some older systems will have the controllers on a card.

IDE supports up to two hard drives per controller (see Figure 1.31). Each ribbon cable therefore has two connectors for hard drives. With two controllers, each controlling two drives, a PC can support up to four IDE drives.

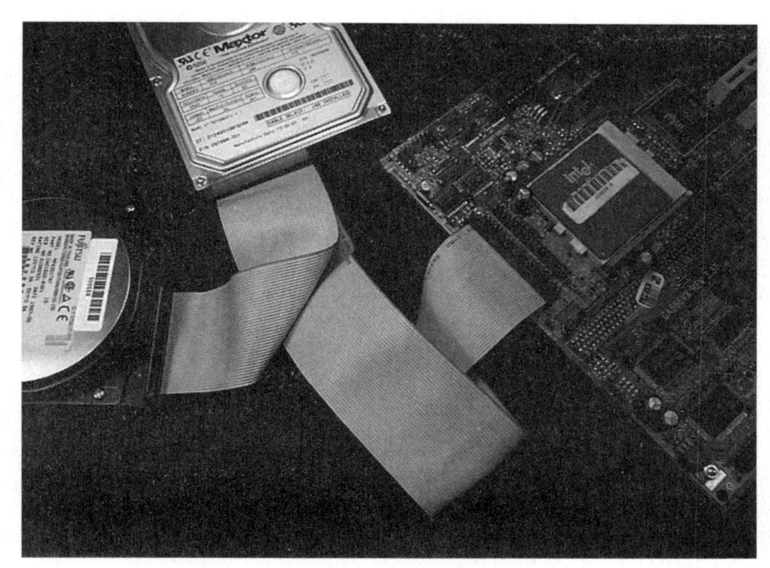

Figure 1.31 Two IDE drives on one controller.

SCSI drives may look like IDE drives, but they are quite different on the inside. First, very few motherboards have SCSI controllers. You usually need to buy a special card called a SCSI host adapter. Also, you can put more than two SCSI drives on the same ribbon. It's not at all uncommon to see CD-ROMs, tape backups, or other devices connected to the same ribbon cable as the SCSI hard drive (see Figure 1.32).

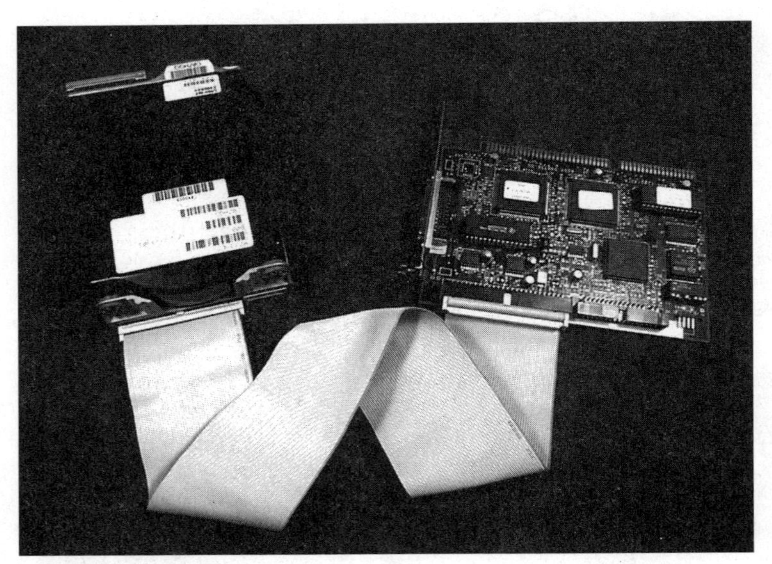

Figure 1.32 SCSI chain.

One thing that IDE and SCSI share is the need for electricity. Every drive needs to be connected to a power connector (see Figure 1.33).

CD-ROM

CD-ROM drives allow the system to access CD-ROM disks. CD-ROM drives are quite large, usually the single largest component inside the PC (see Figure 1.34). With the front of the CD-ROM visible in the front of the PC, and its boxy shape and metallic color, the CD-ROM drive is hard to miss.

Figure 1.33 Hard drive power connector.

Figure 1.34 Typical CD-ROM drive.

When CD-ROMs were first developed, they had their own special controllers. Sound card makers then began to add those special controllers to their sound cards (see Figure 1.35).

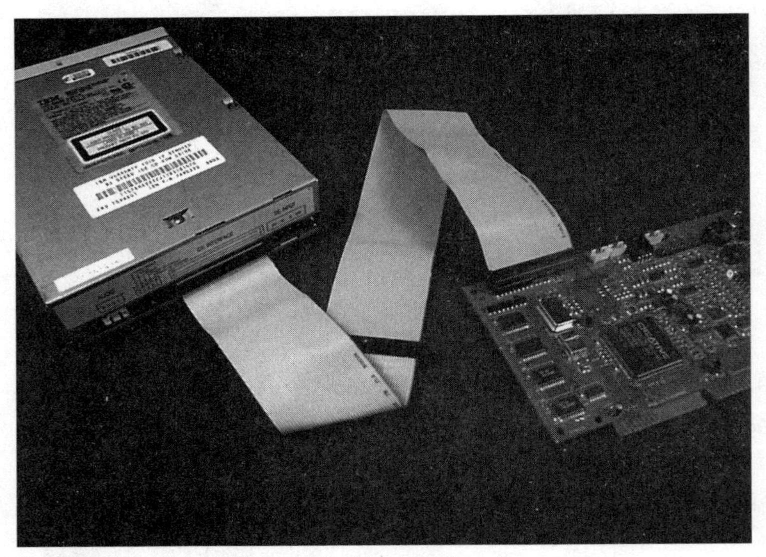

Figure 1.35 CD-ROM controlled by sound card.

These special controllers are now pretty much obsolete; they have been replaced by CD-ROMs that run on either IDE or SCSI controllers, just like hard drives. So there are now basically two types of CD-ROMs: IDE and SCSI. On most PCs, it is common to have an IDE hard drive on one controller and an IDE CD-ROM on the other (see Figure 1.36).

SCSI CD-ROMs go on the same ribbon cable as the SCSI hard drives. One nice feature of SCSI is that you can set up systems with a large number of CD-ROMs because you can have up to seven devices on one ribbon cable. Of course, CD-ROMs, like hard and floppy drives, also need power cables (see Figure 1.37).

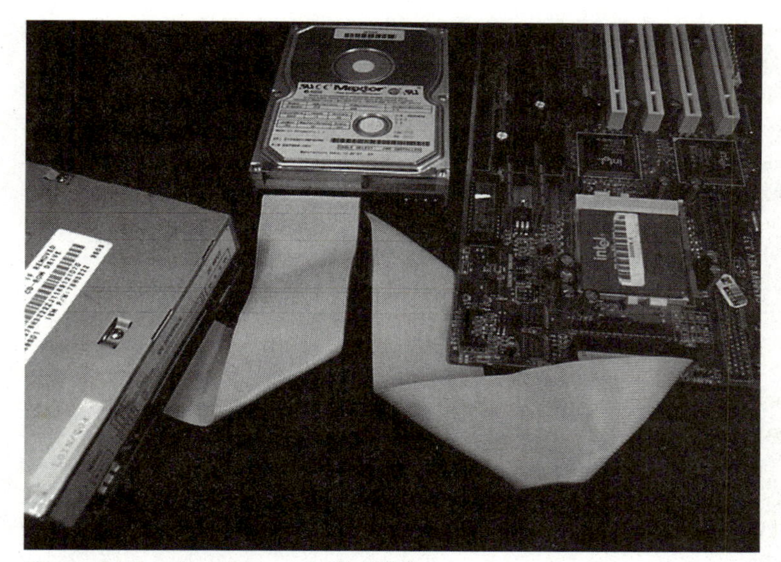

Figure 1.36 Hard drive and CD-ROM.

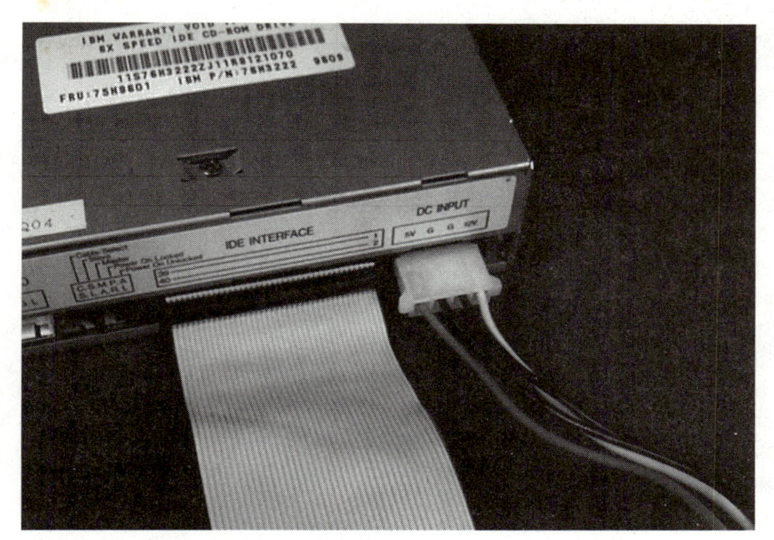

Figure 1.37 CD-ROM power connector.

UNDERSTANDING CONNECTORS

The next sections deal with a number of different devices that are commonly seen in PCs. But before we dive into the realm of soundcards, modems, network cards, and mice, we need to understand that there are many types of connectors (often called *ports*) that these different devices use. These connectors have their own naming conventions. It's not acceptable to go around saying things like "That's a printer port," and "That's a joystick connector." You need to be comfortable with the more commonly used naming conventions so that you can say instead, "That's a male DB-25," or "That's a mini-DIN."

Although there are close to 50 different connectors used with PCs, almost all connectors can all be broken down into six types: DB, DIN, Centronics, RJ, BNC, and Audio.

The DB type connectors are one of the oldest and most common types of connectors used in the back of PCs. They are distinct because of their slight "D" shape, which is designed to allow only one proper way to insert the plug into the socket. Each DB connector has groups of small pins and sockets (male/female) that insert as a group. DB connectors in the PC world have from 9 to 37 pins, although a DB connector with more than 25 pins is now quite rare. Sockets can be either male or female. Some examples are shown in Figure 1.38.

Figure 1.38 "DB" connectors.

DIN connectors are a European design that is also common on every PC. These connectors are round and come in only two common sizes: DIN and Mini-DIN (see Figure 1.39). The sockets are always female.

Figure 1.39 DIN and MINI-DIN.

Centronics connectors are similar to DB connectors, having the same "D" shape to ensure proper insertion. Unlike DBs, Centronics connectors use one large central tab, covered with contacts instead of pins. Even though the Centronics have flat contacts instead of pins, the word *pins* is still used to describe the number of contacts. For example, a Centronics connector with 36 contacts is still called a *36-pin* connector. Centronics connectors are also unique because the sockets have wire *wings* that lock the plug to the socket to reduce the chance of accidental removal. Sockets are always female. With the exception of some obsolete SCSI host adapters, Centronics sockets are rarely seen sticking out of the back of a PC. However, almost every printer in existence has a 36-pin Centronics socket (see Figure 1.40).

Figure 1.40 Centronics port.

Everyone has seen an *RJ* type connector. The little plastic plug used to connect your telephone wire to the jack is a classic example of an RJ type plug. Fortunately, there are only two types of RJ jacks used in PCs: the RJ-11 and the RJ-45 (see Figure 1.41). The phone jack is the RJ-11, which is used almost exclusively for modems. The RJ-45 jack is slightly wider than the RJ-11 and is used for one very popular type of network cabling. Most network cards have an RJ-45 socket.

Figure 1.41 "RJ" jacks.

BNC connectors (better, if incorrectly, known as co-axial or *coax*) are beginning to fade from common PC use, but the large number of PCs that still have coax hanging out the back require their discussion (see Figure 1.42). The coax cable used with PCs looks exactly like the coax that runs into the back of your TV. The connectors, however, are different in that they don't screw in as the TV coax connectors do. The connectors use a twist-type connection —that's really what BNC means. There are two types of cards that can use a BNC connector: network cards that need to link to coax type network cables and old terminal emulation cards.

The emulation cards were direct links to mainframes and are now rare. The older coax networks are fading away, but still have a large presence out there. There is one new way that the screw-type connectors may show up in the back of a PC. There are now cards that you can purchase that allow your PC to do television. They have a screw-type coax connector for, you guessed it, your TV cable! Hmm, Microsoft Word and MSNBC on the same screen at the same time! Can life be any better?

Audio connectors are perhaps the simplest of all. There's really only one type of connector that sees popular use: the *mini-audio* connector (see FIgure 1.43). These small connectors have been around for years. They're the ones we use to plug our headphones into our Walkmans. They're used almost exclusively on soundcards.

Figure 1.42 "BNC" connector.

Figure 1.43 Mini-audio connector.

Keep in mind that there are a virtually endless number of connectors. These six types of connectors cover the vast majority, but there are others. There's no law or standard that requires the maker of a particular device to use a particular connector, especially if they have no interest in making that device interchangeable with similar devices from other manufacturers.

SOUNDCARD

Soundcards perform two functions. First, they take digital information and turn it into sound, outputting the sound through speakers. Second, they take sound, inputted through a microphone, and turn it into digital data. Soundcards are well named: they are cards that deal with sound.

In order to play and record sounds, a soundcard needs to at least connect to a set of speakers and a microphone. Virtually all soundcards have four sockets for mini-type audio jacks (see Figure 1.44). They are Microphone, Speaker, Line In, and Line Out. Many soundcards also have a female 15-pin DB socket that will allow you to connect directly to electronic musical instruments.

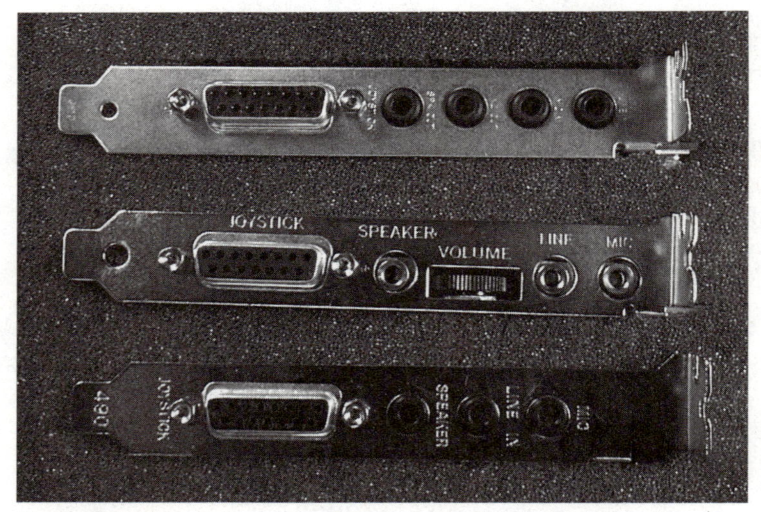

Figure 1.44 Typical soundcard connectors.

The Microphone and Speaker are just as described—to connect a microphone and speakers. Line In allows a soundcard to record from a stereo, tape recorder, etc. Line Out allows the soundcard to output to those same types of devices. On most systems, only the Speaker and Microphone are used.

Most PCs have a small cable running between the soundcard and the CD-ROM (see Figure 1.45). This cable allows the CD-ROM to play audio CD-ROMs through the soundcard, in essence turning your PC into a stereo system.

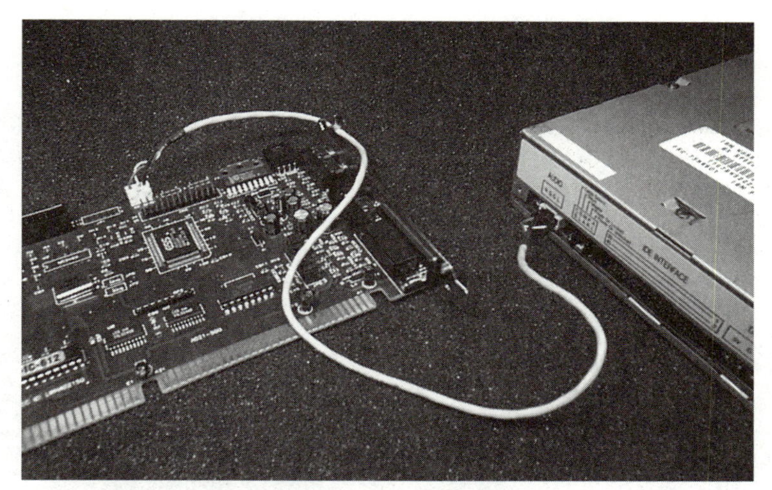

Figure 1.45 CD-ROM on soundcard cable.

VIDEO

Of all the cards in the PC, the video card is by far the easiest to identify (see Figure 1.46). Unless the PC is old, really old, the video card will have a distinct 15-pin female DB connector. Even more unique, although most DB connectors have only two rows of pins, the video card has three rows. There's nothing else like it in the back of a PC. Very old video cards had a 9-pin female DB connector.

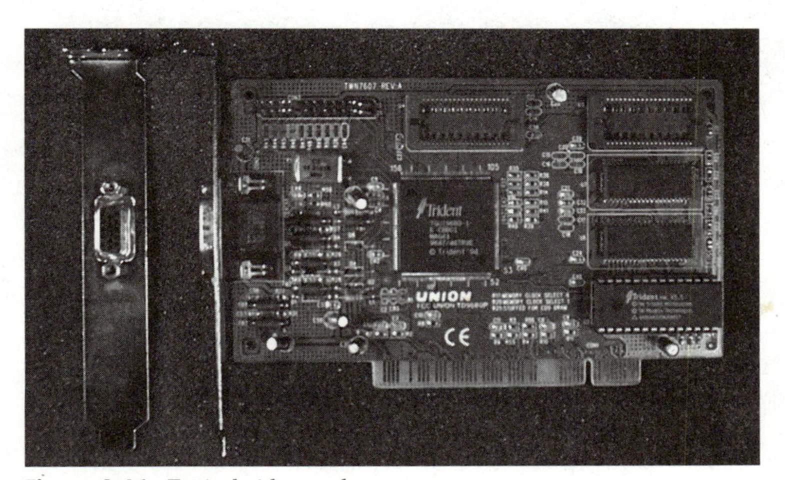

Figure 1.46 Typical video card.

NETWORK CARD

Networks are connected PCs that share information. The PCs are usually connected by some type of cabling, usually an advanced type of phone cable or coax. Network cards (NICs) provide the interface between the network and the PC. A NIC will be distinguished by having one or more of the following types of connectors: an RJ-45, BNC, 15-pin female DB, or 9-pin female DB. It is very common to see NICs with more than one connector (see Figure 1.47). Probably the most common "combo" NIC has an RJ-45 and a BNC.

Figure 1.47 Typical network card connectors.

KEYBOARD

All PCs have a keyboard port directly connected to the motherboard. There are two types of keyboard connectors. The oldest, but still quite common type is a special DIN type connector popularly known as the *AT-style*. It was the keyboard connector on the original IBM PC and is still used in the most modern PCs today. The *AT-style* is quickly beginning to disappear, however, being overshadowed by the smaller *PS/2 style* mini-DIN. You can use an AT style keyboard with a PS/2 style socket (or the other way around) with the use of a converter. Although the AT connector is unique in PCs, the PS/2 style mini-DIN is also used in more modern PCs for the mouse (see Figures 1.48 and 1.49). Fortunately, all PCs that use the mini-DIN for both the keyboard and mouse clearly mark each mini-DIN socket as to its correct use.

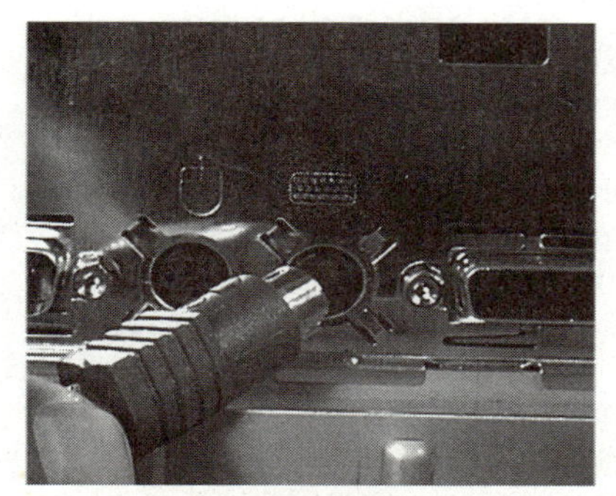

Figure 1.48 Mini-DIN keyboard connector.

Figure 1.49 AT keyboard connector.

MOUSE

A better name for this section might be *what's a serial port, what does it look like and what does a mouse have to do with it?* It's hard to believe, but there was a time, long ago and far away, when PCs worked just fine without mice. When the IBM PC was being created by IBM, mice were not part of the picture. But IBM did something very smart that allowed mice, as well as a lot of other devices that were invented after the PC was first introduced, to easily become part of the PC.

IBM wanted the PC to be easily customized. To that end, the company added a number of ways to add components to the PC.

First were the expansion slots. IBM added lots of unused slots to which anyone (anyone with the technical know-how, at least) could add special cards to the PC to add function to the PC. The original PC had only two cards: the video card and the floppy drive controller. Hard drive controller cards, network cards, soundcards, modems, and a few thousand other devices were all created because IBM had the foresight to add an expansion bus.

The second way that IBM allowed the PC to be easily customized was through the adoption of standardized ports that allowed a person to add devices to the PC without even opening the case. The first of these standardized ports was (still is) called a *serial port.* Now, please understand that IBM didn't invent serial ports, they had been around for a long time, but IBM made sure that every IBM PC came with two serial ports, ready to use.

A serial port is a direct link to the PC. It does only one thing: it takes a stream of serial data (data that runs on only one wire) and converts it into a format that is easily understood by the CPU. Equally, a serial port takes data from the CPU and outputs it in serial format. Think of serial data like a telegraph wire sending Morse code, but instead of sending *dots* and *dashes,* it sends ones and zeroes. Not only did IBM put serial ports in all its PCs, it also told everyone how to write software that could talk to the serial port and do "stuff" with the incoming or outgoing data. To top it all off, IBM standardized the serial connector—defining the size, the shape, and the number and function of all the pins. That way, you knew that if you invented some cool device that worked in one IBM PC, it would also work in all of the others.

The super-standard IBM serial connector was and is either a 25- or a 9-pin male DB connector. No other connector in the back of a PC looks like the serial connectors. The 25-pin connector was the first of the two sizes, but over time it became obvious that only about nine of the pins were needed by most devices. As a result, the 25-pin serial port, although still made, is rarely used (see Figure 1.50). You can get an adapter that allows you to convert 9 to 25 or 25 to 9. You would be hard-pressed to find a PC without at least one 9-pin serial port (see Figure 1.51).

Most of the people reading this book have some PC experience. Somebody out there is right now reading this and asking the question: "Where do COM ports fit into this?" They don't. A COM port is not a physical thing. A COM port is two values called I/O Address and IRQ assigned to a serial port. If you don't know what an IRQ or I/O address is, don't worry. They are covered in detail later. Calling a serial port a COM port is like looking at the White House and saying "That's 1600 Pennsylvania Ave.!" No, it's the White House. Its address is 1600 Pennsylvania Ave.!" Get the difference? Back to serial ports and mice.

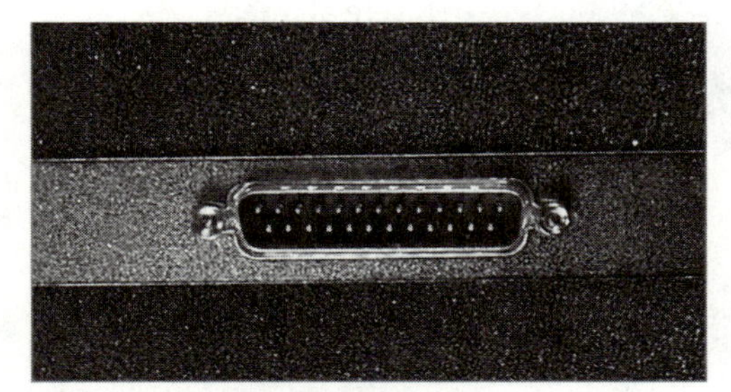

Figure 1.50 25-pin serial port.

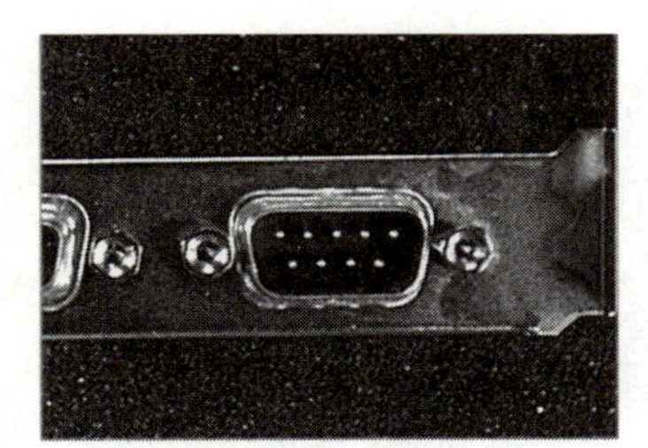

Figure 1.51 9-pin serial port.

Now that we understand and can identify serial ports, we can turn our attention back to mice. For many years, there was no such thing as a mouse port. The mouse was connected into serial ports, either 9- or 25-pin. However, as mice began to become more common, a demand was created for the mouse to have its own connector, just like the keyboard had its own connector. In the mid-eighties, a new type of mouse connection was created. Although still a serial port, it was a mini-DIN connector. This special serial port, just for the mouse, was called the *PS/2* mouse port, out of respect for the first PC that used it, the IBM PS/2 (see Figure 1.52).

In older days, serial ports were on a card, usually called an I/O card. Modern motherboards now have built-in serial ports. The serial ports are either connected directly to the back of the motherboard or are connected to the motherboard via a small ribbon cable. This bit of cable is rather ingloriously referred to as a *dongle* (see Figure 1.53).

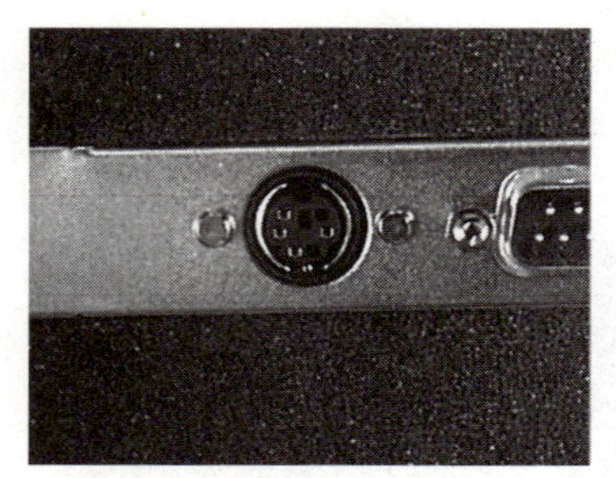

Figure 1.52 PS/2 mouse port.

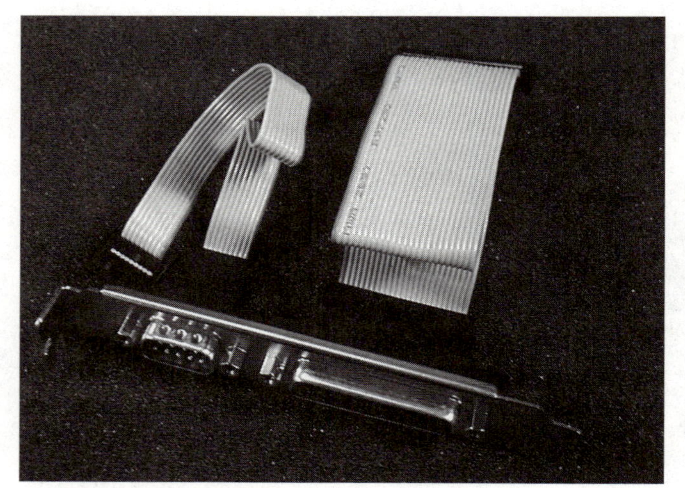

Figure 1.53 Typical dongle.

MODEM

A modem works with your telephone line. A modem is designed to translate analog telephone signals into digital serial data. Modems can also translate digital serial data into analog telephone signals. There are two types of modems: internal and external. An external modem sits outside the PC and is plugged into a serial port. An internal modem is a card that snaps into an expansion slot. Internal modems carry their own onboard serial ports. A modem is another device that is easy to identify in the PC. All modems, internal or external, have two RJ-11 sockets (see Figure 1.54). One connects the modem to the telephone jack on the wall and the other is for an optional telephone, so that you can use the phone line when the modem isn't using it.

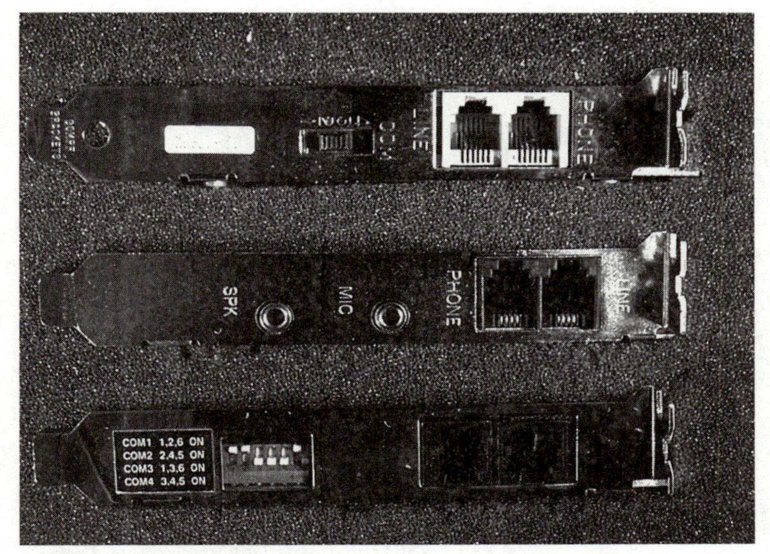

Figure 1.54 Typical modem connections.

PRINTER

The vast majority of printers use a special connector called a *parallel* port (see Figure 1.55). Parallel ports carry data on more than one wire, as opposed to the serial port that only uses one wire. Parallel ports are unique in the PC world: they are 25-pin female DB connectors. Although there are some SCSI host adapters with an identical 25-pin female DB type connector, they are rare in PCs.

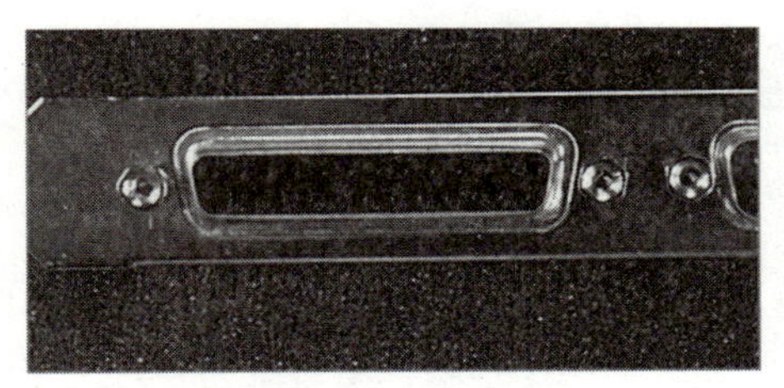

Figure 1.55 Parallel port.

Like serial ports, parallel ports on earlier PCs were mounted on a card, usually the same card that had the serial ports. However, parallel ports today are also directly supported by the motherboard via a direct connection or a dongle (see Figure 1.56).

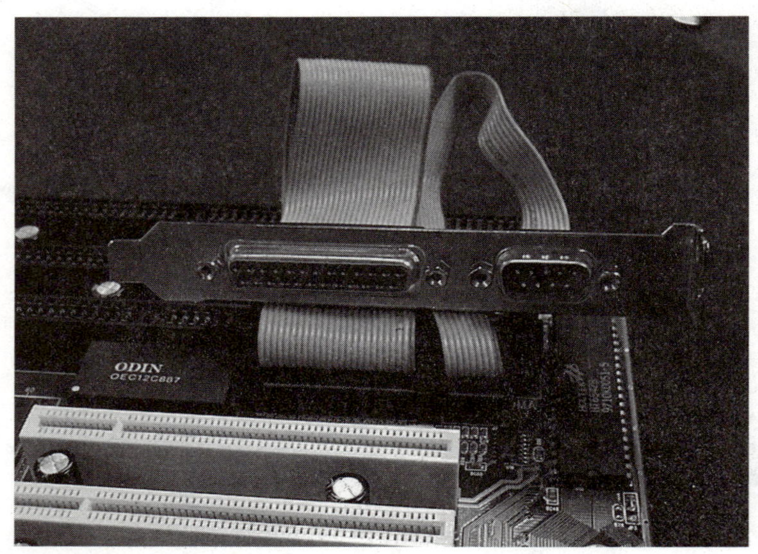

Figure 1.56 Parallel port connected to motherboard.

JOYSTICK

Joysticks weren't supposed to be just for games. When IBM began to add the 15-pin female DB joystick connector for PCs, they were supposed to be a hard-working input device, just as the mouse is today. Nevertheless, that just wasn't to be. Except in the most rare circumstances, the only thing joysticks do today is allow us to play with our $1500 game machine.

But really, is there a more gratifying feeling than easing that joystick (see Figure 1.57) over, pressing the fire button, and watching a Russian SU-27 fighter get wasted from a well-placed Sidewinder? I think not.

Figure 1.57 Joystick port.

JUMPERS AND SWITCHES

All motherboards and cards will need to be setup in one way or another. There are entire chapters of this book devoted to the *hows* and *whys* of setting up these devices. But a moment should be taken to look at the primary tools of hardware setup: jumpers and switches. All motherboards and most cards have circuitry that must be turned on or off for some reason or another. Jumpers and switches are what we use to perform this turning on or off. This section is going to teach you how to recognize jumpers and switches, and how to use them properly.

Switches, or more accurately, *DIP* switches, have been in many PCs since the original IBM PC. DIP switches manifest themselves as tiny, Lego-sized boxes, usually brightly colored (although black is not uncommon), and which have a neat row of tiny rocker-arm or slide switches across the top (see Figure 1.58).

Figure 1.58 DIP switches.

A switch can be turned on or off by flipping the tiny switches (see Figure 1.59). The best way to flip these switches is by using a small screwdriver or a mechanical pencil with the lead removed.

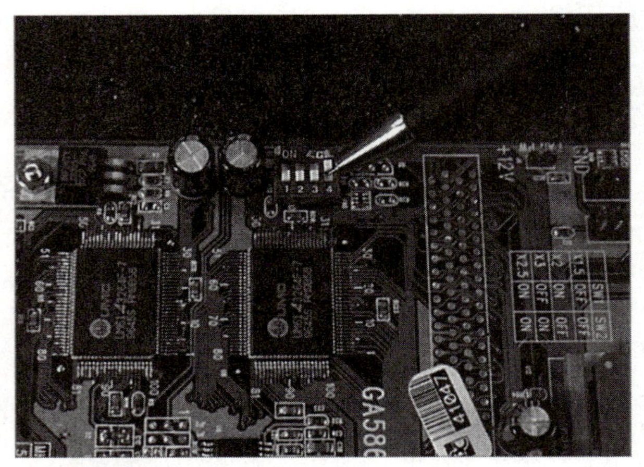

Figure 1.59 Flipping a DIP switch.

Don't use pens or pencils—they leave marks, making it harder to read next time. Worse, they can leave ink residue or lead inside the PC, which is a potential problem if they get in the wrong component. Using your fingers or fingernails is fine but may be difficult, especially if there are a lot of cards and cables in the way.

You usually determine how to set these switches by reading some documentation that came with the device you are configuring. Unfortunately, this documentation can sometimes be a little confusing. One problem is if you have more than one set of DIP switches. How can you tell which one to set? The answer is found by reading the numbers on the board next to the switch. Switches are always numbered with the nomenclature S1, S2 or SW1, SW2, etc. By looking for the S or SW, you can identify one switch from another.

It can also be challenging to determine which way is *on* and which way is *off*. The first problem is that there are a number of ways to say *on* and *off*. In DIP switches, the terms *on, closed,* and *shorted* are synonymous. Equally, *off* and *open* also mean the same thing. Second, most DIP switches will have a word printed on the switch to give you a clue. If there isn't a word, look for a small dot—it usually points to the closed, or on, position. This will identify the state of the switch.

Jumpers are tiny pins, usually about half a centimeter long, which are closely grouped together in twos or threes. A tiny piece, called a *shunt,* is slid down between two pins to create a circuit. Jumpers without a connected shunt are considered open or off; jumpers with a shunt are considered shorted, closed, or on (see Figure 1.60).

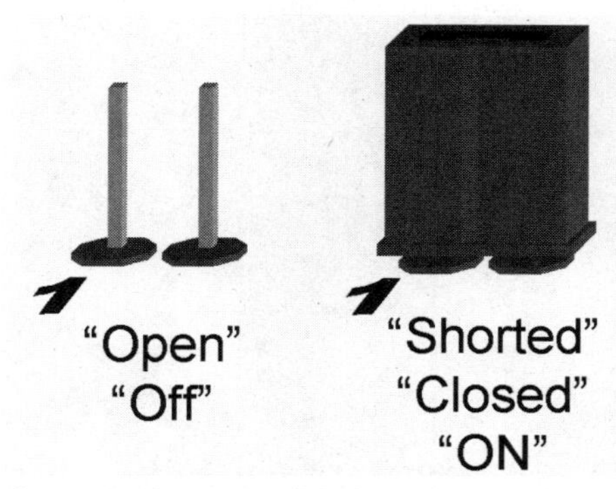

Figure 1.60 Open and closed jumpers.

When there are only two pins, this process is relatively easy. But when three or more pins are involved, it may not be as obvious. Let's use an example with three pins. The documentation only says "2–3." This means you are to place a jumper on the 2nd and 3rd pins (see Figure 1.61). But which two of the three are the 2nd and 3rd pins? If you look closely at the board upon which the jumpers are mounted, you should be able to see a small number "1" on one side or the other, which identifies the 1st pin. You would then short the other two pins.

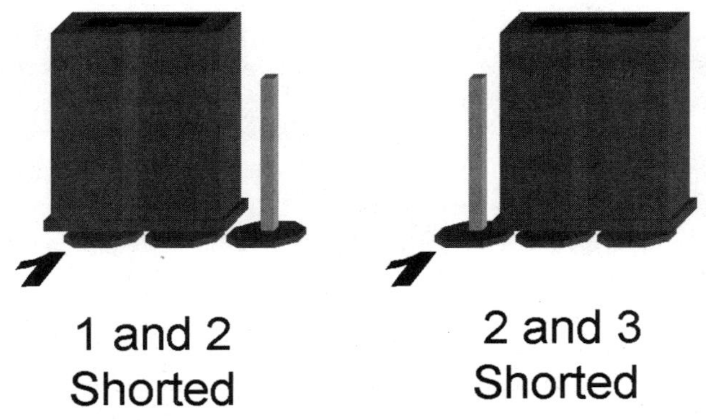

Figure 1.61 Three-way jumpers.

Each group of jumpers will be identified by the nomenclature JP1, JP2, JP3, etc. Use this to identify the jumpers that you wish to set (see Figure 1.62).

Figure 1.62 Jumper labeling.

It is common to see a shunt that is only on one jumper pin. This is called a *parked* jumper (see Figure 1.63). This is used to keep the shunt handy should you ever need to later short that jumper.

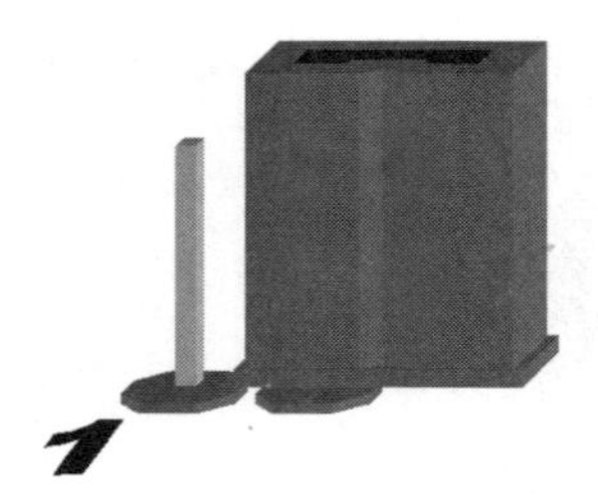

Figure 1.63 Parked jumper.

This book uses a special diagram when discussing jumpers. This diagram looks straight down at the jumpers. For example, a set of jumpers that looks like Figure 1.64 will be represented by a diagram that looks like Figure 1.65.

Figure 1.64 Actual jumpers.

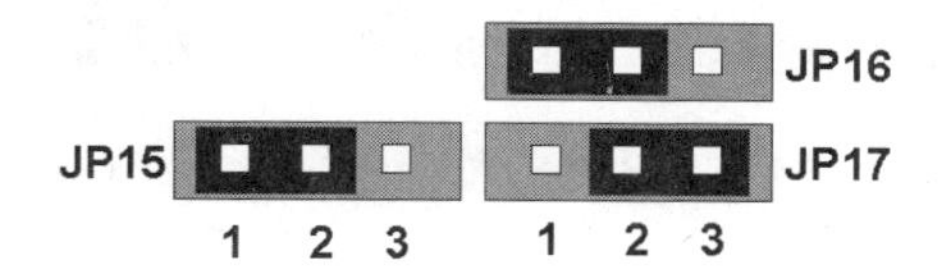

Figure 1.65 Graphic representing jumpers.

If a jumper is shorted, the shunt will be represented by a black rectangle. Otherwise, it will be considered open (see Figure 1.66).

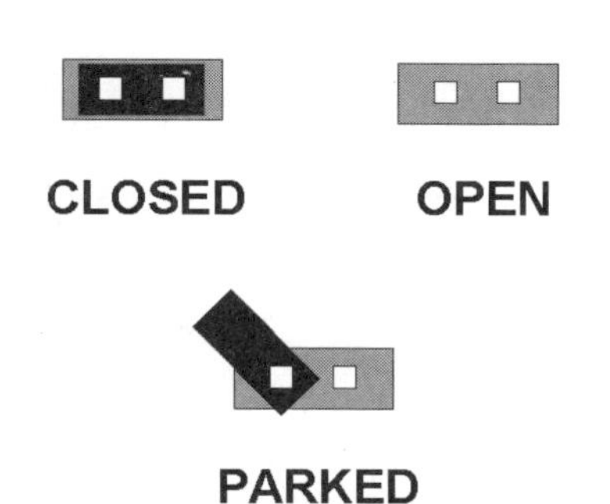

Figure 1.66 Open, closed, and parked jumpers.

DOCUMENTATION

Let's close this chapter with a short mention of documentation. Every modem, every soundcard, and especially every motherboard come with a booklet that describes the proper setting for switches and jumpers. Without this book, you will not know how to set the jumpers and switches. This is particularly important with motherboards. Every motherboard has jumper and/or DIP switches. Every motherboard should also come with documentation, called the motherboard book, to tell you how to set them. If you don't have that book, you will be in for serious frustration and pain. Luckily, the Internet has taken that pain away somewhat by making it relatively easy, if not a little time-consuming, to get a replacement for a lost or never-received motherboard book. Motherboard books are critical, so store them away in a safe place.

This chapter is important! Any decent tech should be able to recognize the main parts of the PC. You should be able to properly name the different types of connectors and to say what types of devices connect to those ports. Make sure you know the difference between types of cards. Good techs can tell the difference by simply running their fingers along the back of a PC. It sure beats pulling a PC out from under a desk!

QUESTIONS

1. Two jumpers have a shunt attached. Which of the following terms does not describe their current state?

   a. Shorted

   b. On

   c. Parked

   d. Closed

2. A DIN connector is always ______, while a DB connector is always ________.

   a. round, d-shaped

   b. d-shaped, round

   c. round, rectangular

   d. rectangular, round

3. A mouse is always plugged into a serial port.
   a. True
   b. False

4. A 25-pin male DB connector will most probably be a ______ port.
   a. parallel
   b. SCSI
   c. serial
   d. joystick

5. The dot on a DIP switch points to the open position.
   a. True
   b. False

ANSWERS

1. The answer is C. The term *park* means to put a shunt on only one jumper wire.
2. The answer is A. A DIN connector is always round and a DB connector is always D-shaped.
3. The answer is True. A PS/2 type mouse port is still a serial port.
4. The answer is C. A 25-pin male DB is a serial port.
5. The answer is False. The dot points to the closed position.

CHAPTER 2

Microprocessors

In this chapter, we will

- Understand the concepts of busses and the function(s) of the data bus and the address bus.
- Understand the clock, clock speed, and concept of clock doubling.
- Understand the relationship of RAM to the CPU and RAM caching.
- Inspect the different types of processors available in the past and today.
- Learn how to install and upgrade processors.

Understanding Microprocessors

For all practical purposes, the term *microprocessor* and *Central Processing Unit* (CPU) mean the same thing: it's that big chip inside your computer that is often described as the *brain* of the system. CPUs have names like *486* or *Pentium,* and are invariably covered up with some huge fan or heatsink so they're often quite easy to locate inside the computer.

Although the computer can certainly seem to act quite intelligently, calling the CPU a *brain* is a huge overstatement of the capabilities of a CPU. The CPU is really nothing more than a very powerful calculator. But, oh, what a calculator! Today's CPUs can add, subtract, multiply, and divide millions of numbers per second. When you can process that much information that fast, it is easy to look intelligent! It's the speed of the CPUs, not some built-in "smarts," that makes our computers capable of performing feats such as accessing the Internet or drawing pictures.

A good PC tech needs to understand some basic CPU functions in order to be able to support PCs. So let's start by choosing an example CPU, O.K.? Now, if you were going to teach someone how an automobile engine works, you would use an example engine that was relatively simple, right? We're going to do the same thing with CPUs. The CPU we're going to look at is the famous Intel 8088 that was invented in the late 70s. So let's begin by visualizing the CPU as a man in a box as shown in Figure 2.1.

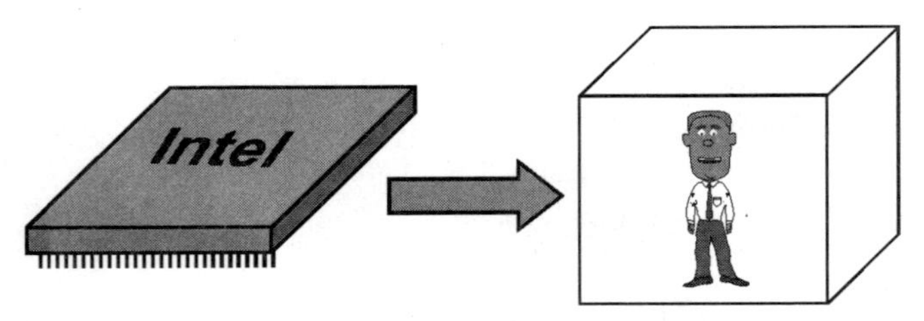

Figure 2.1 Imagine the CPU as a "Man in a box."

This is one clever guy in this box. He can perform virtually any mathematical function, he can manipulate data, he can give us answers to questions, and he can do it FAST. We want to use this guy to get work done. But there's a catch. This man cannot see outside the box. He cannot hear anything outside the box. There is no way for him to communicate with the outside world, and there is no way that we can communicate with him. If we want to take advantage of this guy's skills, we need a way to talk to him (see Figure 2.2).

Figure 2.2 How can we talk to the Man in the Box?

External Data Bus

Fortunately, this box comes with a communication device, consisting of sixteen light bulbs—eight inside the box and eight outside the box. Each light bulb on the inside of the box is connected to one on the outside, creating a pair of lights. Each pair of lights must be either on or off. Also, each connected pair of light bulbs has two switches, one switch on each side. This setup means that the man inside the box or someone outside the box can turn any one of the eight pairs of light bulbs on or off. We need to give this light bulb communication device a name. Let's call it the *external data bus*.

Look at the cutaway view of the external data bus. Understand that if we flip a switch, both light bulbs go on and the switch on the other side is flipped. If we turn a switch off, both light bulbs on each side are turned off and the other switch is turned off (see Figure 2.3).

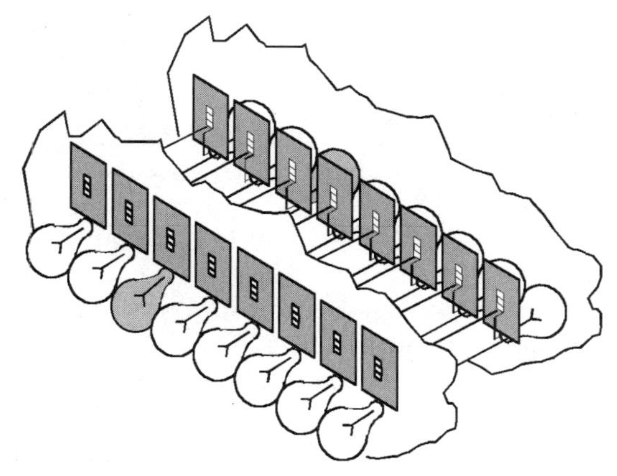

Figure 2.3 Cutaway of the external data bus—note that one light is on.

By turning on different patterns of lights, we can communicate with the guy in the box. However, we need to come up with some common *codebook*, or something that allows us to understand each other's patterns of lights. We'll come back to the external data bus in a moment. Now, we can see that the CPU looks like Figure 2.4 from the outside.

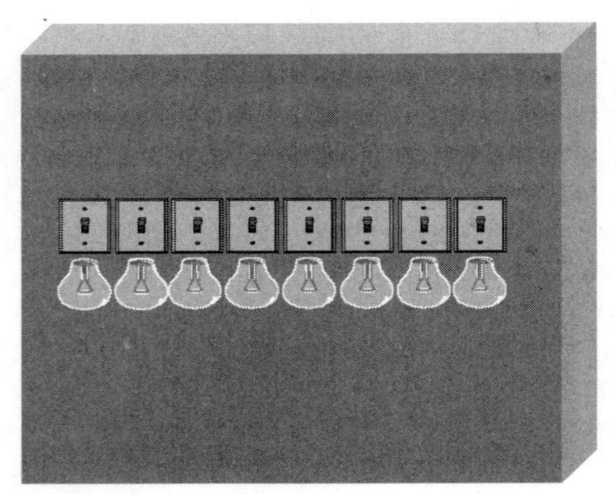

Figure 2.4 The CPU from the outside.

Reality Check

Before we go any further, let's be sure that we're clear on the fact that this is an analogy, not reality. There really is an external data bus, but there are no light bulbs or switches (see Figure 2.5).

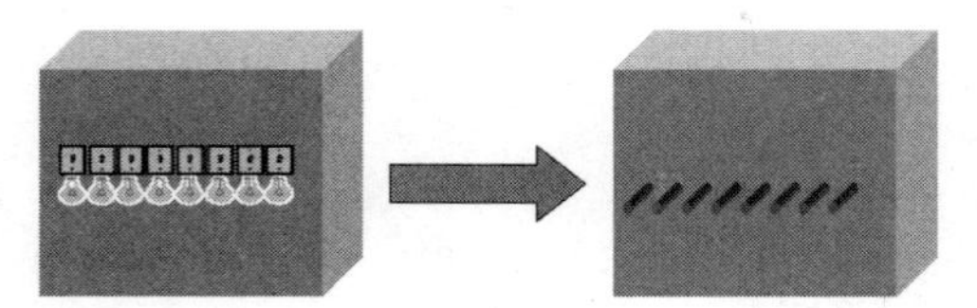

Figure 2.5 Analogy and Reality—side by side.

There are, however, little wires sticking out of the CPU. If we put voltage on one of these wires, we are, in essence, *flipping the switch.* Get the idea? So, if there were voltage on that wire, and if a tiny light bulb *were* on this wire, that light bulb would be shining, wouldn't it? By the same token, if there were no power on the wire, then the light bulb wouldn't be shining, Right? Right. That is why the *switch and light bulb* analogy is used—to help you appreciate that these little wires are *flashing* on and off at a phenomenal rate.

By the way, would it be OK if instead of saying one of the external data bus wires is on or off, I just use the number 1 to represent on and the number 0 to represent off as in Figure 2.6? That way, if I want to describe the state of the lights at any given moment, instead of saying something like on-off-off-off-on-on-off-off, I could say `10001100`.

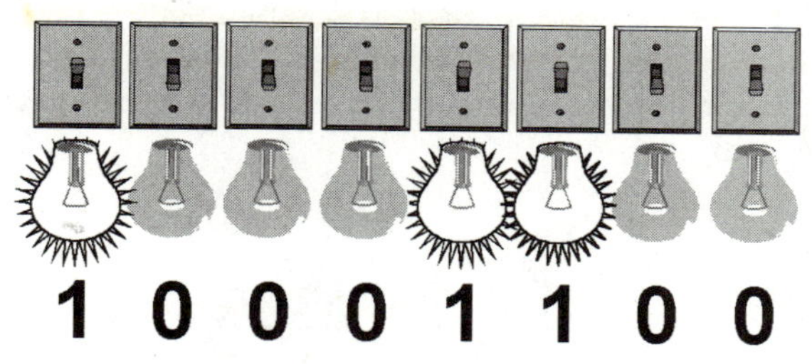

Figure 2.6 "1" means on, "0" means off.

In the world of computers, we are constantly turning wires on and off. As a result, we like to use this "1" and "0,"or "binary," system to describe the state of these wires at any given moment. We will revisit this binary numbering system in greater detail later in the book.

REGISTERS

Go inside the box for a moment. Let's give the guy in the box four *worktables* for him to use. Now, these are not tables in the classic sense; you can't put a pizza on these tables. These four tables really only hold light bulbs. Each table will have 16 light bulbs with switches that the guy in the box can turn on and off. This setup, however, will be substantially different from the external data bus. Here the light bulbs will not be in pairs; just 16 light bulbs straight across with one switch for each bulb. *We will have no access to these light bulbs; only the guy in the box can manipulate them.* These tables are called *registers* (see Figure 2.7).

Figure 2.7 A register.

The function of these registers is to provide the man with a workplace for the problems we are going to give him. We need to be able to identify each register so we will give them names: AX, BX, CX, and DX (see Figure 2.8).

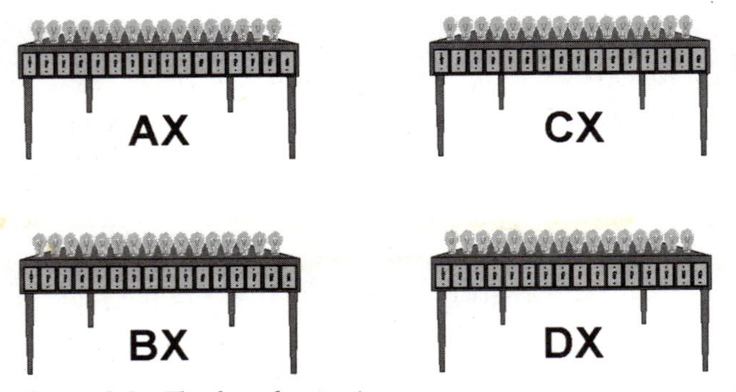

Figure 2.8 The four data registers.

Now, there are more registers than just these four, but these registers are called the *data* or *general purpose* registers. We'll see more registers later, but for now these four are enough.

Before we close the lid on the box, we have to give the man one more tool. Remember the *codebook* that we talked about earlier? Well, let's make one for the external data bus so that we can communicate.

For example, `10000111` (light bulbs 8-3-2-1 on) means MOVE the number 7 into the AX register.

There are some rules here (see Figure 2.9). Counting from right to left, commands start in the last four light bulbs 8-7-6-5 (in techie lingo, we would say the "high-order bits"). Data is in the first four light bulbs 4-3-2-1 ("low-order bits").

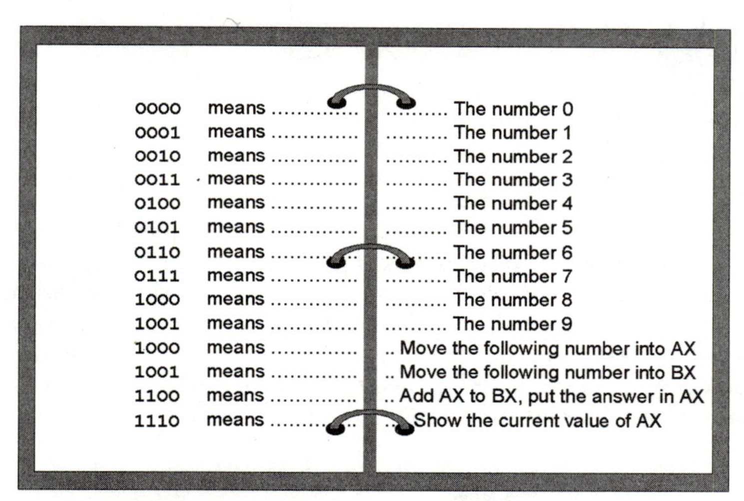

Figure 2.9 The CPU's codebook.

These commands are known as the microprocessor's *machine language*. The commands described here are not actual commands—we have simplified them somewhat to clarify the concept. However, the 8088 has commands that are *very* similar to these, plus a few hundred more!

FYI, here are some examples of real machine language for the Intel 8088:

`10111010`: The next line of code is a number, put that number into the DX register.

`01000001`: Add 1 to the number already in the CX register.

`00111100`: Compare the value in the AX register with the next line of code.

So, here is our CPU so far: the guy can communicate with the outside world via the external data bus, there are four registers with him, and he has the codebook so that he can understand the different patterns on the external data bus (see Figure 2.10).

Figure 2.10 Our CPU so far.

CLOCK

Now, just because we switch the lights on and off does not mean that the guy inside is going to look at his codebook and act upon it. Have you ever seen an old-time manual calculator? The ones with the big crank on one side? You would press the numbers you wanted to deal with, and then press the + key, but that was not good enough. You then had to *pull the crank* on the side of the calculator to get your answer (see Figure 2.11).

Figure 2.11 Nothing happens until you pull the crank!

Well, the CPU also has a *crank*. We *pressed the buttons* by lighting the correct light bulbs on the external data bus, so now we need to pull the crank. The crank of the CPU is a special wire called the *CLOCK* (most diagrams show the clock wire as *CLK*). To continue our analogy, let us put a buzzer inside the box with an activation button outside the box. Once we have the light bulbs on the external data bus set up, we will press the button to activate the buzzer, and the guy will act upon the lights (see Figure 2.12).

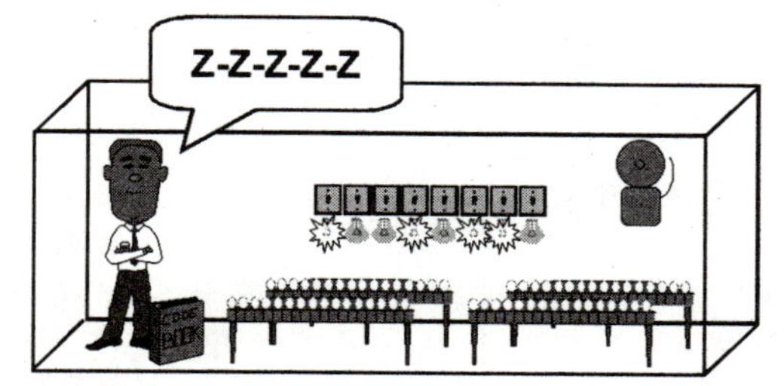

Figure 2.12 The CPU does nothing unless activated by the clock.

Each time the CLK wire is charged is called a *clock cycle*. Once a command has been placed on the external data bus, the clock wire must be raised to a given voltage—a clock cycle—in order for the CPU to process the command.

The CPU needs at least two clock cycles to act upon each command (see Figure 2.13). Using the manual calculator analogy, we need to pull the crank *at least twice* before anything happens. Some commands require hundreds of clock cycles to be processed.

Figure 2.13 The CPU needs more than one CLK to do anything!

Clock Speed

Let's look at the old-time manual calculator one more time. If you tried to pull the crank too quickly, like maybe 30 times per second, the calculator would break because it was not designed to operate that quickly. CPUs have the same problem. If you place too many clock cycles on a CPU, it will overheat and stop working. The maximum number of clock cycles that your CPU can handle is called the *clock speed*. A CPU's clock speed is determined by the CPU manufacturer and is the fastest speed at which the CPU can operate. The Intel 8088 processor had a clock speed of 4.77MHz (millions of cycles per second).

NOTE
1 Hz = 1 Hertz = 1 cycle per second
1 MHz = 1 MegaHertz= 1 Million cycles per second

Understand that a CPU's clock speed is its *maximum* speed, not the speed at which it is running! A CPU can be run at any speed, as long as that speed is slower or equal to its clock speed. The *system crystal* determines the speed at which a CPU is operated (see Figure 2.14). The system crystal is usually a quartz oscillator, very similar to the one in a wristwatch, which is soldered to the motherboard.

Figure 2.14 One of many types of system crystals.

You should never run the CPU above its rated clock speed (see Figure 2.15). The clock speed is always marked somewhere on the CPU itself.

Figure 2.15 A CPU's clock speed is a top speed.

It is critical to understand the relationship of the system crystal to the clock speed of the CPU. It makes sense to visualize the system crystal as a metronome for the CPU as shown in Figure 2.16.

Figure 2.16 The speed of the CPU is determined by the crystal.

A CPU can be pushed by a crystal with a lower clock speed than its own, but it will only operate at the speed of the crystal as shown in Figure 2.17.

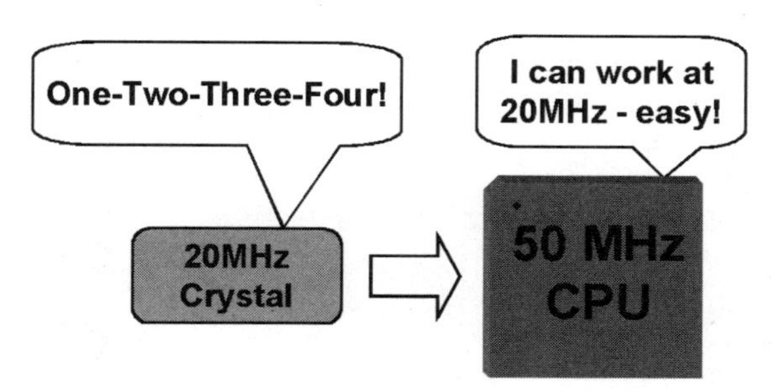

Figure 2.17 Slow crystal, fast CPU.

Don't try to run the CPU faster than its clock speed, or it will overheat and then lock up (see Figure 2.18).

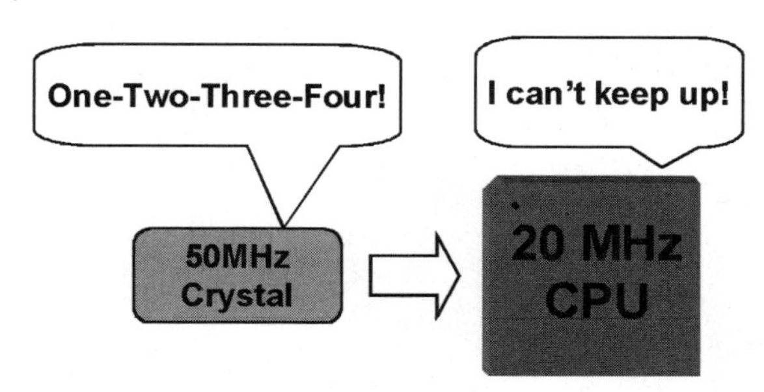

Figure 2.18 Fast crystal, slow CPU.

To run a CPU more slowly than its clock speed is called *underclocking*. To run a CPU faster than its clock speed is called *overclocking*. If you underclock, you are not taking advantage of all of the power of the CPU. If you overclock, the CPU won't work. We will go into more detail later in this chapter.

BACK TO THE EXTERNAL DATA BUS

Now that we have all the necessary components, let's watch how this setup allows a microprocessor to get work done. To do this, we are going to add 2 + 3 and see the answer. We will keep sending commands to the microprocessor until we get the result. So let's refer back to the codebook to tell the guy in the box what to do.

Using the codebook (see Figure 2.19), here are the steps to add 2 + 3:

First we will send	10000010	(MOVE 2 into AX) the command
Then we will send	10010011	(MOVE 3 into BX)
Then we will send	11000000	(ADD BX into AX)
Last we will send	11100000	(SHOW the value in AX)

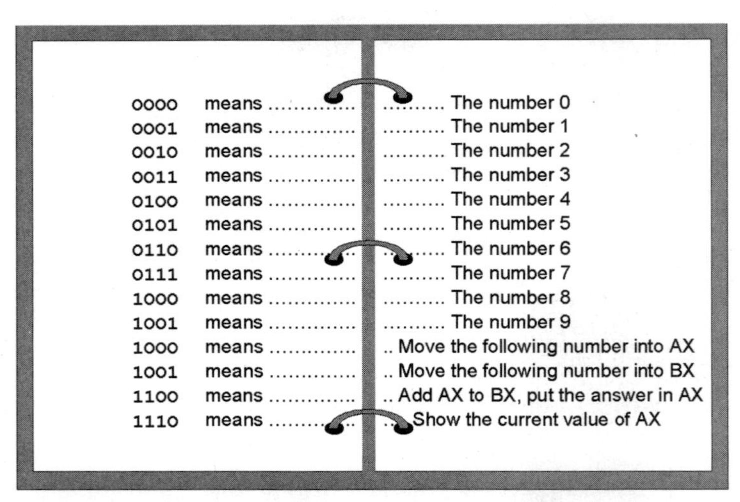

Figure 2.19 The CPU's codebook again (for reference).

This set of commands is known as a *program*. A program is a series of commands sent to a CPU in a specific order to perform work on a CPU. Each discrete setting of the external data bus is called a "line" of code. The previous program, therefore, has four lines of code.

RUNNING THE PROGRAM

Let's watch each step as the program is executed:

1. Flip external data bus switches to `10000010`.
2. Repeatedly add voltage to the clock until the switches on the external data bus suddenly all turn off (that means the guy in the box has acted upon the command).
3. Flip external data bus switches to `10010011`.
4. Repeat step 2.
5. Flip external data bus switches to `11000000`.
6. Repeat step 2.
7. Flip external data bus switches to `11100000`.
8. Repeat step 2, except that this time we see the value `00000101` (five) suddenly appear on the external data bus.

Congratulations! You just added 2 + 3 and got the answer 5! You are a programmer!

ONE MORE REALITY CHECK

Think about the registers again. Clearly, there are no *tables* or *racks of light bulbs*. The four registers we discussed are tiny storage areas on the CPU. They are microscopic semiconductor circuits called TTL logic (not light bulbs); if they are holding a charge they are on, and if they are not holding a charge they are off.

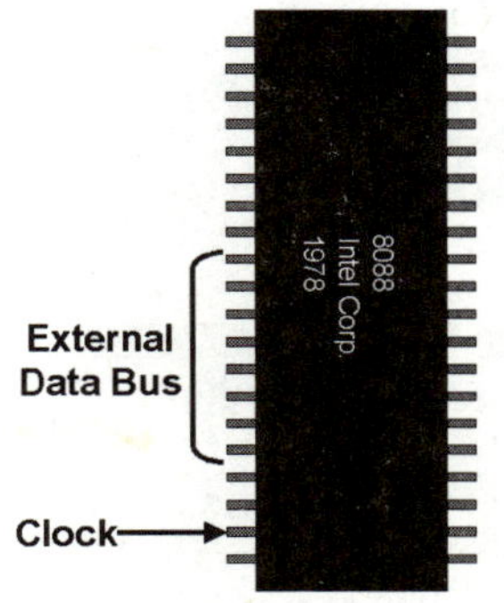

Figure 2.20 Diagram of 8088 showing clock and external data bus.

Here we see a diagram of a real 8088 CPU. This shows the actual wires that compose the external data bus, as well as the single clock wire. Because the registers are inside the CPU, they can't be shown in this figure.

MEMORY

By using the program described previously, we can now add 2 + 3. Because we are manually setting the voltages on the external data bus and the clock wire, however, this is a very slow way to add 2 + 3. Keep in mind that the 8088 has a clock speed of 4.77 MHz, so we need some way to store the programs on something that will feed each line of the program to the CPU at a high rate of speed. That way, the processor can read the data as fast as he can process, or at least a lot faster than we can flip switches!

What can we use to store programs? Because each line of code is nothing more than a pattern of eight ones and zeros, any device that can store ones and zeroes eight across will do the trick. Today's computers use RAM.

Set Random Access Memory (RAM)

Random Access Memory (RAM) provides a storage system that can store both programs and data. This system can also jump to ANY line of code as easily as any other. In the RAM chapter, we will develop the concept of RAM in detail, but at this point think of RAM as an electronic spreadsheet.

Physically, RAM consists of groups of semiconductor chips on small cards that snap into your computer as shown in Figure 2.21.

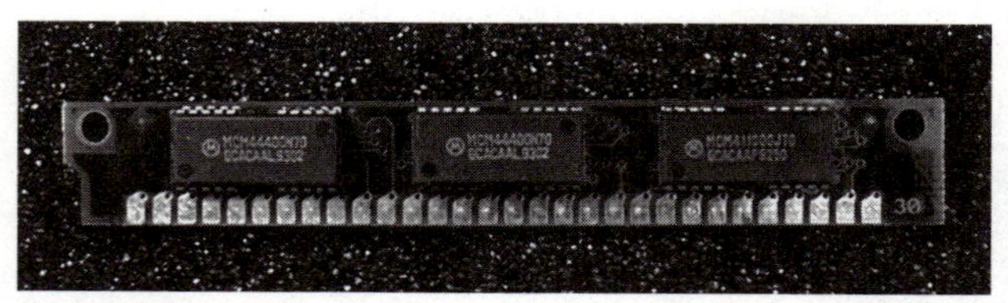

Figure 2.21 Typical RAM (30-pin SIMM).

Electronically, RAM looks like a spreadsheet (see Figure 2.22). Each cell in this spreadsheet can store only a one or a zero. We call each cell a *bit*. Each row in the spreadsheet is eight bits across to match the external data bus of the 8088. We call eight bits a *byte*. So each row is one byte wide. In the PC world, RAM transfers and stores data to and from the CPU in byte-sized chunks (pardon the pun). RAM is therefore arranged in byte-sized rows. The number of rows of RAM varies from PC to PC. RAM can have many rows—hundreds of thousands (later we will see millions, but for the moment, just think in thousands).

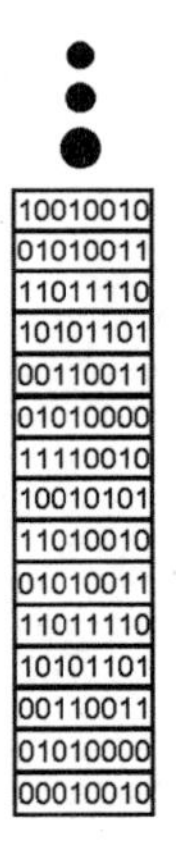

Figure 2.22 To the CPU, RAM looks like a spreadsheet.

Any one row of RAM can be accessed as easily and as quickly as any other row. That's the Random Access part of RAM. Not only is RAM randomly accessible, it is also fast. By storing programs on RAM, the CPU can access and run programs very quickly. RAM is also used to store data that is actively being used by whatever program is currently running.

Don't confuse RAM with mass storage devices like hard drives and floppy drives! We use hard drives and floppy drives to store permanently programs and data that are not currently needed.

Any individual "1" or "0" = a "Bit"

4 Bits = a "Nibble"

8 Bits = a "Byte"

16 Bits = a "Word"

32 Bits = a "Double Word"

64 Bits = a "Paragraph" or "Quad Word"

ADDRESS BUS

So far, we have a CPU and RAM. What we need is some connection between the CPU and the RAM so that they can talk to each other. To do so, we will extend the external data bus (see Figure 2.23).

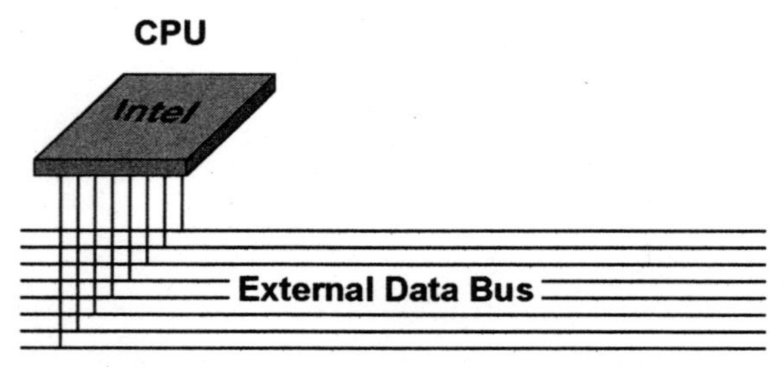

Figure 2.23 Extending the External Data Bus.

WAIT A MINUTE! How can we connect the RAM to the External Data Bus (see Figure 2.24)? This is not a matter of just plugging it in! RAM is a spreadsheet with thousands and thousands of discrete rows, right? We only want to look at the contents of one row of the spreadsheet at a time! What are we going to do?

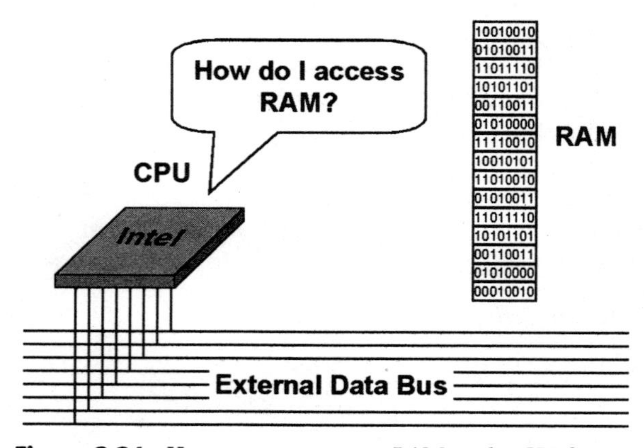

Figure 2.24 How can we connect RAM to the CPU?

In order to allow the CPU to access a row of RAM whenever necessary, we need to add an entirely new set of circuitry that will allow the CPU to "grab" one row of RAM. Let's see how this is done.

We give the CPU access to RAM by adding a new chip to the system. This chip is called a *Memory Control Chip* (MCC). The MCC has circuitry to *grab electronically* any single line of RAM and place that data on the external data bus, thus allowing the CPU to act on that code (see Figure 2.25).

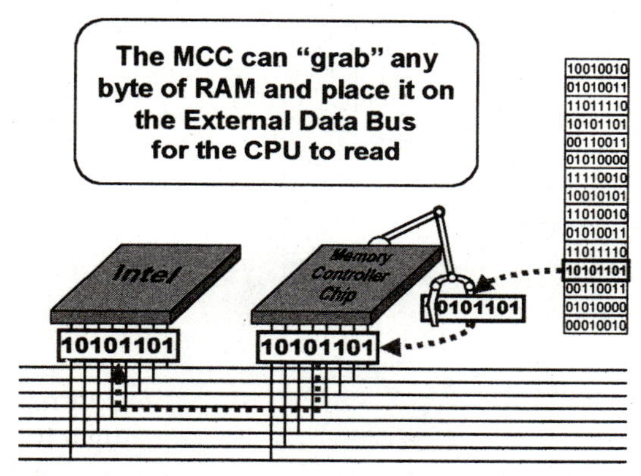

Figure 2.25 The MCC grabbing a byte of RAM.

This is great, but we need to give the CPU the capability to tell the MCC *which line of code* it needs! See Figure 2.26.

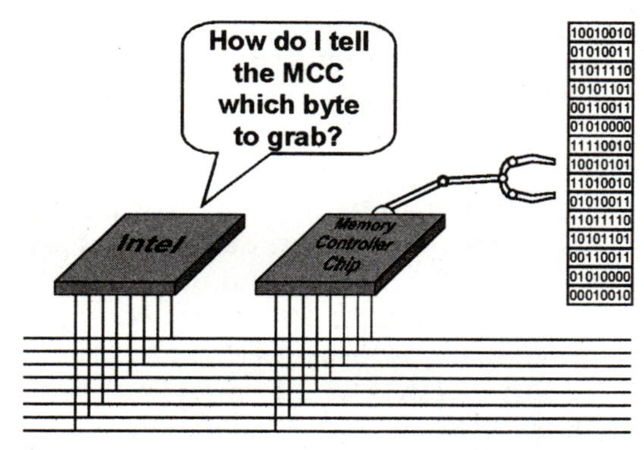

Figure 2.26 How can the CPU control the MCC?

We have to provide the CPU with a way to talk to the MCC, with a new type of data bus called the *address bus*.

The address bus is a set of wires that runs from the CPU and allows the CPU to control the MCC (see Figure 2.27). Different CPUs have different numbers of wires (which, we will soon see, is very significant). The 8088 has 20 wires in its address bus.

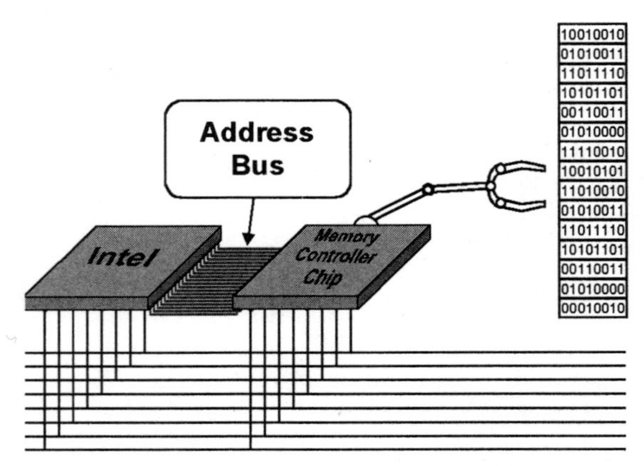

Figure 2.27 The address bus.

By turning wires on and off in different patterns, the CPU can tell the MCC which line of RAM it wants at any given moment. Let's consider these 20 wires. There are two big questions here: 1) How many different patterns of on and off wires can there be in 20 wires? 2) Which pattern goes to which row of RAM?

The answer to the first question is fairly easy. Each wire can only be on or off—it can be in only one of two different states. If there were only one wire on the address bus, it could be either on or off, or 2^1 different combinations. If we had two address bus wires, we would have four different combinations, or 2^2 and so on. If you had 20 wires, you would have 1,048,576 (2^{20}) combinations. Because each different pattern points to one line of code and because each line of RAM is one byte, if you know the number of wires in the address bus, you know the maximum amount of RAM that a particular CPU can handle.

Because the 8088 has a 20-wire address bus, the most RAM it can handle is 2^{20} or 1,048,576 bytes. We say the 8088 has an address space of 1,048,576 bytes.

Counting Wires

Remember that everything in the CPU boils down to ones and zeroes. When we talk about the address bus, we are interested in the maximum number of patterns it can generate (i.e., how much RAM it can take). We know that the 8088 has 20 address wires and the total address space is 1,048,576 bytes. Although this is accurate, no one uses such an exact term to discuss the address space of the 8088. What we say is that the 8088 has a 1 Megabyte (1 Meg) address space. The base value we use in computing is 210 or 1024. We call that a Kilobyte (1 K). So, if someone says he has one kilobyte (1K), he really has 1024 bytes. A Megabyte is 1K x 1K or 1024 x 1024 = 1,048,576 bytes. So, don't confuse 1 Million (1,000,000) with 1 Meg (1,048,576) or one thousand (1000) with one K (1024).

1 K = 2^{10} = 1024

1 Meg = 2^{20} = 1,048,576

1 Gig = 2^{30} = 1,073,741,824

One K is not equal to one thousand

One Meg is not equal to one million

One Gig is not equal to one billion

Now, the second question is a little harder: which pattern goes to which line of RAM? To understand this, we have to take a moment to understand binary counting. In binary, there are only two numbers, 0 and 1, which makes binary a darn handy way to work with wires that are being turned on and off. So, let's try to count in binary. 0, 1, ... what's next? It's not 2! Well, the only thing is 10, so with that idea, let's count to 1000.

```
0
1
10
11
100
101
110
111
1000
```

Very good! Let's think about good old base 10 (regular numbers) for a moment. If you have the number 365, can you put zeroes in front of the 365, like this?

```
000365
```

Sure you can! It doesn't change the value. Same thing in binary —in this case, we will add enough zeroes to make 20 places:

```
00000000000000000000
00000000000000000001
00000000000000000010
00000000000000000011
00000000000000000100
00000000000000000101
00000000000000000110
00000000000000000111
00000000000000001000
```

This would be a great way to represent each line of RAM. The last RAM row would be:

```
11111111111111111111
```

When the CPU turns off all of the address bus wires, he wants the first line of RAM; when he turns on all of the wires, he wants the 1,048,576th line of RAM.

Reality Check

Figure 2.28 is a diagram of an Intel 8088 microprocessor, showing the location of the address wires.

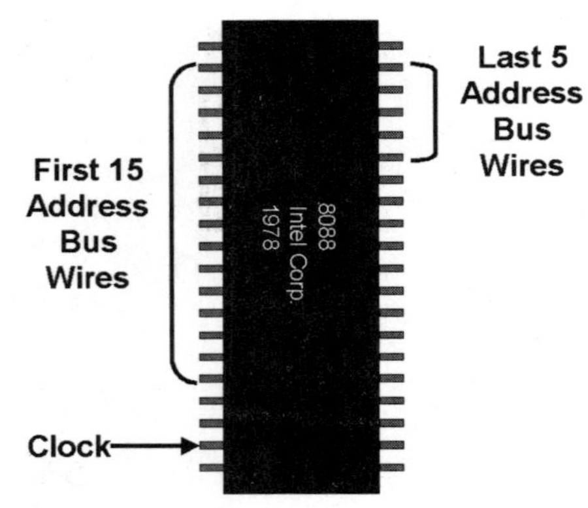

Figure 2.28 Location of address bus wires on an 8088.

If you look at the earlier diagram of the location of the 8088's external data bus wires, you'll notice that some of the external data bus and address bus wires overlap. That's O.K.—some of the wires do both! We call that *multiplexing*.

Intel is King . . . for Now

The original IBM PC used an Intel brand 8088 CPU. Intel's presence from the beginning has allowed it a virtual monopoly on the supply of CPUs for IBM-compatible PCs. Although there are serious competitors, Intel also controls the standards that allow CPUs to be IBM-compatible. As technology progressed from the 8088 to the most current CPU, Intel increased the size of the external data bus, address bus, CPU registers, and amount of RAM storage. This progression from 8-bit technology to 16-bit, 32-bit, and finally 64-bit technology allowed the systems to communicate and process more information faster and more efficiently.

Although Intel definitely has the largest share of the CPU market, a number of other companies, led by Advanced Micro Devices and Cyrix Corporation, continue to grow in technology sophistication. As we discuss the different CPUs, we will see that the early processors were dominated by Intel. But as we move forward, we will see other brands of CPUs begin to show up. In today's CPUs, you have a real choice about which CPU you wish to use.

Now that we have a basic understanding of registers, the external data bus, and the address bus, let's take a tour of the family of Intel processors, as well as some of its more famous competitors.

The 8086 CPU Family

CHIP TYPE	CLOCK SPEED (MHz)	REGISTER SIZE	EXTERNAL BUS	ADDRESS BUS
Intel 8088	4.77–10	16-Bit	8-Bit	20-Bit
Intel 8086	4.77–10	16-Bit	16-Bit	20-Bit

When IBM decided to enter the small computer business, it decided that it would need a more powerful processor than the 8-bit microprocessors that were popular at the time. IBM wanted a chip that was not going to be too hard to integrate into its systems, a chip based on addressing concepts, and machine language that programmers would easily understand. It wanted a chip with flexibility and expandability. Mostly, IBM wanted a chip that would allow existing applications on CPM-based machines to be easily recompiled for the new chip.

Intel Corporation invented an improved version of its very popular 8080 processor called the 8086. The 8086 chip was a full 16-bit chip. Although 16-bit chips were also being produced by some of Intel's competitors, the 8086 had the ability to address up to 1 Megabyte (1 Meg) of memory when everyone else was still addressing only 64 Kilobytes (64K). This addressability was achieved by combining two 16-bit registers (2^{16} = 64K) into one 20-bit (2^{20} = 1 Meg) register. This addressing scheme sliced that 1 Megabyte into 64K chunks, which also made integrating programs written for earlier computers easier to recompile for IBM's computer.

There was one problem with the 8086 chip—it was too powerful. The problem was in the 8086's 16-bit external bus. There were no devices invented that could send or receive the 16-bit data to and from the 8086. In order to get an 8086 to speak to an 8-bit device, the 8086 had to chop its data into two pieces and send each piece separately. Intel was aware of this and created the 8088 processor. The 8088 was identical to the 8086, except it only had an 8-bit external bus. The 8088 was the chip IBM decided to use in its first microcomputer, the IBM PC. The 8088 was also used in the *upscale* PC, the IBM XT. The 8086 was rarely used in comparison to the 8088.

The 80286 CPU Family

CHIP TYPE	CLOCK SPEED (MHz)	REGISTER SIZE	EXTERNAL BUS	ADDRESS BUS
Intel 80286	8 - 20	16-Bit	16-Bit	24-Bit

In 1983, Intel introduced its next generation of chip, the 80286. (There was an interim chip, the 80186, which was little more than a slightly enhanced 8086. It died quickly due to the appearance of the 80286.) The 80286, or as it was more popularly known, the 286, was a significant leap in technology from the 8086. The 286 first appeared in the IBM model *Advanced Technology* (AT) computer.

MODES

When Intel made the 8086/8088, it promised to make every subsequent chip backward-compatible. The 80286 had a number of major enhancements that made it far superior to the 8088/8086 chip. In order to take advantage of these functions, we had to have programs that would use them. But what if you only had programs that were designed to run on the 8088? You wouldn't want the extra features of the 286; you would want the 286 to run like an 8088. The answer that Intel came up with was simple and elegant: starting with the 286 (and this is still true in today's CPUs), all CPUs would start up by acting like an 8088. In order to take advantage of the higher functions, you would then have to run special programs that would "shift" the CPU into a higher *mode*. The 286 had two modes: the first was called *8086 compatible* or *Real Mode*, and the second was the more powerful mode called *Protected Mode*.

PROTECTED MODE

When the 286 was shifted into Protected Mode, it had the capability to use up to 16 megabytes of memory and run more than one program at a time. This could only happen if one had an operating system designed to handle these advanced functions. DOS was designed to run on an 8086, so if you ran DOS on a 286, you were in Real Mode. In order to take advantage of the 286 Protected Mode, you needed a special operating system. In Protected Mode, multiple programs are stored in memory. An operating system designed to run in Protected Mode will create a *focus*, running a few lines of one of the programs stored in memory. After some amount of time, the operating system can then switch the focus to one of the other programs in memory. Technically speaking, this is not multitasking, but if the operating system can switch back and forth between the programs very rapidly, it would certainly look as though multitasking were taking place.

Did anyone write an operating system that would take advantage of this power? Well, some people did. Certain flavors of UNIX were created to run on 286s. Novell NetWare 2.2 needed a 286, as did the first versions of OS/2. These were all very special situations. Also, once you switched into Protected Mode, the only way to go back to regular 8086 mode was to reboot the computer! For the most part, in those days, we all ran DOS on our 286s, which meant that our 286 computers were little more than fast 8086s.

The 80386 CPU—the 386DX Family

CHIP TYPE	CLOCK SPEED (MHz)	REGISTER SIZE	EXTERNAL BUS	ADDRESS BUS	INTERNAL CACHE
INTEL 80386DX	16 - 33	32-Bit	32-Bit	32-Bit	None
AMD AM386DX	20 - 40	32-Bit	32-Bit	32-Bit	None
AMD AM386DXL	20 - 33	32-bit	32-Bit	32-Bit	None
AMD AM386DXLV	25 - 33	32-Bit	32-Bit	32-Bit	8 K

In 1985, Intel unveiled its next generation chip, the 80386 (or 386, for short). The 386 was Intel's first true 32-bit chip—the registers, address bus, and external bus were all 32-bits wide. The 386 also included a number of new registers for debugging and memory management. The 386 could run in three different modes: Real Mode, 286 Protected Mode, and its own very powerful *386 Protected Mode.* Once the 386 was switched to 386 Protected Mode, it had two functions that set it apart from earlier CPUs: *Virtual Memory* and *Virtual 8086.*

VIRTUAL MEMORY

The 386's 32-bit address bus allows for up to 4 Gigabytes of addressable memory, far more than any PC compatible currently needs (232 = 4,294,967,296 = 4 Gig). However, today's PCs can often use more RAM than they have installed. Programs are run in RAM. If you try to load more programs than your RAM can store, you get some kind of *Out of Memory* errors. With the right operating system, the 386 chip can create *pretend RAM,* better known as *Virtual Memory,* by electronically changing a part of your permanent storage (hard drives, in particular) into virtual memory. This virtual memory looks like regular RAM to the operating system. The part of your hard drive that is acting like virtual memory is called a *swapfile* and is used by all of today's operating systems.

VIRTUAL 8086

386s have a more advanced Protected Mode known as *Virtual 8086.* In 286 Protected Mode, it was impossible to run 8086-mode DOS programs. With Virtual 8086, the operating system creates virtual 8086 *bubbles,* which are memory areas that are completely separated and virtually addressed within the 1 Meg 8086 limit. In other words, a DOS program can run within an 8086 bubble while the CPU stays in Protected Mode. The operating system creates *virtual registers* whenever the program wants to use to them. The operating system will then inspect what the program is trying to do and verify that it's not trying to do something dangerous.

The 80386SX CPU Family

CHIP TYPE	CLK (MHz)	REGISTER SIZE	EXTERNAL BUS	ADDRESS BUS	CACHE	VOLTAGE	SMM*
INTEL 80386SX	16–25	32-Bit	16-Bit	24-Bit	None	5 V	NO
INTEL 80386SL	16–25	32-Bit	16-Bit	24-Bit	None	3.3 V	YES
AMD AM386SX	20–40	32-Bit	16-Bit	24-Bit	None	5 V	NO
AMD AM386SXL	16–40	32-Bit	16-Bit	24-Bit	None	5 V	YES*
AMD AM386SXLV	33	32-Bit	16-Bit	24-Bit	8 K	3.3 V	YES
IBM 386SLC	20	32-Bit	16-Bit	24-Bit	8 K	3.3 V	YES

* See Power Saving Strategies

In order to increase the popularity of the 386 chip, Intel recognized the need for a 386 processor that could operate easily on 16-bit motherboards. This need was fulfilled with the 80386SX.

The 386SX differed from the standard 386 (now known as the 386DX) in two ways. First, the external data bus was reduced to 16 bits to match the 286's external data bus. Second, the address bus was reduced to 24 bits. This limited the address range of the 386SX to 16 Megabytes (2^{24} = 16 Meg).

Although the 386SX looked like a 286 on the outside, it was a full 386DX on the inside. The 386SX could handle all of the modes and functions of the DX: 386 Protected Mode, Virtual Memory, and Virtual 8086.

Many people believe that the *SX* stands for *Single Channel* and the *DX* stands for *Dual Channel.* There is no proof of this and Intel has never made any statement to that effect. SX and DX are not acronyms.

POWER-SAVING STRATEGIES

CPUs, like all other electrical components, need electricity. Also, like all other electrical devices, CPUs require a certain voltage of electricity. During the era of the 8086s, 80286s, and 80386s, all CPUs needed 5 volts to operate. During the time of the 80386s, a new type of PC started to become popular—the laptop. There were 80286 laptops, but it wasn't until the 386s that they became truly common. Earlier portable computers derived their power from AC outlets. You turned off the PC, unplugged it, moved to another location, and then plugged it in again. Laptops were designed from the start to derive their power from built-in batteries. As we all can attest, batteries can only work for a relatively short time. The first laptops had batteries that lasted less than half an hour, which was hardly acceptable for any serious work!

It was quickly becoming obvious that if laptops were to become a mainstream product, they were going to have to have battery lives in the multi-hour range. To do that, you must either make better batteries and/or make laptops that used less power. On the *better battery* side, battery makers began to develop longer-lasting battery technologies with names like Nickel-Cadmium and Lithium-Ion. Intel decided to attack the power problem by making CPUs with lower voltage that took less power. Additionally, Intel forwarded a new function for CPUs. This new function, called *System Management Mode* (SMM), could shut down unused, power-draining peripherals.

Lower Voltage

Up to this point, all CPUs ran on 5 volts DC power. Intel invented a special 386SX designed to run in laptops. This CPU ran at 3.3 volts instead of 5 volts. This CPU was called the 386SL. By reducing the voltage usage from 5 to 3.3 volts, the 386SL used roughly half the power of an equivalent 386SX. By reducing the CPU's voltage, Intel led the way for reducing the voltage in every other chip in the laptop. All of the support chips in the laptop were also reduced to 3.3 volts, resulting in a laptop that would use far less power.

Lower voltages have totally taken over the PC world. Although many 486s and even a few of the very first Pentium CPUs used 5 volts, today all CPUs, whether they are in a laptop or on your desk, use 3.3 or even lower voltages. Starting with the 386 table and going forward, we will add another column to the CPU charts, showing the voltage for the CPUs.

On a few late-generation 386 and all 486 systems, you have two voltage issues. First, you need to determine the voltage of the CPU. Second, you need to make sure that the motherboard is supplying the proper voltage to the CPU. Let's look first at determining CPU voltage.

Determining CPU Voltage—386/486 Systems

Non-Intel CPU voltages can be determined by the model of microprocessor. For example, all AMD AM386DLs are 5 volts and all AMD AM386DLVs are 3.3 volts. The tables in this book contain all of the voltage information for the most common 386 and 486 CPUs.

There are a few exceptions to this rule. Certain non-Intel microprocessors are 3.3 volts, but only up to a certain clock speed. Any chips running at a faster clock speed will use 5 volts. One such chip is the AM386DLV. The 25 MHz is a 3.3-volt chip, while the 33 MHz is a 5 volt chip.

Intel sold the exact same model of chips in both 3.3 and 5-volt versions. Intel's rules are as follows:

- The only 3.3 volt 386 is the 386SL; all other 386's are 5 volts.
- On 486s, look for the *SL Enhanced* backwards ampersand &. After the ampersand, there will be a "3" or a "5"; "3" is for 3.3 volts, while a "5" is for five volts.
- On 486s, almost all non-PGA-packaged chips are low-voltage chips. All PGA chips without the backward & are 5 volts.

NOTE
When in doubt, call your supplier or reference this book—but get it right if you want the system to work!

What Voltage is Your Motherboard? 386/486 Systems

Once you know the voltage your CPU needs, you must then begin to verify that the motherboard can give that voltage to the CPU. From a voltage standpoint, there are three different types of 386/486 motherboards: they will be either 5 volt, 3.3 volt, or switchable between 3.3 and 5 volts.

The power supply, as we will see in the following chapter, provides a 5-volt circuit for powering electronic circuits, including CPUs. Some portable computers had power supplies with a special 3.3-volt wire for their low power CPUs. On desktop computers, on the other hand, 3.3-volt CPUs were provided power through a special dampening or regulating circuit on the motherboard itself. The power supplies continued to provide only 5 volt (and 12 volt) power.

The CPU voltage was never an issue for 386 systems. The 3.3 volt 386s were invariably soldered to the motherboard. Such, however, was not the case with 486 CPUs.

Intel (and its competitors) began making 486 CPUs that were identical except in voltages. Motherboard manufacturers wanted to make motherboards that could handle both 5V and 3.3V CPUs and thus not have to make two versions of the same motherboard.

These dual-voltage motherboards used a *voltage regulator* to provide for lower-power CPUs (see Figure 2.29). Technicians simply had to set the jumper(s) or dipswitch(es), depending upon which CPU they were installing.

Figure 2.29 Typical PC voltage regulator.

Take the time to make sure that the motherboard is set up for the particular voltage CPU you want to install. Most 486 motherboards allowed both 5V and 3.3V CPUs, and setting the jumpers could sometimes be a very complex task (see Figures 2.30–2.32). The motherboard manual is your best resource for the settings.

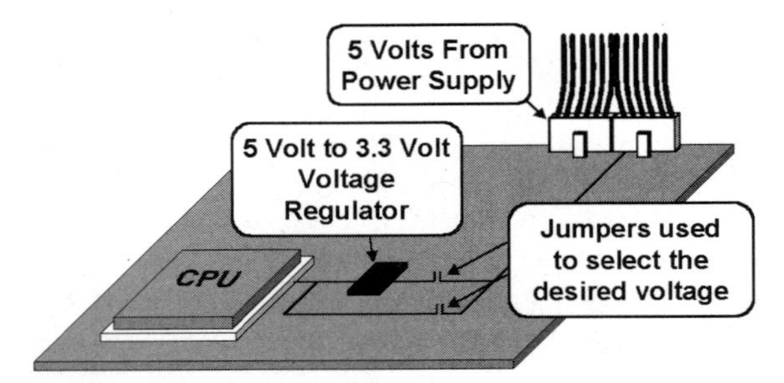

Figure 2.30 A two-voltage motherboard.

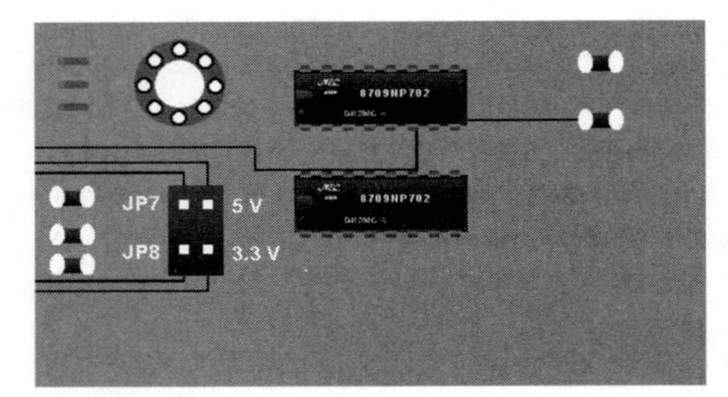

Figure 2.31 Voltage select jumpers.

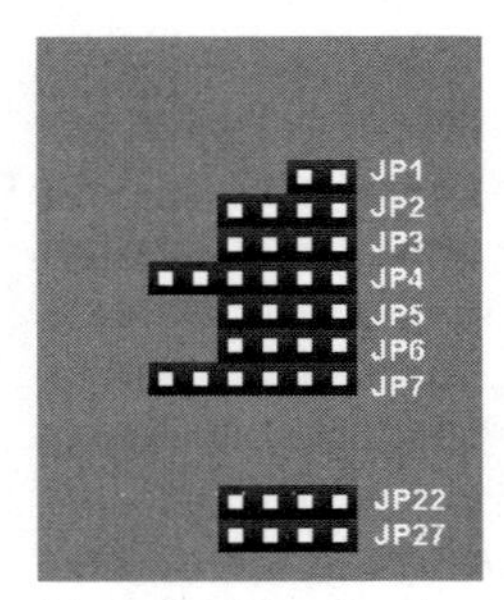

Figure 2.32 Overly complex set of jumpers.

System Management Mode **(SMM)**

The other way to save power is to turn off devices that are not being used by the system. For example, if you walk away from your PC, wouldn't it be nice to have the monitor turn itself off after a set amount of time? How about telling the hard drive to stop spinning if it hasn't been accessed after a few minutes? *System Management Mode* is a hardware-based function, designed by Intel, which allows the CPU to selectively shut down the monitor, hard drives, or any other peripheral not in use in order to save power.

The 486 CPU Family

In 1989, Intel released the i486. The i486 has 32-bit registers, a 32-bit external data bus, and a 32-bit memory address bus, exactly like the 386DX. However, the i486 has far more than the 386DX. It is actually the combination of a slightly improved 386DX, a built-in (and also improved) 387 math coprocessor, and most importantly, a built-in 8K write-through cache, all on the same chip.

NO NEW MODES!

The 486 runs the exact same modes as a 80386. None of the new features of a 486 (math coprocessor and cache) are tied to a specific 486 mode. The most advanced mode the 486 can run is 80386 Protected mode, with Virtual Memory and Virtual 8086, just like an 80386. From a program's point of view, there is no difference between an 80386 with a math coprocessor and a 486!

IMPROVED INSTRUCTION SET

The 486's instruction set includes new functions for optimizing the 486's capability to work in multitasking environments, as well as allowing control over new cache functions. Also, some of the 486's machine language commands act as *Reduced Instruction Set Computing* (RISC) instructions. This means that machine language commands do not have to be "decoded" inside the chip. The computer sees and immediately executes about 20 percent of the 486's most common commands. The other commands still have to be decoded. Because decoding takes at least one clock cycle, removing decode from the processor's functions, whenever possible, is a tremendous asset.

Note: The 486 is not a RISC Chip! It is considered a *Complex Instruction Set Computing* (CISC) chip with a few RISC functions.

MATH COPROCESSOR

All CPUs can add, subtract, multiply, and divide. Remember when we added 2 + 3? There are basic mathematical commands built into every CPU's instruction set. What if you wanted to determine the cosine of a number? There are no built-in commands to perform higher mathematical functions like trigonometrics (sine, cosine, tangent), logarithms (e^x, $\log_{10}x$, ln x) or large floating point numbers ($3.027x10^{24}$). In order to perform high math functions like these, programmers had to write code using approximation formulas. These took hundreds, maybe thousands, of lines of code to get an answer for something like the log (34.2321).

When Intel designed the 8088, it sold a supplementary CPU called the 8087 that could perform these calculations. Why not design the 8088 with all these functions built in? Well, they could have, but it would have increased the cost of the 8088 by at least a factor of two. Plus, very few people needed these extra functions unless they were doing heavy math-intensive calculations. So Intel felt that if you wanted to do extra calculations, you would be willing to pay more. The IBM PC had an extra slot on the motherboard designed for the optional math coprocessor. When the 80286 was created, an improved 8087 called the 80287 was developed. The IBM 286 *AT* had an optional 80287 slot. Same with the 80386—the 80387.

The 486 has basically a 387 math coprocessor built-in to the CPU. The built-in 387 math coprocessor is substantially more powerful than its external 80387 brother. Because it is onboard the CPU, it depends much less on clock cycles. Also, the internal math coprocessor is able to take advantage of the cache, as needed, to store data and code. Finally, there are two different 32-bit pathways to the math unit that can work at the same time, effectively providing a 64-bit program and data path between the math unit and the rest of the 486.

ONBOARD CACHE

The 8K onboard write-through RAM cache allows the 486 to store upcoming lines of instructions as well as data. Although an 8K cache seems small, it can allow for tremendous speed improvements. Let's see how caching works.

CACHE

Reading Webster's, we see that to *cache* means "to set something aside, or to store nearby, for anticipated use." The word *cache* first became popular in the 18th century, when French trappers would bury food and supplies in strategic areas in case they were ever stranded by the weather. In the computer world, to cache means to set aside data that you've used in the past in a special storage area. Then, should you need that data again, it will be easily (and much more quickly) available.

To understand caching, we need to understand that speed is everything in the PC world. If you look at any type of data (program, document, font, whatever . . .), it almost always starts on a hard drive, floppy, or CD-ROM (collectively known as mass storage). It is first read into RAM, and then read into the CPU. Data then returns through the same process: the CPU writes to RAM, and then RAM writes to mass storage (see Figure 2.33).

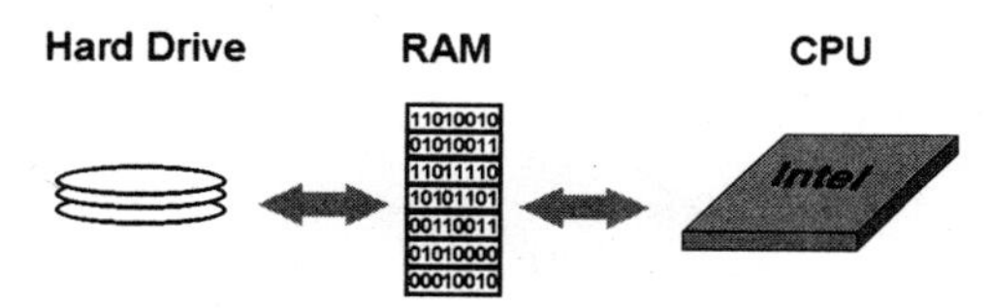

Figure 2.33 Mass storage, RAM, and the CPU.

The problem is that mass storage is much slower than RAM, and RAM is much slower than the CPU. Caching allows us to speed up the system by creating special storage areas for data (see Figure 2.34). That is being moved from the hard drive, RAM, and CPU.

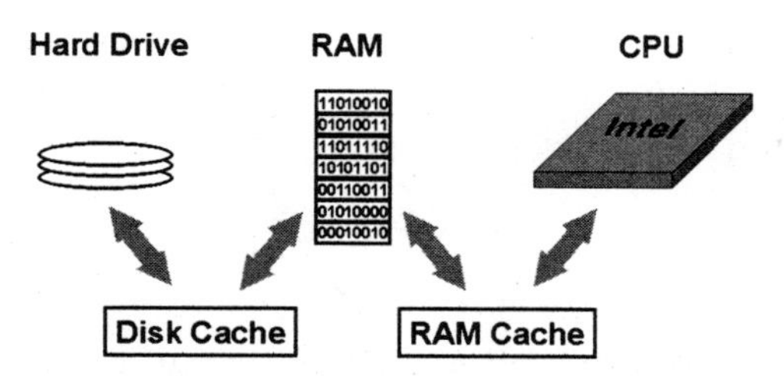

Figure 2.34 Disk cache and RAM cache.

Based on this diagram, we see that we have two distinct types of caches: one for mass storage and another for RAM. At this point, we are going to concentrate on the RAM cache. For an in-depth discussion of hard drive caches, see the DOS chapter.

DRAM (and Why We Cache It)

Dynamic RAM or DRAM is the RAM of choice for the PC world. DRAM is cheap, small, and relatively fast, although not as fast as today's CPUs. DRAM works by making each storage bit into a microscopic capacitor and a microscopic transistor. A charged capacitor is a *1* and a discharged capacitor is a *0* (see Figure 2.35).

Figure 2.35 Each 1 or 0 is a capacitor.

DRAM has a small problem—the capacitors. A capacitor resembles a battery; it holds a charge and then discharges it. Unlike a battery that holds a charge for months, the tiny capacitors in the DRAM hold their charges for about 16 milliseconds. Therefore, the DRAM needs an entire set of circuitry to keep the capacitors charged. The process of recharging these capacitors is called *refresh.* Without refresh, data added to RAM would disappear after 16 milliseconds. This is why DRAM is called *volatile* RAM.

The memory controller chip (MCC) tells the refresh circuitry on the DRAM chip when to refresh. Every few milliseconds, the MCC sends a refresh signal to the RAM and the RAM chips begin their refresh. Unfortunately, if the CPU decides to access the RAM at this point, the MCC will create a *wait state* (see Figure 2.36).

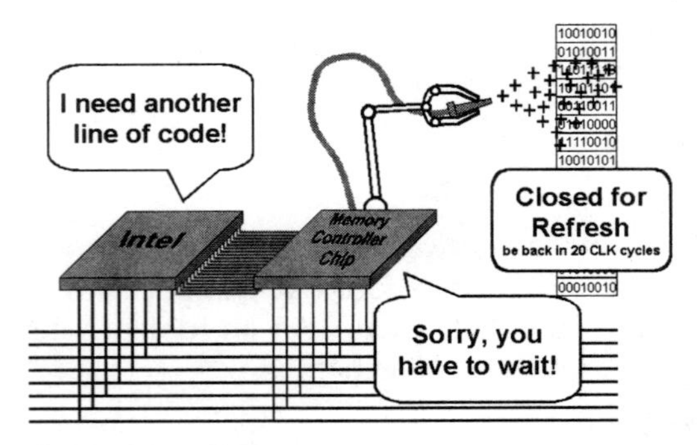

Figure 2.36 Hitting a wait state.

The other problem with DRAM is that it is not as fast as the CPU. The CPU often has wait states, not because the RAM is refreshing, but simply because it has to wait for the DRAM to get the values it needs.

SRAM

Wait states cause the computer to slow down dramatically. If there were some way to get around this problem, we could speed up the computer significantly. We do this by adding special chips called *SRAM* chips to the computer. *Static RAM* (SRAM) is another type of RAM that doesn't use tiny capacitors to store the ones and zeroes. Instead, SRAM uses a special circuit called a flip-flop. Using flip-flops instead of capacitors means that SRAM doesn't have to be refreshed. SRAM is also almost as fast as the fastest CPU.

Now that we have this SRAM, how do we use it? Why not get rid of the DRAM and replace it with SRAM? Because SRAM is at least 10 times more expensive than DRAM, that's why! However, we can afford a small amount of SRAM as a cache.

> **NOTE**
> **DRAM: Fast, cheap, must be refreshed**
> **SRAM: Very fast, very expensive, no refresh**

Internal Cache

The main difference between a 486 and a 386 chip is that a 486 has a small (8192 bytes) SRAM cache built into the chip. All commands for the 486 go through the cache. The 486 will store a backlog of commands in the cache so if a wait state is encountered, the 486 will keep processing from the cache. This is called an internal cache or a Level One (L1) cache (see Figure 2.37).

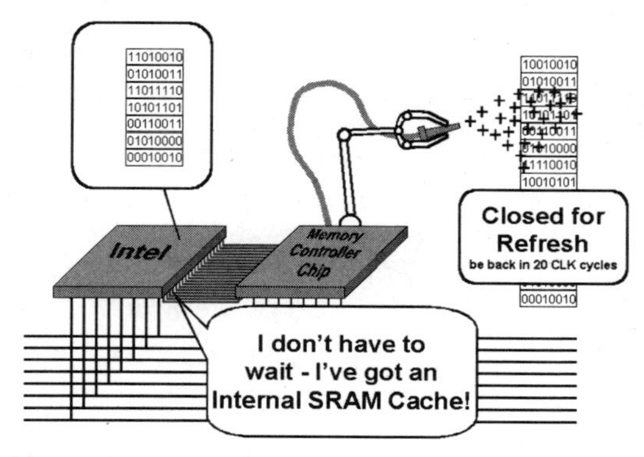

Figure 2.37 Internal cache.

Caching will store any code that has been read in the past. That way, if the CPU asks for that code again, it will already be in the cache and the CPU will not have to wait for DRAM to go get it. All CPUs from the 486 up have internal caches.

External Cache

Although an internal cache on the CPU is very helpful, sometimes more cache would be useful. Therefore, many MCCs are designed to work with an external cache called an L2 cache (see Figure 2.38). An L2 cache is like the same good stuff that you see on an L1 cache, just more of it. An L2 cache is usually around 64K to 1Meg, depending mainly on the size of your wallet. This memory manifests itself with special SRAM chips that sit on the motherboard. Many motherboards have L2 cache soldered permanently to the motherboard.

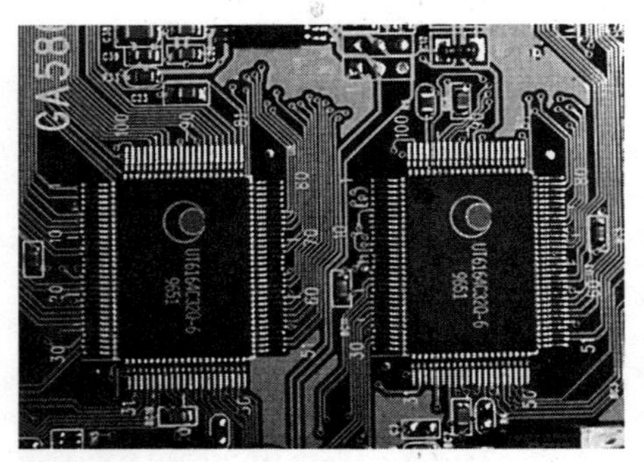

Figure 2.38 Typical external (L2) cache.

Write-back versus Write-through

Everything discussed so far is based only on *reading* from the RAM chips to the CPU. What would happen if we *wrote* data to the RAM? What should the cache do with write data? Some caches will immediately send all data writes directly to RAM, even if it means hitting a wait state. This is called *write-through*. However, some caches will store the write data in the cache and write it to RAM later. These caches are called *write-back* (see Figure 2.39). Write-back caches are harder to implement, but are much more powerful than write-through caches. Write-through caches are cheaper to use, but not as powerful.

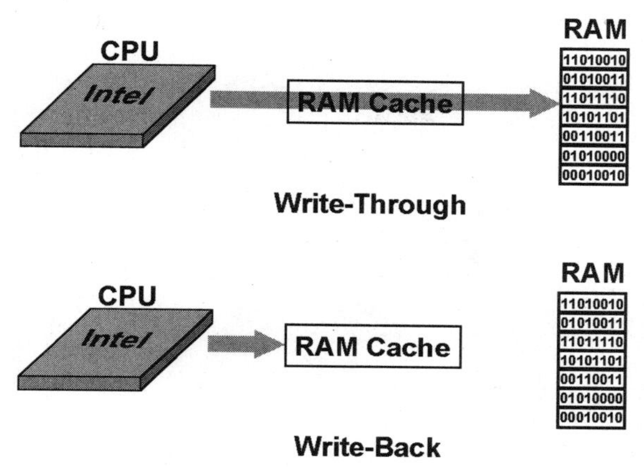

Figure 2.39 Write-through versus Write-back.

Different Caches for Different Chips

Different makers of 486s had different ways of caching. Check the tables in this chapter to see the differences between chipmakers on size of cache and write-through vs. write-back. Cyrix, AMD, and Intel were constantly one-upping each other, touting their respective caches and sizes.

CLOCK DOUBLING

Once 486s got up to 33MHz clock speeds, the PC industry found itself with a bit of a problem. CPU makers wanted to increase their CPU speeds greater than 33MHz, but the motherboards of the time couldn't go faster than 33MHz! This was due to *Radio Frequency Interference* (RFI), among other problems. Oh sure, you could get a motherboard to go faster but they would be expensive because the cheap technology was locked at 33MHz (see Figure 2.40).

To circumvent this problem, Intel came up with the idea of a *clock doubling* CPU (see Figure 2.41). Clock doubling means to run the internals of the PC at one clock speed, while running the external data bus and address bus at another slower speed. CPUs that have internal caches spend the majority of the clock cycles inside themselves, not sending any data on the external busses. These chips can run at some multiplier of the system clock while they are inside themselves. This allows faster processing without having to speed up the entire computer.

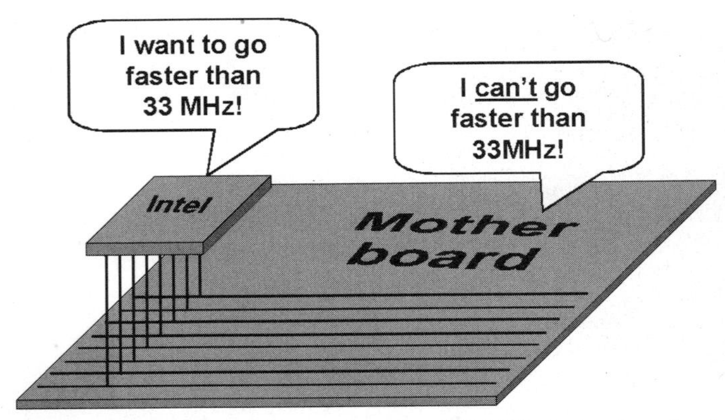

Figure 2.40 CPUs could be made to break 33MHz, but not motherboards.

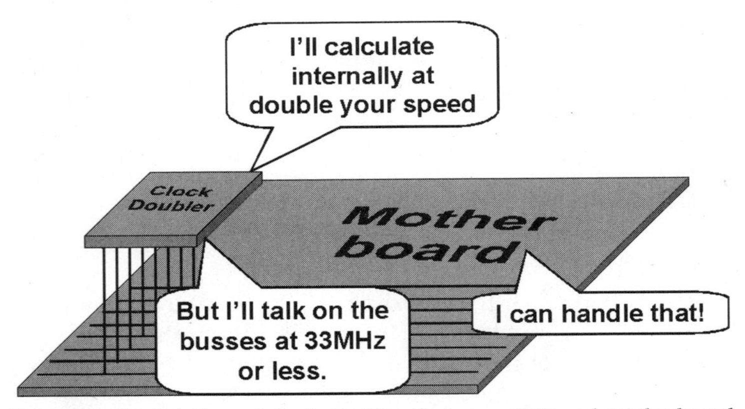

Figure 2.41 Relation of clock doubling between CPU and motherboard.

Clock doubling chips always have two speeds: an internal speed and an external speed. The first clock doubler was the Intel 486DX/2, which came in two different speeds: 25/50MHz and 33/66MHz (see Figure 2.42). The first speed is the external or system bus speed and the second value represents the internal speed of the CPU.

Figure 2.42 A clock doubling 486—the DX/2.

In the 486 world, the multiplier is built-in at the factory. For example, the 486DX/2 multiplies the system crystal's clock speed by two. So, if you have a 486DX/2 33/66 being pushed by a 33MHz crystal, it runs at an internal speed of 66MHz. But remember that the clock speed is a *maximum* speed—you can run a CPU slower than its clock speed by pushing it with a slower crystal (see Figure 2.43). If you decide to run the 486DX/2 with a 25MHZ crystal, the 486DX/2 33/66 will double the clock speed to 50MHz.

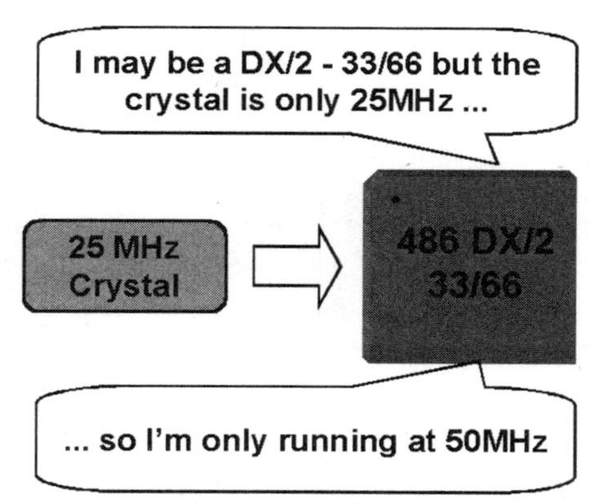

Figure 2.43 Underclocking a clock doubler.

Clock doubling has come to mean *any multiplier*. For example, the 486DX/4 actually triples the clock speed, but is still called a doubler. Just because someone says doubler, don't assume *times two.*

486 CPUs Note: All 486s have a 32-bit Address Bus. and 32-bit Registers

CHIP TYPE	CPU SPEED	CLK MULT	XTRL BUS	INT'L CACHE	MATH UNIT	VOLTS	SMM
INTEL 80486DX	25,33,50	1 X	32-Bit	8 K	YES	3.3/5 V	YES *
INTEL 80486DX/2	25/50 33/66	2 X	32-Bit	8 K	YES	3.3/5 V	YES *
INTEL 80486DX/4	25/75 33/100	3 X	32-Bit	16 K	YES	5 V	YES *
INTEL 80486SX	16,20,25	1 X	32-Bit	8 K	None	5 V	YES *
INTEL 80486SL	16,20,25	1 X	32-Bit	8 K	None	3.3 V	YES
AMD AM486DX	33,40	1 X	32-Bit	8 K	YES	5 V	NO
AMD AM486DXLV	33	1 X	32-Bit	8 K	YES	3.3 V	YES
AMD AM486DX2	25/50 40/80	2 X	32-Bit	8 K	YES	3.3/5 V	NO
AMD AM486DX4	33/100 40/120	3 X	32-Bit	8 K	YES	3.3 V	YES
AMD AM486DX4 "Enhanced"	40/120, 33/133	3 X 4 X	32-Bit	16 K W/B	YES	3.3 V	YES

CHIP TYPE	CPU SPEED	CLK MULT	XTRL BUS	INT'L CACHE	MATH UNIT	VOLTS	SMM
AMD AM486DXL2	25/50 40/80	2 X	32-Bit	8 K	YES	5 V	NO
AMD AM486SX	33,40	1 X	32-Bit	8 K	None	5 V	NO
AMDAM486SXLV	33	1 X	32-Bit	8 K	None	3.3 V	YES
AMD AM486SX2	25/50	2 X	32-Bit	8 K	None	5 V	NO
CYRIX CX486DX	33	1 X	32-Bit	8 K W/B	YES	3.3/5 V	YES
CYRIX CX486DX2	25/50 40/80	2 X	32-Bit	8 K W/B	YES	3.3/5 V	YES
CYRIX CX486DLC	33 - 40	1 X	32-Bit	1 K W/T	YES	5 V	YES *
CYRIX CX486SLC	20 - 33	1 X	16-Bit	1 K W/T	NO	3.3/5 V	YES
CYRIX CX486SLC2	25/50	2 X	32-Bit	1 K W/T	NO	3.3/5 V	YES

*See SMM

UPGRADING 486 CPUS

A CPU is useless until you insert it into a motherboard. The device into which you insert the CPU has classically been called a *socket.* During the reign of the 8088s, 286s, and 386s, there was little interest in sockets because upgrading a CPU was an extremely rare occurrence. However, towards the end of the 386s, a number of innovations came about that created the desire and the capability to upgrade CPUs.

The first innovation that made upgradability practical was a motherboard that had more than one clock speed. Remember that the system crystal is on the motherboard. If you removed a 25MHz CPU and inserted a 33MHz CPU, the 33MHz would still only run at 25MHz. Starting with a few 386 motherboards, but becoming mainstream in the 486 motherboards, we began to see the capability to change the system crystal speed via jumpers on the motherboard (see Figure 2.44).

Figure 2.44 Jumpers to adjust motherboard speed.

The second innovation was the strong adoption of the PGA-type CPU package. There were (still are) many types of CPU packages, but by the time of the 486s, the vast majority of CPUs made were in the PGA package. Because the CPUs were all PGA, the motherboards all had PGA sockets. As long as the motherboard had adjustable voltage and motherboard speed, you could easily change the CPU in the system.

The third innovation was the *Zero Insertion Force* (ZIF) socket. ZIF sockets have a lever arm that allows for simple removal and installation of CPUs. Before ZIF sockets came along, you had to use a special removal tool to take the CPU off the motherboard (see Figure 2.45).

ZIF sockets allow for a much easier, and safer, removal (see Figure 2.46).

There are many types of ZIF sockets - the following table and diagram show the different types of 486 ZIF sockets.

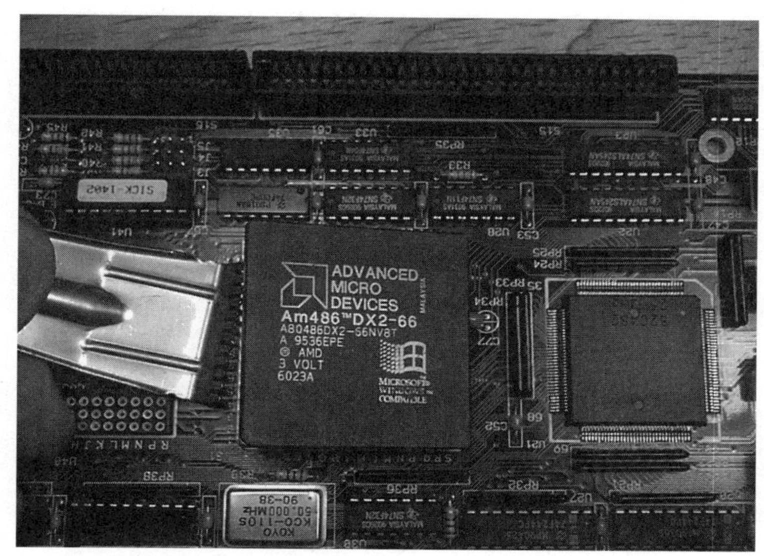

Figure 2.45 CPU removal tool.

Figure 2.46 ZIF socket.

Socket	No. Of Pins	Pin Layout	Voltage	CPU Type
1	169	17 x 17 PGA	5V	486SX/SX2, DX/DX2, 486 Overdrive
2	238	19 x 19 PGA	5V	SX/SX2, DX/DX2, DX4, Pentium OverDrive
3	237	19 x 19 PGA	5V/3.3V	SX/SX2, DX/DX2, DX4, Pentium OverDrive
6	235	19 x 19 PGA	3.3V	486 DX4, Pentium OverDrive

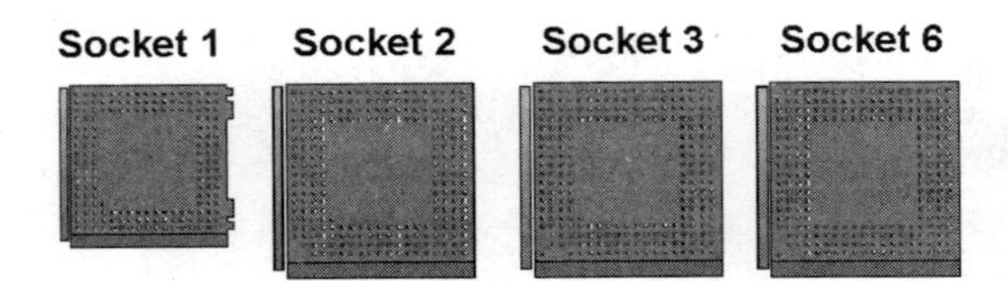

Figure 2.47 486 ZIF sockets.

OVERDRIVE CPUS FOR 486S

When the 486 chip was first released, a number of computer manufacturers began to make *upgradable* systems. These systems had proprietary CPU cards (often called daughter cards) that could be removed and replaced with a daughter card having a more powerful CPU. Intel realized, as 486s that were more powerful came into the market, that first-generation 486s running at 25MHz could be good candidates for upgrading. Intel unveiled the 486 *Overdrive* chips to take advantage of this anticipated market. The 486 Overdrive Chips were nothing more than a 486DX/2 or DX/4 with an extra pin. In order to take advantage of an Overdrive processor, one normally needed a special, extra 169-Pin PGA/ZIF socket, designed especially for the Overdrive chip.

Although Overdrives were a simple, effective upgrade for systems that were prepared for their use, there were some major downsides. First, if you plugged in an Overdrive, the old processor was disabled, BUT YOU COULDN'T REMOVE IT! This was frustrating, considering that you could have sold that old 486SX or DX. Second, most 486 motherboards could accept multiple types of regular processors, which negated the need for an Overdrive. However, if you already had an Overdrive Ready motherboard, it was often a cost-effective option.

The term "OverDrive" is now used by Intel to describe a broad family of replacement processors, not only for 486 systems, but also for older Pentium systems. Here's a list of Intel 486 OverDrive processors.

486 OverDrive CPUs for 486 Systems

Chip	Speed (MHz)	Recommended Upgrades
486DX/2	25/50	486SX-25 486DX-25
486DX/2	33/66	486SX-33 486DX-33
486DX/4	25/75	486SX-25 486DX-25 486DX/2 25/50
486DX/4	33/100	486SX-33 486DX-33 486DX/2 33/66

The 486 Overdrive CPUs are no longer produced. Intel now sells a series of Overdrive CPUs that can convert a 486 system to a Pentium level. These 486-to-Pentium level Overdrive CPUs are covered in the Pentium section.

Upgrading 386s: the CYRIX CX486DRx²–CX486SRx²

To say that no one upgraded before 486s is not exactly true. Motherboard manufacturers began to create upgradable systems as early as the 286 era. As mentioned earlier, these systems usually had a CPU-on-a-board type strategy that allowed the replacement of the CPU, crystal, and a few other support chips all in one.

However, there were some attempts at replacement CPUs for 286 and 386 systems. The 286-to-386 replacement chips were universally buggy and were generally rejected by the end users. There was better luck with the 386-to-486 replacement chips. Due to the fact that the 386 and 486 shared the same size address and external data bus, it was a lot easier to create upgrade CPUs.

By far the most popular of all 386-to-486 replacement CPUs was the Cyrix DRx2 and the SRx2 for 80386DX and 80386SX systems, respectively. The upgrade was performed by replacing the 386 with the Cyrix chip. The Rx2 chips were clock-doubled versions of the Cyrix DLC and SLC chips. These chips were extremely dependable and were an excellent alternative to motherboard replacements for older 386 computers. With the upgrade, one received all the benefits of a 486DX/2: a 1K write-back cache and clock doubling.

The Pentium CPU—the Early Years

1993 saw the introduction of the Pentium processor. The Pentium was a major technological leap forward from the 486 and included many new functions. The Pentium has a 64-bit external data bus that splits internally as two *dual-pipelined* 32-bit data busses. These give the chip the ability to process two separate lines of code simultaneously. The Pentium also sports an 8K write-back cache for data and an 8K write-through cache for programs (see Figure 2.48). The program cache is capable of *branch prediction*. In branch prediction, the program cache will attempt to anticipate branching within the program it is running. The CPU will store a few lines of code from each branch so that when the code reaches the branch, the Pentium already has the lines of code stored within the cache.

Figure 2.48 Pentium CPU.

DUAL PIPELINE

All CPUs have a pipeline (see Figure 2.49). The pipeline is all of the discrete steps that each command must go through to be processed. If one were to look at the steps of a 486 for example, you would see the following:

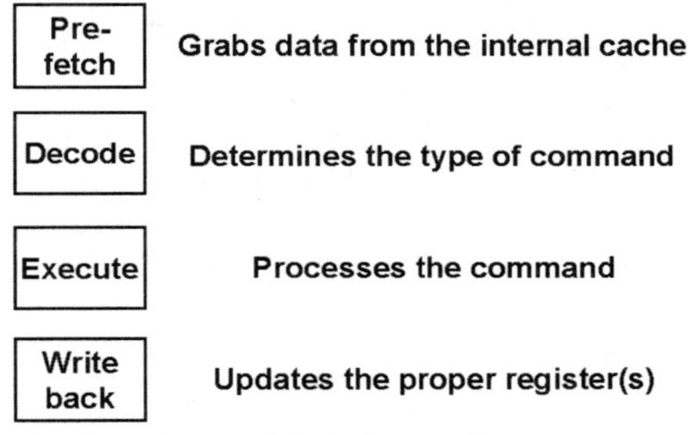

Figure 2.49 Simplified CPU pipeline.

The problem is the execute stage. Inside the CPU are different sets of circuitry to handle different types of commands. There are four main different circuits inside the CPU for different commands as shown in Figure 2.50.

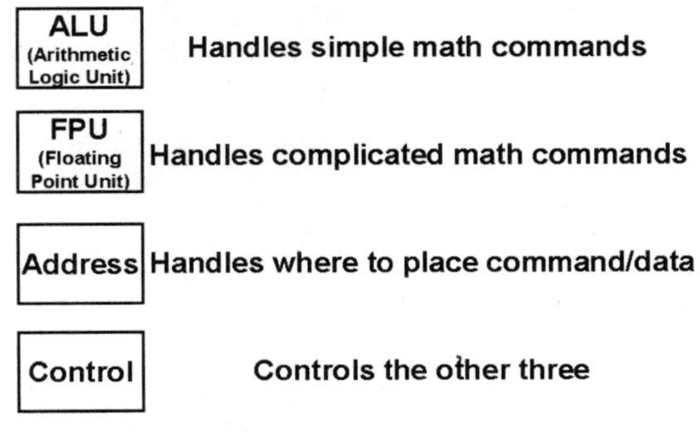

Figure 2.50 Four main processes in a CPU.

So, a command passes through some or all of these circuits as it is processed (see Figure 2.51).

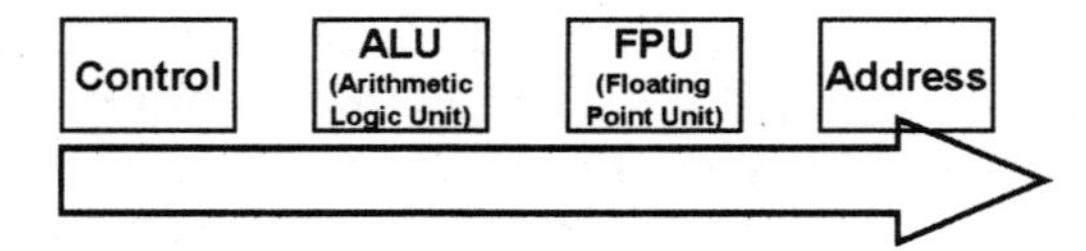

Figure 2.51 Possible pipeline.

Think of pipelining like washing clothes (see Figure 2.52). You don't sort, wash, dry, fold, and iron one load at a time. You get it all sorted, then you start one load in the washer. After that washer load is finished, you put that load in the dryer and start another load in the washer, so that the washer and dryer are running at the same time. You keep this up until you are washing, drying, folding, and maybe even ironing at the same time. This is far more efficient.

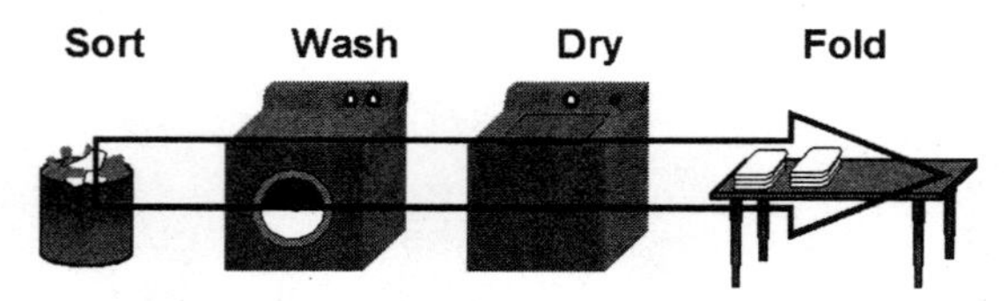

Figure 2.52 Pipelines are like washing clothes.

Imagine that you had an extra washing machine and an extra dryer. That would certainly speed up the process, wouldn't it? Sure, you would sometimes have to wait for some of the other steps in the pipeline, but it would help (see Figure 2.53).

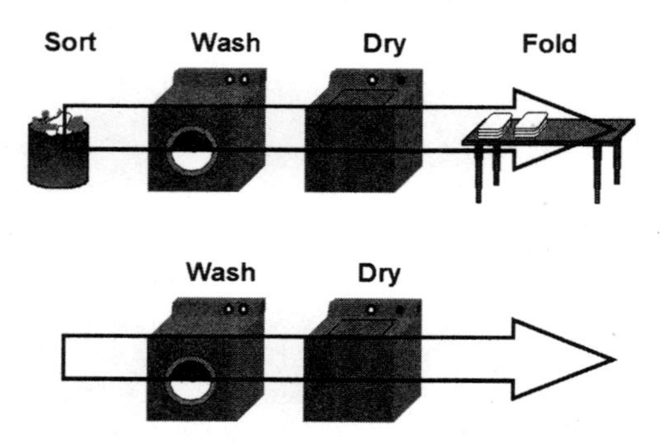

Figure 2.53 Not all stages are required.

Well, a Pentium has a second, separate set of circuitry that allows more than one command (of certain types) to be processed at a time. This is called *dual pipelining* (see Figure 2.54).

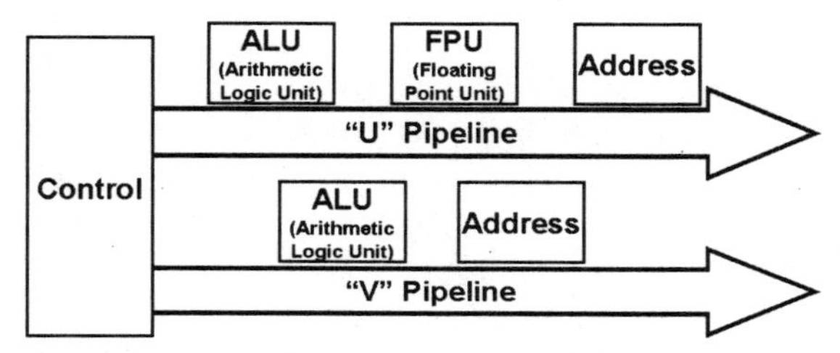

Figure 2.54 Dual-pipelining, Pentium style.

The names of the pipelines are called *U* and *V*. The *U* pipeline is the main one that can do anything; the *V* pipeline can only handle simple commands such as integer addition.

CPU Voltages: Pentium Systems

A CPU is little more than a huge conglomeration of tiny transistors. Millions of transistors. Now, all transistors create heat; the faster you make a transistor work, the more heat it generates. The tiny transistors in a CPU generate a trivial amount of heat individually but, as you add more and more transistors to faster and faster generations of CPUs, the amount of heat becomes significant. If a CPU gets too hot, it will lock up and not operate. If you look at a CPU, what you are looking at is a plastic or ceramic outer case. The electronics of the CPU are much smaller than the case (see Figure 2.55).

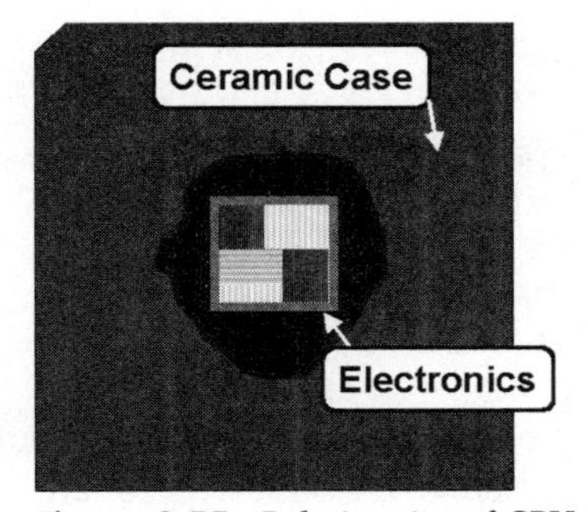

Figure 2.55 Relative size of CPU case to electronics.

Why? The case is used to dissipate the heat generated by the CPU. The heat from 8088, 286, and 386 systems was relatively low due to the relatively low speeds and low number of transistors. The outer case could easily handle the necessary dissipation. By the time of the 486s, plastic cases were no longer acceptable and ceramic cases became standard. Heat first became a serious problem in the late-generation 486 CPUs. This could be easily resolved for the most part by using cooling fans or fins that could be attached to the CPU. However, the Pentium created some very serious heat problems that simply adding a fan could not repair. The first two Pentium CPUs, the 60MHz and the 66MHz, needed 5 volts for operation, and they were hot— very hot. If you can make a CPU that can run at a lower voltage, usually by making the tiny transistors even tinier, the CPU will run at a much lower temperature. So why didn't Intel make the first Pentiums to be 3.3 volt instead of 5 volt? Intel simply didn't have the technology at the time to make a 3.3-volt CPU with that many transistors. Consequently, the original 5-volt Pentiums had much larger cases than the later 3.3-volt versions.

As Intel developed the technology to make lower-power CPUs, the Pentium shrunk down to the common size seen today.

Low-Voltage CPUs: the Early Pentiums

CPU voltage in the early Pentium world was relatively simple. With the exception of the Pentium 60 and 66 that operated at 5 volts, all of the early Pentiums ran at 3.3 volts.

What Voltage is Your Motherboard? Early Pentium Systems

Even as 3.3-volt CPUs began to dominate the early Pentiums, there was talk of even lower-voltage CPUs. This potential made it hard for motherboard makers to sleep. How could they make a motherboard to support both 3.3 and lower voltages? How could they keep the motherboards they were making today from being obsolete tomorrow? People don't want to buy computer parts, especially hard to replace motherboards, which have a high potential of being obsolesced too quickly.

The first way to support lower-voltage CPUs was by adding more than one voltage regulator to the motherboard (see Figure 2.56). The motherboard makers knew that the lower voltage was going to be in the range of 2.9 volts. Taking a chance, many motherboard makers simply added a second voltage regulator that dropped the voltage from 5 to 2.9 volts. Here's an example of a motherboard with two voltage regulators.

Figure 2.56 Two voltage regulators.

You would activate the proper voltage regulator by moving the four jumpers located directly below the voltage regulators.

The second concept, proposed by Intel, was to have CPUs that came with their own standardized voltage regulators! Whatever voltage regulator was needed was soldered to a small card and was called a *voltage regulator module* (VRM). The VRM would fit into a special VRM slot next to the CPU (see Figure 2.57).

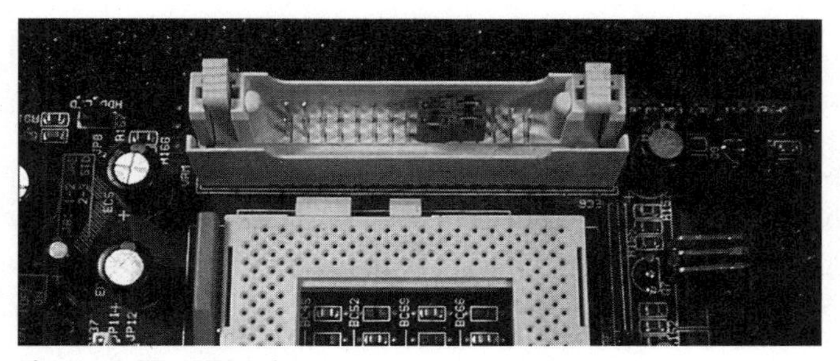

Figure 2.57 VRM slot.

The previous example has both a VRM as well as soldered voltage regulators. The jumpers inside the VRM slot control the voltage regulators. When a VRM is installed, the jumpers are removed. This disables the voltage regulators and gives the VRM control.

Pentium Clock Doubling

Remember the 33MHz-motherboard speed limit in the 486 world? Well, this limit was soundly crushed with the Pentium. All Pentium motherboards run at speeds up to 66MHz. However, early Pentium

CPUs had/have clock speeds up to 200MHz. How can they do that on motherboards that only run at 66MHz? Simple—they are all clock doublers. Plus, Pentium clock doubling (better known as the *multiplier* in the Pentium world) isn't limited to whole numbers like 2 or 3 times the motherboard speed (see Figure 2.58). An early Pentium can have multipliers of 1, 1.5, 2, 2.5, and 3.

Figure 2.58 Pentiums are clock doublers.

Equally interesting is the fact that you have to configure the multiplier on a Pentium. With 486s, if you bought, say a 486DX/2-33/66, the multiplier was 2 and there was no way to change it. Sure, you could use different speed motherboards, but you couldn't change the multiplier from times two to something like times three. The 486 multiplier was built-in by the CPU manufacturer.

Pentium CPUs don't have a built-in multiplier. All Pentium motherboards come with a set of jumpers or switches that allow you to set the proper multiplier. So, when you install a Pentium, not only do you have to set the motherboard speed, but you also need to set the multiplier. Here's a drawing of a nice Pentium motherboard that clearly shows both the motherboard speed and the multiplier jumpers (see Figure 2.59).

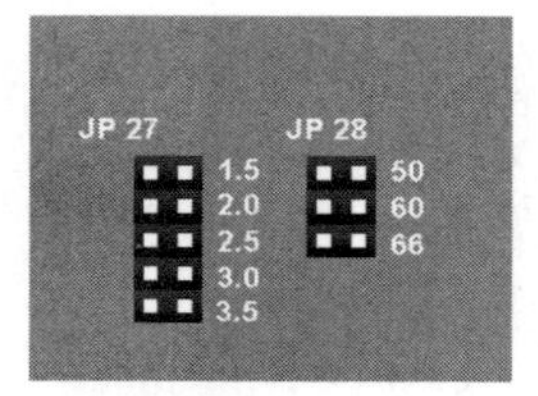

Figure 2.59 Pentium motherboard clock and multiplier jumpers.

So how do you know what is the correct clock speed and multiplier? Simple—the manufacturers tell you and you do what they say! For example, if you buy a Pentium 200, you set the clock to 66 and the multiplier to 3—'cuz Intel said so, that's why!

In other words, when you buy a Pentium, the first question you ask is "What is the clock speed and multiplier?" If the supplier can't quickly answer, run away!

Early Pentium Competitors

Because "Pentium" is a copyrighted product name, competitors to Pentium have chosen to call their chips by a variety of names, each intended to imply compatibility with the Intel x86 family of processors. Unlike some of their later CPUs, the early Pentium competitors had little success against the true Intel Pentium (see the table on the following pages).

AMD K5

The AMD K5 was pin-compatible with the Pentium. Although it was pin-compatible, the K5 was a different animal on the inside. It was basically a RISC (Reduced Instruction Set Computing) CPU designed to be compatible with the Pentium. AMD sold them cheaply and they made some serious sales in the low-end area. The K5 was quickly eclipsed by other CPUs.

Cyrix 6x86/6x86L

The Cyrix 6x86 delivered true Pentium-level performance at a very low price. Early in this chapter, we saw how the 486 offered improved performance over the 386 by streamlining the operating instructions within the processor. Because similar improvements were made within the architecture of the 6x86, it could process instructions as quickly as a Pentium at a lower clock rate. The 6x86 CPU ran at a clock rate that was substantially slower than the Pentium chip it was designed to replace, yet it delivered comparable performance. Unfortunately, the first 6x86 CPUs were very hot and had a few small bugs. The 6x86L eliminated these early problems and was a powerful, inexpensive CPU.

Early Pentium CPUs

CPU	Maker	Core Speed	Ext Speed	Mult	Cache	Voltage	Package[2]
Pentium—P5	Intel	60	60	1	8T/8W	5	Socket 5
Pentium—P5	Intel	66	66	1	8T/8W	5	Socket 5
Pentium—P54C	Intel	75	50	1.5	8T/8W	3.3	Socket 7
Pentium—P54C	Intel	90	60	1.5	8T/8W	3.3	Socket 7
Pentium—P54C	Intel	100	66	1.5	8T/8W	3.3	Socket 7
Pentium—P54C	Intel	120	60	2	8T/8W	3.3	Socket 7
Pentium—P54C	Intel	133	66	2	8T/8W	3.3	Socket 7
Pentium—P54C	Intel	150	60	2.5	8T/8W	3.3	Socket 7
Pentium—P54C	Intel	166	66	2.5	8T/8W	3.3	Socket 7
Pentium—P54C	Intel	200	66	3	8T/8W	3.3	Socket 7
K5—PR75[1]	AMD	75	50	1.5	8T/8W	3.3	Socket 7
K5—PR90[1]	AMD	90	60	1.5	8T/8W	3.3	Socket 7

CPU	Maker	Core Speed	Ext Speed	Mult	Cache	Voltage	Package[2]
K5—PR100[1]	AMD	100	66	1.5	8T/8W	3.3	Socket 7
K5—PR120[1]	AMD	90	60	1.5	8T/8W	3.3	Socket 7
K5—PR133[1]	AMD	100	66	1.5	8T/8W	3.3	Socket 7
K5—PR166[1]	AMD	116	66	1.75	8T/8W	3.3	Socket 7
6x86/6x86L–P120[1]	Cyrix	100	50	2	8T/8W	3.3[3]	Socket 7
6x86/6x86L–P133[1]	Cyrix	110	55	2	8T/8W	3.3[3]	Socket 7
6x86/6x86L–P150[1]	Cyrix	120	60	2	8T/8W	3.3[3]	Socket 7
6x86/6x86L–P166[1]	Cyrix	133	66	2	8T/8W	3.3[3]	Socket 7
6x86/6x86L–P200[1]	Cyrix	150	75	2	8T/8W	3.3[3]	Socket 7

1 See P–Rating

2 See Pentium Socket Types

3 The 6x86L used 2.9 volts

P-Rating

Intel's competitors have a problem—they can't compare apples and oranges. Let's say Cyrix makes the 6x86, which runs at 100MHz. Now, Cyrix knows that its 6x86-100 can handle more calculations per second than an Intel Pentium-100, due to improvements in caching, pipelining, and program execution. In fact, the 6x86-100 runs as fast as a Pentium-120. In order to show this improvement, Cyrix, IBM Microelectronics, SGS-Thomson, and AMD developed the *P-Rating*. The P-rating allows you to quickly compare a Cyrix or AMD CPU against the Intel chips.

The problem with P-ratings is that they can cause some confusion. For example, if a person buys a Cyrix P-120, they are really getting a 100MHz CPU. Therefore, when purchasing AMD and Cyrix CPUs, be prepared to install the CPU with different values than the ones printed on the CPU!

Here are a few examples:

CPU	"P" Rating	External Speed	Multiple	Internal Speed
Cyrix 6x86–P200+	200	75 MHz	X 2	150 MHz
AMD K–5–166	166	66 MHz	X 1.75	116.5 MHz

There is nothing wrong with P-ratings! In fact, they are an excellent way to compare AMD and Cyrix CPUs with Intel processors. However, it is not an absolute, perfect gauge. Use it as a rough guideline only.

PENTIUM SOCKET TYPES

The Pentium CPU had significantly more pins and therefore needed a larger case than the 486. The original Pentium 60 and 66 simply used a larger PGA-type package (see Figure 2.60). All other Pentiums used a totally different type of case called a *Staggered Pin Grid Array* (SPGA). The SPGA, as its name describes, staggers the pins, allowing a higher pin density and a smaller case. The SPGA package continues to be the most popular package for many Pentium CPUs.

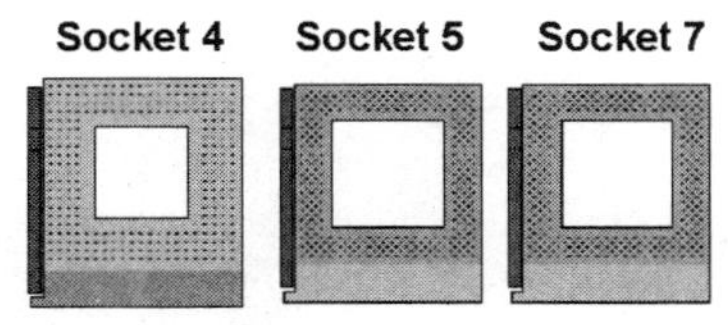

Figure 2.60 Early Pentium socket types (Graphic courtesy of Intel Corp.)

Socket Number	No. of Pins	Pin Layout	Voltage	CPU Type
4	273	21 x 21 PGA	5V	Pentium 60/66
5	320	37 x 37 SPGA	3.3V	Pentium 75/90/100/120
7	321	21 x 21 SPGA	2.5/3.3V	Pentium 75–233

PENTIUM OVERDRIVE CPUS FOR 486 SYSTEMS

Known as the P24T before its release in early 1995, the Pentium Overdrive is touted as a plug-in upgrade for 486 systems. The Pentium Overdrive is a Pentium with a 32-bit external data bus and two 16K caches instead of two 8k caches. A more realistic name for the Pentium Overdrive might be something like *Pentium SX*. Intel specifies a special 238-pin PGA ZIF socket for the Pentium Overdrive that most motherboard manufacturers integrate into their 486 boards. However, the price of true Pentium motherboards has dropped so dramatically that there is relatively little demand for the Pentium Overdrive. One can simply purchase a real Pentium processor with a superior motherboard tuned to run a true Pentium 64-bit expansion bus for little more than the price of the Pentium Overdrive. Nevertheless, the Pentium Overdrive is a convenient and easy upgrade that many end users find attractive.

Chip	Speed (MHz)	Recommended Upgrades
Pentium	25/63	486SX-25, 486DX-25, 486DX/2–25/50, 486DX/4 - 25/75
Pentium	33/83	486SX-33, 486DX-33, 486DX/2–33/66, 486DX/4 - 33/100

AMD 5x86

First on the list is the AMD 5x86. Despite the eye-catching name, this processor is simply a pin-compatible 486 that is running at a clock-quadrupled 133MHz. At this clock speed, it offers performance comparable to a 75MHz Pentium. Before you say "no way," remember that the 75MHz Pentium is running on a 50MHz system bus, compared to 60/66MHz for its faster siblings.

Pentium OverDrive CPUs for Pentium Systems

The Pentium Overdrives for Pentium systems are still being sold by Intel, although the "writing is on the wall" for Intel to stop producing these processors. Like their earlier Overdrive brothers, the price of these CPUs makes them a little too pricey for most pocketbooks, although there are many motherboards that can only be upgraded with these chips.

Chip	Speed (MHz)	Recommended Upgrades
Pentium	180	Pentium 75 to 150
Pentium	200	Pentium 100 to 166

The Pentium Pro (P6)

In 1995, Intel released the next generation of CPU, the Pentium Pro, often called the P6 (see Figure 2.61). The P6 has the same bus and register sizes as the Pentium. What makes the P6 so powerful are three new items: Quad-pipelining, Dynamic Processing and On-Chip L2 cache. However, the P6 is optimized for true 32-bit code and will often run more slowly than a Pentium when running 16-bit (DOS, Windows 3.X) code. The Pentium Pro has a distinct, rectangular SPGA package.

Figure 2.61 Pentium Pro.

QUAD PIPELINING

Where the Pentium is a dual pipeline CPU, the P6 is able to handle four separate pipelines simultaneously. This allows the equivalent of three simultaneous processes, on average.

DYNAMIC PROCESSING

From time to time, all CPUs must go to DRAM to access code—no matter how good its cache. When a RAM access takes place, the CPU must wait a few clock cycles before processing. Sometimes the wait can be ten or twenty clock cycles. When the P6 is forced into wait states, it looks at the pipeline to see whether there are any commands that can be run while the wait states are active. If it finds commands that it can process (that are not dependent on the data being fetched from DRAM) it will run these commands OUT OF ORDER! After the DRAM fetch is given to the P6, it will then rearrange the commands and continue processing.

ON-CHIP L2 CACHE

The P6 has both the L1 and the L2 cache on the CPU. Because the L2 cache is on the chip, it will probably be near 0-wait state and almost as fast as the L1 cache. You can even see this cache in the picture; it's the interior square on the right.

CHIP TYPE	CPU SPEED	CLK MULT	EXT'L BUS	L2 CACHE
PENTIUM PRO	166	2.5 X	64-Bit	512K
PENTIUM PRO	180	3 X	64-Bit	256K
PENTIUM PRO	200	3 X	64-Bit	256K,512K, 1 Meg

The Pentium Pro has a unique SPGA case that fits into a special socket called Socket 8 (see Figure 2.62). No other CPU uses this type of socket.

The Pentium Pro has made strong inroads in the high-end server market. However, its poor performance running DOS and Windows 3.X programs, combined with its high cost, have made it unacceptable to be most people's desktop computer.

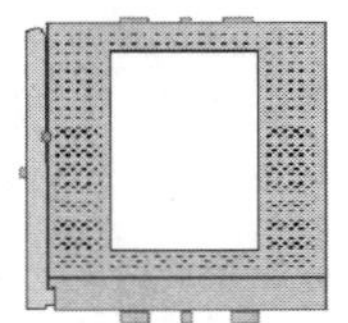

Figure 2.62 Socket 8.

Later Pentiums

Intel's usual game plan in the nasty business of chip-making is to introduce a new CPU and simultaneously declare all previous CPUs obsolete. However, the Pentium Pro was never really developed for most users. It was to be the CPU for more powerful, higher-end systems. This kept the Pentium as the CPU of choice for all but the most power-hungry systems. After the development of the Pentium Pro, a new generation of Pentium CPUs were developed by Intel, AMD, and Cyrix, which incorporated a series of powerful improvements, some of which were taken from the Pentium Pro. These improvements require them to be looked at as a new family of CPUs that we'll call the *Later Pentiums*. Although there are certainly some profound differences between these CPUs, they all carry four groups of similar improvements: MMX, split voltage, increased multipliers/clocks and improved processing.

This group of CPUs marks a major shift in Intel's control of CPUs. Both AMD and Cyrix have produced CPUs that are considered by many to be superior to Intel's Pentium. In particular, AMD's K6 is so good that most consider it to be on par with the latest generation of CPUs: the Pentium II. See the table on the following page.

MMX

In 1996, Intel forwarded a new enhancement to its Pentium CPU called Multimedia Extensions—better known as MMX. MMX is manifested as four new registers and 57 new commands added to the Pentium codebook. These commands can be used to move and manipulate large chunks of data. This capability is particularly helpful (and was designed for) graphical applications (a.k.a. GAMES). Both Cyrix and AMD have copied the MMX extensions in their CPUs. The downside to MMX is that applications (games) need to be written to take advantage of MMX. Although few applications are currently written to take advantage of MMX, the number is growing.

CPU	Make	Internal Speed	External Speed	Mult	Cache	Ext. Volt	Core Volt	Package
Pentium - P55C	Intel	166	66	2.5	16T/16W	3.3	2.8	Socket 7
Pentium - P55C	Intel	200	66	3	16T/16W	3.3	2.8	Socket 7
Pentium - P55C	Intel	233	66	3.5	16T/16W	3.3	2.8	Socket 7
Pentium - P55C	Intel	266	66	4	16T/16W	3.3	2.8	Socket 7
Pentium - P55C	Intel	300	66	4.5	16T/16W	3.3	2.8	Socket 7
Pentium - P55C	Intel	333	75	4.5	16T/16W	3.3	2.8	Socket 7
K6	AMD	166	66	2.5	32T/32W	3.3	2.9	Socket 7
K6	AMD	200	66	3	32T/32W	3.3	2.9	Socket 7
K6	AMD	233	66	3.5	32T/32W	3.3	3.2	Socket 7
K6	AMD	266	66	4	32T/32W	4.3	3.2	Socket 7
6x86MX - PR166	Cyrix	133	66	2	64W	3.3	2.9	Socket 7
6x86MX - PR166	Cyrix	150	60	2.5	64W	3.3	2.9	Socket 7
6x86MX - PR200	Cyrix	150	75	2	64W	3.3	2.9	Socket 7
6x86MX - PR200	Cyrix	166	66	2.5	64W	3.3	2.9	Socket 7
6x86MX - PR233	Cyrix	188	75	2.5	64W	3.3	2.9	Socket 7

MMX is kind of like the built-in math coprocessor. You get it whether you need it or not. All new CPUs from all manufacturers are MMX-enabled. You can't save money by trying to buy a non-MMX CPU.

SPLIT VOLTAGE

Improvements in CPU manufacturing have continued, resulting in Pentium CPUs that run even lower than 3.3 volts. Yet these CPUs still need 3.3 volts for communication with other chips on the motherboard. To fulfill both needs, all later Pentiums are now called split voltage. They literally need two different voltages to operate properly. Yet once again, a whole new family of motherboards has to be created to take advantage of split voltage CPUs. Even though the later Pentiums use exactly the same Socket 7 used by most earlier Pentiums, you can't install a later Pentium into these motherboards because they can't provide the proper voltage.

INCREASED CLOCKS AND MULTIPLIERS

Later Pentiums all have vastly increased multipliers, resulting in higher speeds. Whereas most early Pentiums used 2.5 multipliers at best, later Pentiums are up to 4.5 multipliers; by the time you read this, they will be even higher.

Intel has recently created a very fast series of Pentium II CPUs that can run with an external speed of 100MHz. These Pentium IIs are physically identical to their slower siblings. The first Pentium II of this new group has a 4x multiplier giving it a 4x100—400MHz clock speed, with even faster clock speeds imminent.

IMPROVED PROCESSING

All of the later Pentiums have some improvement in plain ol' Pentium branch prediction. The Intel Pentium has made a slight improvement by making the branch prediction a little smarter, allowing it a better chance of getting the correct code. The Cyrix 6x86MX and the AMD K6 have incorporated the Pentium Pro features of speculative execution and out-of-order execution, making them more like the Pentium Pro and Pentium II (see Pentium II, next) than the Pentium.

Pentium II

Intel's current "hot" CPU is the Pentium II (see Figure 2.63). In reality, the Pentium II is little more than a faster Pentium Pro with

MMX. The Pentium II is distinct with the new SEC cartridge, replacing the older style SPGA socket of the Pentium Pro and allowing more room on the motherboard.

Figure 2.63 Pentium II (Photo courtesy of Intel Corp.).

Although the Pentium II is an excellent CPU, it has some limitations that may cause trouble in the future. For example, it generates the >200 Mhz speeds by large multipliers of a 66MHz bus clock (see table on following page), while Cyrix and AMD CPUs are handling bus speeds approaching 100MHz. This points to easier upgradability for the non-Intel chips in the future.

Finally, the SEC cartridge might be a problem because it is licensed by Intel. This prevents other CPU manufacturers from making CPUs that fit in the SEC's special *Slot 1* connection. Although this may point as a big opportunity for Intel to take even more market share, it virtually guarantees that many systems will continue to use the older SPGA type Socket 7.

INSERTING A CPU

Inserting and removing CPUs is a relatively simple process—just don't touch the pins or you may destroy the CPU. Note that on the inside square in the lower right hand corner there is a notch and a black dot. That is to help you align the CPU correctly. Look at the CPU diagram shown in Figure 2.64.

Note the notch and dot. That is the *Orientation Notch* or *Index Corner.* The Index Corner of the CPU must line up with the notch on the socket. Be careful! Improper installation of the CPU will almost certainly destroy the CPU and/or the motherboard!

Installing a CPU into a ZIF socket is as simple as making sure that the orientation notches line up on the CPU and the ZIF socket. Here are all of the ZIF sockets from previous sections combined to help verify the type of socket you are using (as shown in Figure 2.65).

CHIP TYPE	CPU SPEED	CLK MULT	EXT'L BUS	ADDRESS BUS	L1 CACHE	L2 CACHE
PENTIUM II	233	3.5 X	64-Bit	32-Bit	16 K W/B & 16 K W/T	512K
PENTIUM II	266	4 X	64-Bit	32-Bit	16 K W/B & 16 K W/T	512K
PENTIUM II	300	4.5 X	64-Bit	32-Bit	16 K W/B & 16 K W/T	512K
PENTIUM II	333	5.0 X	64-Bit	32-Bit	16 K W/B & 16 K W/T	512K
PENTIUM II	400	4.0 X	64-Bit	32-Bit	16 K W/B & 16 K W/T	512K

ZIF Socket Types

Socket Number	No. Of Pins	Pin Layout	Voltage	CPU Type
1	169	17 x 17 PGA	5V	486SX/SX2, DX/DX2
2	238	19 x 19 PGA	5V	SX/SX2, DX/DX2, DX4, Pentium OverDrive
3	237	19 x 19 PGA	5V/3.3V	SX/SX2, DX/DX2, DX4, Pentium OverDrive
4	273	21 x 21 PGA	5V	Pentium 60/66
5	320	37 x 37 SPGA	3.3V	Pentium 75/90/100/120
6	235	19 x 19 PGA	3.3V	486 DX4, Pentium OverDrive
7	321	21 x 21 SPGA	2.5/3.3V	Pentium 75 - 233
8	387	21 x 24 SPGA	2.5V	Pentium Pro

*ODPR = OverDrive Processor with voltage regulator. PGA = Pin Grid Array
SPGA = Staggered Pin Grid Array. VRM = Voltage Regulator Module

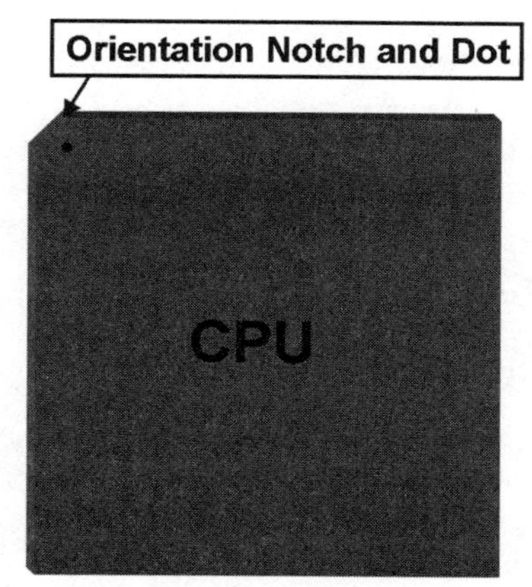

Figure 2.64 Location of orientation notch.

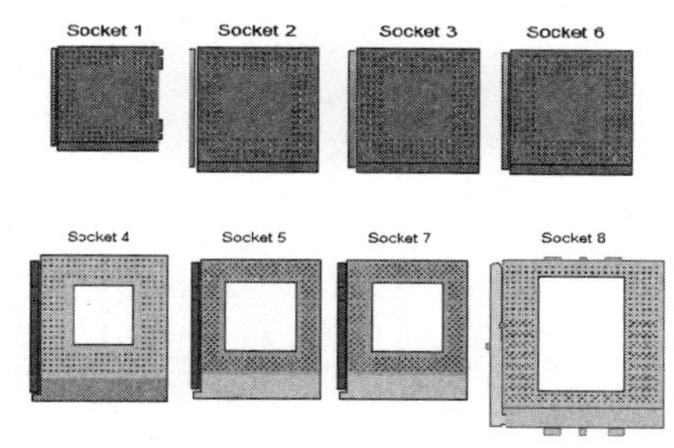

Figure 2.65 Socket diagrams (Graphics courtesy of Intel Corp.).

Figure 2.66 is a diagram of the ZIF socket and CPU. Let's see how they go together.

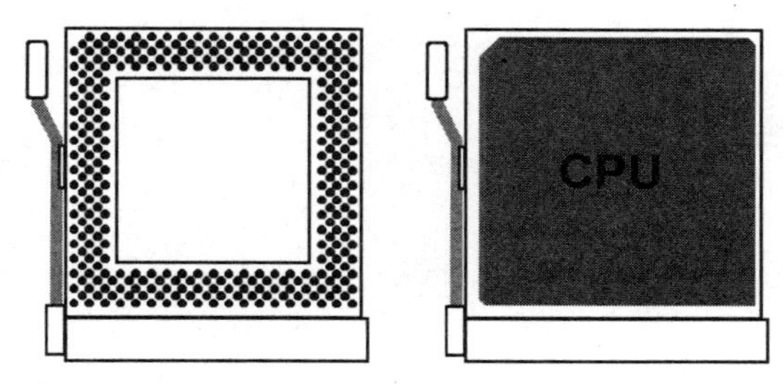

Figure 2.66 Proper insertion of CPU.

In this chapter, we have seen the basic concepts of the components and functions of the PC's CPU. We have taken a historical view to help us understand better the amazing evolution of CPUs in the less than 20-year life span of the personal computer.

This knowledge will be referred to again and again throughout this book. Take the time to memorize certain facts such as the size of the external data busses and clock-doubling features. These are things that good techs can spout off without having to refer to a book and will help you be a better tech.

CHAPTER 3

Power Supplies

In this chapter, we will

- Be introduced to the standards of PC-compatible power supplies
- Inspect the different types of power connectors and their different functions
- Learn how to install a power switch properly
- Learn how to use a voltmeter to perform a basic test of a power supply

The One Truly Standard Piece of Equipment in Your PC

In a break from traditional computer marketing, IBM allowed the development of an *open architecture* for the IBM PC. What constitutes an IBM-compatible PC has often been more a matter of opinion than fact. To be classified as an IBM-compatible PC, a computer must comply with a very loosely enforced set of standards. This loose enforcement has been a mixed blessing. On one hand, it has fostered an environment of constant innovation and creativity. If a PC manufacturer develops a new and better way to do things, he needs no approval from anyone to begin production. The consumer judges the merits of a new PC technology. This has led to wonderful innovations that have been embraced by the entire industry (i.e., Sound Blaster-compatible sound cards, Enhanced IDE, Iomega ZIP drives, scanners, etc.) and to some notable failures (i.e., Microchannel, light pens, 2.88Meg floppies). It also led to the nightmare we refer to as "hardware incompatibility." Although not as much of a problem as it once was, we occasionally run into two devices that either require special configuration to work together or simply will not work together.

With the possible exception of floppy drives, the power supply is the only truly standard piece of equipment in a PC (see Figure 3.1).

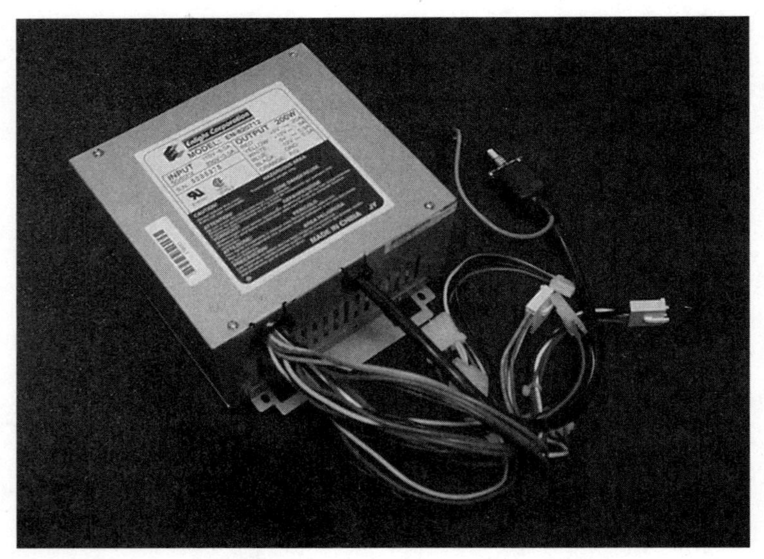

Figure 3.1 Typical power supply.

The power supply does not supply the power. After all, the electricity comes out of the wall socket and ultimately from the utility company. The *power supply* in a PC actually acts as a step-down transformer, converting 115V AC (volts of alternating current) into voltages of +/-5 volts, +/-12 volts, and sometimes 3.3 volts DC (direct current). The PC uses the 12-volt current to power motors on devices like hard drives and CD-ROMs, and the 5-volt/3.3-volt voltages for support of on-board electronics. Manufacturers are free to use these voltages any way they wish, however, and may deviate from these assumptions.

Motherboard Connections

The most popular type of power supply used today is known as the *AT* power supply. This chapter will focus on the AT power supply. The AT has been around for almost twenty years and is beginning to show its age. A new type of power supply, called the ATX power supply, is quickly supplanting AT as the power supply of choice. See the Motherboards and BIOS Chapter for a discussion of ATX, including the ATX power supplies.

A pair of connectors, called P8 and P9, links the power supply to the motherboard. These connectors are easily recognized because of the row of "teeth" along one side and a small guide on the opposite side that helps to hold the connection in place. Because the connectors are "faced" (i.e., they have a front and a back), they cannot be installed backward. However, they can be reversed. When connecting P8 and P9 to the motherboard, keep the black ground wires next to each other. All motherboards and power supplies follow this rule. Be careful: incorrectly inserting P8 and P9 can damage both the power supply and other components in the PC (see Figure 3.2).

Figure 3.3 shows the plug on the motherboard.

Figure 3.2 The P8 and P9 connectors.

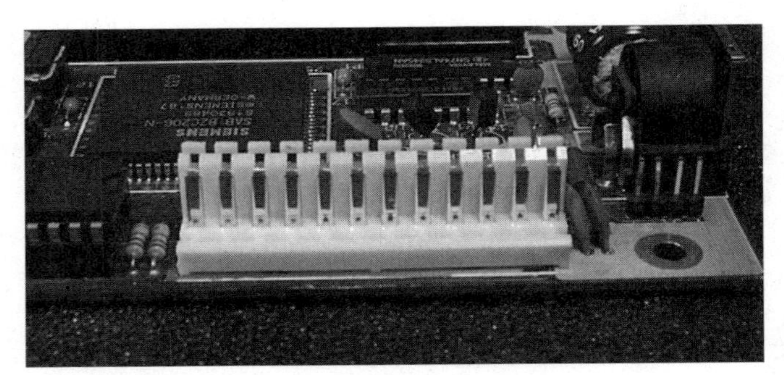

Figure 3.3 Standard P8 & P9 connection.

There are a few PC makers today who do not use these standard connections. Dell, IBM, and Compaq have proprietary connections on some models. If these power supplies need to be replaced, you must go to the manufacturers and pay their prices. Figure 3.4 shows how P8 and P9 should be installed.

Figure 3.4 P8 & P9 Installed—Note that the black grounds on each connector are together.

You must install P8 and P9 so that the two black grounds on each connector are together (see Figure 3.5)! Installing them backward can damage your motherboard and/or the power supply.

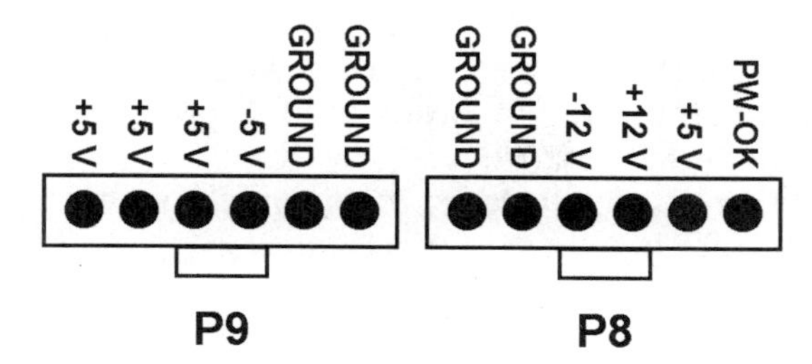

Figure 3.5 Diagram of P8 & P9.

Connections to Peripherals

Many different devices inside the PC require power. These include hard drives, floppy drives, CD ROMs, ZIP drives, and fans. Your power supply has two or possibly three different types of connectors to which you can install your peripherals. Let's take a look at each of these power connections.

MOLEX CONNECTORS

The first and most common type of connection is called the *Molex* (see Figure 3.6). The Molex connector is primarily used for devices that need both 12V and 5V power.

Figure 3.6 Standard Molex connector.

The Molex connector has chamfers (notches) that make for easy installation. These chamfers can be defeated if you push hard enough, so always inspect the Molex connection to ensure proper orientation before you install.

Installing a Molex backward will almost certainly destroy the device into which the Molex is connected (see Figure 3.7).

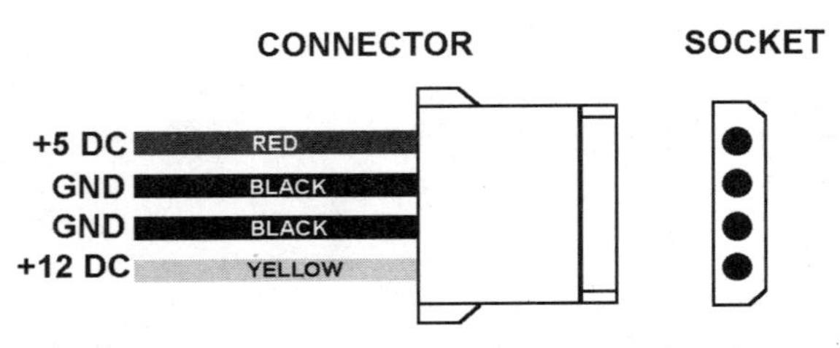

Figure 3.7 Diagram of Molex connector and socket.

MINI-CONNECTORS

Most systems also provide a *mini-connector* (see Figure 3.8). The mini is used primarily on 3.5-inch floppy drives because floppy drive makers have adopted the mini-connector for that use.

Figure 3.8 Standard mini-connector.

Be careful when installing these connectors! Whereas Molex connectors are extremely difficult (but not impossible) to install incorrectly because of the notches (a.k.a. chamfers) on the Molex socket, minis can be inserted upside-down with very little effort. Installing a mini incorrectly will almost certainly destroy the device.

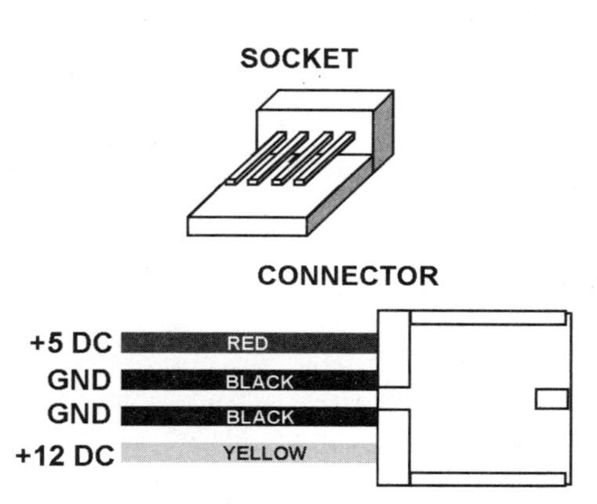

Figure 3.9 Mini-connector with plug.

Look at a picture of a correctly oriented mini connection as shown in Figure 3.10.

Figure 3.10 Correct orientation of mini-connector.

SUB-MINI CONNECTORS

Most power supplies will also provide a small, two-hole connector, which is known most commonly as a *sub-mini* (see Figure 3.11).

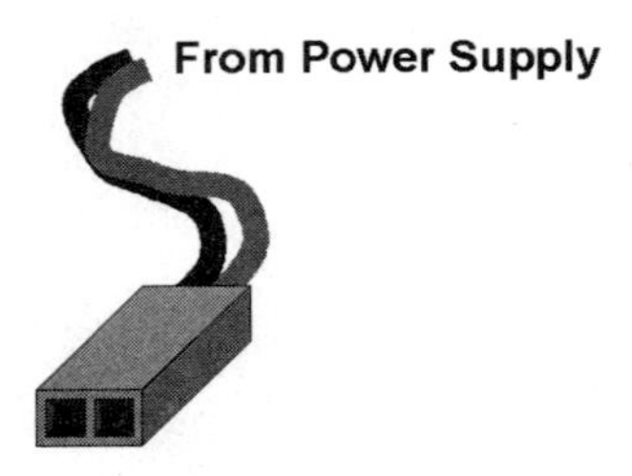

Figure 3.11 A sub-mini.

Although the main purpose of these small connectors is to provide 5-volt power to the LED lights in the front of some computers, they can be used in other rather unique ways (see Figure 3.12). One of these *other* uses of sub-minis is to provide power to the floppy drive because the floppy drive needs only a ground and +5 DC.

Figure 3.12 Sub-mini used to power front displays.

Be careful! It is easy to install a sub-mini backward on a floppy drive because it has no guides for proper orientation. The only way to orient the connector properly is by the color of the wires: the red + 5V DC wire to the extreme outside of the floppy, and the black ground wire to the inside. You will notice that the floppy may not work, will get warm to the touch, and then will eventually smoke if you inadvertently reverse this connection (see Figure 3.13).

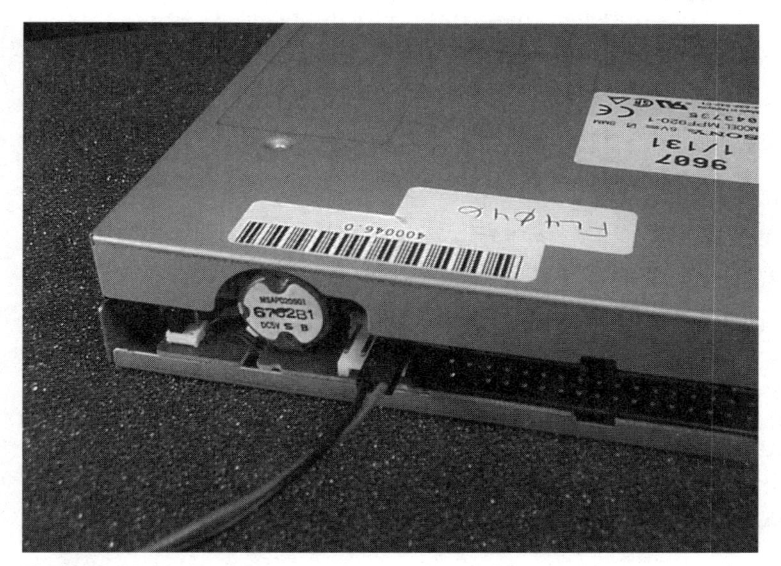

Figure 3.13 Sub-mini connector on 3.5 inch floppy (red wire on the far right).

SPLITTERS AND CONVERTERS

You may occasionally find yourself not having enough connectors to power all of the devices inside your PC. In this case, you can purchase splitters to create more connections.

Figure 3.14 Molex splitter.

WATTAGE

Power supplies are rated in watts. A PC requires sufficient wattage in order for the machine to run properly. The average desktop PC with two hard drives and a CD-ROM will need, on average, ~115 to ~130 watts while running; and up to 200 watts when booting up. Play it safe and buy 200- to 230-watt power supplies. They are by far the most common wattage of power supplies and will give you plenty of extra power for bootup as well as whatever is added in the future.

SIZES

Power supplies are available in a variety of shapes and sizes. Although the sizes are very standardized, the names for these sizes are not. For most desktop or mini-tower PCs, the power supply will be an *AT Mini* sized power supply in the 200- to 230-watt rating. To save time and repeat visits to your friendly neighborhood electronics parts shop, do yourself a favor—remove the suspect power supply and take it in with you to guarantee that you select the correct replacement.

When Power Supplies Die

Power supplies fail in two ways: *easy* and *hard*. When they die *easy*, the computer does not start and the fan in the power supply does not turn. In this case, verify that electricity is getting to the power supply before you do anything! Avoid the embarrassment of trying to repair a power supply when the only problem was a bad outlet or an extension cord that was not plugged in. Assuming that the system has electricity, the best way to absolutely verify that a power supply is working or not working is to check the voltages coming out of the power supply with a voltmeter (see Figure 3.15).

Do not panic if your power supply puts out slightly more or less voltage than its nominal value. The voltages supplied by most PC power supplies can vary by as much as -10 percent to +8 percent of its stated value. This means that the 12-volt line can vary from 10.8 to 12.9 volts without exceeding the tolerance of the various systems in the PC.

Be sure to test every connection on the power supply! That means the P8, P9, and every Molex, mini, and sub-mini. Because all voltages are between -20 and +20 DC, simply set the voltmeter to the 20 volt DC range for everything. Figure 3.16 shows how I set my voltmeter.

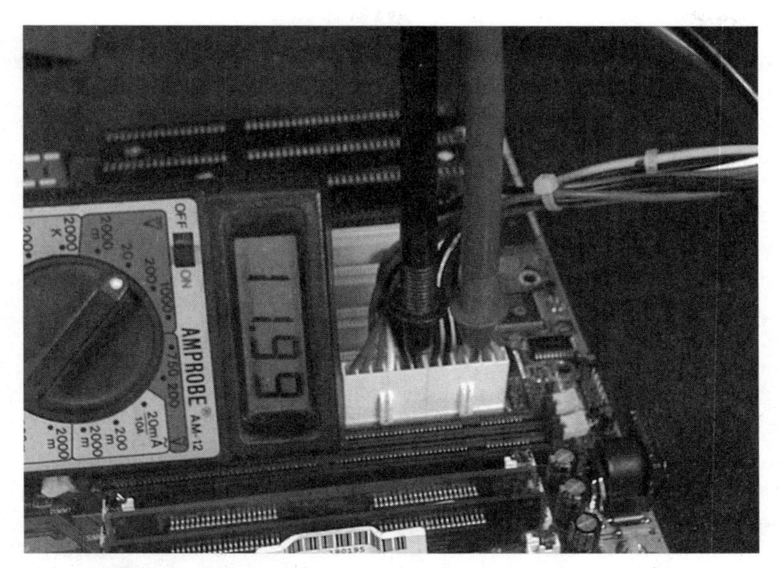

Figure 3.15 Testing one of the +12DC connections (looks OK!).

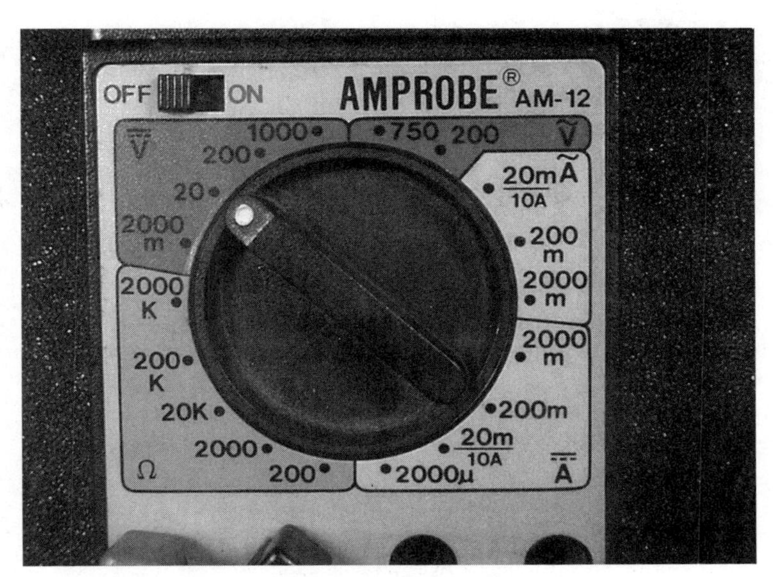

Figure 3.16 Voltmeter set to 20-volt DC range.

If the power supply is not providing any power, be sure to check the fuse within the power supply. Open the power supply and locate the fuse—it will look like a tiny glass cylinder with silver-colored metal caps on each end. Look closely at the fuse: if it has *blown,* it should show up as a dark smoky spot on the glass. It is a simple matter to unsolder the fuse from the printed circuit board and test it for continuity with a *Volt Ohm Meter* (VOM), and to replace the fuse if necessary (see Figure 3.17).

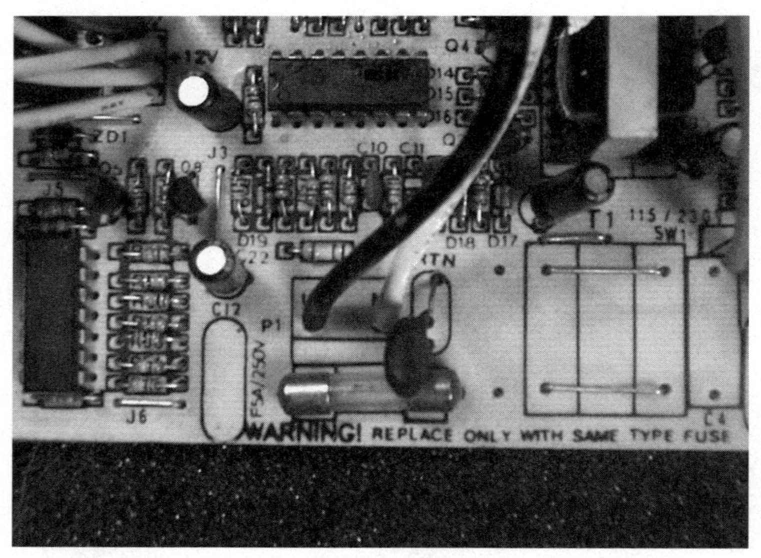

Figure 3.17 Fuse within the power supply.

Another indication of power supply failure is a dead fan. If you turn on the computer and it boots up just fine, but you notice that the PC seems quiet, the power supply fan is bad and needs to be replaced as quickly as possible. This fan not only keeps the voltage regulator circuits cool within the power supply, but it also provides a constant flow of outside cool air through the computer's interior. Without this airflow, the CPU can quickly overheat and destroy itself. Replacement fans are inexpensive and easy to come by at any Radio Shack or other electronics parts outlet. As you can see in Figure 3.18, there are only four easy-to-remove screws holding the fan in the power supply. Note also the connector on the fan's power cord. It may be necessary to cut off the connector from the old fan and solder it onto the power leads of the replacement fan.

Figure 3.18 Fan removed from power supply.

Switches

The power switch is behind the on/off button on every PC (see Figure 3.19). It is usually secured to the front cover or inside front frame on your PC, making it a rather challenging part to access.

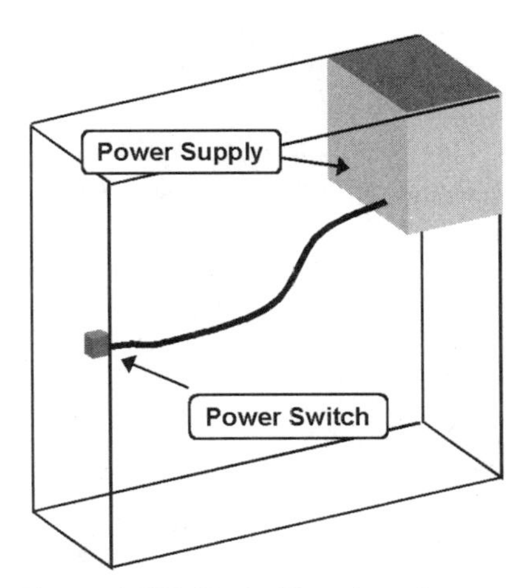

Figure 3.19 Typical location of power switch.

Familiarity with the power switch is important for two reasons. First, a broken power switch is a common source of problems for power supplies that will not start. Second, when replacing a power supply, one usually plugs the new power into the original switch.

TYPES OF SWITCHES

Fortunately, there are only two common types of switches: *rocker* and *plunger* (see Figure 3.20). Each of these switches has four tab connectors that attach to four color-coded wires leading from the power supply. These switches handle 120V current and are interchangeable. The type of computer box determines the type of switch used in a system.

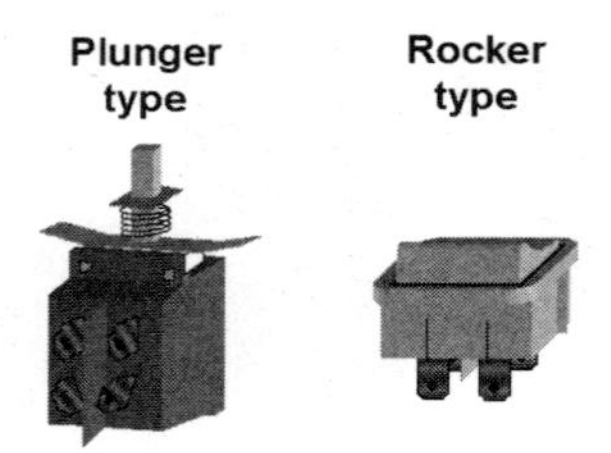

Figure 3.20 Types of switches.

Replacement switches are cheap and readily available at any electronics store. When replacing a switch, remember: Black to Brown and Blue to White. All power supplies have these four colors and they must be properly matched or, when you turn on the power supply, you will be in the dark—literally—because you will blow a circuit breaker. So remember, *Black to Brown and Blue to White.*

Figure 3.21 shows you the proper placement of the power wires into the switch.

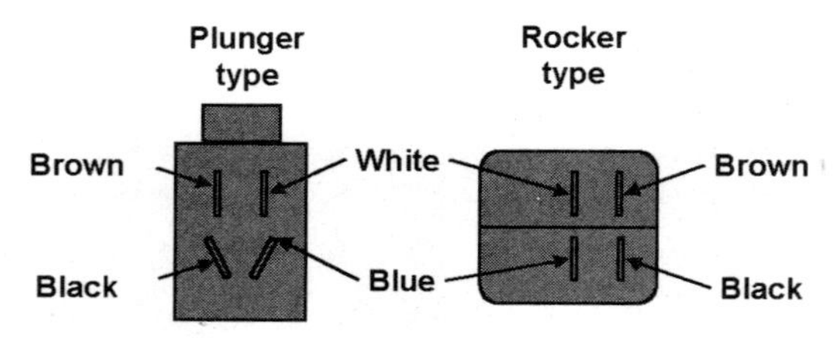

Figure 3.21 Correct wire placement.

The four plugs that go into the PC are 115 volts! Be careful! Make sure the power supply is unplugged.

When Power Supplies Die Hard

If all power supplies died easy, this would be a much shorter chapter. Unfortunately, the majority of PC problems occur when power supplies die *hard*. This means that one of the internal electronics of the power supply has begun to fail. The failures are *always* intermittent and tend to cause some of the most difficult-to-diagnose problems in PC repair. The one secret to discovering that a power supply is dying is one word: intermittent. Whenever I have intermittent problems, my first guess is that the power supply is bad. Here are some other clues:

"Whenever I start my computer in the morning, it starts to boot and then locks up. If I hit Ctrl-Alt-Del two or three times, it will boot up fine."

"Sometimes when I start my PC, I get an error code. If I reboot, it goes away. Sometime I get different errors."

"My computer will run fine for an hour or so. Then it locks up. Sometimes once or twice an hour."

Sometimes something bad happens and sometimes it does not. That's the clue for replacing the power supply. And don't bother with the voltmeter. The voltages will show as within tolerances, but *once in awhile* they will spike and sag (far more quickly than your voltmeter can measure), and cause these *intermittent* errors. When in doubt, change the power supply. Power supplies break in computers more often than any other part of the PC, second to the floppy drives. I keep power supplies in stock for swapping and testing.

Danger, Will Robinson, Danger!!

Electricity can kill you, especially electricity from the wall outlet.

A power supply might appear innocuous, but if you do not unplug the power supply before you open it, you could end up as a baked potato. Although when a power supply is closed it is safe, once you get access to the 115 VAC lines on the inside, you must be very careful not to touch anything unless the power supply is unplugged.

CHAPTER 4

RAM

In this chapter, we will

- See the different types of RAM packaging
- Understand RAM banking
- Understand different types of DRAM
- See how to install RAM properly
- Understand RAM access speed

What is RAM?

Random Access Memory (RAM) is the *working memory* of your PC. Although this was touched on in Chapter 1, let's review RAM's function in the PC. When not in use, programs are held in mass storage. Mass storage usually means a hard drive but it can also mean floppies, a CD-ROM, or some other device that can hold values when the computer is turned off. When a program is loaded by typing its name in DOS or by clicking an icon in Windows, the program is copied from the mass storage device to RAM and then run.

Any device that can hold data is memory. *Random Access* means that any part of the memory can be accessed with equal ease. A single sheet of paper with names can be called random access because we can see any one name as easily as another. A cassette tape is not random access because we have to rewind or fast forward the tape to access a particular piece of information. When we use the word RAM in the PC world, however, we are referring to a specific type of electronic storage device known as *Dynamic Random Access Memory* (DRAM).

DRAM

The most popular type of electronic memory in the PC world is called *Dynamic Random Access Memory*. As mentioned in the CPU Chapter, DRAM is a special type of semiconductor that stores individual ones and zeroes using a microscopic capacitor and transistor.

DRAM comes to us in many different ways. Usually, DRAM is soldered onto a card of some type. We will talk about these different cards later in this chapter. But for the moment, we're going to concentrate on the individual chips on the card as shown in Figure 4.1.

Figure 4.1 Typical DRAM, single chip encircled.

Once we understand how the individual chips are organized, we will return to these cards and see how they work together.

ORGANIZING DRAM

Due to its low cost and the capability to pack a lot of data into relatively small packages, DRAM is the de facto standard RAM that is used in all computers today. Even Macintoshes and mainframes use DRAM. In fact, DRAM can be found in just about everything—from automobiles to automatic bread makers.

So what kind of DRAM do we need for PCs? Remember that the original 8088 processor had an 8-bit external data bus. All of the commands given to an 8088 processor were in discrete, 8-bit chunks. (Refer back to the CPU chapter if this is not clear!) Therefore, we need RAM that can store data in 8-bit chunks. Even today's most modern CPUs still can run 8088 commands, so the *width* of RAM that we need is still eight bits wide. When we talk about PC memory, we say things like "32 Megabytes," "8 Megabytes" or, if the computer is really old, "640K bytes." We never say things like "16 Megawords" or "32 Megabits." That's because memory is always eight bits or one byte across. So, when we talk about memory in PCs, we always talk about *byte-wide* memory.

When we speak of individual DRAM chips, we are primarily interested in two values: the *depth* and the *width*. To explain this, let's use a couple of analogies. Have you ever taken film in to be developed? You usually have an option about how large you want the photographs to be, right? You can get the 3 × 5, the 4 × 6 and if you're willing to pay more, you can even get the 6 × 8 size. When you say "3 × 5," what does that mean? Of course, it means 3 inches high by 5 inches wide (see Figure 4.2).

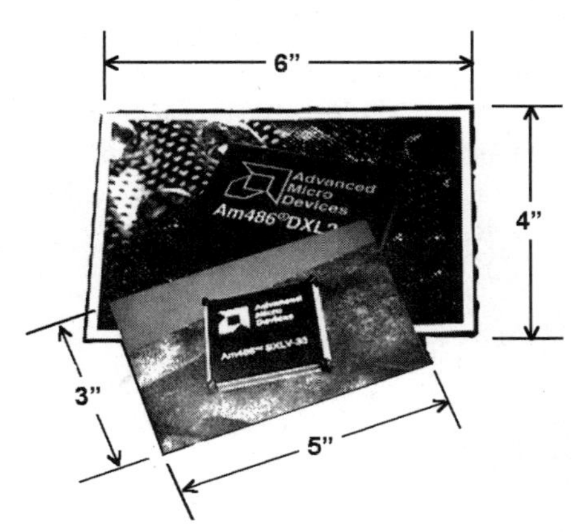

Figure 4.2 Height and width of photos.

Well, DRAM works exactly the same way. DRAM has a depth and a width. This depth and width is measured in units of bits. First, we want to know how *deep* the chip is. Some common depths are 256K, 1Meg, 4Meg, and 16Meg. Second, we want to know how *wide* the chip is. Some common widths are one bit, 4 bits, 8 bits, or 16 bits. When we combine the depth with the width we get the *size* of the DRAM chip (see Figure 4.3). So, when talking about individual DRAM chips, we say something like 256Kx1 or 1Megx4.

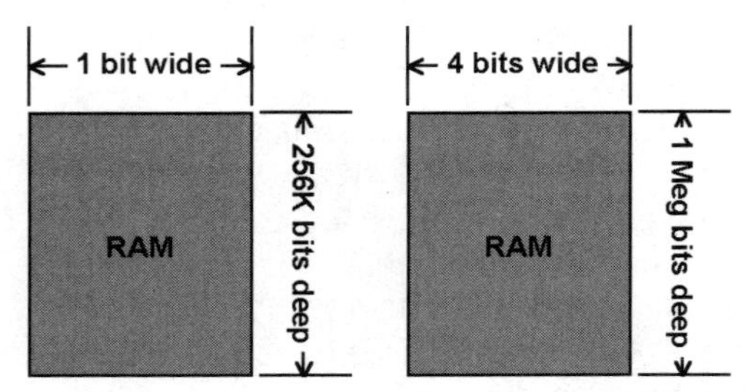

Figure 4.3 Height and width of DRAM.

If someone held up a 3 × 5 photo and asked you, "How large is the photo I am holding?" You could probably *eyeball it* and say: "That's a 3 × 5 size photo!" Unfortunately, it is virtually impossible to do that with DRAM. Two chips that look identical can be very different on the inside (see Figure 4.4)! The only way you can tell one DRAM from another is by reading the information printed on the chips itself. There is no direct correlation between physical size and the internal organization of the chip.

Figure 4.4 Different DRAM may look identical.

Here are some current common DRAM sizes (there are more):

Table 4.1 Sizes of RAM

256Kx1	=	262,144 bits
256Kx4	=	262,144 nibbles
256Kx16	=	262,144 words
512Kx8	=	524,288 bytes
1Megx1	=	1,048,576 bits
1Megx4	=	1,048,576 nibbles
1Megx16	=	1,048,576 words
2Megx8	=	2,097,152 bytes
4Megx1	=	4,194,304 bits
4Megx4	=	4,194,304 nibbles
16Megx4	=	16,777,216 nibbles
16Megx8	=	16,777,216 bytes

NOTE
Remember: 1K = 1024, 1Meg = 1,048,576

So, if you were to go up to a DRAM salesman and say: "I'd like 32 Megabytes of RAM, please!" he would look at you funny. DRAM makers don't think in terms of bytes. DRAM is sold in depth by width units like *256K × 4*. We need to put the DRAM makers' world into our PC world and understand how the two work together. Let's do it!

AN HISTORICAL LOOK

Wait a minute. Before we get started, I need to warn you about something. We're going to go back in time here, back to the original IBM PC and to the first DRAMs used in the PCs. I know how most folks HATE to talk about old stuff (I do, too), but if you want to understand how DRAM works today you've got to talk about how DRAM worked a long time ago. You'll be surprised how much of the original technology is still used today!

In the original IBM PC, the most DRAM that the PC could use was 640K (655,360) bytes. Later in the book, I'll explain this limitation, but for now I need you to do a *Trust Me.* I promise to completely clarify this limit later.

NOTE

The single greatest truism of the PC business—"Everything old is new again!"

PCs need *byte-wide* RAM. Although today's DRAM chips can have widths of greater than one bit, back in the old days, all DRAMS were one bit wide. That means you only had sizes like 64K × 1 or 256K × 1—always one bit wide.

So how did we take one-bit wide DRAM and turn it into 8-bit wide memory? To help us understand what was done, we visualize RAM as an *electronic spreadsheet.* We've all used a spreadsheet like Excel, Lotus 123, or Quattro Pro. Imagine a spreadsheet in which the only values you can enter are `0` and `1`. The number of columns is the width and the number of rows is the depth. This *electronic spreadsheet* concept is exactly how the CPU sees RAM.

So, 640K of RAM would look like Figure 4.5 to the CPU.

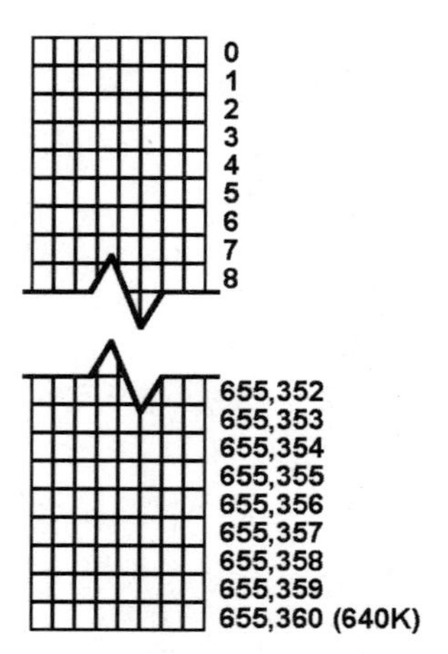

Figure 4.5 RAM spreadsheet.

So here's the goal: how do we take a bunch of one-bit wide DRAM chips and turn them into 8-bit wide RAM? The answer is quite simple—we just take eight one-bit wide chips and electronically organize them with the memory controller chip. First, we put eight one-bit wide chips in a row on the motherboard, and then we wire up this row of DRAM chips to the Memory Controller Chip (the memory controller chip has to be designed to handle this) to make byte-wide memory (see Figure 4.6).

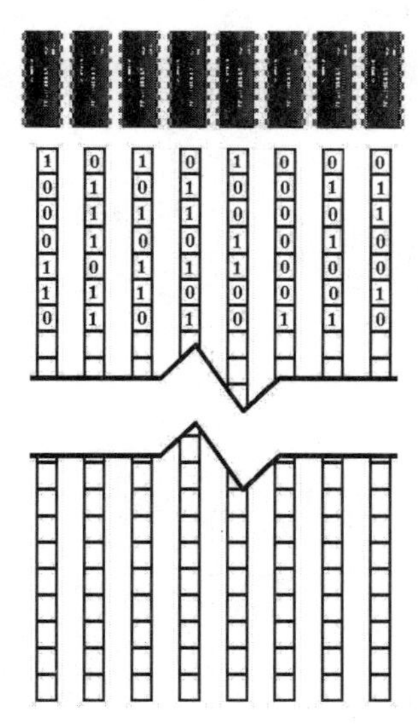

Figure 4.6 Each chip handles one column.

The Memory Controller Chip accesses one byte of code by grabbing one bit from each chip (see Figure 4.7). To the CPU, this process is transparent. The CPU, remember, only thinks in terms of memory addresses.

MULTIPLE ROWS

Well, great! We can use multiple DRAMs to create byte-wide memory. But there's a little problem. You see, back in the days of the 8088 processor, the biggest DRAM chip you could get was 256K × 1. With eight of these, the biggest row you could have was 256K bytes, but we wanted more RAM. Because the biggest row was 256K bytes, the only way to get more RAM was to add more rows! In order to add more rows, we needed an improved memory chip that could control more than one row of chips. So new types of *Memory Controller Chips* (MCCs) were created that could handle two rows or more rows of RAM as shown in Figure 4.8.

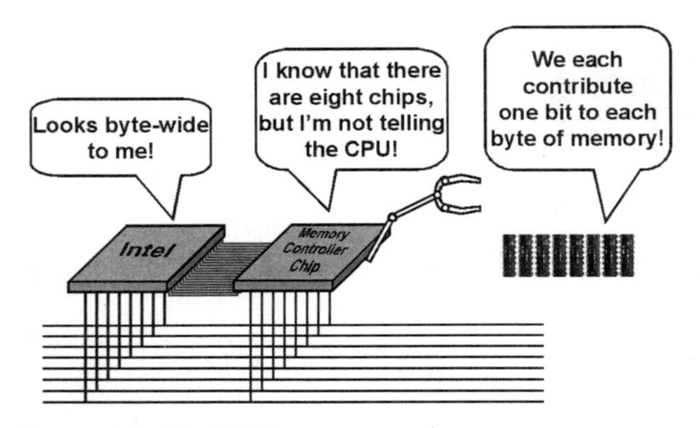

Figure 4.7 The MCC in action.

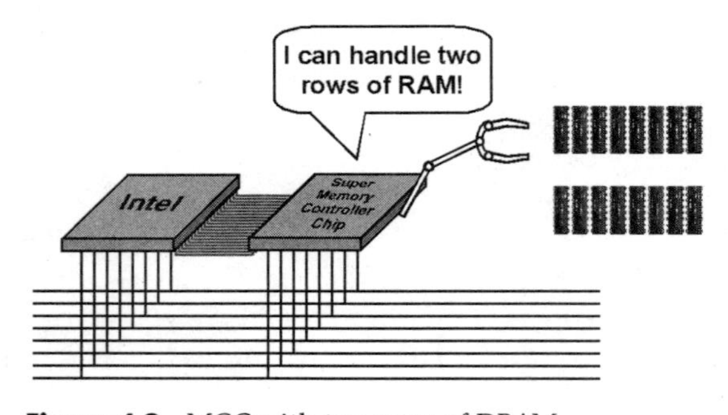

Figure 4.8 MCC with two rows of DRAM.

Now, when the CPU needs a certain byte of memory, the CPU requests that byte via the address bus. *The CPU has no idea where the byte of RAM is physically located* (see Figure 4.9). The MCC keeps track of this and just gives the CPU whatever byte it requests.

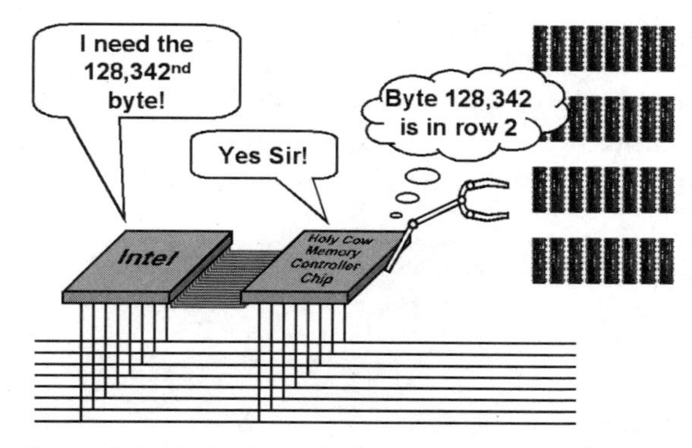

Figure 4.9 Only the MCC knows the real location of the DRAM.

It is easy to determine whether your CPU can handle more than one row of RAM. All you have to do is to look at the motherboard: you can see rows of sockets ready for you to add RAM (see Figure 4.10).

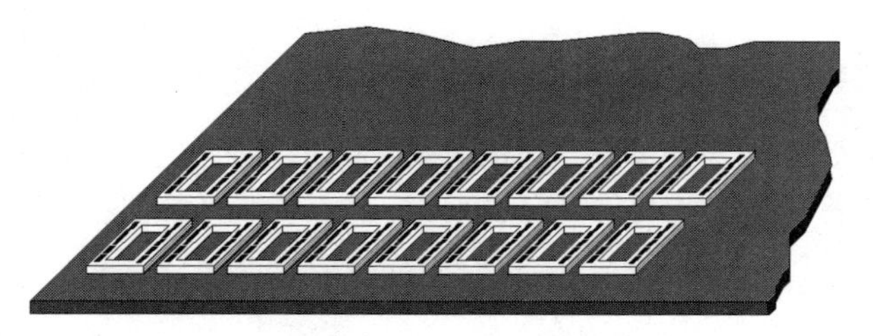

Figure 4.10 Empty rows, ready for DRAM to be added.

PARITY

Parity is for error-detection. Parity is usually manifested through an extra chip that is one bit wide and as deep as all the other chips in the row. This ninth bit allows the MCC to compare the number of ones stored in a byte with the number of ones found when the byte is accessed. In order for parity to work, you must have a MCC that is designed to use the parity chip. Every time that data is placed in RAM, the parity bit is set. Every time you access that byte of RAM, the parity bit is checked. If something has happened between data storage and retrieval to change one of the bits, you will get the infamous *Parity error, system halted* message. Parity checking was useful in the early days of desktop computers when DRAM had a relatively high failure rate, but today's DRAMs are much more dependable—so much so that very few PCs still support parity (see Figure 4.11).

Figure 4.11 Here's an older PC with four rows of DRAM in old style DIPP packages with a ninth parity chip. Note that this motherboard numbers each bit, including the parity chip!

RAM Packaging: Part I

There have been many popular types of RAM packages over the years. In this section, we'll take a quick look at the more common ones used in the early days of the PC industry. After a short diversion, we will return to the RAM packages used in modern machines.

DIPPS

The first-generation DRAM chips used a package called *Dual In-line Pin Package* (DIPP); see Figure 4.12. These types of chips are distinguished by their two rows of pins extending from either side of the package.

Figure 4.12 Classic DIPP package.

Installing DIPPs was, at best, a hassle. It was easy to break a pin or to insert the DRAM improperly into its socket. Plus, as RAM chips began to drop in price during the late eighties and early nineties, it became obvious that when we were dealing with DRAM, we were dealing more with complete rows than with individual chips. Think about it. When you want to add RAM, you have to populate an entire row, right? If you are going to remove RAM, again you are going to remove an entire row. So why mess with individual chips when 99 percent of the time you are going to be dealing with entire rows?

This demand created a new type of DRAM package. Instead of individual chips inserted into individual sockets, the RAM was soldered to a small board, which was then inserted into the motherboard. This type of package was called a *Single In-line Pin Package* (SIPP).

30-PIN SIPPS

The SIPP used a standardized set of pins that mounted into the motherboard. This eliminated the need for individual mounts for each DRAM. The SIPPs board revolutionized the way DRAM was used in a PC. For example, by then new DRAM chips had been invented that were more than one bit wide—you could find 256K × 4 chips. Now the *rule of the row'ed* says that each row must equal eight bits. That used to mean that you had to use eight one-bit chips. But now you could use two four-bit chips to do the same thing. With DIPPs, you could only use whatever chips were designed to use the sockets soldered to the motherboard. If you had eight little sockets on the motherboard, that was what you were going to use, period.

But with SIPPs, the 30-pin connectors were independent of the type of chips soldered onto it. So you could take out a 30-pin SIPP (see Figure 4.13) with eight 256K × 1 chips and replace it with a 30-pin SIPP with two 256K × 4 chips, and the system wouldn't know the difference! The SIPP package really made installing and removing RAM much simpler.

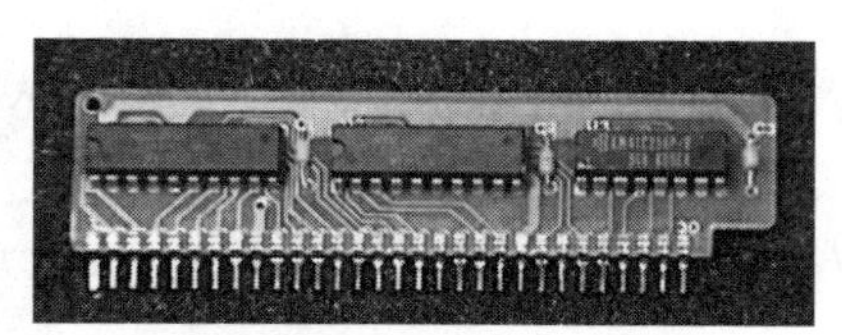

Figure 4.13 30-pin SIPP.

SIPPs packages plugged directly into the motherboard via its own special socket. It was relatively easy to install; all you had to do was push down.

Unfortunately, the SIPP had a rather nasty Achilles heel. The 30 pins that connected the package to the motherboard were just as delicate as the pins on the DIPP chips. Like the DIPP chips, it was just too easy to break off one of the pins accidentally—which made the whole SIPP garbage. So, although SIPPs were revolutionary, they were quickly replaced by their much more robust successor, the 30-pin SIMM.

30-PIN SIMMS

Single In-Line Memory Modules (SIMMs) are the next rungs on the memory evolutionary ladder. Physically, they look very similar to SIPPs, but with one exception: no pins. There is nothing to bend and no way to inflict serious bodily harm to you or the chips.

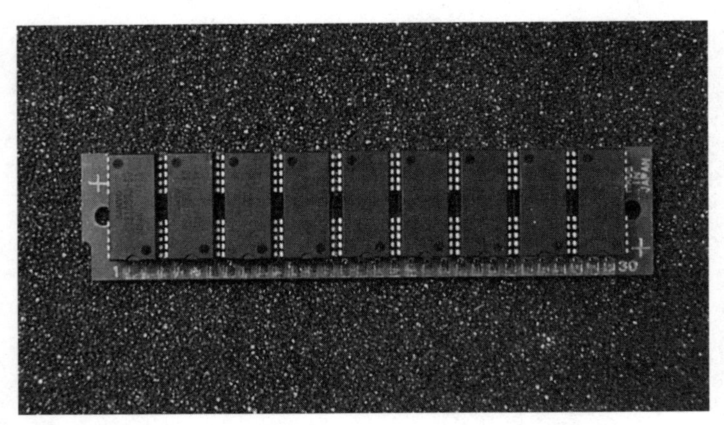

Figure 4.14 30-pin SIMM.

SIMMs are inserted into a special SIMMs socket (see Figure 4.15). It is virtually impossible to install SIMMs improperly, due to the notch on one side of the card. Electronically, 30-pin SIMMs are identical to 30-pin SIPPs. You can even purchase a simple converter that allows SIPPs to be inserted into SIMMs sockets and vice versa.

Figure 4.15 Eight rows for 30-pin SIMMs.

30-pin SIMMs are so-called because each printed circuit card has 30 pins or contacts along the edge. The most important thing to remember about 30-pin SIMMs is that although their depths may vary they are always 8 data bits (one byte) wide. Although the SIMMs chip is always 8 bits wide, the chips on the package can differ widely. Some examples of different chip layouts on 30-pin SIMMs are shown in Figure 4.16.

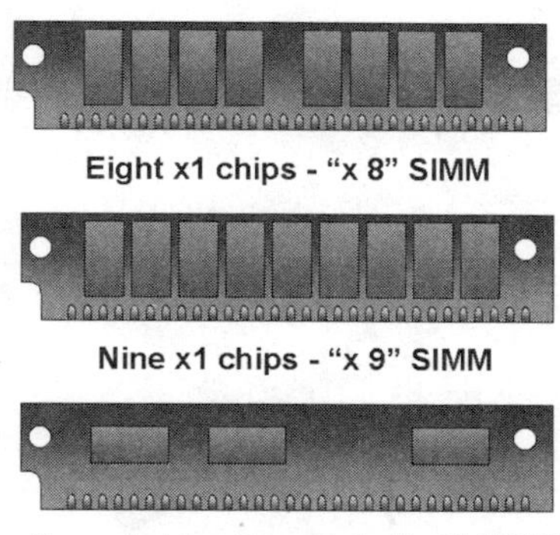

Figure 4.16 Different chip layout on SIMMs.

Keeping Track of Your SIMMs

One unfortunate aspect of 30-pin SIMMs (we will see this is true for all DRAM) is that you can't tell how deep a SIMMs chip is simply by looking at it. The following figure shows a 4 × 3 SIMM and a 1 × 3 SIMM. Notice in Figure 4.17 that they look almost identical.

Figure 4.17 Identical looking, but very different SIMMs.

The best way to know what depth of SIMM you have is to label the SIMM when you buy it. Every SIMM I own has a small label on it that tells me its size—that way, there's never any guessing (see Figure 4.18).

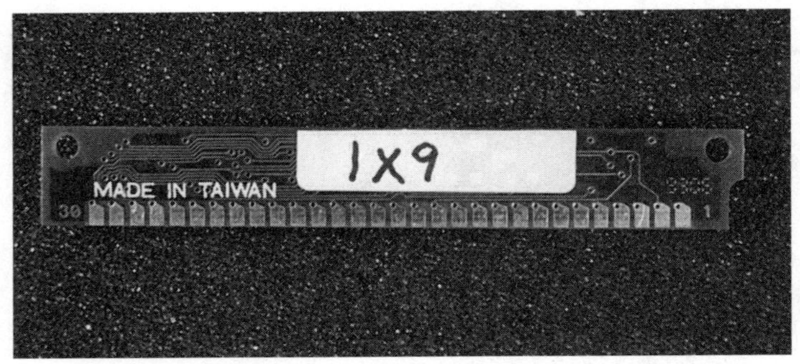

Figure 4.18 How to be sure of the size of SIMM—labeled 1 x 9.

It's easy to tell a parity from a non-parity 30-pin SIMMs. All non-parity 30-pin SIMMs have an even number of chips; all parity 30-pin SIMMs have an odd number of chips.

SIMMs and Parity

When purchasing SIMMs chips, the question is this: do I need parity or non-parity? This is decided exclusively by the motherboard. Refer to the motherboard book to determine whether your machine requires parity or non-parity chips. Another way is to look at the chips currently in your PC. Are there an odd (parity) or even (non-parity) number of chips? Some PCs allow you to turn off the parity—look at the following figure that shows a screen from a PC's advanced CMOS settings (see Figure 4.19). On these machines, you can mix parity with non-parity chips, as long as the parity is turned off.

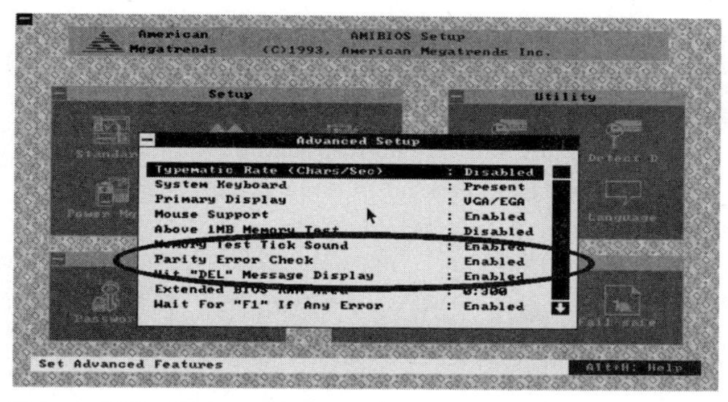

Figure 4.19 Parity option on older CMOS.

Access Speed

It takes a certain amount of time for the DRAM chip to respond to the MCC with the requested data. This is called the *access speed,* which is typically given in nanoseconds and is commonly abbreviated as *ns*. The faster the chip, the smaller the access speed. Therefore, a 100ns chip is slower than a 60ns chip.

NOTE
A lower number shows a faster access speed

Every motherboard requires a certain speed of DRAM. Therefore, it is critical that you can *eyeball* a DRAM chip and determine its access speed. You can determine the access speed by looking at the chip. Access speeds range from as slow as 200ns on ancient 8088s up to 50ns on the newest DRAMs.

Look at some examples of chips and determine their access speeds in Figure 4.20.

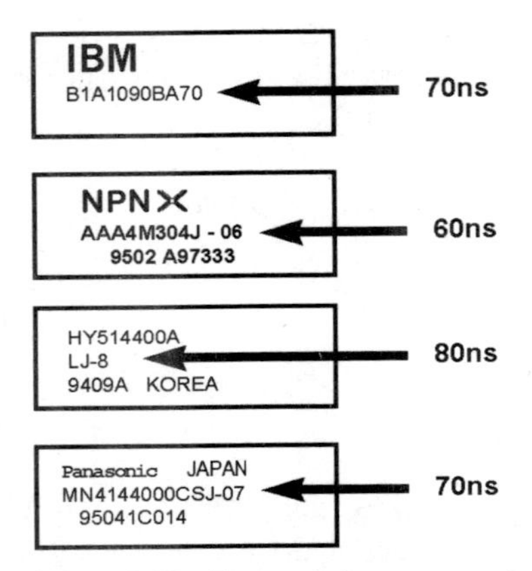

Figure 4.20 Determining access rates.

Although there are some exceptions that we will visit later, the easiest rule of DRAM access speeds is simply to put in the proper speed based on your motherboard book and to make sure that every piece of DRAM is that speed.

Talking the Talk

If you want to purchase DRAM at the cheap wholesale places, it is imperative to be able to speak the language of DRAM. For example, each individual package of SIMM or SIPP is called a *stick*. So if you want four SIMM packages, you would say: "Give me four sticks of RAM!"

Never ask for parity or non-parity. There are only three widths of DRAM in 30-pin SIMMs or SIPPs: x8, which is by definition non-parity; x9, which is by definition parity; and x3, which is simply a x9 SIMM with a three-chip package and is also parity. So by saying, "x8" or "x3," you're telling the other person whether you want parity or not.

There are only three common sizes in 30-pin SIMMs or SIPPs: 256K, 1Meg, and 4Meg. These three sizes make up 95 percent of all

30-pin SIMMs. Therefore, when we describe these sizes, we drop the unit values and just say the number. So when we talk about a size of 30-pin SIMM or SIPP, we simply say "4 × 8" or "1 × 3."

NOTE
If you say "× 3," "× 8," or "× 9," you are talking about 30-pin SIMMs or SIPPs

Always say "SIMMs" or "SIPPs" so that you get the right package.

Finally, when you specify an access speed, don't say, "fifty nanoseconds." Just say, "fifties" or "eighties." If you're just buying one stick, say, "fifty" or "sixty."

So, if you were going to order some SIMMs, the conversation would go something like this: "I'd like 16 sticks of 1 × 8 sixties SIMMs and 4 sticks of 256 × 9 eighties SIPPs, please."

Hey man, you're talking the talk!

Banking

The 8088 processor inside the original IBM PC defined many of the rules that are still in force today about how RAM is accessed. But that's not to say that RAM access functions have stood still. The first major improvement to RAM access from the IBM PC was a concept known as *banking*. Simply put, banking means to access more than one row of DRAM at a time. Every PC since the 286 performs this banking function. Let's see how banking came to be and how we use it today

One concept that we must clarify immediately is the idea that every command in the 8088 CPUs machine language is one byte wide. Many commands are 16 or even 32 bytes wide. So how can the 8088, with only an 8-bit external data bus, handle commands that are more than one byte wide? The answer is simple: it chops the commands up into one-byte chunks.

So, every time the 8088 CPU runs into commands like these, it must access RAM at least twice before it can act on the command due to its 8-bit external data bus. When the 286 CPUs arrived, an opportunity arose. As we remember from the CPU chapter, a 286 has a 16-bit external data bus. So, with the right MCC, a 286 can access 16 bits every time memory is accessed (see Figure 4.21). It would be much faster to access two bytes every time we go to RAM instead of just one.

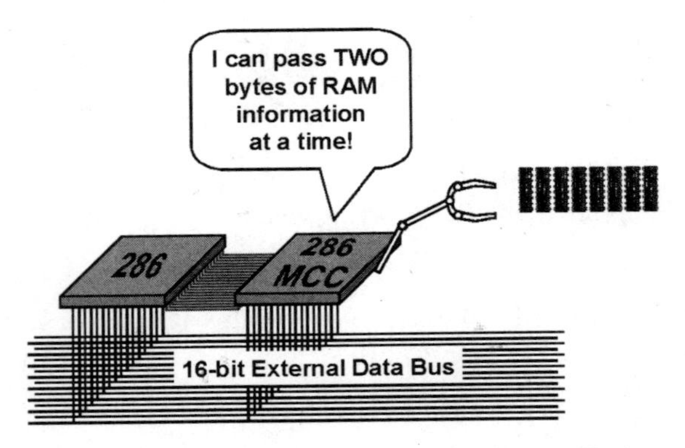

Figure 4.21 Most MCCs can pass more than eight bits at a time.

The only problem with this was that one row (or one SIMM) could only give one byte each time it was accessed—that's all they were designed to do (see Figure 4.22).

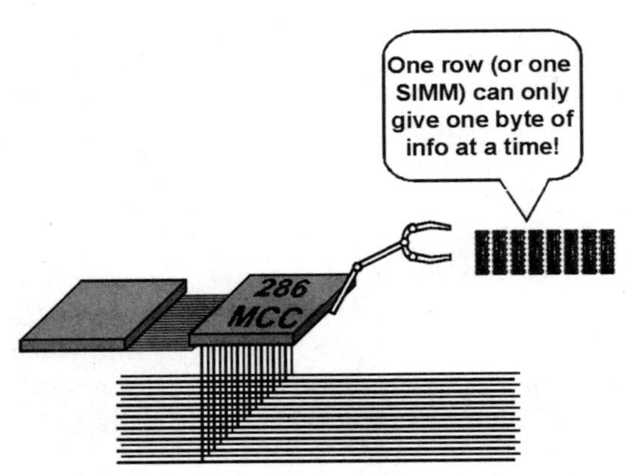

Figure 4.22 One 8-bit row can only pass one byte.

So we could either invent a new type of 16-bit wide DRAM (which nobody wanted to do back then) or we could just install DRAM in pairs, which worked together as a team (see Figure 4.23).

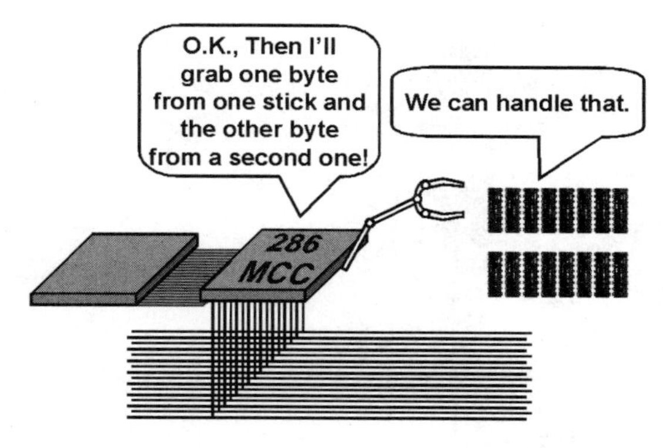

Figure 4.23 Passing more than eight bits with two rows.

When the 386s and 486s with their 32-bit external data busses came out, we simply added two more rows or two more SIMMs to the two we already had to make four 8-bit rows. We needed to be sure that the RAM was wide enough to match the size of the external data bus. Combining the widths of DRAM to match the width of the external data bus is called *banking*. The number of SIMMs that make up a bank depends on the MCC, which in turn depends on the CPU's external data bus size.

NOTE

The number of rows or SIMMs that can be simultaneously accessed by the MCC is a BANK

Figure 4.24 shows some *Rules of Thumb* for banking with 30-pin SIMMs.

THE RULES OF BANKING

The most important rule of banking is that all SIMMs in the same bank must be identical. For example, if you have a 486 (32-bit external data bus) and 30-pin SIMMs (8-bits wide), you must have four identical 30-pin SIMMs to make a bank (see Figure 4.25). You can have four 1 × 8s, four 4 × 3s, four 256 × 9s . . . it doesn't matter, as long as they are identical. They also should be the same speed.

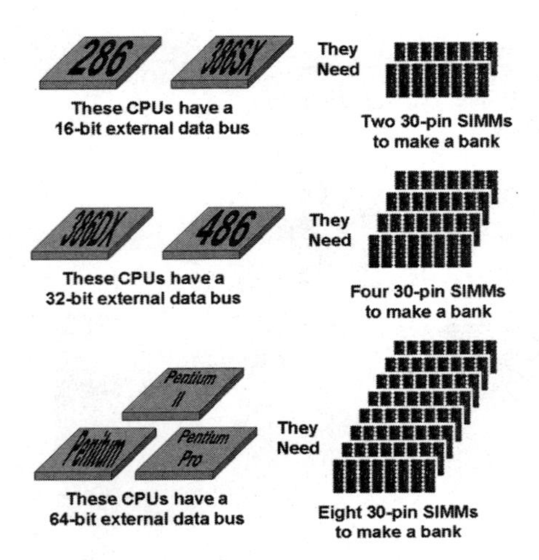

Figure 4.24 Banking rules.

Figure 4.25 All rows in the bank must be identical.

The amount of RAM in each bank combined is the total amount of RAM in the system. Using the earlier example of the 486, if you have four 1 × 8 SIMMs, you have four times one megabyte, or four megabytes of RAM. If you have a 286 with two 256 × 9 SIMMs, you have 512K of RAM.

Almost all PCs have more than one bank. Figure 4.26 shows a picture of an old 486 system with connectors for up to eight rows of 30-pin SIMMs.

Because we know that you need four 30-pin SIMMs to make a bank, the fact that there are eight connectors on this motherboard tells us that this motherboard is designed to have two banks. Having more than one bank on a motherboard allows for flexibility in the amount of RAM in your system. You can have different sized SIMMs in *different banks*. For example, assuming you have a 486 system with two banks, you can install 4 × 8 SIMMs in one bank (total of 16Meg) and 1 × 8 SIMMs (total of 4Meg) in another for a total amount of 20Meg of RAM.

Imagine how limited RAM installation would be if you didn't have multiple banks! Virtually all systems today have multiple banks for RAM (see Figure 4.27).

Figure 4.26 Eight 30-pin SIMM slots in a 486 make two banks.

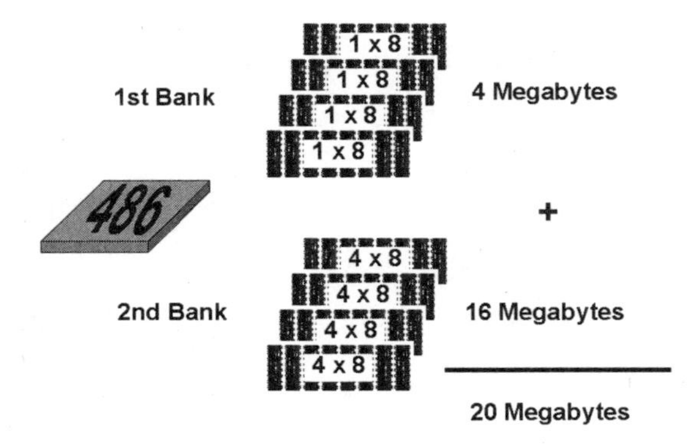

Figure 4.27 Banks are cumulative.

NOTE
The connectors where you install a bank are also collectively called a bank. Therefore, a bank without any SIMMs is called an "Unpopulated" bank; a bank filled with SIMMs is called a "Populated" bank

A bank must be completely populated or completely unpopulated. This is almost obvious, but let's hit on this concept just to be clear. Let's say you have a 486 system that needs four sticks to make a bank. You have two banks. You will have either four or eight sticks in the system. You won't have three, you won't have five—only four or eight because that's the only proper way to fill four-stick banks.

RAM Packaging: Part 2

Now that we have a basic understanding of the different types of early DRAM packages, we can now move forward into the more modern types of DRAM with the necessary conceptual tools to appreciate why we use them in today's machines.

72-PIN SIMMS

In the previous section, most of the examples used 486 CPUs. Why didn't I use Pentiums? Well, Pentium motherboards don't use 30-pin SIMMs—for a very good reason. You see, you would need eight 30-pin SIMMs to make a bank to match the 64-bit external data bus of the Pentium. Although this is no problem electronically, it takes up a massive amount of physical space on the motherboard. You would need 16 slots just to create two banks! What was needed was a new type of DRAM packaging that was more than eight-bits wide.

Enter the 72-pin SIMM. Like its little brother, the 72-pin SIMM is so called because it has 72 pins on each stick. Unlike 30-pin SIMMs, each 72-pin SIMM is 32-bits wide. This means that for a 386DX or a 486 motherboard we can replace 4 rows of 30-pin SIMMs with 1 row of 72-pin SIMMs (see Figure 4.28). For a Pentium, we only need two 72-pin SIMMs.

Although similar to the 30-pin SIMM, the 72-pin SIMM is about an inch longer and has a distinct notch in the middle of the pins to assist in inserting the stick (see Figure 4.29).

Because 72-pin SIMMs are 32-bits wide, we use the term *x32* for non-parity and *x36* for parity to describe them. When you hear, *1Megx32 SIMM*, you are inclined to think that it is one Megabyte. That is incorrect. A *1Megx32* means 1Meg of *32 bits*. This means that SIMM holds four Megabytes of RAM (1,048,576 × 32 = 4 Megabytes).

Figure 4.28 72-pin SIMM.

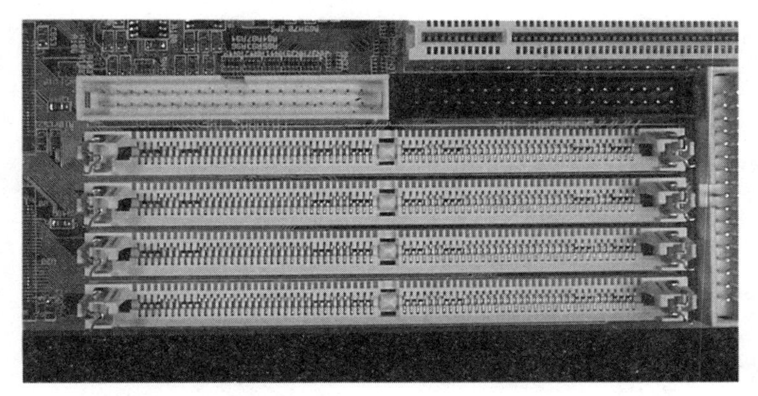

Figure 4.29 72-pin SIMM slots.

Here are some common 72-pin SIMMs and their sizes in Megabytes:

1x32	=	4 Megabytes, no parity
1x36	=	4 Megabytes, parity
2x32	=	8 Megabytes, no parity
2x36	=	8 Megabytes, parity
4x32	=	16 Megabytes, no parity
4x36	=	16 Megabytes, parity
8x32	=	32 Megabytes, no parity
8x36	=	32 Megabytes, parity

16x32	=	64 Megabytes, no parity
16x36	=	64 Megabytes, parity

Because 72-pin SIMMs are 32 bits wide, you only need one 72-pin SIMM to make a bank in a 386 or 486. You need two 72-pin SIMMs to make a bank on a Pentium or Pentium Pro.

Other than the width, 72-pin SIMMs are just like the older 30-pin SIMMs. They have an access speed, the choice of parity or non-parity, and are used in banking. Like 30-pin SIMMs, it is virtually impossible to install a 72-pin SIMM incorrectly since it is also notched.

NOTE
If you say "× 32" or "× 36," you are talking about 72-pin SIMMs.

72-Pin SIMMs and Parity

Unlike the 30-pin SIMMs, there is no definite way to tell a parity 72-pin SIMM from a non-parity 72-pin SIMM. Just make sure you write the type of SIMM on the back of the stick and you'll never have a problem (see Figure 4.30). In fact, many DRAM makers and distributors print this information right on the SIMM. (They're not being nice, they just don't want you to bother them with stupid questions).

Figure 4.30 Labeling is the secret to identification.

Interestingly, there are two types of parity SIMMs available: True and TTL parity. True parity is just as it sounds. A real parity chip for every eight data bits. TTL parity emulates parity and costs less. The few systems that use parity will be clear to tell you which one to use.

168-PIN DIMMS

The most popular new package in use today is the 168-pin *Dual In-Line Memory Module* (DIMM), which is more than just a bigger, wider SIMM (see Figure 4.31). The "Dual" in DIMM comes from the fact that each side of each pin has a separate function, while each side of each pin is the same on a SIMM. DIMMs have the extra pins necessary to enable rather interesting options like buffering, ECC, and SDRAM (these will be discussed next). A DIMM stick is 64-bits wide, which means you only need one to create a bank in a Pentium-class motherboard.

Figure 4.31 168-pin DIMM.

There is another type of DIMM that is most commonly used in laptops: the SO-DIMM. SO-DIMMs are much shorter than 168-pin DIMMs. They only have 72-pins (pure coincidence) and they only have a 32-bit data path (see Figure 4.32). Their convenient size, however, has made them extremely popular with laptops.

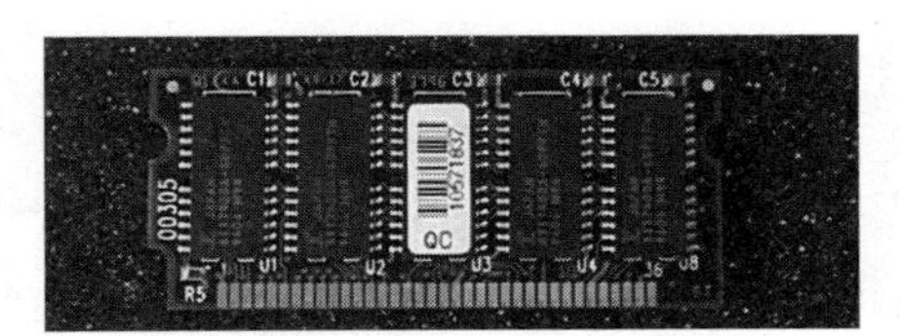

Figure 4.32 72-pin SO-DIMM.

Because a 168-pin DIMM is 64-bits wide, a 1 × 64 DIMM is 1Meg of 64 bits wide or 8 Megabytes.

Here are some common 168-pin DIMMs and their sizes in Megabytes:

1x64	=	8 Megabytes
2x64	=	16 Megabytes
4x64	=	32 Megabytes
8x64	=	64 Megabytes
16x64	=	128 Megabytes

DIMMs rarely do parity in the PC world.

NOTE
Although 168-pin DIMMs are officially "× 64"-wide chips, many techs just say "16 Megabyte 168-pin DIMMs." Be ready to "talk the talk" either way.

THE MAGIC BANKING FORMULA

With 30-pin SIMMs, 72-pin SIMMs, SO-DIMMs, and 168-pin DIMMs, it can get a little challenging to remember how many sticks of each type of DRAM are needed to make a bank on different systems. Don't bother trying to memorize them—the powers-that-be are just gonna come out with wider SIMMs/DIMMs and wider external data busses, and you're going to be right back where you started. Instead, I've got a little formula that you can use to determine the number of SIMMs/DIMMs sticks needed to make one bank. I call it my Magic Banking Formula;

So, for a 486 with 30-pin SIMMs:

486 (32-bit External data bus) and
30-pin SIMMs (8-bit wide data) = 32/8
= 4 (30 pin SIMMs per Bank on a 486)

For a Pentium II with 168-pin DIMMs:

Pentium II (64-bit EDB) and
168-pin DIMM (64-bit wide data) = 64/64
= 1 (168-pin DIMM per bank on a Pentium II)

Stick with this formula, no matter what they throw at you in the future; this will always tell you the number of sticks to make a bank.

MIXING DRAM PACKAGES

Many motherboards have slots for more than one type of DRAM. This is done to add more flexibility to motherboards and to allow you to move from an older type of DRAM to a newer type without losing your investment in the older type of DRAM. For example, here's an old 486 motherboard that can handle both 30-pin and 72-pin SIMMs (see Figure 4.33).

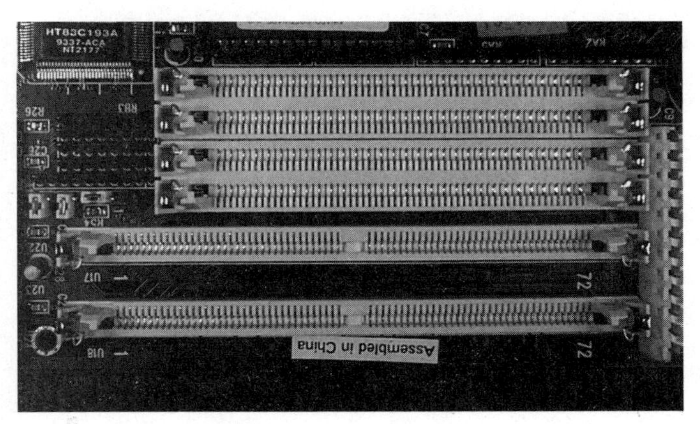

Figure 4.33 30- and 72-pin SIMM slots.

Nothing wrong with this at all—just be aware that you may have to move a jumper or two around to get them to work. Also be aware that some types of SIMMs take precedence over others. On this particular board, if you populate both of the 72-pin banks and the 30-pin bank, one of the 72-pin banks is ignored (I have no idea why!)

Figure 4.34 shows a modern motherboard that can take both 72-pin SIMMs and 168-pin DIMMs.

In this case, you can only install SIMMs or DIMMs. I have another virtually identical motherboard that allows them to work together—go figure.

Figure 4.34 SIMMs and DIMMs.

Improvements on DRAM

As we look at RAM, we need to inspect some of the improvements on the classic *Fast Page Mode* (FPM) DRAM of the original 8088 days. When I say improvements, I'm talking about functional technology improvements, not just widening the RAM via a new type of stick, as we saw in the previous sections. My goal here is not to go into great depth on these improvements, but rather to help you recognize these improvements and take advantage of them when they are available.

EDO

As was explained in the CPU chapter, all DRAM needs to be refreshed in order to keep the data and programs that it stores valid. The process of refresh creates a big bottleneck in RAM access. Sure, things like SRAM caches certainly reduce the impact, but any way to minimize the frequency of refresh will improve the overall speed of the computer. Thus enters *Extended Data Out* (EDO) DRAM. EDO DRAM is nothing more than a moderate improvement on old-style FPM DRAM. EDO needs to be refreshed much less often, thereby allowing an extended period where data can be taken out of RAM.

EDO RAM is either on a 72-pin SIMM or DIMM (168 or SO), and looks exactly like regular DRAM. There is no standard way to tell EDO from FPM DRAM, so be sure to label your EDO RAM as such (see Figure 4.35).

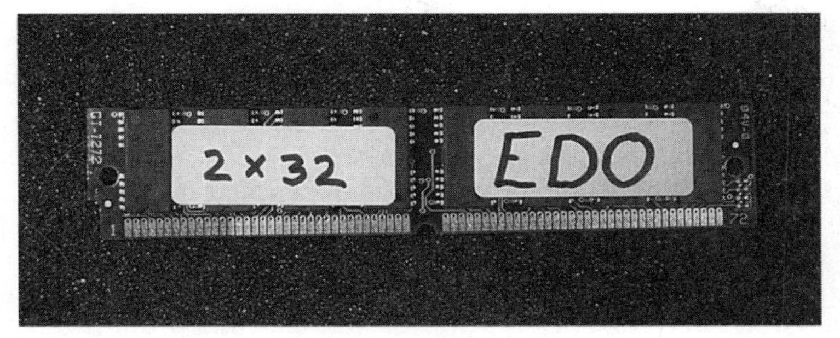

Figure 4.35 How to tell EDO from FPM—another label!

You want to use EDO whenever possible. Unfortunately, you can't just put EDO RAM in any computer. In order to take advantage of EDO, you need a motherboard that is designed to handle it. The majority of today's Pentium systems can use EDO RAM. Refer to your motherboard book to see if your system can use it.

Mixing EDO and FPM RAM is not a good idea. Most systems that use EDO will run with FPM RAM, but you lose the benefit of EDO. Equally, most systems that need FPM RAM will also work with EDO, but the EDO will be treated as regular FPM RAM and you won't get any benefit. Some systems simply won't work unless the proper type of RAM is installed.

SDRAM

The "hot" RAM that everyone is using today is called *Synchronous Dynamic Random Access Memory* (SDRAM). SDRAM is still DRAM, but it is synchronous—tied to the system clock. Let me explain.

Regular DRAM (EDO or FPM) is not tied like the CPU to any clock. If the CPU wants some data from RAM, the MCC sends the necessary signals to the DRAM, waits a certain number of clock ticks, and then accesses the RAM again to get the data. The number of clicks of the clock to wait is either set up through CMOS or determined by the MCC every time the system boots up. The number of clicks is not exact and is rounded up to ensure that the MCC won't access the DRAM before the DRAM is ready with the data it needs. This is wasteful of system time, but until recently DRAM was too slow to be handled any other way.

With SDRAM, the DRAM is tied to the system clock. As a result, the MCC knows when data is ready to be grabbed from the SDRAM, resulting in little wasted time. Plus, SDRAM is just plain faster than DRAM. Finally, SDRAM pipelines instructions from the MCC that allow commands to be ready as soon as the previous one is taken by the MCC. Collectively, these improvements make SDRAM 4–6 times faster than regular DRAM.

Currently, SDRAM is only available on 168-pin DIMMs. This makes many people think that every time they see a 168-pin DIMM, it is SDRAM. This is incorrect: 168-pin DIMMs can also be regular DRAM, although that is pretty rare.

NOTE

SDRAM is always a DIMM, but a DIMM isn't always SDRAM

In order to take advantage of SDRAM, you must have a system that is designed to use it. Chances are that if you have a system with a slot for 168-pin DIMMs, your system can handle SDRAM.

Because SDRAM is tied to the system clock, it doesn't have an access speed, it has a clock speed just like a CPU. There are four clock speeds that are commonly found: 66, 75, 83, and 100MHz. These speeds are marked on the DIMM. You need to get a clock speed that is faster than or equal to the motherboard speed. For example, if you have a Pentium 200, the motherboard speed is 66MHz, so 66MHz SDRAM is fine.

Although most motherboards still run at 66MHz or less, those times are changing. I always get 83 or 100MHz SDRAM—not because I need it today, but because I want RAM that will last for awhile.

A lot of people say that SDRAM provides little speed improvement over regular/EDO DRAM. That is true. However, both FPM and EDO have a lot of trouble running on motherboards that pass 66MHz, and SDRAM will easily handle speeds up to 100MHz. Get SDRAM.

ECC

Error Correction Code (ECC) DRAM is becoming very popular in higher-end systems. ECC is a major advancement in error checking on DRAM. As I mentioned earlier, although DRAM rarely goes bad anymore, it is still prone to occasional *hiccups* that can cause data loss while not destroying hardware. Although parity is virtually useless for these types of occasional problems, ECC is excellent at detecting problems in RAM and *at fixing most of them on the fly*. ECC

DRAM can be in any form, although it is most common as 72-pin SIMMs. In order to take advantage of ECC RAM, you need a motherboard that is designed to use ECC. Check your motherboard book.

You rarely see ECC RAM in the standard home or office system.

WORKING WITH RAM

All DRAM chips are extremely static-sensitive, so be sure to use caution when working with DRAM. When I install DRAM, I always use an anti-static wrist pad, available at any electronics store. Always handle SIMMs/DIMMs like a piece of film: keep your fingers on the edges. There is nothing worse than destroying a 64Meg DIMM chip because of static discharge.

A Word on Speed

There is often a temptation to mix speeds of DRAM in the same system. There are some situations in which you can get away with mixing speeds on the system, but the safest, easiest rule is always use the speed of DRAM specified in the motherboard book and make sure that every piece of DRAM is that speed!

Unacceptable mixing of DRAM speeds will almost always manifest itself by a system lockup every few seconds to every few minutes. You might also get some data corruption, so don't do your income tax on a machine with mixed DRAM speeds until the system has proven itself to be stable for a few days. The important thing to note here is that you won't break anything, other than possibly data, by experimenting.

O.K, enough of the disclaimers. First, you can use RAM that is faster than what the motherboard specifies. For example, if the system needs 70ns DRAM you can put in 60ns, and it will work fine. Faster DRAM is not going to make the systems run any faster, so don't look for any system improvement.

You can usually get away with putting one speed of DRAM in one bank and another speed in another bank, as long as all of the speeds are as fast or faster than the speed specified by the motherboard.

Don't bother trying to put different speed DRAM in the same bank. Yeah, it does work once in a while, sort of, but it's too *chancy.* I avoid it.

A Word on Banks

Although banks are generally straightforward and rarely cause problems, you need to be aware of a few situations that might cause trouble.

All systems number their banks, usually starting with the number 0. Some systems require you to populate bank 0 before you populate any other bank. Most systems don't care. So, if you install some RAM and the system doesn't boot up, always try the RAM in another bank to be sure that your system isn't *bank-sensitive.*

Not all banks take all sizes of DRAM. For example, I've got some older Pentium motherboards that take 72-pin SIMMs. These motherboards, however, won't use any SIMMs bigger than 4 × 32. So the biggest DRAM sticks I can put in there are 16 Megabytes. There is no way around it.

Watch out for interleaved banks. It is usually a safe assumption that the connectors are grouped together by banks. In a Pentium system with four rows of 72-pin SIMMs, the first two rows are usually one bank and the second two rows are another. You may occasionally run into a system, however, in which the banks are *interleaved.* Using the same example, the first and third rows are one bank, while the second and fourth rows are the other bank.

Finally, be aware that not everybody banks according the Magic Banking Formula. Many Pentium systems will run with just one 72-pin SIMM. In many of these systems, however, you end up with a serious system slowdown; so on the rare occasion where I stumble into one of these systems, I will still bank the way I know to be correct.

Installing SIMMs

All SIMMs have a notch on one side that prevents them from being installed improperly. When installing SIMMs, be sure to insert the SIMMs at an angle, as shown in the following diagram (see Figure 4.36). When I install SIMMs, I visualize the same motion as a chip shot in golf. If you're not a golfer, visualize scooping ice cream out of a container.

After the SIMM is securely seated into the slot, push it upright until the holding clamps on either side are secured (see Figure 4.37). Make sure that holes on either side show the small retaining tabs coming through.

If the SIMM will not insert relatively easily, it's probably backward. Also, most SIMMs will stand up vertically when properly installed, so if it isn't vertical, it is probably backwards.

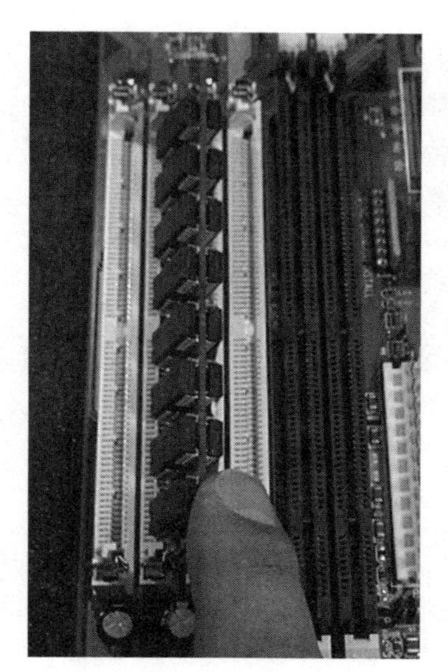

Figure 4.36 Inserting a SIMM.

Figure 4.37 SIMM not all the way in.

Take advantage of the fact that more than one SIMM is being installed to give you the ability to see how they line up across their tops. An improperly installed SIMM will almost always give itself away by not giving a nice uniform appearance across the top when compared to the other SIMMs (see Figure 4.38).

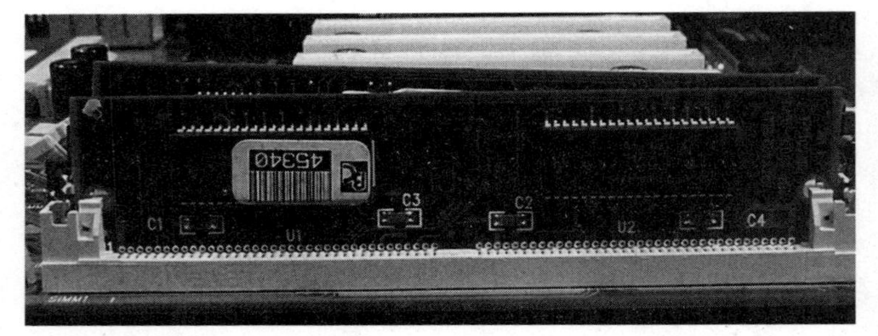

Figure 4.38 Improperly inserted SIMM.

Installing DIMMs

DIMMs are far easier to install than SIMMs (see Figure 4.39). A good hard push down is usually all you need to ensure a solid connection. Make sure that the DIMM snaps into position to show it is completely seated. You will also notice that the two side tabs will move in to reflect a tight connection.

Figure 4.39 Inserting a DIMM.

CMOS

After the SIMMs are installed, turn on the PC. If the DRAM is physically installed correctly, you will notice the RAM count on the PC reflects the new value. If the RAM value stays the same, you probably have either a disabled bank or the SIMM is not properly installed. Check the motherboard book to see if a jumper needs to be changed to turn it on. If the computer does not boot and there is nothing on the screen, you probably have not installed all the RAM sticks correctly. Usually a good second look is all you need to see if that's the problem.

Once the RAM is installed and the RAM count reflects the new value, your CMOS needs to be updated to show the new amount of installed RAM. On most machines, this is done automatically and you do not have to do anything. However, if your machine says the following

```
CMOS Memory Mismatch
Press F1 to continue
```

or something like that, you'll have to access your CMOS with your CMOS setup program, and then simply save and exit. Your CMOS will be reset. Reboot again and your RAM is installed.

When your PC is booting, all RAM counts are based on units of 1024 bytes (Ks). So, 4 Megabytes will show as 4096, 8Meg as 8192, 16Meg as 16384, etc. Most RAM counts, however, will stop before they get to the value you expect. For example, a machine with 8Meg may only count to 7808. This is acceptable—some of your memory is *skipped* during the count up, but it's all there.

Troubleshooting RAM

Today's DRAM chips are tough—the MTBF (mean time between failure) rate for 16Meg of RAM in a post-1995 computer is something like 30-35 years! The overwhelming majority of errors that look like bad RAM are usually something else.

Bad RAM chips manifest themselves in only two ways: parity errors and lockups/Page Faults. Parity errors are simply errors that the MCC detects from the parity chips (if you have them). These errors are reported by the operating system if you are using DOS, OS/2, or Windows 95. Windows will intercept the errors and report them in a window. They look something like this:

```
Parity Error at XXXX:XXXX
```

where XXXX:XXXX is a hexadecimal value. If you get an error like this, write down the XXXX:XXXX value! The secret of parity errors is that they always happen at the same place. If you get another parity error and it shows a different XXXX:XXXX value, it's a bogus error. If the error shows up at the same place every time, you probably have a bad SIMM chip.

My favorite SIMMs tester is the Troubleshooter by Forefront: (813)724-8994. Although the Troubleshooter does a lot of things other than just checking RAM, the RAM checker is all that I use. My second choice would be Norton's Diags, which is part of Norton's Utilities.

There is another product that's for only the most serious users: QAPlus /FE from Diagsoft (813)207-7000. The RAM-testing functions of QAPlus work best on RAM when it's used before something goes wrong. It will literally draw a picture of your RAM and give you a snapshot of your memory layout. When the RAM tester is used, it will tell you which SIMM is bad!

If you are using DOS 6.20 or higher, you already have a very good RAM checker in HIMEM.SYS. HIMEM.SYS by default will check all RAM in your system every time it runs. It's accurate, but if it finds bad RAM, all it says is that you have *unreliable* memory. This is O.K., but then you are reduced to finding the bad SIMM by using the "replace and pray" method.

The "replace and pray" method is to open the system case and replace each SIMM, one at a time, with a known good replacement SIMM (you've got one of those lying around?). Although this certainly is a valid method for troubleshooting, the only drawback is that requires you to open the case—and to have an extra SIMM.

If you get parity errors that are intermittent, it's almost certain to be a bad power supply. (See the power chapter.)

The last place that bad RAM tends to manifest itself is within Windows. Whenever Windows 3.1 gives a General Protection Fault or Windows 95 gives a Page Fault, they will always give a long string of hexadecimal digits that say something like the following:

```
KRNL386 Caused a Page Fault at 03F2:25A003BC
```

When I get these, I document that crazy string of letters and numbers. If I keep getting the same error at the same value, there is a good chance that I have a bad RAM chip. I then again use the "replace and pray" method to determine which DRAM stick is the bad one.

CHAPTER 5

Motherboards and BIOS

Motherboards & BIOS

In this chapter, we will

- Understand the function of BIOS
- See the different types of BIOS
- Examine various CMOS setups
- Properly configure and maintain CMOS

The Communications Gap

In Chapter 2, we saw how the address bus and the external data bus connect the RAM to the CPU in order to run programs and transfer data. However, the computer needs more than just a CPU and RAM. It needs input devices such as keyboards and mice to accept input from the user. The computer needs output devices like monitors or sound cards to display the current state of the programs being run. A computer needs permanent storage devices, such as floppy drives and hard drives, so you can store data when you turn off the computer. The external data bus joins together all of these parts of the computer (see Figure 5.1).

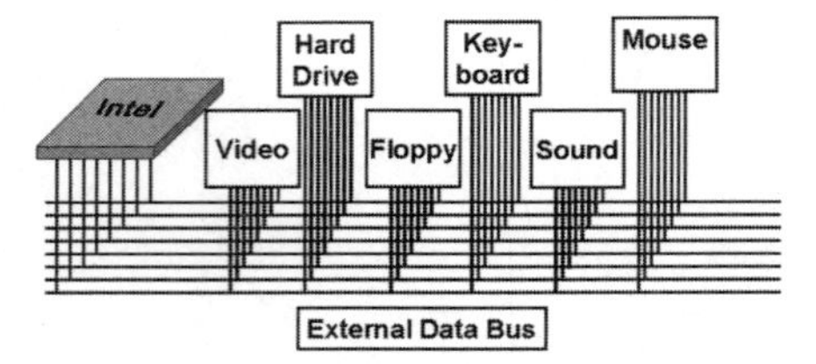

Figure 5.1 Everything is connected to the EDB.

The external data bus is not the only bus that connects all the parts of the PC. The address bus is also connected to the different parts of the PC (see Figure 5.2).

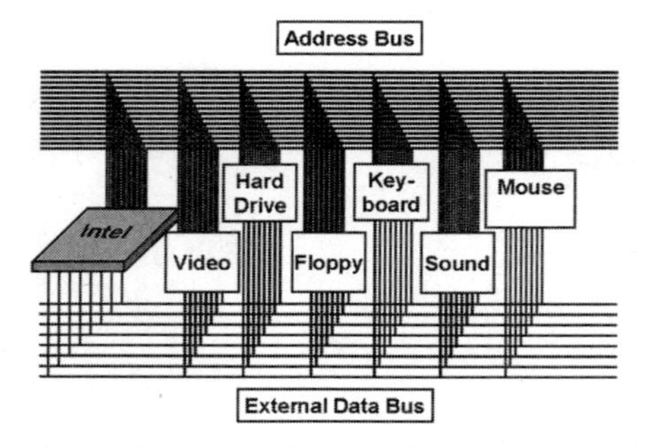

Figure 5.2 Everything is also connected to the address bus.

Knowing this, two big questions come to mind. First, where are these busses and how are they physically organized? Second, how can we use these wires to perform communication between the CPU and the different components of the PC? In this chapter, we will answer these questions through the discovery of BIOS and motherboards. Let's begin by discussing BIOS.

BIOS

So far, we understand how programs can be written to get simple work done like adding 2 + 3. Now, we see that all these devices are attached to the CPU. How do we put data on the screen? How do we tell the hard drive to send us a file? How do we read the mouse to tell if it's being moved? We need to take advantage of the data and address busses to communicate with these devices. The interaction between the keyboard and the CPU provides a good example of how all this works.

The keyboard connects to the external data bus via a special chip known as the keyboard controller. An early keyboard controller was the Intel 8042 (see Figure 5.3). The 8042 has long since been obsolesced by more advanced keyboard controllers, but the name has stuck. All keyboard controllers are generally called *the 8042.* Although the 8042 and the CPU exchange data through the external data bus, they need some type of programming to allow that communication.

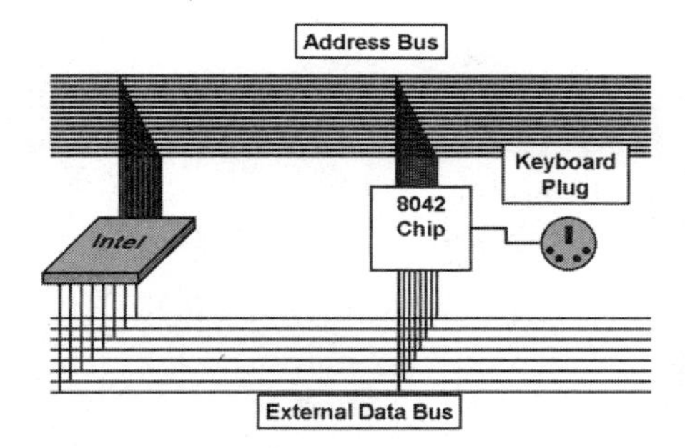

Figure 5.3 The 8042 chip.

Every time you press a button on the keyboard, a scanning chip in the keyboard notices which button has been pressed. Then the scanner sends a coded burst of ones and zeroes to the 8042 chip (see Figure 5.4). This pattern of ones and zeroes is called the *scan code.* Every button on your keyboard has a unique scan code. The 8042 chip stores the scan code in its own memory registers.

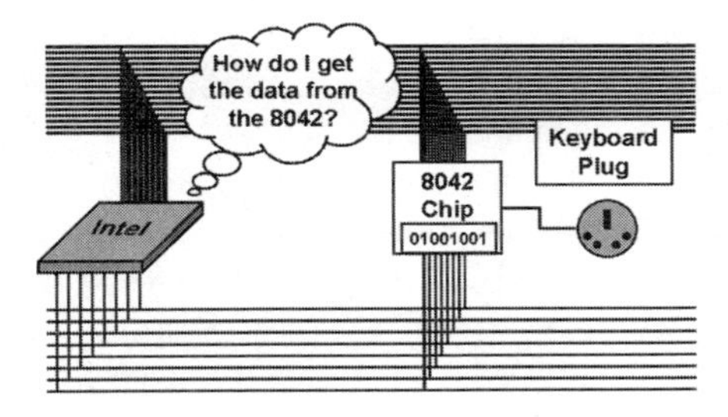

Figure 5.4 How does the CPU communicate with the 8042?

How does the CPU get the scan code out of the 8042? Well, the 8042 chip accepts commands exactly like the 8088 CPU does. Remember when we added 2 + 3 with the 8088? We used a specific command from the *instruction set* that told the 8088 to take the value stored in the AX register and put it on the external data bus. The 8042 has its own *code book*—much simpler than a CPU's, but conceptually the same. In order to find out the scan code stored inside the 8042, we need to know the command (or series of commands) to make the 8042 put the scan code of the letter on the external data bus so the CPU can read it.

The CPU needs a program to enable it to talk to the 8042. This creates two big issues. First, all 8042 chips are not alike. The original 8042 chip, designed in 1978, has been redesigned and improved upon many times over the years. With each redesign, the code book of the 8042 has been expanded and/or changed. Second, where is this program stored? You can't store the program on hard drives or floppy drives. As we will see later in this chapter, you will need the keyboard installed and working before you can install a floppy drive or hard drive.

So how do we handle these issues? Let's think about this for a moment. Yes, there are lots of different 8042 chips out there, but once you have your motherboard, it will have a particular 8042 chip soldered on it. You're not going to be changing an 8042 chip. So what we need to do is put the program that knows how to talk to the specific 8042 chip *on the motherboard with the 8042 chip*. Now, where do we store this program? On DRAM? No, that would be erased every time we turn off the computer. We need some type of program storage device that is permanent and doesn't depend on other peripherals in order to work.

Let's put the specific program on a special type of memory chip called a ROM. ROM chips can store programs exactly like RAM chips, but with two major differences (see Figure 5.5). First, ROM chips are *non-volatile*. Non-volatile means that the program(s) stored on the ROM will not be erased, even when the computer is turned off. Second, ROM chips are read-only. This means that once the programs are stored, they can't be changed.

Now, when the CPU wants to talk to the 8042, it goes to the ROM chip to access the proper program to talk to the 8042. Understand that there are *many* programs on the ROM chip. For example, there's more than one program to talk to the 8042. The program we described previously accesses the scan code, but there are other programs that do things like change the typeamatic buffer rate (when you hold down a key and the letter is repeated). There are programs on that ROM chip to talk to the keyboard (via the 8042), the floppy drive(s), the hard drive(s), the monitor, and a few other devices on your computer. So clearly there is not just one program on that ROM chip! To talk to all that basic hardware requires hundreds of little programs (2–30 lines of code each). We call these hundreds of little programs stored on the ROM chip the *Basic Input/Output System* (BIOS) (see Figure 5.6). Each of these tiny programs is called a *service.*

Figure 5.5 Typical ROM BIOS.

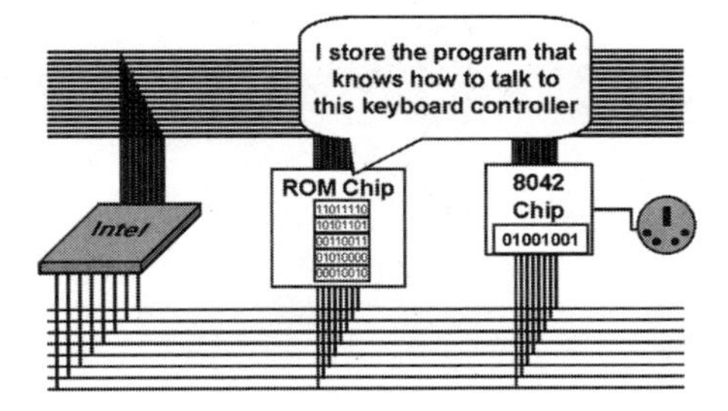

Figure 5.6 Function of the ROM chip.

Please say the following sentence out loud. *BIOS is software.* BIOS is hundreds of little programs designed to talk to the most basic parts of your computer. We store these programs on a ROM chip because a ROM chip can hold the programs even when you turn off the computer. Although there is some variance, most ROM chips store around 65,536 lines of BIOS programming.

BIOS AND THE RELATIONSHIP TO MEMORY ADDRESSING

BIOS is software, right? So how does the CPU run software? Well, if the software is in RAM, we use the address bus to tell which byte of RAM we want to run, correct? On the original 8088 chip, the address bus consisted of 20 wires. These twenty wires could be turned on and off in 1,048,576 (1 Meg) different combinations, and each combination was kind of like the *phone number* for every byte of RAM. Turning wires on and off on the address bus allowed us to tell the memory controller chip which byte of RAM we wanted to access. Now, however, we have a ROM chip loaded with 65,536 bytes of BIOS code. How do we access this code? The same way we access RAM—through the address bus.

All of the patterns that the address bus can generate are called the *address space*. A good analogy for this is the phone company. In the 713 area code, all of the phone numbers from (713) 000-0000 all the way to (713) 999-9999 are all of the numbers that our phones can generate, correct? That's exactly 10,000,000 different telephone numbers. We could say the address space of the 713 area code is 10,000,000. The address space for the 8088 processor is 1,048,576.

When IBM invented the IBM PC, IBM declared that the last 65,536 patterns on the address bus would be *reserved* for the BIOS on the ROM chip (see Figure 5.7). That means that you cannot add 1 Megabyte of RAM to a computer that runs on an 8088 chip. At this point, it looks as if the most RAM you can add is about 1 Megabyte minus 65,536 bytes. Using the telephone analogy, it would be like the phone company keeping all the phone numbers from 777-7777 up to 999-9999 for its own use.

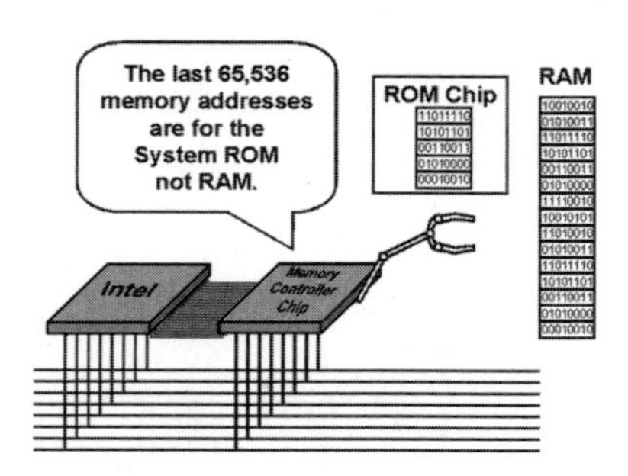

Figure 5.7 Reserving address space for ROM.

The CPU must be able to communicate with every piece of hardware in your computer. You have to be able to tell the sound card to play a song or tell the video card to put a graphic on the monitor. There must be some kind of software to talk to all of the hardware of your computer. All hardware, therefore, needs BIOS.

NOTE
All hardware needs BIOS.

The BIOS stored on the ROM chip welded to the motherboard is officially known as the SYSTEM BIOS, to differentiate it from other BIOSs that may be on the computer.

When IBM designed the original IBM PC back in 1981, they knew that other devices would be invented in the future and would need BIOS support. IBM did not want to get into a game where every time you added a device, you had to replace the system ROM. So, IBM decided that the easiest way to handle the problem was to have devices with their own ROM chip. Therefore, in the original 8088, IBM decided to reserve 384K out of the 1024K (1 Meg) of memory addresses for ROMs. That leaves 640K of memory addresses for RAM.

What if you have a computer that runs on a 286, 386, 486 or Pentium? They have much larger address busses, as big as 32 wires, which means they can put a lot more RAM on their PCs. However, they still must reserve the last 384K of the first megabyte of memory space for their BIOS to be backwardly compatible to the 8088. We will go into this concept in more detail in the memory chapter.

THE MANY DIFFERENT FACES OF BIOS

A computer's hardware breaks down into three groups: Core, CMOS, and Everything Else. Core hardware include devices that are common, necessary, and never change. The BIOS for core devices, such as the keyboard, is stored on the System BIOS ROM chip. CMOS group devices are also common and necessary, but may change from time to time. This group includes RAM (we can add RAM), hard drives (we can add a larger or a second hard drive), or floppy drives (same as hard drives). The BIOS for these devices is also stored on the System BIOS chip. But some BIOS information that changes must be stored on a separate, special RAM chip called a *Complimentary Metal-Oxide Semiconductor* (CMOS) chip. All other *non-core* devices, such as mice, sound cards, tape backup units, CD-ROMs, etc., fall into the Everything Else Group.

CORE GROUP: THE SYSTEM ROM

The Core group contains hardware that is essential for all PCs, and does not change after the initial integration into the motherboard. We have seen an example of a core device with the keyboard/8042 chip. Other examples of core devices are parallel ports, serial ports, the PC speaker, and support chips on the motherboard. The BIOS for Core devices is written into the System ROM chip, which provides a stable and unchanging source for the CPU to access. For the most part, technicians need never mess with the System BIOS ROM because it almost never fails. On those rare occasions when it does break, however, the result is catastrophic and obvious. We will discuss failed system BIOS later in this chapter.

CMOS GROUP: THE CHANGEABLE ONES

Some devices in the PC are necessary and common, but have certain parameters that are changeable. Every PC, for example, must have RAM to operate, but the type, speed, and size of that RAM can change, according to what is installed. The basic BIOS for this assumed and necessary hardware—like RAM, hard drives, floppy drives, and video—is stored in the System BIOS ROM chip. However, if we change one of these items, such as upgrading a hard drive or adding a second hard drive, we must be able to change certain parameters to reflect those modifications to the hardware. We cannot change the BIOS routines on the ROM, so we need to add another type of storage chip that can be modified to reflect these changes. This changeable chip is called the *Complimentary Metal-Oxide Semiconductor* (CMOS) chip. In the PC world, CMOS chips do not store programs; they only store data that is read by BIOS to complete the programs needed to talk to changeable hardware. The CMOS chip also acts as a clock to keep the date and time.

We will go into the parameters stored on the CMOS chip in minute detail as we talk about the different types of hardware, so we need not concern ourselves with the details here (see Figure 5.8). For now, simply appreciate that there is a system BIOS chip and a CMOS chip in your computer.

The information stored in the CMOS chip must accurately reflect the hardware installed in the system. If the data referencing a particular piece of hardware stored on the CMOS is different from the actual hardware, the computer will not be able to access that particular piece of hardware. It is critical that this information is correct. If you change any of the previously mentioned hardware, the CMOS must be updated to reflect those changes. So we need to know how to change the data on the CMOS chip.

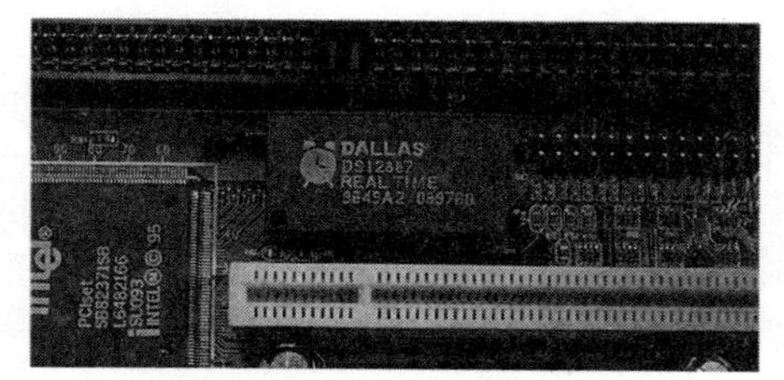

Figure 5.8 Typical CMOS chip.

Updating CMOS: The Setup Program

Because the CMOS must be changed when you make certain hardware changes, we need a way to access and update the data on the CMOS chip. This is the function of the CMOS setup. The CMOS setup is a special program that allows you to make changes on the CMOS chip. The CMOS setup is stored on the system ROM. There are many ways to start the CMOS setup program, and it usually depends on the brand of BIOS you have on your computer. Let me explain. When you fire up your computer in the morning, the first thing you see is the BIOS information. For example, you may see:

```
AMIBIOS (C) 1998 American Megatrends Inc.
PRESS <DEL>, if you want to run setup
(C) American Megatrends Inc.,
40-0100-006259-00101111-060692-SYMP-F
```

Or maybe something like this:

```
Phoenix BIOS(TM) Pentium Version 1.03 (2.25B)
Copyright (C) 1985-1998 Phoenix Technologies Ltd.
All Rights Reserved
```

Who or what is *American Megatrends*? Who or what is Phoenix Technologies? These are brand names of BIOS companies. They write BIOS and sell them to computer makers. In the bad old days, the days of XTs and 286s, when companies made a motherboard, they usually hired a few programmers to write the BIOS. In today's world, almost nobody writes their own BIOS. Instead, they buy their BIOS from third-party BIOS makers like American Megatrends and Phoenix Technologies. Although there are about ten different companies that write BIOS, there are three big companies that control 99 percent of the BIOS business: American Megatrends (AMI), Award Software (Award) and Phoenix Technologies

(Phoenix). AMI, Award and Phoenix pretty much control the entire BIOS market these days and they each have different ways to access the CMOS setup program. Here are the most common ways to access their CMOS setup programs.

For AMI and Award, press the DEL key when the machine first begins to boot.

For Phoenix, press <CTRL>, <ALT>, and <ESC> simultaneously at any time.

Watch your screen as your computer boots up. Most BIOS makers will tell you how to access the CMOS setup right on the screen. Look at the bottom of this diagram:

```
Award Modular BIOS v4.51PG, An Energy Star Ally
Copyright (C) 1984-97, Award Software, Inc.
Intel 430VX CHIPS, AUTO CPU VOLTAGE DETECT START Ver. 2.3
Award Plug and Play BIOS Extension v1.0A
Copyright (C) 1996, Award Software, Inc.

Press DEL to enter Setup
12/30/96-i430VX-8663-2A59GG0BC-00
```

Note that you simply press the Delete key to access the CMOS setup. Motherboard makers can change the key combinations to access the CMOS setup. If these do not work, try these key combinations:

```
<CTRL><ALT><INS>, <CTRL><A>, <CTRL><S>, <CTRL><F1>, <F10>
```

AMI, Award, and Phoenix are not the only BIOS makers in the world. Watch your computer when it boots to determine your manufacturer. You can also take off the cover from your PC and see whose name is on the system ROM chip. Read your motherboard book to determine the process to access the CMOS Setup Program.

If you are not sure how to access your CMOS setup, there are a number of good third-party utilities to let you edit your CMOS. Try Touchstone's Checkit PRO, available at almost any software store.

Another way that works is to reboot the PC and hold down a bunch of keys. That will often cause an error and prompt you with something like:

```
Keyboard Error
Press F1 to enter Setup
```

You can often generate the same error by simply unplugging the keyboard. After you get the error, plug the keyboard back in and press whatever key the machine tells you to press.

A Quick Tour through CMOS Setup: Award

Every maker of BIOS has a different-looking CMOS setup program. Do not let screens that look different confuse you! They all say basically the same thing—you just have to be comfortable poking around. The only secret is not to save anything unless you know it is right. Award Modular BIOS is the most popular CMOS today. We will therefore touch on Award first and continue to use Award screens throughout the book.

When you boot a machine with Award BIOS, you see something like this:

```
Award Modular BIOS v4.51PG, An Energy Star Ally
Copyright (C) 1984-97, Award Software, Inc.
Intel 430VX CHIPS, AUTO CPU VOLTAGE DETECT START - Ver. 2.3

Award Plug and Play BIOS Extension v1.0A
Copyright (C) 1996, Award Software, Inc.

Press DEL to enter Setup
1/30/98 - i430LX - 8663-2A59GG0BC-00
```

Press the DEL key and the screen in Figure 5.9 appears.

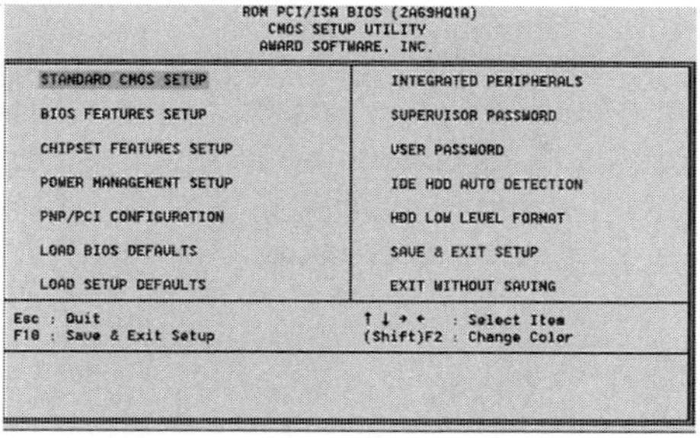

```
ROM PCI/ISA BIOS (2A69HQ1A)
CMOS SETUP UTILITY
AWARD SOFTWARE, INC.

STANDARD CMOS SETUP          INTEGRATED PERIPHERALS
BIOS FEATURES SETUP          SUPERVISOR PASSWORD
CHIPSET FEATURES SETUP       USER PASSWORD
POWER MANAGEMENT SETUP       IDE HDD AUTO DETECTION
PNP/PCI CONFIGURATION        HDD LOW LEVEL FORMAT
LOAD BIOS DEFAULTS           SAVE & EXIT SETUP
LOAD SETUP DEFAULTS          EXIT WITHOUT SAVING

Esc : Quit                   ↑ ↓ → ←    : Select Item
F10 : Save & Exit Setup      (Shift)F2 : Change Color
```

Figure 5.9 CMOS screen.

You are now in the CMOS setup program. This program is stored on the ROM chip, but all it does is edit the data on the CMOS chip. Although we will describe all the contents of the CMOS setup program, concentrate on the most basic part, the standard CMOS setup. Select `STANDARD CMOS SETUP` and the standard CMOS screen shown in Figure 5.10 appears.

```
                 ROM PCI/ISA BIOS (2A69HQ1A)
                     STANDARD CMOS SETUP
                    AWARD SOFTWARE, INC.

 Date (mm:dd:yy) : Mon, May 5 1998
 Time (hh:mm:ss) : 16 : 13 : 59

 HARD DISKS          TYPE   SIZE  CYLS HEAD PRECOMP LANDZ SECTOR MODE

 Primary Master    : Auto      0     0    0       0     0      0 AUTO
 Primary Slave     : Auto      0     0    0       0     0      0 AUTO
 Secondary Master  : None      0     0    0       0     0      0 ------
 Secondary Slave   : None      0     0    0       0     0      0 ------

 Drive A : 1.44M, 3.5 in.
 Drive B : None                          Base Memory:     0K
                                     Extended Memory:     0K
 Video    : EGA/VGA                     Other Memory:   512K
 Halt On  : All Errors
                                        Total Memory:   512K

 ESC : Quit          ↑ ↓ → ←    : Select Item     PU/PD/+/- : Modify
 F1  : Help          (Shift)F2  : Change Color
```

Figure 5.10 Typical standard CMOS screen.

Here, we can change floppy drive, hard drive, and date/time settings. We will learn how to set up CMOS properly for these devices, as we discuss them individually in later chapters.

The first BIOS was nothing more than a standard CMOS setup. Today, virtually all computers have many extra CMOS settings. These extra settings encompass items such as memory-management, password and booting options, diagnostic and error handling, and power management. At this point, my goal is only for you to be aware of the *existence* of CMOS setup and how to access the CMOS setup on a PC. As we understand more and more of the computer, we will return to CMOS many times to setup properly whatever device we are discussing. (See also the CMOS Settings Appendix for an alphabetical listing that describes the majority of these settings.)

It is important to note here that motherboard makers buy a basic BIOS from Award and can then add options based on the needs of the motherboard. This can cause problems because seemingly identical CMOS setups can be extremely different. Options that show up on one computer may be missing from another.

Phoenix BIOS

Phoenix BIOS is the *Mercedes Benz* of BIOS. Phoenix custom creates each BIOS for optimal use in the machine for which it is designed. As a result, Phoenix BIOSs have fewer options (see Figure 5.11). You will usually see Phoenix BIOS in machines with proprietary motherboards such as laptops.

```
PhoenixBIOS Setup - Copyright 1992-97 Phoenix Technologies Ltd.
Main   Advanced   Security   Power   Exit

                                                 Item Specific Help
System Time:                 [16:19:20]
System Date:                 [03/02/1994]

Legacy Diskette A:           [1.2 MB, 5¼"]       <Tab>, <Shift-Tab>, or
Legacy Diskette B:           [Not Installed]     <Enter> selects field.

▶ Primary Master:            C:  121 MB
▶ Primary Slave:             None
▶ Secondary Master:          None
▶ Secondary Slave:           None

▶ Memory Cache
▶ System Shadow              [Enabled]
▶ Video Shadow               [Enabled]

System Memory:                640 KB
Extended Memory:             1024 KB

F1  Help   ↑↓ Select Item   -/+   Change Values        F9  Setup Defaults
ESC Exit   ↔  Select Menu   Enter Select ▶ Sub-Menu    F10 Save and Exit
```

Figure 5.11 Phoenix BIOS.

AMI BIOS

American Megatrends BIOS competes directly with Award, providing highly flexible BIOSs. AMI was the most-used BIOS for many years until Award became more predominant, starting around 1994–95 (see Figure 5.12). Although AMI no longer holds the virtual monopoly it once had on BIOS, it is still quite common in many popular systems.

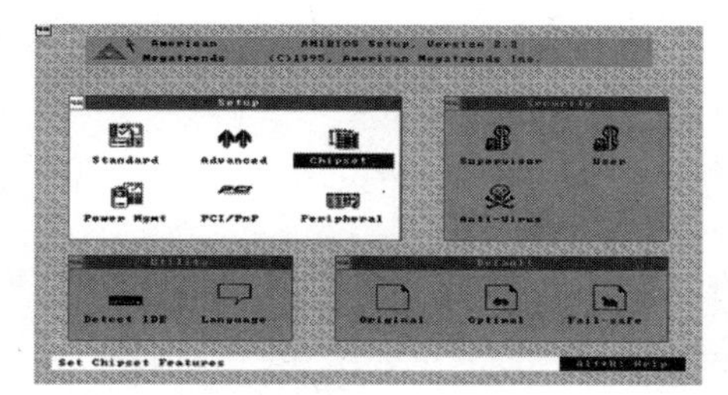

Figure 5.12 AMI BIOS.

Care and Feeding of Your CMOS

Losing CMOS information is a common problem. If the information on the CMOS chips is erased, the computer will not be able to boot up and/or you get nasty-looking errors. Unfortunately, it is easy to lose CMOS information. Some of the more common reasons for losing CMOS data are:

- The on-board battery runs out
- Pulling and inserting cards
- Touching the motherboard

- Dropping something on the motherboard
- Dirt on the motherboard
- Faulty power supplies
- Electrical surges

Losing the CMOS just happens and is accepted as *one of those things* in the world of computing. The errors that point to lost CMOS information usually take place while the computer is booting. Watch for errors like:

- CMOS configuration mismatch
- CMOS date/time not set
- No boot device available
- CMOS battery state low

Although these errors sometimes point to other problems, when they show up at boot, the first place to check is the CMOS settings. In order to check the CMOS settings, you need to either have all of your CMOS settings memorized or you need to compare the current CMOS settings to a backup copy. Because it is impossible to prevent, the correct course of action is to prepare for losing the CMOS by keeping backups of CMOS information. So, make a backup copy of your CMOS information. The best way to do this is to use a shareware CMOS save and restore program, like `CMOSSAVE`, which is readily found on the Internet.

Running CMOSSAVE

Run CMOS Save by inserting a blank diskette into the `A:` drive and type:

```
CMOSSAVE a:filename
```

The filename is anything you want, preferably something that describes the computer whose CMOS is being saved. The CMOS information for hundreds of computers can be placed on one diskette. You can lose your CMOS information by inserting or removing cards at an angle, by not using a good surge suppressor, or by letting the computer get dirty; so be careful.

Battery

The beauty of CMOS chips is that the data stored on them can be changed. The trade-off for this capability is that the CMOS chip needs a trickle voltage, whether the computer is turned on or not. To provide the CMOS with power when the computer is turned off, all motherboards come with a battery. These batteries are mounted in two ways: on-board and external (see Figure 5.13). On-board batteries are mounted directly to the motherboard; external batteries are not. Many PCs today no longer need a battery because the CMOS chip itself has enough battery power to keep itself running.

Figure 5.13 Typical batteries.

The voltage for this battery is either ~3.6 or ~6 volts, depending on whether you have a low-power (3.3 volt) or standard (5 volt) motherboard. Most low-power motherboards will work with either voltage, but you should always check the motherboard documentation to verify the correct voltage. On-board batteries are usually rechargeable Nickel Cadmium (NiCd) or Nickel Metal-Hydride (NiMH), and will last, on average, from five to seven years. External batteries are usually non-rechargeable AA-size alkaline batteries that tend to last for two to four years (see Figure 5.14).

Figure 5.14 External battery pack.

It's usually pretty clear when the battery needs to be replaced. The first clue that the battery is going is that the CMOS clock begins to slow down. Go to a `C:\>` prompt and type `time`—if you notice that you are losing time, it's time to change the battery. However, remember that if you are on a DOS (this includes Win95) machine, DOS only uses the CMOS clock to get the date on boot. Once the PC is running, DOS uses the memory refresh timer on the memory controller to keep time. This is fine, except that the refresh timer does not do seconds very well and as a result, you will lose one or two seconds a day. Many people never turn off their computers and as a result, their clocks lose time. Do not confuse this with a bad battery. If you reboot, the computer will then update itself from the CMOS and show the correct time. If the CMOS battery is low, it will still show the incorrect time.

When the CMOS battery really dies, the effect is painfully clear. The scenario looks something like this: you get lost CMOS errors as previously discussed, so you reconfigure the CMOS settings. You reboot and the errors return. It's definitely time to change the battery. Sometimes, the PC will hold the CMOS information during the week, but over the weekend, when the PC is off for two days, the CMOS data are lost. Do not let these seemingly *intermittent* problems fool you.

NOTE

Any time a PC loses the CMOS information more than once within a week, replace the battery immediately to eliminate it as a possible problem.

The CMOS chip contains a capacitor that allows you to replace the battery without losing the data. For motherboards with welded on-board batteries, there is usually a connection provided to add an external battery to replace a worn-out, on-board battery. Remember to be sure that the external battery has the same voltage as the on-board battery you are replacing.

If you have a motherboard that doesn't have a battery, you're in luck. The latest motherboards have CMOS chips with very long-lasting batteries. These batteries virtually never go out. Unfortunately, these machines almost never have an external battery connector. I've only had one go out on me and I just replaced the motherboard. Sure, you could get a new CMOS chip, but it's not worth the time or the price.

FLASH ROM

The use of ROM chips for BIOS has a huge shortcoming: you can't change the BIOS without physically removing the ROM. A few years ago, a new type of ROM chip, called a Flash ROM, was developed, which has now become the primary type of system ROM used in PCs today. Flash ROMs look exactly like regular ROM chips —you can't tell whether you have a flash or not just by looking at the system BIOS chip (see Figure 5.15).

Figure 5.15 Flash ROM and clock.

Flash ROMs can be reprogrammed without removing the chip! This is a huge advantage in today's systems. Every time some new type of technology comes out, there is invariably a need to update the BIOS to take advantage of this technology. Let's use MMX as an example. If you buy an MMX CPU, you may not be able to take full advantage of it unless your BIOS can be updated to handle the new features of MMX. If you have a regular ROM, you can either physically yank out the ROM chip or buy a new motherboard. This can be a little expensive—and difficult. But with Flash ROM, all you do is run a small DOS program that combines with an update file to update your BIOS. Although the exact process varies from one BIOS maker to another, it usually entails booting off of a floppy diskette and running a command that looks like this:

```
A:\>AW P55T2.BIN
```

It's really that simple! Most of these utilities will allow you to make a backup of your BIOS in case the update causes trouble—always make the backup! If, for some reason, a flash update messes up your computer, you may end up throwing the motherboard away without a good backup.

NOTE
As a rule, don't update your BIOS unless you have a strong compelling reason to do so. If it ain't broke . . .

It's actually fairly easy to determine if you have a Flash ROM. Peel back the little sticker on the chip—if you see a small, round glass window, you don't have a FLASH. If you see the number 28 or 29 in the chip's numbers that looks something like this:

```
29XXXXX or X28XXXXXX
```

You've got a flash!

EVERYTHING ELSE GROUP

The last group of hardware is *Everything Else*. IBM could not possibly add all the necessary BIOS routines for every conceivable piece of hardware. When programmers wrote the first BIOSs, network cards, mice, and sound cards did not exist. Early PC designers (IBM) understood that they could not anticipate every new type of hardware. So, IBM gave us a few ways to BYOB (Bring Your Own BIOS).

Option ROM

The first way to BYOB is to put the BIOS on the hardware device itself. Look at a popular expansion card, an Adaptec 2940 SCSI host adapter (see Figure 5.16). There is a chip on the card that looks a lot like the ROM chip on a motherboard because it is a ROM chip and there is BIOS on it! The system BIOS does not have a clue about how to talk to this card, so the card has to bring its own BIOS with it.

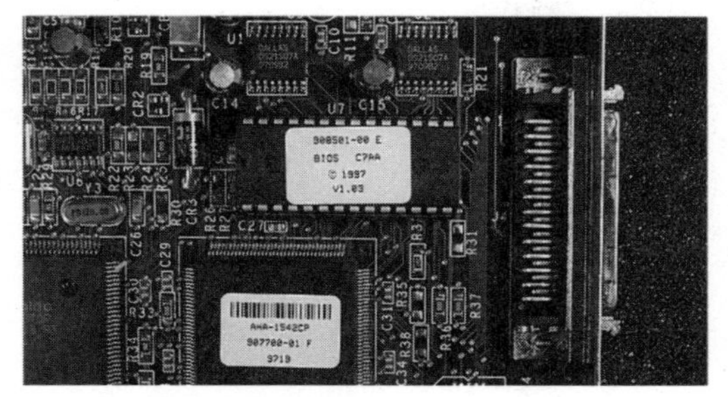

Figure 5.16 ROM on adapter.

Leave It to Software

Installing BIOS on a ROM is extremely inflexible and is rarely used on most devices. Far more popular is to add special programs, called *device drivers* to the system. All PCs have a *list* of device drivers that are loaded into RAM every time the computer starts. This list can be one text file, many text files or, in the case of Windows 95/98, a special database.

> **NOTE**
> **If you're uncomfortable with the concept of text files, directories (folders), or file extensions, jump ahead to the DOS chapter in the *Accelerated A+ OS* book for clarification!**

CONFIG.SYS

The most popular way to add BIOS for DOS PCs is through a special file called `CONFIG.SYS`. `CONFIG.SYS` is a text file in the root directory of your `C:\>` drive. It can be changed with a text editor like `EDIT.COM`. The main (but not the only) reason `CONFIG.SYS` exists is for you to load extra BIOS for hardware that your system BIOS does not support. This is where the BIOS for *Everything Else* is initialized in DOS. BIOS routines that are initialized by `CONFIG.SYS` are stored on the hard drive in special files called *device drivers*. These files usually end with a `.SYS` or `.EXE` extension.

These device drivers come with the device when you buy it. For example, when you buy a sound card, it comes with a diskette or CD-ROM that holds all of the necessary device drivers. There is usually some install program that automatically installs the necessary drivers and updates the `CONFIG.SYS` file. Device driver files are easily identified in the `CONFIG.SYS`. Any line that begins with `DEVICE=` or `DEVICEHIGH=` is loading a device driver. Let's look at a few lines of a typical `CONFIG.SYS` and identify the device drivers:

```
DEVICE=C:\DOS\HIMEM.SYS                         <- BIOS
DEVICE=C:\DOS\EMM386.EXE noems highscan         <- BIOS
BUFFERS=30                                      <- NOT BIOS
DOS=UMB                                         <- NOT BIOS
LASTDRIVE=m                                     <- NOT BIOS
DEVICEHIGH=C:\SCSI\ASPI2DOS.SYS /D /Z           <- BIOS
DEVICEHIGH=C:\SCSI\ASPICD.SYS /D:ASPICD0        <- BIOS
```

When the computer is booted up, DOS reads the CONFIG.SYS file and loads the device drivers from the hard drive to RAM. We will return to CONFIG.SYS when we discuss memory and cover these lines in detail.

SYSTEM.INI

Device drivers that are run through CONFIG.SYS have certain limitations. DOS can only use 640K bytes of RAM. Every device driver in your CONFIG.SYS takes up some of these precious 640K bytes. Also, DOS is a single-tasking operating system, and is therefore incapable of running more than one program simultaneously.

Windows 3.X runs in protected mode (Microsoft calls it 386 Enhanced Mode. (See the CPU chapter for a discussion of *modes*.) Although Windows 3.X can use the device drivers from CONFIG.SYS, it is beneficial to use device drivers that can run in extended memory and can be accessed by more than one program at a time. Therefore, Windows has its own drivers for accessing hardware in protected mode. These drivers are loaded in the SYSTEM.INI file. The SYSTEM.INI file is located in the \Windows directory and is a text file like CONFIG.SYS. The SYSTEM.INI is broken up into groups. Each group can be identified by the name of the section in square brackets that start the section. The standard sections have names [boot], [keyboard], [boot description], [386Enh] and [drivers]. The majority of drivers that are loaded after the installation of Windows 3.X are located in the [386Enh] section. They are distinguished by their device= line, just like in CONFIG.SYS. Here's a small piece of an example [386Enh] section from a SYSTEM.INI file:

```
[386Enh]
device=vwpd.386                <- BIOS
device=dva.386                 <- BIOS
device=*vmcpd                  <- BIOS
SystemROMBreakPoint=false      <- NOT BIOS
device=mach.386                <- BIOS
DebugLocalReboot=TRUE          <- NOT BIOS
device=vshare.386              <- BIOS
device=lpt.386                 <- BIOS
device=serial.386              <- BIOS
VirtualHDIrq=OFF               <- NOT BIOS
```

This begs the big question: If I have a device driver in `CONFIG.SYS`, do I also need a device driver in `SYSTEM.INI`? The fast answer is No, but there are some big exceptions. First, Windows programs can use `CONFIG.SYS` drivers, but DOS programs can't use the Windows protected mode drivers. Second, many devices can only have a device driver in `CONFIG.SYS` or `SYSTEM.INI`—not both. I usually just let the install program do what it wants to do and only worry about these details if something goes wrong.

Also, Windows will add device drivers that completely take over the function of the system BIOS. These device drivers are often generically called *32-bit drivers* and are indistinguishable from any other driver in the `SYSTEM.INI` file.

Registry

One of the big problems of the DOS/Windows 3.X combination was the fact that you could have device drivers installed in more than one location. One of the more powerful features of Windows 95 was the consolidation of all of these files into a new type of configuration file called the Registry (see Figure 5.17). Every configuration setting in Windows 95 is stored in the Registry, including all of the device driver information.

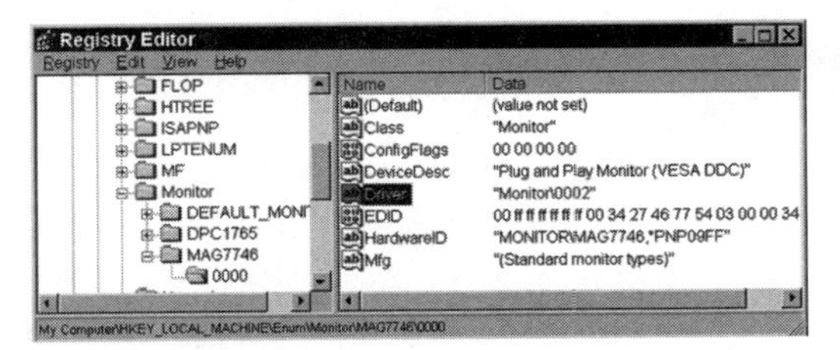

Figure 5.17 Registry.

Unlike `CONFIG.SYS` and `SYSTEM.INI`, the Registry is not a text file. It can only be edited with a special program called the *Registry editor* (REGEDIT). Even though we can directly access the Registry through REGEDIT, there is no *normal* reason to edit the Registry manually to add or delete device drivers.

In the overwhelming majority of situations, we use two programs, the Add New Hardware Wizard and the Device Manager, to edit the Registry (see Figure 5.18). These two programs provide a far more intuitive interface for installing hardware and the necessary drivers. The Add New Hardware Wizard is used to install new devices. The Device Manager is used to change or remove the drivers for any particular device (see Figure 5.19).

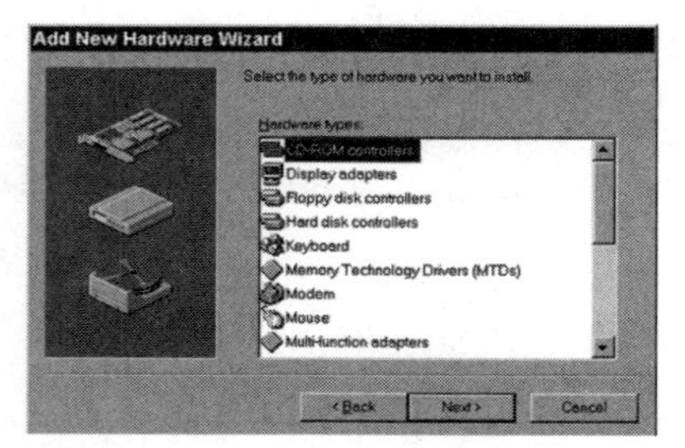

Figure 5.18 Add New Hardware Wizard.

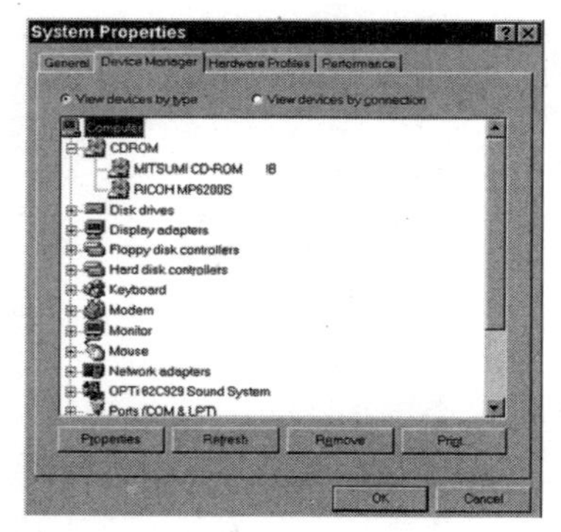

Figure 5.19 Device Manager.

The only downside to the Windows 95 system is the fact that it is backwardly compatible with `SYSTEM.INI` and `CONFIG.SYS`. For example, you can install a sound card into `SYSTEM.INI` or `CONFIG.SYS`, and it will work perfectly. Unfortunately, if you go into the Device Manager, you won't see any information about a sound card. This is bad because most of the newer techs out there today only know to look in the Device Manager; they don't see any information on the sound card and immediately assume that there is some kind of witchcraft going on inside the PC.

Device Drivers versus ROMs

Using device drivers is the most popular way to provide BIOS support for hardware. The main reason for this popularity is flexibility. Imagine the difficulty of only using ROM chips; for example, if we discovered that the Adaptec SCSI card would not work under Windows. We would call the company that sold us the card, and they would tell us that it did not work because the BIOS routines are not designed to run under Windows.

How would we upgrade the BIOS? Because the BIOS is stored on an on-board ROM chip, we would have to open the computer, remove the card, and replace the chip with a new ROM chip that has the new BIOS. It is much easier to use device drivers. If an upgrade is necessary, the card maker can send a diskette with the new device driver, with no need to open the PC or replace ROM chips. However, as we delve further into different devices, we will see that ROMs are still alive and well, and are being used on a broad cross-section of devices.

We now know that there are two different sets of programs on the system ROM: the BIOS routines and the CMOS setup program. Let's take a look at the third and last aspect of the system ROM: the POST.

POST—Power on Self Test

When the computer is turned on or reset, it initiates a special program, also stored on the ROM chip, called the Power On Self Test or POST. The function of the POST is to allow the system to be *checked out* every time the computer is turned on. To perform this check, the POST sends out a standardized command that says to all the devices *Check Yourself Out!* All the devices in the computer then run their own internal diagnostic. The POST doesn't say what to check, it only tells the devices to run their checks. The quality of the diagnostic is up to the people who made that particular device.

Let's consider the POST for a moment. Suppose that the 8042 chip runs its diagnostic and determines that it is not working properly. What will the POST do about it? There's only one thing to do —tell the human being in front of the PC! So how does the computer tell the human? The first thought is to put some information on the monitor. That's fine, but what if the video card is faulty? What if some really low-level device (there are still a ton of devices we haven't even covered yet) isn't operational? Well, all POSTs will first run a test of all of the most basic devices. If anything goes wrong on this first group of devices, the computer will beep, using its built-in speaker. But what if the speaker does not work? Trouble! The POST assumes that it always works. In order to know whether the speaker is working or not, all PCs beep on startup to let the user know whether the speaker is working.

Now you know why every computer always beeps when it first starts!

So we can break the POST into two parts. First is the test of the most basic devices, up to and including the video—if anything goes wrong, the computer will beep. Second are the rest of the devices. If anything goes wrong here, a text error message will appear onscreen.

BEFORE/DURING THE VIDEO TEST: THE BEEP CODES

The computer tests the most basic parts of the computer first. If anything goes wrong at this point, the computer will send a series of beeps. The meaning of these beeps varies from one BIOS manufacturer to another. Here are beep codes for AMI and Phoenix BIOS.

Table 5.1 AMI BEEP CODES

# of Beeps	Problem
1	The memory controller is not refreshing DRAM
2	64K RAM parity error
3	64K RAM error
4	System timer doesn't work
5	The CPU is generating an error
6	Keyboard controller is bad
7	A Card mounted CPU generated an error
8	Video card is missing or bad
9	ROM Chip is bad
10	CMOS chip is bad
11	Cache memory is bad

Table 5.2 TABLE OF POST BEEP CODES FOR PHOENIX BIOS

1-1-3	CMOS write/read test in-progress or failure
1-1-4	BIOS ROM checksum in-progress or failure
1-2-1	Programmable Interval Timer test failure
1-2-2	DMA initialization in-progress or failure
1-2-3	DMA page register write/read test fail
1-3-1	RAM refresh verification in-progress or failure
1-3-3	1st 64K RAM chip or data line failure - mullet-bit
1-3-4	1st 64K RAM odd/even logic failure
1-4-1	1st 64K RAM address line failure
1-4-2	1st 64K RAM parity test in progress or failure
2-1-1	1st 64K RAM chip or data line failure - bit 0
2-1-2	1st 64K RAM chip or data line failure - bit 1
2-1-3	1st 64K RAM chip or data line failure - bit 2
2-1-4	1st 64K RAM chip or data line failure - bit 3
2-2-1	1st 64K RAM chip or data line failure - bit 4
2-2-2	1st 64K RAM chip or data line failure - bit 5
2-2-3	1st 64K RAM chip or data line failure - bit 6
2-2-4	1st 64K RAM chip or data line failure - bit 7
2-3-1	1st 64K RAM chip or data line failure - bit 8
2-3-2	1st 64K RAM chip or data line failure - bit 9
2-3-3	1st 64K RAM chip or data line failure - bit A
2-3-4	1st 64K RAM chip or data line failure - bit B
2-4-1	1st 64K RAM chip or data line failure - bit C
2-4-2	1st 64K RAM chip or data line failure - bit D
2-4-3	1st 64K RAM chip or data line failure - bit E

continues

Table 5.2 Continued.

2-4-4	1st 64K RAM chip or data line failure - bit F
3-1-1	Master DMA register test in-progress or failure
3-1-2	Slave DMA register test in-progress or failure
3-1-3	Master interrupt mask register test fail
3-1-4	Slave interrupt mask register test fail
3-2-4	keyboard controller test in-progress or failure
3-3-4	screen memory test in-progress or failure
3-4-1	screen initialization in-progress or failure
3-4-2	screen retrace tests in-progress or failure
4-2-1	timer tick interrupt test in progress or failure
4-2-2	shutdown test in progress or failure
4-2-3	gate A20 failure
4-2-4	unexpected interrupt in protected mode
4-3-1	RAM test i failure above address 0FFFFh
4-3-3	Interval timer channel 2 test failure
4-3-4	Time-Of-Day clock test in progress or failure
4-4-1	Serial port test in progress or failure
4-4-2	Parallel port test in progress or failure
4-4-3	Math Coprocessor test in progress or failure

Some error codes are chipset or custom-platform specific, and will vary from system to system. However, these codes are basically constant. Refer to your motherboard book for details.

What to Do If You Beep

Here is a list of the most common problems and how to deal with them.

Table 5.3 Common POST Beep Errors and Solutions

Problem	Solution
RAM Refresh Failure Parity Error RAM BIT Error Base 64K Error	1) Reseat and clean the RAM chips. 2) Replace individual chips until the problem is corrected.
8042 Error Gate A20 Error	1) Reseat and clean keyboard chip. 2) Replace keyboard. 3) Replace motherboard
BIOS Checksum Error	1) Reseat and clean ROM chip 2) Replace BIOS Chip
Video Errors	1) Reseat video card 2) Replace video card
Cache Memory Error	1) Reseat and clean cache chips 2) Verify cache jumper settings are correct 3) Replace cache chips
Everything Else	1) Clean motherboard 2) Replace motherboard

Many computers will generate beep codes when the only problem is a bad power supply! The secret to determining whether you have a bad power supply is to turn the computer on and off 3 or 4 times, and see whether you generate the same beep code every time. If you get the same beep code, it's probably a legitimate beep code. If the beep codes are different, if the machine stops working, or if the computer seems to heal itself, check or replace the power supply.

AFTER THE VIDEO TEST: THE ERROR MESSAGES

Once the video has been tested, the POST will display any error messages on the screen. These errors, known as POST Error Messages, are displayed in one of two different ways: old style *numeric* error codes or more modern *text* error messages.

Numeric Error Codes

When a computer generates a numeric error code, the machine locks up and the error code appears in the upper left-hand corner of the screen. For an example, see Figure 5.20.

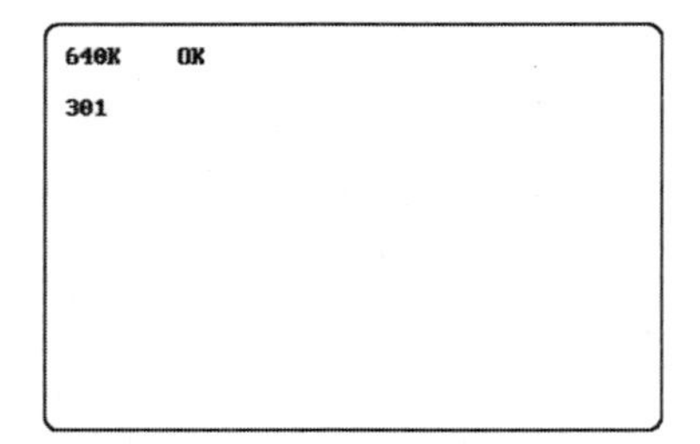

Figure 5.20 Old style numeric error code.

This indicates that the keyboard is not responding. There are hundreds of error codes, but Table 5.4 shows five most common codes and the probable cause of the problem.

Table 5.4 Common Numeric Error Codes

Error Code	Problem
301	The keyboard is broken or not plugged in
1701	The hard drive controller is bad
7301	Floppy drive controller bad
161	Dead battery
1101	Bad serial card

Please refer to Appendix A for a complete list of IBM error codes.

Text Errors

No BIOS uses numeric error codes any longer. Because the overwhelming majority of numeric error codes are never used, AMI reduced the number of error codes to about 30 and uses text instead of numbers to describe the problem. Instead of mysterious numbers, you get text that is usually, but not always, self-explanatory. Here is an example of an AMI text error message:

```
AMIBIOS (C) 1997 American Megatrends Inc.
PRESS <DEL>, if you want to run setup
HDD Controller Failure
Press <F1> to continue
(C) American Megatrends Inc.,
40-0100-006259-00101111-060692-SYMP-F
```

Text errors are far more useful because one can simply read the screen to determine the bad device.

POST Cards

Beep codes, numeric codes, and text error codes, although helpful, can sometimes be misleading. Worse than that, an inoperative device can sometimes disrupt the POST, forcing the machine into an endless loop. This causes the PC to act *dead*: there are no beeps, nothing on the screen, nothing. In this case, we need a device to monitor the POST and report which piece of hardware is causing the trouble.

There are devices designed to do just that! They are known as POST cards. Manufacturers make POST cards for all types of PCs. They will work with any BIOS, but you need to know the type of BIOS you have in order to use them properly. When a computer is giving an error code that does not make sense or is locking up and will not boot, turn off the computer, install the POST card in any expansion slot, and restart the PC. All POST cards have some type of display, usually a two-digit hexadecimal display that the tech must decode by referring to a manual that comes with the POST card. Use Appendix B in the back of the book to help you diagnose POST error codes.

There are a lot of people selling POST cards today, with prices ranging from 50 up to 1500 dollars. You should spend the absolute least amount of money to purchase POST cards. The more expensive cards add bells and whistles that you do not need, like diagnostic software and voltmeters. Try JDR Microdevices for a good, cheap, POST card (see Figure 5.21). JDR's number is 1-800-538-5000. Ask for wholesale, mention Total Seminars, and they should sell it to you for about $30. In addition, they have the JDR-PDI card, a combination Post card and DMA/IRQ tester card (I'll explain IRQ/DMA later) for under $100 that is an excellent value.

Figure 5.21 POST card in action.

Using POST Cards

Turn off the PC, install the POST card in any unused slot, and turn on the PC. As you watch the POST card, notice the different hex readouts. Refer to them as your POST progresses. You will recognize many of them! Good techs will often memorize 50–100 different POST hex codes. Memorizing them is faster than looking them up in a book.

O.K. So you got a beep code, a text error code, or a POST hex error. Now what do you do with that knowledge? We have covered the explanation of beep code problems previously. What about text or POST hex errors? The important thing to remember is that a POST error does not fix the computer—it only tells you where to look. Use common sense—if you get a text error code that says the floppy drive controller is bad, don't worry about the video. Check the floppy drive cabling, connections, power, etc. The only thing a POST error will do for you is tell you where it hurts. You then have to know how to deal with that bad or misconfigured component.

THE BOOT PROCESS

All PCs need a process to begin their operations. Unfortunately, there is no START button on the front of the PC. Instead, when the first PCs were developed, IBM decided to create a process in which all the user has to do is provide electricity to the computer (flipping the ON/OFF switch). Once power was fed to the PC, a tight interrelation of hardware, firmware, and software would be used to allow the PC to start itself—to *pull itself up by the bootstraps* or *boot* itself. All PCs still follow the original boot process, as described by IBM for the original IBM 286 AT computer. Let's take a look at the boot process.

The first electrical component to *wake up* when the computer is turned on is the CPU itself. As soon as the power supply provides the proper voltage, the CPU reads a special wire called *voltage good* and knows that it can safely start. Every Intel and clone CPU has a built-in memory address to which it will immediately send on its address bus. This special address is on the system ROM—it's the first line of programming of the POST! The POST is then run.

After the POST has finished, there must be a way for the computer to find the programs on the hard drive, and to start the main program called the *operating system* (e.g., DOS). The BIOS begins to look for the operating system by first checking to see if a diskette is in the floppy drive. If there is a floppy diskette inserted, the PC assumes that the operating system is on the floppy. If there is no floppy, the system then looks for an operating system on the hard drive. All floppy and hard drives have a very specific location on the drive called the boot sector. If the drive is bootable, there will be special programming designed to tell the system where to locate the operating system. A drive that has a functional operating system is called a bootable drive/disk or a system drive/disk. The term *bootable drive* is usually associated with hard drives; the term *system disk* is more commonly used by floppy drives. Either way, if there is no bootable drive, you get the error:

```
Non-System disk or disk error
Replace and press any key when ready
```

Many CMOS have settings that allow you to change the order in which devices are searched for an operating system (see Figure 5.22). This system has reversed the standard: it first checks the hard drive `C:` and then the floppy `A:`.

This is commonly done to prevent a hacker from inserting a bootable floppy and accessing the system, or to speed up the boot process.

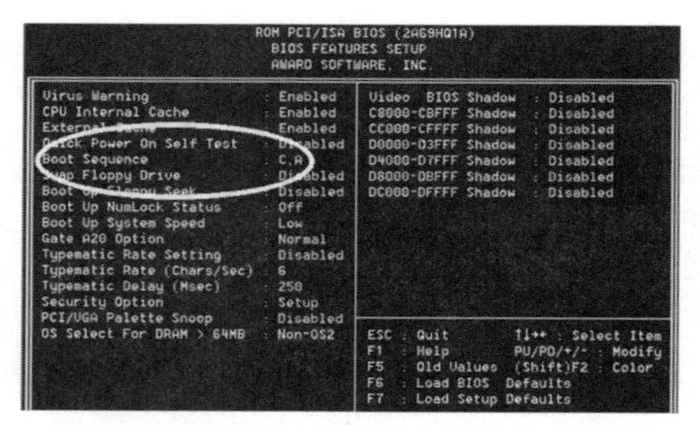

Figure 5.22 CMOS changing boot sequence.

Motherboard Layouts

The *form factor* of a motherboard describes the particular way that components are positioned on a motherboard. Currently, there are two standard form factors used by most motherboards, AT and ATX. The AT form factor, invented by IBM in the early eighties, has been the predominant form factor for motherboards. The AT type motherboard always has the keyboard plug in the same relative spot (about 1 inch from the expansion bus edge), and has the split P8/P9 style of power socket, as discussed in the Power Supply chapter.

The AT motherboard has a few size variations (see Figure 5.23). The original size of the AT motherboard was almost the same size as two pieces of paper laid side-to-side. It needed to be quite large because the first PCs carried a lot of individual chips. As technology improved, there was a strong demand for a smaller AT motherboard. A smaller size was created and dubbed the *Baby AT*. The original size AT motherboard was then called the *Full AT*, *Regular AT*, or sometimes just *AT*. The Baby AT has been and continues to be the most common size of AT form factor used.

There is even some variation in size within Baby AT! One motherboard may be slightly larger or smaller than another (see Figure 5.24). That's okay as long as the keyboard and the expansion slots stick to the form-factor specifications.

Even though the AT form factor has predominated for many years, there have been a number of problems with the AT motherboards. The single greatest problem is the connectors. Clearly, PCs are going to have quite a few cables hanging out of the back. When PCs were first invented, the only devices plugged into the average PC were a monitor and a keyboard. That's what the AT was designed to handle. The only dedicated connector on an AT motherboard was the keyboard plug. If you wanted to add connectors for anything else you had to do it through the expansion slots.

Figure 5.23 Different sizes of AT motherboards.

Figure 5.24 Commonality between AT motherboards.

Well, over the years the number of devices that have to be plugged into the back of the PC has grown tremendously. Your average PC today has a keyboard, a mouse, a printer, some speakers, a monitor, and a phone line connected to it. These added components have created a demand for a new type of form factor, one that would have more dedicated connectors for more devices. There were many attempts to create a new standardized form factor. Invariably, these new form factors integrated new dedicated connectors for at least the mouse and printer; and many even added connectors for video, sound, and phone lines. Although many excellent designs were created by motherboard manufacturers, no single new form factor was able to become very popular. One new form factor that did have a small degree of success was known as LBX (see Figure 5.25).

The main problem with form factors like LBX was their inflexibility. Certainly, there was no problem with new dedicated connections for devices like mice or printers, but the new form factors would also add connectors for devices like video or sound. These devices were prone to obsolescence, making the motherboard useless the moment a new type of video or sound card came into popularity.

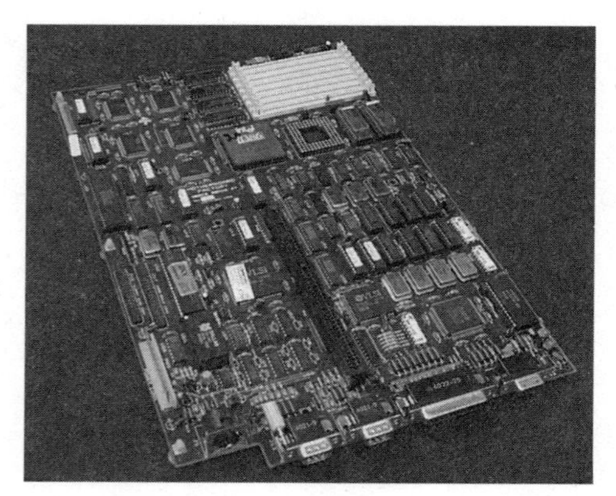

Figure 5.25 LBX motherboard.

Yet there continued to be a tremendous demand for a new form factor—a form factor that had more standard connectors, but that would also be flexible enough for possible changes in technology. This demand led to the creation of ATX (see Figure 5.26).

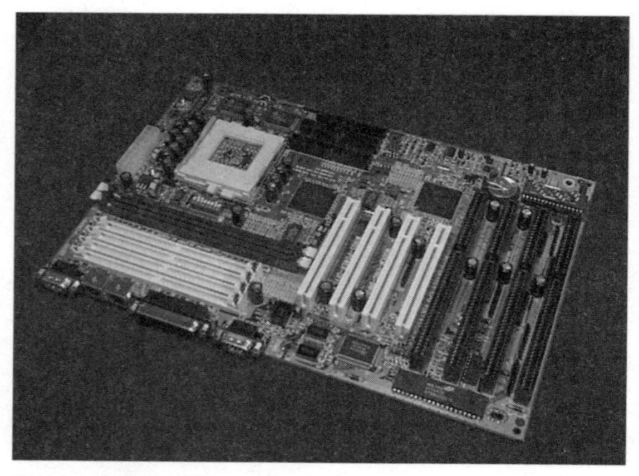

Figure 5.26 ATX motherboard.

Although relatively new, ATX has taken a strong position in motherboard form factors and today is quite common—and easily as popular as AT. ATX is exactly the same size as a Baby AT, but it is turned 90 degrees relative to the computer's box.

ATX is distinct from the AT because of the lack of an AT keyboard port. This port is replaced with a rear plate that allows access to all necessary ports (see Figure 5.27).

Figure 5.27 ATX ports.

The ATX form factor includes many improvements over AT. The position of the power supply allows for better air movement. The CPU and RAM are placed in such a way to allow easier access.

Unlike AT power supplies, ATX uses a feature called soft power—it uses software to actually turn the PC on and off. The physical manifestation of soft power is the power switch. Instead of the thick power switch cord used in AT systems, an ATX power switch is little more than a pair of small wires leading to the motherboard. ATX uses a P1 power connector instead of P8 and P9, which are commonly found on AT systems. P1 connectors include a 3.3 volt wire along with the standard 5V and 12V wires (see Figure 5.28).

There is no performance enhancement in ATX over AT. The motherboard you choose will be based on other areas such as price, cache, motherboard top speed, etc. The form factor is secondary. Keep in mind that AT uses a different box from an ATX. You cannot upgrade an AT system with an ATX motherboard, or vice versa. ATX has definitely made some inroads and is bound to continue to take market share over the next few years.

Figure 5.28 P1 connector.

Motherboard Installation and Replacement

To most techs, the concept of adding or replacing a motherboard can be extremely intimidating. It really shouldn't be because motherboard installation is a common and necessary part of PC repair. It is inexpensive and easy, although it can sometimes be a little tedious and messy due the large number of parts involved. This section covers the process of installation/replacement and will show some of the tricks that make this necessary process easy to handle.

CHOOSING THE MOTHERBOARD AND CASE

First, determine which motherboard you need. What CPU are you using? Will the motherboard work with that CPU? Because most of us buy the CPU and the motherboard at the same time, make the seller guarantee that the CPU will work with the motherboard. How much RAM do you intend to install? Are there extra RAM sockets available for future upgrades? There are a number of excellent motherboard manufacturers available today. Some of the more popular brands are Tyan, Asus, Shuttle, and Gigabyte. Your supplier may also have some lesser-known but perfectly acceptable brands of motherboards—as long as there is an easy return policy, it's perfectly fine to try one of these.

Second, do not worry about size. Virtually any motherboard will fit into any case made today. Usually a quick visual inspection will be sufficient to see if it will fit. Keep form factor with form factor—AT motherboards for AT boxes and ATX motherboards with ATX boxes.

Third, all motherboards come with a technical manual, better known as the *motherboard book*. You must have this book! This book is your only source for all of the critical information about the motherboard! For example, if you have an on-board battery and that battery decides to die, where would you install a replacement external battery? Where do you plug in the speaker? Even if you are letting someone else install the motherboard, insist on the motherboard book—you will need it.

Fourth, pick your case carefully. Cases come in four basic sizes: Slimline, Desktop, Mini-Tower, and Tower. The Desktop and Mini-Tower are the most popular choices, but, as mentioned earlier, pretty much any motherboard will fit in any case. Power supplies come with the case. Watch out for very inexpensive cases—they often have very poor quality power supplies that can stop working, or worse, damage your new motherboard. Cases come with many different options, but there are two more common options that point to a better case. One option is a removable face—many cheaper cases will screw the face into the metal frame using wood screws. A removable face makes disassembly much easier! Another is a detachable motherboard mount. Clearly, the motherboard will have to be attached to the case in some fashion. In better cases, this is handled by a removable tray or plate, allowing you to attach the motherboard to the case separately, saving the difficult chore of sticking your arms into the case to turn screws.

Installing the motherboard

To replace a motherboard, first remove the old motherboard. Begin by removing all the cards. Also remove anything else that might impede removal or installation of the motherboard, such as hard or floppy drives. Keep track of your screws—the best idea is to return the screws to their mounting holes temporarily until the part is to be reinstalled. Sometimes, even the power supply has to be removed temporarily to allow access to the motherboard. Document the positions of the little wires for the speaker, turbo switch, turbo light, and reset button in case you need to reinstall them.

Unscrew the motherboard. IT WILL NOT SIMPLY LIFT OUT. The motherboard is also mounted to the case with plastic connectors called *standouts* that slide into keyed slots at the bottom of the box. Screws hold the motherboard in place. If the CPU or RAM has been removed, be sure to replace them before installing the new motherboard. Don't forget to set the motherboard speed, voltage, and clock multiplier if necessary—check the motherboard book.

When you put in the new motherboard, do not assume that you will put the screws and standouts in the same place as they were in your old motherboard. When it comes to the placement of screws and standouts (see motherboards), there is only one rule: anywhere it fits. Do not be afraid to be a little tough here! Installing motherboards can be a wiggly, twisty, scraped-knuckle process.

Once the motherboard is mounted in the case with the CPU and RAM properly installed, it's time to insert the power connectors and test the installation. A POST card can be a real help here because you won't have to add a video card, monitor, and keyboard to verify that the system is booting. If you have a POST card, start the system and see whether the POST is taking place—you should see a number of POST codes before the POST stops. If you don't have a POST card, install a keyboard, video card, and monitor. Boot the system and see if the BIOS information shows up on the screen. If it does, you're probably O.K. If it doesn't, it's time to refer to the motherboard book to see where you messed up.

Wires, Wires, Wires

The last, and often the most frustrating, part of motherboard installation is connecting the lights and buttons on the front of the box. These usually, but not always, include the following:

- Soft Power
- Turbo Switch
- Turbo Light
- Reset Button
- Keylock
- Speaker
- Hard Drive Active Light

These wires have specific pin connections to the motherboard. Although you can refer to the motherboard book for their location, usually a quick inspection of the motherboard is sufficient. There is no hard and fast rule for determining the function of each wire. Often, the function of each wire is printed on the connector. If not, track each wire to the light or switch to determine its function.

There are a few rules to follow when installing these wires. The first rule is: *The lights are LEDs (Light Emitting Diodes), not lightbulbs —they have a positive and negative side. If they don't work one way, turn the connector around and try it the otherway.*

The second rule is: *When in doubt, guess. Incorrect installation will not result in damage to the computer.* The device that was incorrectly wired simply will not work. Refer to the motherboard book for the correct installation.

The third and last rule is: *With the exception of the soft power switch on an ATX system, you do not need any of these wires for the computer to run!* The only possible downside is that the PC will only run in non-turbo (slow) mode, but it will run.

THE NEXT STEP

We have described the motherboard's function as providing easy access to the wires of the external data bus and the address bus for all of its devices. This chapter has described the devices (ROM chips, CMOS chips, keyboard controllers, etc.) that mount directly onto the motherboard. What if we want to add other devices? For other optional devices, an additional bridge is required: the expansion bus.

CHAPTER 6

Expansion Bus

In this chapter, we will

- Understand the function of an external data bus
- See how I/O addressing works
- See how IRQs and DMA work
- Understand COM and LPT ports
- Understand the different types of expansion busses

This chapter dwells on a fairly broad, but closely linked set of topics that I have decided to call Expansion Bus. A better title would be something like How Do I Add Cards and Motherboards to an Existing System—but I might have a little trouble getting all that on the title page! The function of an expansion slot is to allow flexibility in configuration when adding devices to your PC. Expansion slots are standardized connections that provide a common access point for any device to be installed.

In today's world of *Plug and Play* (PnP) devices, many people would say this topic isn't so important. They would be wrong. Granted, the capability of a new device to be snapped in and then automatically work is wonderful, but it is also very problematic because it doesn't always work. As we will see, many PnP devices today have some rather nasty habits of not working properly. I might also add that quite a few devices that are being sold today are still not able to configure themselves. Understanding how motherboards and the expansion slots that are soldered to them work together to allow a soundcard or modem to run properly is absolutely vital. Let's take the time to understand the expansion bus and motherboard by starting with something we already know: the external data bus.

It's The Crystals, Dammit!

Considering what the book has described up to this point, there should only be one data bus on the PC, the external data bus. Everything in the computer is connected to everything else in the computer via the external data bus. Whether a device is welded to the motherboard or snapped into a socket should make no difference. Every device in the computer—RAM, keyboard, network card, soundcard—is connected to the external data bus.

All integrated circuits are regulated by a quartz crystal oscillator, just like the one that runs a watch. The crystal acts like a drill sergeant calling a cadence, setting the pace of activity across the computer. Every device welded to the motherboard is designed to run at the speed of the system crystal. If there is a 66MHz keyboard chip, there is also a 66MHz *Memory Controller Chip* (MCC) and a 66MHz everything else, all timed by a 66MHz crystal.

Now, consider what happens when you buy a device that did not come with your computer. Take a soundcard as an example. Like most every other electronic device, the chips on the soundcard need to be pushed by a crystal. At what speed should these chips run? 25MHz? 33MHz? 66MHz? If you used the system crystal, that would mean you would need to have soundcards for every possible computer speed. You would not be able to just buy a soundcard. You would have to find one that ran at the same speed as your motherboard. That also means that if you make soundcards for a living, you have to make them for every possible speed that may be needed.

This is ridiculous, and IBM knew it when they designed the PC. They had to make an extension to the external data bus that *ran at its own standardized speed*. This part of the external data bus would be used for devices to be snapped into the PC. That was achieved by adding a different crystal, which controlled the part of the external data bus that was connected to the expansion slots (see Figure 6.1).

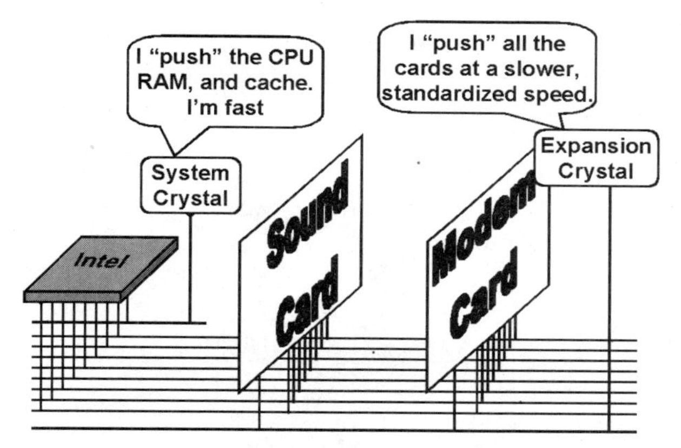

Figure 6.1 Function of System and expansion crystal.

This way, no matter what speed CPU you had, the expansion slots all ran at a standard speed. In the original IBM PC, that speed was about 14.31818MHz/2, or about 7.16MHz.

We now have, in essence, two different busses. The first bus is the external data bus running at the speed of the system crystal. The second bus is the expansion bus that runs at the speed of the expansion bus crystal. How can this work? Wouldn't data being moved from the faster bus overrun the other? No. Expansion devices can tell the CPU that they are not ready (they generate a wait state, just like the DRAM). Also, most expansion devices have buffer areas to store extra data coming from the CPU (or vice versa).

NOTE

The external data bus is the primary data path for the entire computer. All devices on the external data bus run at the speed of the system crystal. The expansion bus is an extension of the external data bus that runs at the speed of the expansion bus crystal.

We distinguish between the two different busses by using two different names. The *expansion bus* is the part of the external data bus that supports the expansion slots. The *system bus* is the part of the external data bus that is timed by the system crystal and supports the CPU, RAM, and other important components on the motherboard.

History of PC Expansion Busses—Part 1

8-BIT ISA

On first generation IBM XTs, the 8088 processor had an 8-bit external data bus and ran at a top speed of 4.77MHz. Therefore, IBM made the expansion slots on the XT with an 8-bit external bus connection. IBM settled on a standard expansion bus speed of 8.33MHz maximum, although most machines ran their expansion busses at around 7MHz. This speed was fast enough—at the time, it was faster than the CPU! This expansion bus was called the *PC bus* and the slots looked like Figure 6.2.

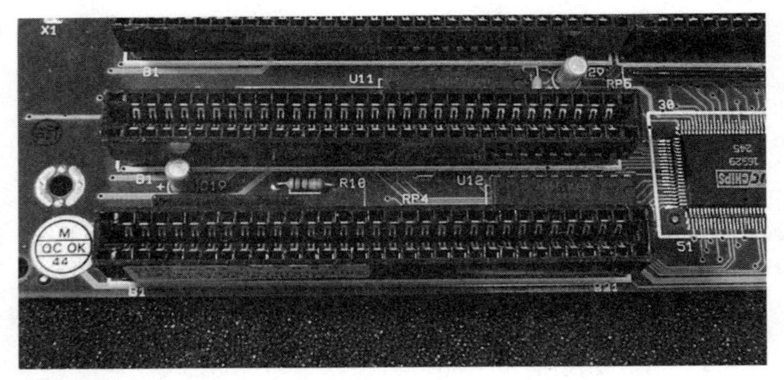

Figure 6.2 8-bit ISA or XT slots.

The address bus wires also go out to the expansion slots. The connections that start with A are the 20 address bus wires. The connections that start with D are the eight external data bus wires. We will discuss the function of most of the other connections as we progress through this chapter.

IBM did something nobody had ever done before. They allowed competitors to copy the PC Bus They also allowed third parties to make cards that would snap into their PC Bus. Remember that IBM invented the PC expansion bus. It was (and still is) a patented product of IBM Corp. By allowing everyone to copy the PC expansion bus technology, IBM established the industry standard and created the clone market.

16-BIT ISA

When the 286 was invented by Intel, IBM wanted to create a new expansion bus that would take advantage of the 286's 16-bit external data bus, yet still be backwardly compatible with older 8-bit cards. This was achieved by simply adding an extra slot to the PC bus, creating a new 16-bit bus, AT bus bus, AT bus. This was called the AT bus because IBM used it in their 286-based IBM AT computer (see Figure 6.3).

Figure 6.3 16-bit ISA or AT slots.

Notice that the connectors add eight more external data bus wires and four more address wires. This new 16-bit bus also ran at a top speed of 8.33MHz, but just about every motherboard maker used the same crystal as on the 8-bit ISA bus to ensure total compatibility.

IBM, while retaining the patent rights, allowed third parties to copy their bus architecture. However, IBM never released the complete specifications for these two types of expansion busses. Today, we call these busses 8-bit and 16-bit ISA slots. Because the term *Industry Standard Architecture* (ISA) did not become official until 1990, these busses are often referred to as the XT or AT busses.

So, we have two types of standardized expansion slots: the 8-bit ISA and the 16-bit ISA. These slots are extensions of the external data bus, yet they run at only around 7MHz, regardless of the speed of the system. So, the best throughput we can have is 16 bits wide at 7MHz. This is fine, as long as the external data bus on the CPU is

16 bits or less—8088 and 80286s. The 7MHz speed is only slightly slower than the 12MHz of the fastest 286s.

The 8-bit and 16-bit ISA busses were for many years the only serious options for PC users. It was these expansion busses upon which the PC industry was built. Although other expansion busses are now coming into the forefront of PC use today, we need to take time to discuss some generic features of card installation with a focus toward the ISA bus. Once we have understood these concepts, we will move on to the more advanced expansion busses with a solid, clear understanding of their benefits.

Now that we understand the overall function of the expansion bus, we can move toward understanding the details of their function. Over the next few sections, we will delve deeply into the card installation *big three*: I/O addresses, IRQs, and DMA. These three topics combined are probably the single greatest headache that confronts PC techs. We will take the time to go over each of these in detail, starting with I/O addresses.

I/O Addresses

The external data bus is used to transfer lines of programs between memory (RAM and ROM's) and the CPU. The external data bus is also used to send data back and forth from peripherals (keyboard, hard drives, CD-ROMs, whatever) to the CPU. We know that we can run BIOS routines from ROM to tell peripherals to do whatever it is they are supposed to do. The question is this: if everything is plugged into the external data bus, how does the CPU know how to talk to a particular device (see Figure 6.4)? How do particular devices know the CPU is talking to them?

Remember the other bus used in a PC: the address bus. We communicate with devices by assigning them unique *I/O addresses*. I/O addresses are patterns of ones and zeroes transmitted across the address bus by the CPU to address memory. The CPU uses an extra wire, called the IO/MEM (Input/Output or Memory) wire, to notify the devices that the address bus is not being used to specify an address in memory. Instead, it is being used to read to or write from a particular device. The address bus has at least 20 wires. However, when the IO/MEM wire has voltage, only the first 16 wires are monitored.

Figure 6.4 How can the CPU talk to one device?

All devices, both those embedded on the motherboard (like the 8042 keyboard controller) and those inserted into expansion slots (like a video card), respond to special, unique patterns built into them. For example, the hard drive controller responds to 16 unique commands. If the CPU lights up the IOW wire and puts the pattern `0000 0001 1111 0000` onto the address bus, the hard drive controller will send back a message describing its error status.

All of the different patterns used by the CPU to talk to the devices inside your computer are known as the I/O addresses (see Figure 6.5).

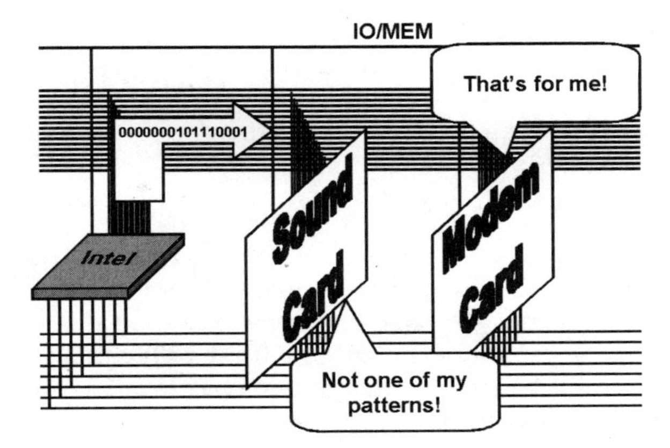

Figure 6.5 Sending an I/O address.

HEXADECIMAL

Sorry, but before I go any further, we are going to have to talk about hexadecimal numbers. I know that most of us hate the thought, but if you are going to fix computers, you are going to have to know how to talk THE DREADED HEX!

DON'T PANIC. Hex is really almost trivial once you understand the secret. Hexadecimal, also known as base 16 mathematics, is a complete numbering system based on 16 instead of 10 digits. You can add, subtract, or do trigonometry with hex. *We Don't Care.* The only part of hex that we need to know is how it is used in the PC world. To help us understand hex, we will use the address bus. When the IO/MEM wire is asserted, it uses the first 16 wires to talk to the devices in the computer. These wires can have voltage on them or they can have no voltage. We represent a wire with voltage by showing a one; we represent a wire with no voltage by showing a zero. With 16 wires, there are 65,536 different combinations of ones and zeroes, from:

```
0000000000000000
```

to

```
1111111111111111
```

Each different combination of charged and uncharged wires represents one pattern that the CPU can send down the address bus to talk to some device. The problem here is that it is a real pain to say things like, "The command to tell the hard drive controller to show its error status is `000000111110000`." Think how difficult it would be to try to talk to someone about these different patterns of ones and zeroes! For example, try telling another person to write down the following series of ones and zeroes as you dictate them:

```
00100100010010010010001001001001000010011111110101010101010100
00101011100
```

I guarantee that they will mess up somewhere as they try to write them down. Forget it! Although your computer is very good at talking in ones and zeroes, we human beings find it very difficult.

What we need is some kind of shorthand, some way to talk about ones and zeroes so that our fellow human beings can understand. This is where hexadecimal becomes very useful. *We use hex as a shorthand description of the state of wires.*

NOTE

In the PC world, hexadecimal is nothing more than a shorthand method of describing a series of binary values.

Pretend that we have a computer with a 4-wire address bus. How many different patterns can we create? Well, look at all the possibilities of ones and zeroes we can make with four wires:

```
0000
0001
0010
0011
0100
0101
0110
0111
1000
1001
1010
1011
1100
1101
1110
1111
```

So, there are 16 different possibilities. There are no computers with only a 4-wire address bus, but just about every processor ever built has an address bus with a multiple of four wires (8,16,20,24,32). The largest common denominator of all these address bus sizes is four. So we can use this four binary digit grouping to create a shorthand by *representing any combination of four ones and zeroes with a single character*. Because there are 16 different combinations, the 16 unique characters of the base-16 numbering system called hexadecimal were the natural choice. The hex shorthand looks like this:

Table 6.1

Binary Number		Hexadecimal Value
0000	all wires off	0
0001	only 4th wire on	1
0010	only 3rd wire on	2

continues

Table 6.3 Continued.

0011	3rd and 4th on	3
0100	only 2nd wire on	4
0101	2nd and 4th wire on	5
0110	2nd and 3rd wire on	6
0111	only 1st wire off	7
1000	only 1st wire on	8
1001	1st and 4th on	9
1010	1st and 3rd on	A
1011	only 2nd off	B
1100	1st and 2nd on	C
1101	only 3rd off	D
1110	only 4th off	E
1111	all wires on	F

So, when we talk about a particular pattern being sent to a device on the address bus, we do not say things like:

```
0000000111110000
```

First, we mentally break these sixteen digits into four sets of four:

```
0000   0001   1111   0000
```

We then give each four character set its hex shorthand (refer to the previous chart):

0000	0001	1111	0000
0	1	F	0

So, instead of a bunch of ones and zeroes, we say something like: `01F0`.

To represent all the possible I/O addresses, we will always have four digits, from all zeroes:

0000	**0000**	**0000**	**0000**
0	0	0	0

to all ones:

1111	**1111**	**1111**	**1111**
F	F	F	F

All of the possible I/O addresses can be represented by four digit hexadecimal values, starting at `0000` and ending at `FFFF`.

This explanation of hexadecimal is heavily slanted to the concept of I/O addresses. However, *hex* is used in many other areas of the PC. Memory management, for example, requires a solid understanding of hexadecimal.

THE RULES OF I/O ADDRESSES

All devices respond to more than one pattern. The I/O address is a *range* of patterns. The pattern of ones and zeroes that represent each address is used to give various commands to each device or for the device to talk to the CPU. For example, the hard drive's I/O address range is `01F0-01FF`. If the CPU sends a `01F0` pattern, it is asking the hard drive controller if there is an error anywhere. The command `01F1` is a totally separate command. No device has only one I/O address.

All devices must have an I/O address. This is how the CPU talks to everything in your computer, and there is no exception. Every device in your computer either has a preset I/O address, or you will have to give it an I/O address. Basic devices in the computer have preset I/O addresses. For example, if you buy a hard drive controller, it will have preset I/O address of `01F0-01FF`. A soundcard will have to have its I/O address configured when you install it into a system.

Once a device is using an I/O address, no other device can use it. For example, when you install that new soundcard in your system, you will have to know what I/O addresses are already used and make sure that the soundcard uses I/O addresses that no other device is currently using.

NOTE
Every device in your computer has an I/O address. No two devices can share any I/O addresses, or else the device(s) won't work.

So the big question here is: *How do I know what I/O addresses are being used in my computer?* Fortunately, most of the I/O addresses were set up by IBM a long time ago. When IBM released the PC to the public domain, they gave users a list of I/O addresses that must be used in order to be *IBM-Compatible.* This list is still followed by every PC in the world today.

Table 6.2

I/O Address Range	Usage
0000-000F	DMA Controller
0020-002F	Master IRQ Controller
0030-003F	Master IRQ Controller
0040-0043	System Timer
0060-0063	Keyboard
0070-0071	CMOS Clock
0080-008F	DMA Page Registers
0090-009F	DMA Page Registers
00A0-00AF	Slave IRQ Controller
00B0-00BF	Slave IRQ Controller
00C0-00CF	DMA Controller
00E0-00EF	Reserved
00F0-00FF	Math Coprocessor
0170-0177	Secondary Hard Drive Controller

I/O Address Range	Usage
01F0-01FF	Primary Hard Drive Controller
0200-0207	Joystick
0210-0217	reserved
0278-027F	LPT2
02B0-02DF	Secondary EGA
02E8-02EF	COM4
02F8-02FF	COM2
0378-037F	LPT1
03B0-03BF	Mono Video
03C0-03CF	Primary EGA
03D0-03DF	CGA Video
03E8-03EF	COM3
03F0-03F7	Floppy Controller
03F8-03FF	COM1

TALKING THE TALK

I/O addresses are 16-bit addresses that are always displayed through four hexadecimal numbers, such as `01F0`. However, when discussing I/O addresses, most people drop the leading zeroes, so `01F0` is usually referred to as `1F0`. Also, almost no one talks about the I/O address range. What is usually discussed is the I/O *base* address. The I/O base address is the first pattern of ones and zeroes. If the I/O address for a hard drive is `1F0-1FF`, the I/O base address is just `1F0`. Last, when discussing any hex value, many people put a lower-case *h* on the end to show you that it is hex value. For example, some people show the I/O base address for the floppy controller as `3F0h`.

NOTE
When talking about I/O addresses, always drop the leading zero.

The I/O address is a range of addresses: The I/O address for the joystick is `200-207`.

The I/O base address is the first I/O address for a device: The I/O base address for the joystick is `200`.

Many people put an *h* on the end of a hex value to show that it is hex: The I/O base address for the floppy is `3F0h`.

Take a close look at the I/O address map one more time. Notice that there are no I/O addresses for soundcards, are there? No I/O addresses for network cards either. In fact, IBM only mapped out the I/O addresses for the most common devices. So if we want to install a soundcard, what I/O addresses are available? Well, look at I/O base address `210h`. Then look at the next I/O base address—it's `278h`, isn't it? All of the I/O base addresses between them are open for use! There are plenty of unused addresses! By the way, you'll notice that the last address is only `3F8h`. Couldn't we use all of the addresses from `3F8` all the way to `FFFF`? Unfortunately, we can't, due to a limitation of DOS/Windows. (O.K., there is a way, but bear with me for a moment and assume that we can't. I promise to explain later!)

We now see that I/O addresses provide a two-way communication pathway between peripherals and the CPU. If the CPU wants to talk to a device, BIOS routines or device drivers *device drivers* can use I/O addresses to initiate conversations over the external data bus. Later in this chapter, we will put this theory into practice.

Interrupts

Now that we have a way for the CPU to communicate with all of the devices inside the computer, we still have a small problem. I/O addressing is a two-way communication, but it must be started by the CPU. A device, like your mouse, can't send its own I/O address to the CPU to get the CPU's attention. So how does a device initiate a conversation with the CPU (see Figure 6.6)? For example, how does the mouse tell the CPU that it has moved? How does the keyboard tell the CPU that somebody just pressed the *J*? We need some kind of mechanism to tell the CPU to stop doing whatever it is doing and talk to a particular device.

This mechanism is called *interruption*. Every CPU in the PC world has a wire called the INT (Interrupt) wire. If this wire is charged, the CPU will stop what it is doing and deal with the device. Pretend that we have a PC with only one peripheral, a keyboard. The CPU is running WordPerfect. The user then presses the *J* key. The keyboard is connected to the CPU's INT wire and charges the wire. The CPU temporarily stops running WordPerfect and runs the necessary BIOS routine to query the keyboard.

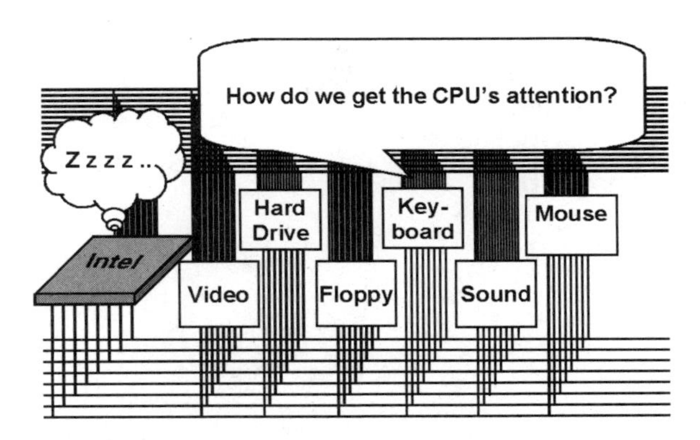

Figure 6.6 How do devices tell the CPU they need attention?

This would be fine if there was only one device in the computer. However, we know that there are lots of devices, and at some time or another, almost all of them would like to interrupt the CPU. So we need some kind of *traffic cop* chip to act as an intermediary between all of the devices that may want to interrupt the CPU's INT wire. In the original IBM PC, a chip known as the 8259 served this function.

The 8259 was hooked to the INT wire of the CPU on one side, and had eight wires called IRQs (Interrupt Requests) that extended out from the chip into the motherboard. Every device that needed to interrupt the CPU got an IRQ. If a device needed to interrupt the CPU, it lit its IRQ, and the 8259 then lit the INT wire on the CPU. Whenever the INT wire was lit, the CPU then talked to the 8259 via its I/O address to determine which device was interrupting. The 8259 told the CPU which IRQ was lit, which allowed the CPU to know which BIOS to run.

Most of the IRQ wires were dedicated to certain devices. IRQ 0 went to a device called the system timer that told the RAM when to refresh (see Figure 6.7). IRQ 1 went to the keyboard. The other six wires ran straight to the ISA expansion bus.

So any ISA card could use IRQs 2 through 6. This system of IRQ usage, although developed way back in the early eighties, is still used on today's most modern PCs. Now, there are some important rules here. The first rule is that no two devices can share an IRQ. If one device is using IRQ3, for example, no other device can use that IRQ.

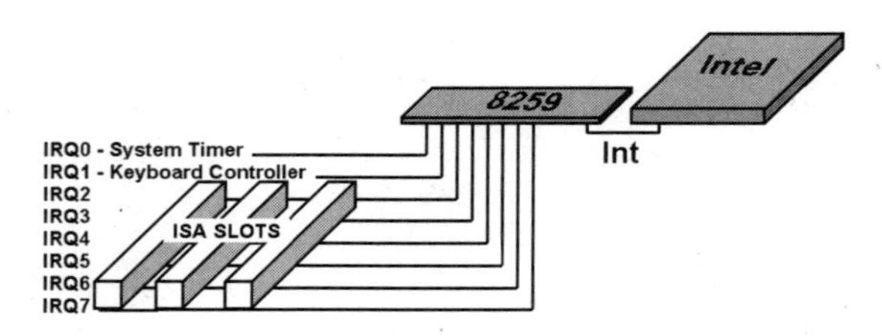

Figure 6.7 IBM PC—Function of IRQs.

NOTE
Under almost all circumstances, no two devices can share an IRQ.

To prevent devices from sharing IRQs, IBM gave an IRQ map to tell card manufacturers which IRQs to use for certain types of devices, just like they did for I/O addresses.

Table 6.3 IRQs assignments on IBM PC and XT

IRQ	Default Function
IRQ 0	System Timer
IRQ 1	Keyboard
IRQ 2	Reserved
IRQ 3	COM2
IRQ 4	COM1
IRQ 5	LPT2
IRQ 6	Floppy Drive
IRQ 7	LPT1

So where's the IRQ for the hard drive? Where's the IRQ for soundcards? Friend, this IRQ map was for the original IBM PC—they hadn't been invented yet! You may notice that IRQ2 is *reserved*. IBM didn't want anyone to use IRQ2 because they reserved it for something special: a mainframe card called the 3270. You see, IBM thought that most PCs would be hooked to mainframes so they wanted to keep IRQ2 just for these 3270 cards.

Virtually every device in your computer needs an IRQ, although there are a very few exceptions. A joystick, for example, doesn't use an IRQ. If you write a program to use a joystick, you have to write the program so that it constantly checks the joystick to see whether a button has been pressed or the stick has been moved.

NOTE
If you install something in your computer, it will have an I/O address. It will also almost certainly have an IRQ.

You may notice items called COM1, COM2, and LPT1. Let's take a moment to understand what they are and how they function in the PC.

COM and LPT Ports

IRQs and I/O addresses were not invented for the IBM PC. Mainframes, minis and pre-PC microcomputers all used IRQs and I/O addresses. When IBM was designing the PC, they wanted to simplify the installation, programming, and operation of devices. Because virtually every peripheral needs both an IRQ and I/O address, IBM created *standard preset combinations* of IRQs and I/O addresses. For serial devices, the presets are called COM ports. For parallel devices, the presets are called LPT ports. The word *port* is used to describe a *portal* or a two-way access. Look at the list of the preset combinations of I/O addresses and IRQs:

Table 6.4 COM and LPT Assignments

Port	I/O Address	IRQ
COM1	3F8	4
COM2	2F8	3
LPT1	378	7
LPT2	278	5

Ports do make installation easier. Look at modems. A modem does not have any setting for IRQs or I/O addresses. Instead, you set its COM port. Most people do not realize that they are really setting the IRQ and I/O address when they select a COM port. If you set a modem to COM1, what you are really doing is setting the modem's IRQ to 4 and the modem's I/O address to 3F8 (refer to the previous table).

NOTE
COM and an LPT ports are nothing more than preset combinations of IRQs and I/O addresses.

Programmers also enjoy the benefits of ports. All ports are built into the system BIOS. Programmers do not have to know the I/O address for a modem. They simply run the BIOS routine to output data or commands to the appropriate COM port. The BIOS routine will then translate and send the command or data to the correct I/O address. Even operating systems understand ports. That is why you can type commands like `DIR>LPT1` and DOS will know which BIOS routine to activate so that the DIR will output to the printer instead of the monitor.

COM3 AND COM4

Back in the original PCs, IBM dedicated two IRQs to serial ports: IRQ4 for COM1 and IRQ3 for COM2. Many systems needed more than two serial devices, and there were a lot of complaints about this lack of COM ports. IBM established two more COM port standards, COM3 and COM4, and assigned two previously unused I/O addresses to these ports: `3E8-3EF` for COM3, and `2E8-2EF` for COM4.

Table 6.5 COM Port Assignments

COM Port	IRQ	I/O Base Address
COM 1	4	3F8H
COM 2	3	2F8H
COM 3	4	3E8H
COM 4	3	2E8H

Remember, this was in the days when there was only one 8259, so there were no extra IRQs. So IBM just doubled them up. COM3 used IRQ4 and COM4 used IRQ3.

HEY WAIT A MINUTE! The #1 rule of setting IRQs is not to let two devices ever share the same IRQ. Well, there is an exception to that rule. Two (or more) devices can share the same IRQ *as long as they never talk at the same time!*

Back in the old days, there were lots of devices that could share IRQs. For example, you could have a dedicated fax card and a modem on the same IRQ. Neither device had a device driver, and the fax would never run at the same time as the modem (this was before Windows). So these two devices could be set to COM1 and COM3. In today's computers, you can no longer set one device as COM1 and another device as COM3, or one device as COM2 and another as COM4. If you do, the computer will lock up.

NOTE

If you accidentally have two devices sharing the same IRQ, the computer will eventually lock up. However, you won't destroy anything—just correct the problem and try again.

LPT PORTS

LPT ports are for parallel connections. In the old days, the only function for parallel ports was for high-speed printers, so when IBM standardized ports for parallel devices, they were called LPT ports for Line printer. LPT ports work well. Because IBM standardized the LPT port not to talk back, IRQ7 for LPT1 and IRQ5 for LPT2 were never used by the LPT port. IRQ5 and IRQ7 could be used for other device.

Of course, there is also an exception to this rule. Many devices are being made today to plug into the parallel plug in the back of your PC. Many devices that plug into a parallel port (for example, tape backups or ZIP drives) *do* use an interrupt. So, if you use IRQ7 for another device, do not plug anything other than your printer into LPT1. Buy a new LPT2 parallel port card. Also, many printers now interrupt, so be careful.

PHYSICAL VERSUS I/O PORTS

One thing we need to clarify right away: A serial port is a physical item, a 9- or 15-pin male DB connector in the back of your PC. A

COM port is just the I/O address and IRQ assigned to it (see Figure 6.8). A parallel port is a 25-pin female DB connector on the back of your PC. An LPT is just the I/O address and IRQ assigned to it. Think of a telephone. If someone pointed to your phone and said, "That is a 324-5444!" you would look at them funny and say, "No, that's a telephone. The number assigned to it is 324-5444." Same with serial and parallel ports. Just as you would not look at a phone and say, "That's a 324-5444!" you would not look at a serial port and say "That's COM1!"

Figure 6.8 Physical versus I/O ports.

Back to the 8259

Because it was discovered with the original IBM PC that six IRQs were not enough for most systems, IBM added another 8259 when the 286 AT was invented. The 8259 was designed to run in a *cascade*. This means that you can hook another 8259 to the first 8259, but the INT connection on the second 8259 has to take one of the IRQs from the first 8259 (see Figure 6.9). IBM decided to take the INT wire from the second 8259 and hook it into the IRQ2 of the first. However, this created a problem in that a lot of cards were already using IRQ2. So IBM ran the IRQ9 wire over to the IRQ2 position on the ISA slot, allowing older cards to work. So, this cascading adds eight more IRQs, but you lose one in the process. The eight new wires run to the extension on the 16-bit ISA expansion slot.

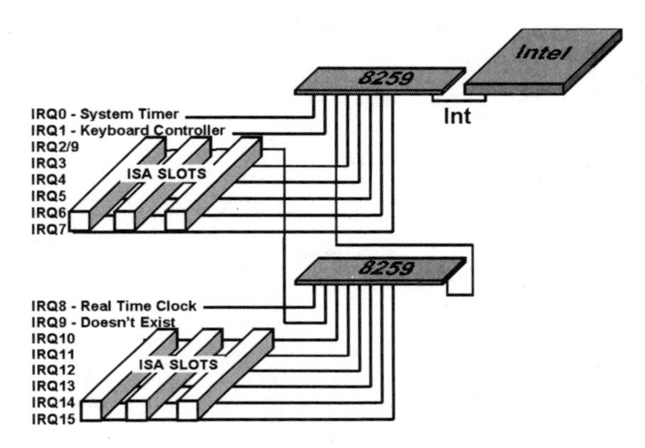

Figure 6.9 Dual 8259 cascade.

Table 6.6 below displays the IRQ map, as designed for the two 8259s in the original IBM AT computer. Again, notice that the cascade removes IRQ2. IRQ9 is hooked to the old IRQ2 wire, so if there is a device designed to run on IRQ2, it will now run on IRQ9. In essence, IRQ2 and IRQ9 are the same IRQ. Three IRQs are hard wired (0,1 and 8). Four IRQs are so common that no PC or device maker dares to change them, for fear that their devices will not be compatible (6,13,14,15). Four IRQs default to specific types of devices, but are very changeable as long as the hardware device allows it (IRQ3,4,5 and 7). The rest (IRQ2/9,10,11 and 12) are not specific and are open for use.

NOTE
There is no IRQ2 or IRQ9. We call it IRQ 2/9.

These settings are somewhat flexible. If a device that uses a certain IRQ is not present, that IRQ is available. For example, if you do not have a secondary hard drive controller, IRQ 15 can be used by another device.

Table 6.6 IRQ Assignments with COM3 and COM4

IRQ	Default Function
IRQ 0	System Timer

continues

Table 6.6 Continued

IRQ 1	Keyboard
IRQ 2/9	Open for use
IRQ 3	Default COM2, COM4
IRQ 4	Default COM1, COM3
IRQ 5	LPT2
IRQ 6	Floppy Drive
IRQ 7	LPT1
IRQ 8	Real-Time Clock
IRQ 10	Open for Use
IRQ 11	Open for Use
IRQ	**Default Function**
IRQ 12	Open for Use
IRQ 13	Math-Coprocessor
IRQ 14	Primary Hard Drive Controller
IRQ 15	Secondary Hard Drive Controller

I/O PORTS TODAY

There's a lot of confusion about I/O ports. But now that we understand what they are, we can eliminate that confusion. First, even though IBM dictated what the I/O address and IRQ for a particular COM or LPT port might be; the IRQ can be changed to another IRQ, as long as the device can actually do it and the software that talks to that device knows about the change. So you can change, say, COM1's IRQ from 4 to 5 if the hardware and software allow it. Let's use my motherboard as an example. Like most computers today, I have two built-in serial ports. You can change the COM port settings by accessing the CMOS (see Figure 6.10).

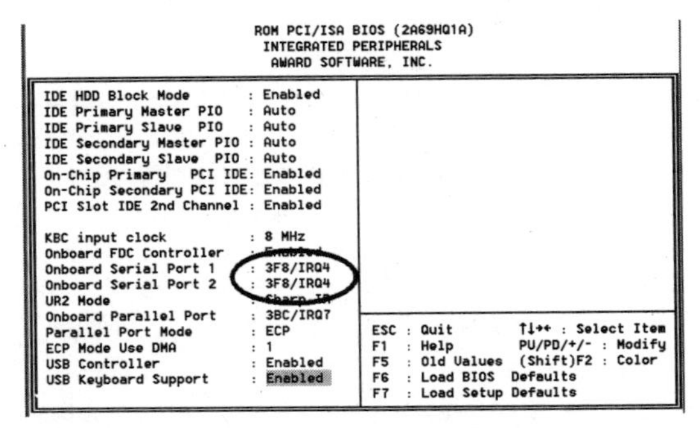

Figure 6.10 Port settings for an onboard serial port.

Note that serial port 1 is set to I/O address 3F8 and IRQ4. What COM port is that? It's COM1. In this CMOS I could change the COM port to any of the following settings:

`3F8/IRQ4`—standard COM1

`2F8/IRQ3`—standard COM2

`3F8/IRQ5`—COM1, but with the non-standard IRQ5

`2F8/IRQ5`—COM2, but with the non-standard IRQ5

It is also important to state that if a standard device isn't using the IRQ assigned to it, or if you don't have that device, the IRQ is open for use. The most common example of this is LPT2, which uses IRQ5. Most PCs today don't have a second parallel port, so it is common for devices to use IRQ5. A great example of this is soundcards. When a soundcard is installed, it will almost always want to be set at IRQ5.

Don't forget that if you set a device to a COM/LPT port, you are using an IRQ. This is always a big problem for new techs who don't understand IRQs and their relationship to COM/LPT. Most people have already heard that you don't let more than one device use an IRQ. But because they don't know that a COM/LPT port is by definition an I/O address and an IRQ, they get into trouble. If someone has a COM1 and then tries to install some other device to IRQ4, the system will lock up. But they don't see the error—they don't realize that COM1 is IRQ4!

The combination of I/O address and IRQ is the cornerstone of CPU/device communication. There is but one more aspect of the CPU/device communication system that must be discussed. This is the badly misunderstood concept of DMA.

DMA

CPUs do a lot of work. The CPU runs the BIOSs, operating system, and applications. CPUs handle interrupts and access I/O addresses. They are busy little chips. CPUs also deal with one other item—data. Data is constantly being manipulated. One of the biggest data manipulations is *moving* data. CPUs move data from one place in RAM to another. Peripherals send data to RAM (for example, a scanner) via the CPU, and the CPU sends data from RAM to peripherals (for example, a laser printer).

All of this data movement is obviously necessary, but it is also very simple to do. Moving data is a waste of the CPU's power and time. Moreover, with all of the caches and such on today's CPUs, most of the time the system is doing nothing while the CPU is handling some internal calculation. So, why not make devices that can access memory directly, without involving the CPU?

The process of accessing memory without using the CPU is called Direct Memory Access, or DMA (see Figure 6.11). DMA allows the system to run background applications without interfering with the CPU, which is excellent for having background sounds in games, accessing floppy drives, and accessing hard drives (see Figure 6.12).

Figure 6.11 The need for DMA.

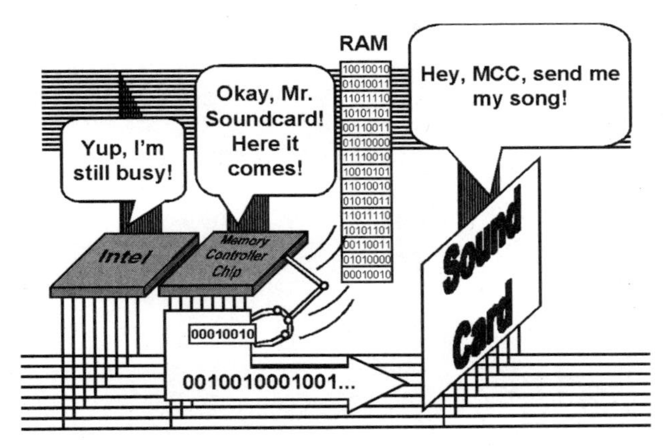

Figure 6.12 DMA in action.

However, the concept of DMA as we show it here has a problem. What if more than one device wants to DMA? Who is to keep these devices from stomping on the external data bus at the same time? Plus, what if the CPU suddenly needs the data bus? How can we stop the device that is DMAing so that the CPU, which should have priority, can access the bus?

Knowing this, IBM installed another, very simple CPU called the 8237 chip to control all DMA functions. This primitive CPU can handle all the data passing from peripherals to RAM, and vice versa. This takes necessary but simple work away from the CPU so the CPU can spend more time doing more productive work. The DMA chip passes data along the external data bus when the CPU is busy and not using the external data bus. This is perfectly acceptable because the CPU only accesses the external data bus a small percentage of the time—only 20 percent of the time on a 486 and only 5 percent of the time with a Pentium.

The 8237 chip was linked to the CPU via the HRQ wire to inform the CPU that the data bus was going to be busy. The 8237 had four wires called DRQs (DMA Requests), which led to the DRAM refresh circuitry and the ISA slots. DRQs were, and still are, more commonly known as DMA channels. If a device wants to perform a DMA transfer, it must activate its assigned DMA channel.

NOTE

DMA channel and DRQ are identical terms.
No two devices can share DRQs.

DRQs work exactly like IRQs, with all the same rules (no two devices can share the same DMA channel, for example). In 286s on up, there are two cascaded DMA chips (see Figure 6.13), giving a total of seven DRQs (DRQ0 and DRQ4 are the same, just as IRQ2 and IRQ9 are the same). However, we never say DRQ 0/4, we just say DRQ0.

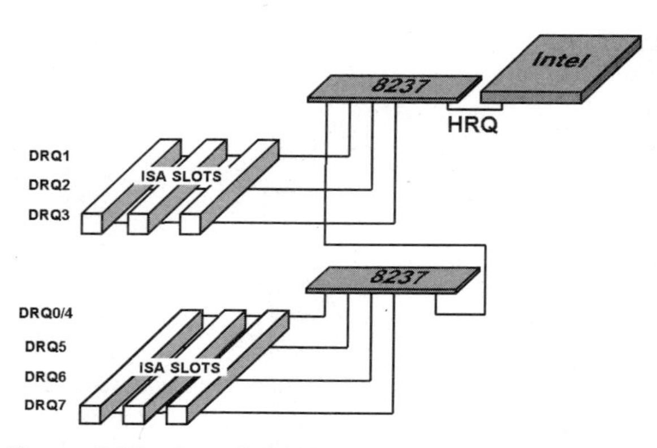

Figure 6.13 Cascaded 8237s

DMA LIMITATIONS

DMA, as originally designed by IBM, has some serious limitations. First, DMA is designed to run from cards installed on the ISA bus. As a result, DMA is limited to a maximum speed of roughly 8MHz. Second, each 8237 can only handle byte-wide data. Although this wasn't a problem in the first IBM PC, as PCs moved from 8088s through 286s, 386s, and 486s, it was faster to skip DMA and just wait for the CPU to move data. DMA can be moved in two-byte chunks in 286s and up, which have dual 8237s by using eight bits from each 8237. But even 16-bit data is too slow for more modern systems. This slowness has relegated DMA to low speed, background jobs like floppy access, sounds, and tape backups. However, there has been a bit of a renaissance in the use of DMA through the use of bus mastering.

NOTE

There are two types of DMA transfers, 8-bit and 16-bit. If a device wants to use 8-bit transfers, it should use a lower DMA channel: 0 through 3. If a device wants to use 16-bit transfers, it should use a high DMA channel: 5 through 7.

BUS MASTERING

Some devices have the capability to DMA without accessing the 8237s or the CPU. These devices are known as bus masters. Bus-mastering devices are usually created for high-speed data transfers —they are doing something *weird* to the system that would confuse the 8237s or the CPU. Bus mastering is powerful but not too commonly done. We will revisit bus mastering later in this chapter to discuss a few special installation issues.

WHO USES DMA?

Not very many devices use DMA. Although the only devices that commonly use DMA are soundcards and floppy drives, virtually any device can be designed to use DMA.

Table 6.7 DMA Assignments

DMA Channel	Type	Function
0	8-Bit	None
1	8-Bit	Open for Use
2	8-Bit	Floppy Drive Controller
3	8-Bit	Open for Use
5	16-Bit	Open for Use
6	16-Bit	Open for Use
7	16-Bit	Open for Use

Although it is important to understand the WHY of I/O address, IRQ, and DMA, we need to take the time to discuss the HOW of installation, configuration, and troubleshooting the *Big Three.* The following sections are designed to give you a solid methodology to ensure that you can set up any device in any PC with a minimum of effort and a maximum of speed.

CHIPSETS

Before we dive into device installation, I want to make a quick tangent. We've been talking about a lot of different chips in your PC, haven't we? Take a look at a motherboard. You see the CPU and

RAM, but do you see the 8259 chips? Can you find the 8237s? How about that *memory controller chip*? You don't, do you! But you may notice two (sometimes three or even one) chip(s). They are distinct in that they say *Intel, Opti,* or *VIA*, as shown in Figure 6.14.

Figure 6.14 Typical chipset.

This is the chipset, which is a specialized chip that has consolidated ALL of the functions of the many chips we have discussed. All chipsets act exactly like the original chips they have replaced. Even though you don't have an 8259, all of the IRQs are there. Same with the DMA and memory-management functions.

NEED FOR A BETTER BUS

The first-generation expansion busses, 8- and 16-bit ISA, were both excellent busses in their time. In fact, the 16-bit ISA (which we will refer to going forward as just ISA) continues to soldier on, in even the most modern PCs available today. Yet the ISA bus suffers from some tremendous limitations. It is slow, running at only roughly up to 8.33MHz. It is narrow and unable to handle the 32- and 64-bit external data busses of more modern processors. Last, it was stupid. If you added a device to the system, you had to (and still do today) configure the I/O address, IRQ, and DMA manually (or at best semi-manually) to allow that device to work correctly. At the time of the creation of the 386, there was tremendous demand to improve/replace the ISA bus to correct these deficiencies. Let's look at the evolution of later generation expansion busses to bring us up to date to the systems of today.

History of Expansion Busses—Part 2

So far, we have only talked about two types of expansion busses: 8-bit ISA and 16-bit ISA. The ISA busses run at a maximum of 8.33MHz, although most run at around 7MHz. The busses require the user to configure I/O addresses, IRQs, and DMAs manually. The technology is free, however, because IBM released the design to the public domain.

MCA

When the 386 started to appear in 1986, IBM decided to create a new type of expansion bus called *Micro-Channel Architecture* (MCA) (see Figure 6.15). This bus is 32-bit to match the 386's (and the 486's) 32-bit external data bus. It is also faster than the ISA bus, running at about 12MHz. What really makes the MCA bus different is its capability to self-configure devices. When you buy a micro-channel device, it always comes with a diskette called an *options disk*. You simply install a new device in the micro-channel computer, insert the options disk when prompted, and the IRQs, I/O addresses, and DMA channels are automatically configured. MCA is an excellent bus.

Figure 6.15 Microchannel slots.

MCA has some major drawbacks, however. First, the slots are different. MCA cards are incompatible with ISA. Second, MCA is a licensed product of IBM, meaning that they did NOT release it to the public domain, so it is expensive. Also, MCA devices are much more sophisticated than ISA devices, making them two or three times more expensive than the equivalent ISA device.

MCA is now a dead technology. Virtually no manufacturers other than IBM made MCA computers, primarily because of licensing and manufacturing costs. Today, there are newer busses that perform all the functions of MCA at a fraction of the cost. Although you can still purchase MCA cards, the cold fact that the technology is no longer supported by new systems virtually guarantees that you are wasting your money. MCA is dead.

Figure 6.16 MCA is dead.

EISA

When MCA came out in the mid-1980s, it created quite a stir. IBM was not only trying to regain control of bus standards, but also charging for licensing of that standard. An industry group of clone makers created a competitor to MCA called *Enhanced ISA* (*EISA: ee-suh*) in 1988 (see Figure 6.17). Basically, EISA does everything that MCA does: it is a faster, 32-bit, self-configuring expansion bus. EISA has two aspects that make it an attractive alternative to MCA. First, it is much cheaper than MCA, although not nearly as cheap as ISA. Second, EISA uses a double slot connector that is compatible with ISA devices.

Although considered the high-end expansion bus for years, EISA also seems to be a dying technology for many of the same reasons mentioned for MCA. However, EISA still has a strong installed base of machines and you can still find new systems today that support EISA. Although EISA will certainly be around for at least a few more years, I'd recommend going with the newest busses.

Figure 6.17 EISA slots.

VESA VL-BUS

Although MCA and EISA were fine busses, neither gained any significant following. Before Windows, the expansion bus speed of the ISA slots (7MHz) was sufficient for most tasks. As a result, virtually all 386 and early 486 systems were a strange combination of a 32-bit external data and address bus, running at the speed of the CPU, connected to a 7MHz, 16-bit expansion bus. In essence, you had two data busses, the fast, wide local bus and the slow, narrow expansion bus (see Figure 6.18).

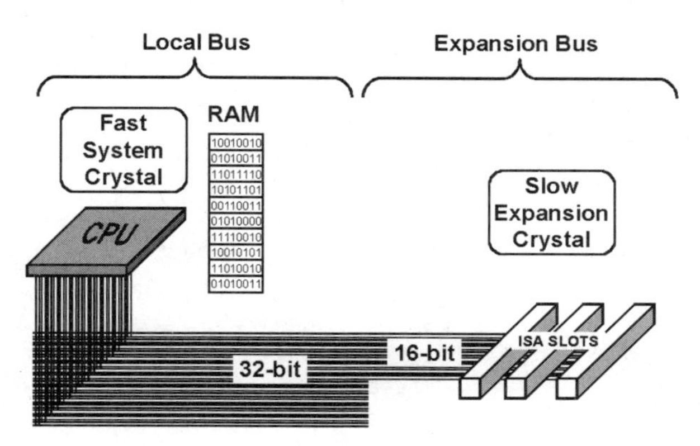

Figure 6.18 Local versus expansion bus.

Microsoft Windows changed that. The graphical user interface (GUI) of Windows put huge new demands on video. The 16-bit data path and 7MHz top speed of the ISA video cards could not keep up with these new demands. Two solutions presented themselves: the first was the creation of co-processed video cards. These video cards were preprogrammed with Windows objects such as scroll bars and menus. The video BIOS of all VGA video cards have similar programming for the ASCII character set. On a standard VGA card, if the video card receives instruction to output the letter *j* on the monitor, it does not specify each pixel. It is preprogrammed with the ASCII character set and would output a predefined *j*. The new Windows co-process video cards were preprogrammed with common Windows GUI features such as scroll bars, title bars, mouse cursors, etc. Instead of having to draw each feature of the interface, these new video cards could pop out a *scroll bar* the same way that earlier cards could pop out a *j*. These cards could probably have kept the average computer user happy for a time, avoiding the need for a new, faster expansion bus. One problem remained—the new, Windows-ready co-processing video cards would not be available for more than a year after the introduction of Windows 3.0.

Another way to increase throughput is to tap back into the local bus. The *Video Electronics Standards Association* (VESA) created the *VESA Local* (VL) BUS (see Figure 6.19). The VL-BUS solution to both of these problems was to tap back into the local bus. Remember that although there is only one external data bus that connects everything in the PC, the external data bus is divided into two parts: the system bus and the expansion bus. The system bus ran at the speed (or 1/2 the speed) of the system crystal, usually between 25–33 MHz on a 386 or 486. The expansion bus, into which ISA cards are snapped, ran off a different crystal at a standard 7MHz to ensure backward-compatibility.

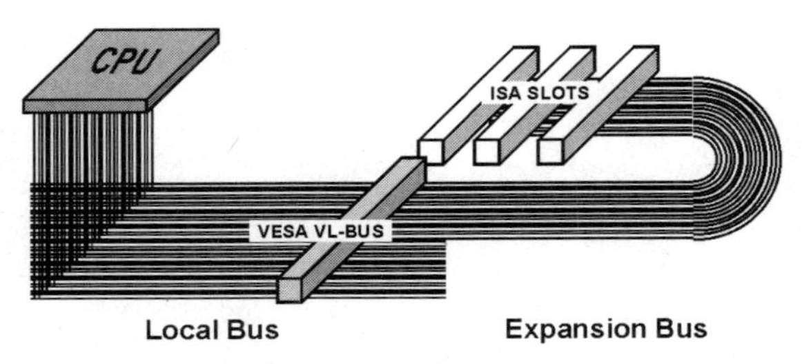

Figure 6.19 VESA VL-BUS.

By tapping directly into the local bus, VL-BUS devices can use the full 32-bit data bus available on 386 and 486 machines. In addition, VL-BUS devices can run at either the speed of the system bus (synchronously) or at the speed of a crystal on the VL-BUS itself (asynchronously). VL-BUS has a top practical speed of 33MHz. Most CMOS setup programs on motherboards with VL-BUS allow you to set the speed of the VL-BUS to either synchronous or asynchronous. Although either will work, for optimum performance you should set it to run at whichever speed is faster (see Figure 6.20).

Figure 6.20 VESA VL-BUS slots.

VL-BUS slots are *parasitic slots*. The reason a VL-BUS must work with another bus is that each VL-BUS slot is paired with another bus slot, usually a 16-bit ISA slot (the specifications allow for the VL-BUS to work with MCA and EISA slots, but in practice this is not done). VL-BUS relies on the ISA slot for all basic control functions (I/O addressing, IRQs, DMA, etc.). The VL-BUS slot controls only those functions specific to VL-BUS devices, including burst mode, bus mastering, and 32-bit data transfers.

VL-BUS devices are capable of bus mastering. We have already met two other *bus mastering* devices: the CPU itself and the 8237 DMA chip. As you recall, the 8237 can take control of the external data bus if the CPU is not currently using it. Each VL-BUS device can act in the same fashion, taking control of the external data bus if the CPU is not using it. The VL-BUS can *arbitrate* between up to three VL-BUS devices that want to use the external data bus at the same time, assigning different priorities to each device. VL-BUS devices are capable of a limited *burst mode*. The VL-BUS device can take control of the external data bus for up to four bus cycles. By doing so, it can pass up to 16 bytes (128 bits) of data in a single burst. This significantly reduces the number of clock cycles needed to pass that data by sending the addressing information only once. Because the VL-BUS can only arbitrate among three bus mastering devices, the practical maximum number of VL-BUS slots is three.

VL-BUS is a cheap, simple way to get a fast, wide data path. Except for the extra slot connection, installation of VL-BUS devices is identical to the installation of any ISA device. Plug the card in, set the IRQ, I/O address, and DMA (if applicable), and you are ready to go.

Although VL-BUS presents huge advantages over ISA technology, it has one severe limitation in that it is designed to run with a 486 CPU. With 64-bit Pentium systems, VL-BUS is rather limited by its 32-bit data path. As a result, virtually no Pentium systems use VL-BUS and VL-BUS has quickly died (although there is still a solid market for VL-BUS devices).

PCI

The latest type of expansion bus is *Peripheral Component Interconnect* (PCI). Designed by Intel and released to the public domain, PCI provides a stronger, more flexible alternative to any other expansion bus (see Figure 6.21). As a result of this great power and flexibility, combined with low price, PCI is now the predominant expansion bus in the PC world (see Figure 6.22).

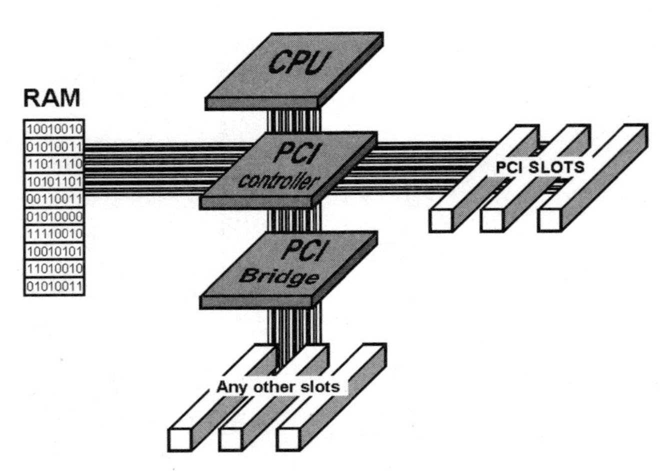

Figure 6.21 PCI bus.

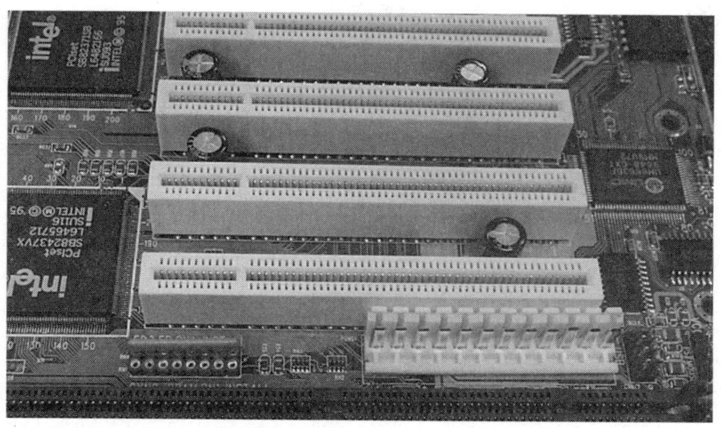

Figure 6.22 PCI bus slots.

PCI is far more than VL-BUS. Although VL-BUS is limited to 486s, PCI is independent of the CPU. Even Apple is using PCI. PCI can exist by itself on the motherboard, or it can exist with any other expansion bus, including VL-BUS, MCA, and EISA. Because of this flexibility, PCI offers motherboard manufacturers great flexibility in the creation of *transitional motherboards* that allow the use of the newest, most advanced bus with any and all previously purchased equipment (see Figure 6.23).

Figure 6.23 Motherboard showing PCI and ISA slots.

The PCI bus can support more than just expansion slots. On-board I/O controllers and video controllers can also hook into the PCI bus. With the first PCs and their ISA expansion busses, the external data bus was divided into two busses: the system bus and the expansion bus. With PCI, we add a third player: the PCI mezzanine bus.

PCI is known as a *mezzanine* bus because it actually sits between the system bus (local bus) and the expansion bus. PCI expansion slots do not connect devices to the same expansion bus used by ISA and VL-BUS slots. Instead, they connect to a PCI bus, which acts as an intermediary between PCI devices and the system bus. The PCI bus acts as a *bus master,* taking full control of the external data bus when it can, in order to pass data more quickly. We have already met two other *bus mastering* devices: the CPU itself and the 8237 DMA chip. As you recall, the 8237 can take control of the external data bus if the CPU is not currently using it. The PCI bus acts in the same fashion, taking control of the external data bus in order to transfer data.

PCI's bus-mastering capabilities are much more powerful than those of the 8237 DMA chip. For example, while DMA is limited to either 8- or 16-bit data transfers, PCI devices can use 32-bits of the external data bus for data transfers. In a Pentium system, the 64-bit external data bus is currently only used for transfers between the CPU and the main memory or level-2 cache. PCI-2 takes advantage of the full 64-bit external data bus. Better yet, two PCI devices can transfer data between themselves while the CPU uses the external data bus, provided that the CPU is not communicating with another PCI device. If the CPU uses the external data bus to communicate with a PCI device, the CPU must also use the PCI mezzanine bus. However, if the CPU uses the external data bus to talk to some non-PCI device, such as the main memory or an ISA modem or network card, the PCI bus remains dormant. The PCI mezzanine bus is sufficiently separate from the system bus that two PCI devices (for example, a hard drive controller and a video card) can exchange data at the same time that the CPU uses the system bus to access a non-PCI device. PCI devices do not have to wait for the system bus to become available before they can transfer data among themselves, provided there is no activity on the PCI bus itself.

The PCI mezzanine bus also features a powerful burst mode. The PCI bus uses the same wires for both addresses and data. Although this clearly saves money for the motherboard manufacturers, it also seems inefficient. The PCI bus more than makes up for this limitation with its speed, through the use of its powerful *burst mode.* The PCI bus recognizes when the reads or writes in its buffer have consecutive addresses. Instead of addressing each byte individually, the PCI bus groups them into packets and sends them to the PCI devices as a single burst. The receiving unit assumes that consecutive bytes are to be written to consecutive addresses, eliminating the need to use up a clock cycle to relay addressing information. The PCI bus employs this burst mode completely independently of the CPU. Data sent by the CPU hit the PCI bus as individually addressed bytes of data and are converted by the PCI bus into bursts. Additionally, unlike VL-BUS, which is limited to bursts of four clock cycles, the PCI bus possesses great flexibility with regard to the length of these bursts. Because the PCI bus remains functionally separate from the system bus, the PCI controller can use longer bursts than the VL-BUS or a DMA chip, which must check much more frequently for CPU activity on the external data bus. Remember that the expansion bus and the system bus are directly linked, while the PCI bus (a mezzanine bus) is not *directly* linked with either. The separation of the PCI mezzanine bus from the system and expansion busses creates the opportunity for these long bursts.

PCI devices are self-configuring. Although they still need interrupts and I/O addresses, they are set by the PCI bus. Remember when we installed a hard drive controller? Did we set its I/O address and interrupt (IRQ)? No. Why not? Because ISA (the Industry Standard Architecture) had already defined the I/O address and IRQ for that device, as well as for video cards, keyboard controllers, etc. These were considered *assumed hardware.* The reason we had to assign I/O addresses and IRQs for devices such as soundcards and network cards is that those devices did not exist when the ISA specifications were written. PCI SIG (the organization that defines the PCI standard) *assumes* that you will have a soundcard, a network card, SCSI controller, etc. In fact, they assumed that you might have multiple soundcards, network cards, SCSI controllers, etc. PCI SIG defined the I/O addresses and interrupts for multiple occurrences of virtually every device commonly in use today, as well as some not-yet-common devices. The intelligent PCI mezzanine bus interrogates PCI cards as they are installed and assigns them to preset I/O addresses.

PCI handles interruption differently as well. Instead of setting a device to an IRQ, the PCI bus assigns each device an interrupt channel. Each PCI device has four interrupt channels, A–D. The PCI bus has its own registers that keep track of the IRQs in use by the system, and *channels* the interrupt requests of PCI devices onto unused IRQ wires on a case-by-case basis. The only restriction appears to be that Interrupt A for a PCI hard drive controller must access IRQ14 for backward-compatibility reasons. (Remember that IRQ14 was preset in the ISA/VL-BUS specifications for the primary hard drive controller.) Because the PCI bus can arbitrate between devices, multiple devices can share the same interrupt channel.

PCI is currently 32-bit, but the latest generation of PCI, PCI-2.1, is 32- or 64-bit to take advantage of the Pentium and P6 external data busses. PCI-2.1 has optional SCSI connections as standard equipment, just like a Macintosh. PCI also supports the use of multiple processors.

It is impossible to purchase a new motherboard today that is not PCI. The only real option you can get in expansion slots is PCI and ISA or PCI and EISA slots. No doubt about it, PCI is King.

CHAPTER 7

Floppy Drives

In this chapter, we will:

- See how to install floppy drives
- Learn basic floppy drive maintenance

History

Floppy drives have the unique distinction of being the only component on the PC to maintain basically the same technology as in the original IBM PCs. Certainly, there have been tremendous gains from the first 160K, 5.25" dual-sided, single-density drives to the 2.88 megabyte, 3.5" dual-sided, quad-density drives; but the cabling, configuration, and BIOS routines have remained the same as the first floppy drives in the IBM PC.

There are two basic types of floppy drive sizes: 5.25" and 3.5". 5.25" drives can accept two different capacities of floppy diskettes (see Figure 7.1). These sizes are the now obsolete 360K diskettes and the virtually obsolete 1.2 megabyte diskettes.

3.5" drives come in three different capacities. First are the 720K drives, which are extremely rare. Second are the 1.44 megabyte drives that are by far the most common drives in use today. The third and last type are 2.88 megabyte drives, which were virtually stillborn and basically don't exist. There is no way to tell the difference between any of these 3.5" drives by observation (see Figure 7.2). The capacity can only be determined by installing the drive.

Figure 7.1 5.25" floppy drive.

Figure 7.2 3.5" floppy drive.

DOS/Windows has reserved drive letters `A:` and `B:` for floppy drives. You cannot name them anything other than `A:` and `B:`. DOS and Windows 95 are designed to look for a floppy drive called `A:` at boot. So, if you have only one floppy drive, it should be called `A:`. The second floppy drive will be called `B:`.

Floppy drives are connected via a 34-pin cable. This cable has a seven-wire twist that creates the difference between the `A:` and `B:` drives. If the floppy drive is installed on the end connector, the drive will be the `A:` drive; if the drive is installed on the middle connector, it will be the `B:` drive. The floppy drive BIOS routines are designed to support no more than two floppy drives. The cabling looks like Figure 7.3.

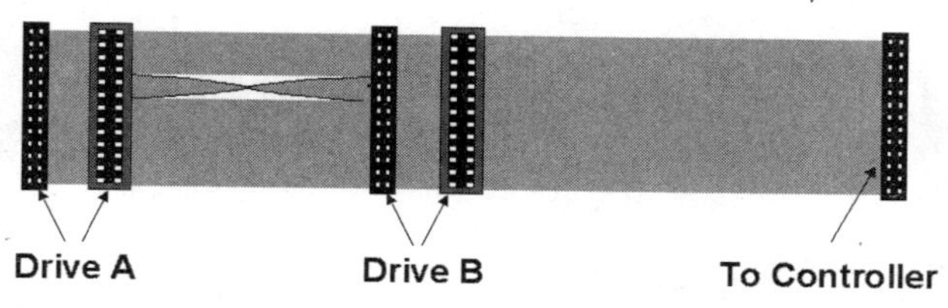

Figure 7.3 Floppy drive cable.

Some of the older cables have only the *push* style connections for the older 5.25-inch drives (see Figure 7.4). There are readily available conversion plugs that will allow 3.5-inch drives (which generally use *pin* style connectors) to plug into the older 5.25-inch connectors (see Figure 7.5).

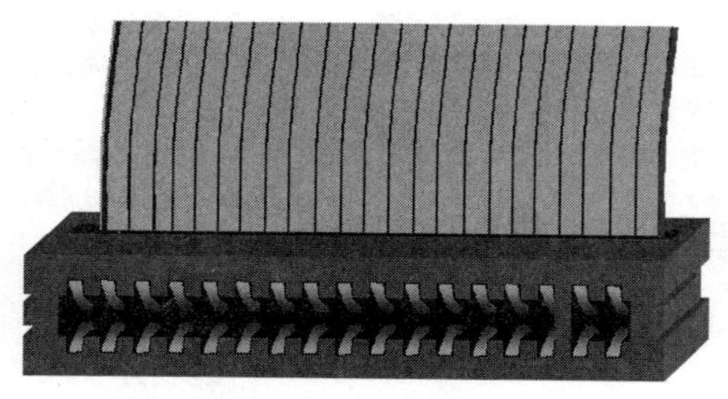

Figure 7.4 5.25 inch *push* connector.

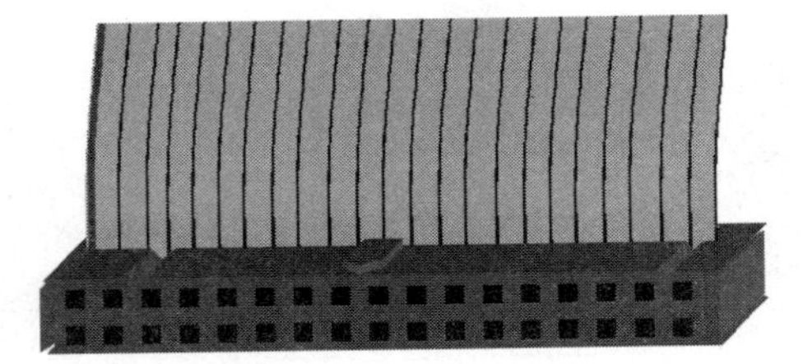

Figure 7.5 3-inch *pin* connector

The power connection will be either the large Molex type connector on the 5.25-inch drive or the smaller mini connector on the 3.5-inch drive (see Figure 7.6).

Figure 7.6 Properly inserted mini-connector.

After the floppy is installed, the next step is to configure the CMOS settings. The CMOS settings must correspond to the capacities of the drives (see Figures 7.7 and 7.8). Simply select the drive (`A:` or `B:`) and enter the correct capacity.

Many older CMOSs will not contain settings for either 1.44 megabyte or 2.88 megabyte 3.5-inch floppies, simply because the older CMOSs were developed before these drives were. If one of these more advanced floppy drives is installed without CMOS support, there are many third-party utilities, such as Checkit Pro by Touchstone Corp., which allow the CMOS to accept the necessary values to support these drives.

There are a few other interesting settings that can be seen in most of today's Pentium-class CMOSs (see Figure 7.9). One of the most handy is the *Swap Floppy Drive* setting that allows you to change the

A: and the B: drives without moving the cables. We also often see a *Boot Up Floppy Seek,* which tells the PC not to look for a floppy during the POST—not very handy, except for speeding up the boot process.

```
        PhoenixBIOS Setup - Copyright 1992-97 Phoenix Technologies Ltd.
   Main    Advanced    Security    Power    Exit

                                                          Item Specific Help
   System Time:                     [16:19:20]
   System Date:                     [03/02/1994]

   Legacy Diskette A:               [1.2 MB, 5¼"]     <Tab>, <Shift-Tab>, or
   Legacy Diskette B:               [Not Installed]   <Enter> selects field.

 ▶ Primary Master:                  C:  121 MB
 ▶ Primary Slave:                   None
 ▶ Secondary Master:                None
 ▶ Secondary Slave:                 None

 ▶ Memory Cache
 ▶ System Shadow                    [Enabled]
 ▶ Video Shadow                     [Enabled]

   System Memory:                      640 KB
   Extended Memory:                   1024 KB

 F1  Help   ↑↓ Select Item   -/+   Change Values        F9  Setup Defaults
 ESC Exit   ↔  Select Menu   Enter Select ▶ Sub-Menu    F10 Save and Exit
```

Figure 7.7 Phoenix CMOS, showing floppy drive selection.

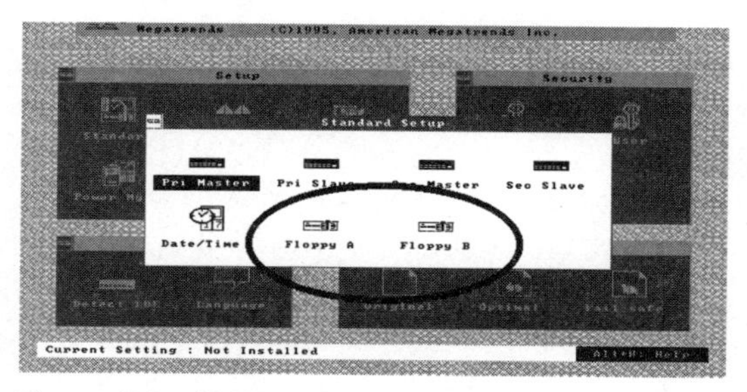

Figure 7.8 AMI WinBIOS, giving floppy options.

A third option, which is very popular, is the Boot Sequence. This allows the system to seek out the C: drive first, and then look for a floppy drive. The Boot Sequence option is a powerful security tool —preventing would-be hackers from accessing a PC by loading a boot diskette.

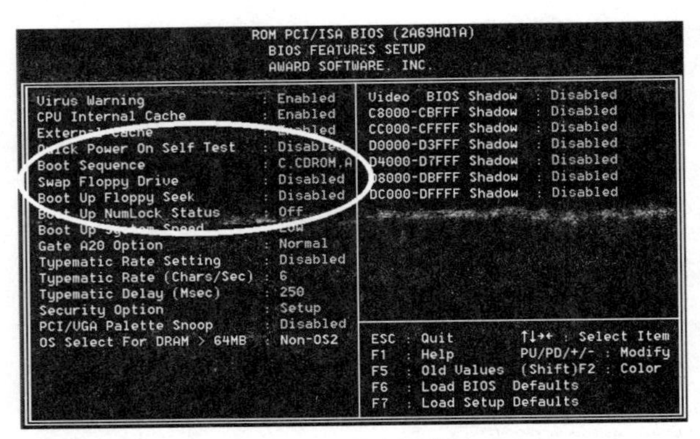

Figure 7.9 Common *extra* CMOS floppy options.

Care and Feeding of Floppy Drives

There are no parts of the computer that break more often than the floppy drives. They are the only components that have internals directly exposed to the outside environment. There is only a small door (or, in the case of 5.25-inch drives, not even a door) that divides the read/write heads from dust, grime, and cigarette smoke. Floppy drives are also exposed to the threat of mechanical damage. Floppy drives are often the victims of inverted disks, paperclips, and other foreign objects.

As a result of this abuse, it is imperative that serious preventive maintenance be performed on all floppy drives. This *PM* is simply to KEEP THE FLOPPY DRIVE CLEAN! Excellent cleaning kits are available everywhere, and should be used at least once a month to ensure the best possible performance from floppy drives.

Repairing Floppy Drives

When a floppy drive dies, follow these steps to resolve the problem:

FIRST, BLAME THE FLOPPY DISK

The vast majority of the time, when the floppy drive decides not to read the floppy disk, the bad guy is the floppy DISK, not the floppy DRIVE. When the disk can't be read, insert another diskette. If a new diskette from a fresh box won't work, don't insert another diskette from the same box. Find another diskette, preferably from another person's desk, to retest. If two disks are unreadable, then the floppy drive can be considered the problem.

SECOND, CHECK FOR DATA ERRORS ON THE DISK

If other floppy disks work in the drive, it's the floppy disk. If a floppy disk is bad, the best thing to do is to throw it away. But often there is data on the disk that is needed. Since other disks operate in the drive, the errors must be those ominous types that look like:

Data error reading drive A:

Seek error writing drive B:

Sector not found reading drive A:

Or any error that ends with one of those two happy little phrases:

Abort, Retry, Fail?

Abort, Retry, Fail, Ignore?

These are problems with the floppy disk, not the drive. The process for repairing floppy diskettes is *identical* to the process for repairing hard drives. Refer the Hard Drive chapter to review the process of running the Norton's Disk Doctor/Spinrite combo for data repair.

THIRD, CHECK THE CMOS SETTING

CMOS settings for floppies rarely cause problems. Most current BIOS manufacturers set the default CMOS settings for the `A:` drive to 3.5" High Density, so that even if the CMOS is accidentally erased and everything else fails, at least the floppy will still work (assuming you have a 3.5" for your `A:` drive). The rarity of CMOS errors for floppy drives can be dangerous because techies rarely look there. Certain errors can point to the CMOS as a problem:

Not ready error reading drive `A:`

General failure reading drive `A:`

Insert diskette for drive `A:` and press any key when ready

Note that these errors are not exclusive to CMOS problems! But do double-check the CMOS. A quick peek can save a lot of time!

BLAME THE FLOPPY CONTROLLER

The floppy controller is extremely sensitive to static and trauma. It is common for floppy drives to fail after a move, after a few months in a high static environment, or, most frustrating of all, when a new computer is first delivered. (I'm convinced that delivery people use boxes with computer parts for their lunchtime volleyball games.)

If the data cable or the power plug is loose, the POST will flag with either *FDD Controller Failure* or *Drive Not Ready* errors. At this point, open the machine and verify the connections. If the connections are good, remove and reseat the controller. If the same errors show up again, replace the controller.

It's impossible to find a floppy drive controller card that is only a floppy drive controller card. All floppy drive controllers are welded onto I/O cards that usually include hard drive controllers, serial ports, parallel ports, and joystick ports.

Try to keep an extra I/O card around, just to check floppies. I keep an old I/O card with a bad hard drive controller to test systems. I make sure to turn off all the other devices on the card, *including* the bad controller.

MAYBE THE CABLE

The 34th wire on the floppy drive cable is called the *Drive Change Signal* (or *Diskette Change Signal*). When a floppy drive is inserted or removed, this wire is active. When DOS or Windows first reads a floppy drive, a copy of the directory is left in RAM and is not updated unless the Drive Change Signal is activated. This stops the system from constantly re-reading the very slow floppy drive unless it needs to be read. If a bent pin or bad cable disconnects the Drive Change Signal, however, you will keep seeing the same directory, even if you change the diskette! This problem can almost always be traced back to a bad floppy cable, so replace and retry.

LAST, REPLACE THE FLOPPY DRIVE

At this point, if the floppy drive isn't working, the only recourse is to replace the drive. Replace the bad drive and *throw it away*. Keeping a bad floppy drive is a study in frustration. Almost all *bad* floppy drives aren't always bad, just sometimes bad. Techs are tempted to give a bad floppy drive *one more chance*. They install the drive and voila! It works! They're convinced they made a mistake and declare the drive to be *good*. If the drive is reinstalled somewhere else, it will soon die again. Throw it away.

Floppy drives fail more than any other part of a computer system. Given any five PCs, at least one floppy drive will be replaced in a year. So keep floppy drives in stock. Floppy drives should be purchased in quantity, at least five drives at a time, so that they can be discounted. Buying floppy drives one at a time is expensive and a time waster.

CHAPTER 8

Hard Drives

In this chapter we will

- Understand the concept of geometry
- See the different types of hard drives
- Learn how to install hard drives

Technicians need to understand how to install, troubleshoot, and repair hard drives. Hard drives are the primary data storage devices in personal computers. Techs therefore must also know techniques for making that data as secure as possible.

The most common form of hard drive today is called EIDE, and it has been standard in most PCs for almost five years. Other hard drive technologies, however, are still available in many machines. Techs need to understand many older concepts, technologies, and terminology in order to service the wide variety of computers still in service.

Inside the Drive

All hard drives are composed of individual disks, or platters; with read/write heads on actuator arms, controlled by a servo motor; all contained in a sealed case that prevents contamination by outside air (see Figure 8.1).

Figure 8.1 Inside of typical IDE drive.

The platters are made of aluminum and are coated with a magnetic media, usually cobalt or ferro-ceramics. There are two tiny read/write heads for each platter, one to read the top and the other to read the bottom of the platter (see Figure 8.2).

Figure 8.2 Close up of read/write heads and armatures.

This coating is phenomenally smooth! It has to be because the read/write heads actually *float* on a cushion of air above the platters that are spinning at 3500–7200 rpm. The distance (flying height) of 0.2-0.5uM between the heads and the disk surface is less than the thickness of a fingerprint. The closer the read/write heads are to the platter, the more densely the data can be packed onto the drive. This is why the platters can never be exposed to outside air. Even a tiny dust particle would be like a mountain in the way of the read/write heads and would cause catastrophic damage to the drive.

All hard drives do, however, have a tiny aperture, complete with air filter, to keep the air pressure equalized between the interior and the exterior of the drive.

DATA ENCODING

Although data is stored in binary form on the hard drive, it is not a simple matter of a magnetized spot representing a one and a non-magnetized spot representing a zero. Although there are magnetized and non-magnetized positions on the hard drive, the ones and zeroes of the binary code are stored in terms of *flux reversals*, which are the transitions between magnetized and non-magnetized positions on the hard drive. There are several methods for encoding and interpreting the flux reversals.

The first method used on hard drives was called *Frequency Modulation* (FM); it used the time spent in a magnetized state to determine ones and zeroes. FM depended on every one or zero to be preceded by a *timing bit* that took up significant disk space. FM was quickly supplanted by *Modified Frequency Modulation* (MFM). MFM reduced the number of timing bits by more than 50 percent by using the preceding data bits to indicate whether the current bit was a one or a zero. MFM was the predominant way to encode data on hard drives for many years. Starting around 1991, hard drives began using a data encoding system known as *Run Length Limited* (RLL), which is the only data encoding scheme used today.

RLL uses patterns of ones and zeroes to represent longer patterns of ones and zeroes. For example, 1000 in RLL represents 11. This seems inefficient, but RLL eliminates the need for timing bits, and combinations of RLL patterns can represent long strings of ones and zeroes.

Because of the overwhelming utilization of RLL-type data encoding, it is unimportant to know what type of data encoding is used by a hard drive unless you are working with older (pre-1989) equipment.

You're never going to have to deal with data encoding, just a lot of techs who like to throw the terms around!

MOVING THE ARMS

The read/write heads are moved across the platter on the ends of the actuator arms. To move these arms quickly across the hard drive, hard-drive manufacturers use two methods.

The *stepper motor*, the first method developed, moved the arm in fixed increments, or steps. This early technology had several limitations. Because the interface between motor and actuator arm required minimal slippage in order to ensure precise and reproducible movements, over time the positioning of the arms became less precise. This physical deterioration caused data transfer errors. Another problem with stepper motors is heat deformation. Just as valve clearances in automobile engines change with operating temperature, so does positioning accuracy change as a PC operates and its various components get warmer. Although these changes were very small, it can make accessing the data, written while the hard drive is cold, difficult if the disk is warm. In addition, the read/write heads can damage the disk surface if they are not parked (set in a non-data area) when not in use.

Most hard drives that are made today employ a linear motor to move the actuator arms. The linear motor is also called a *voice coil motor* because its design is the same in principle as the voice coil found in an audio loudspeaker. A permanent magnet surrounds a coil on the actuator arm through which an electrical current passes, thus generating a magnetic field that moves the actuator arm. The direction of the actuator arm depends upon the polarity of the electrical current through the coil. Because there is no mechanical interface used between the motor and the actuator, there is no degradation in positional accuracy over time. The one drawback is the inability to accurately predict the movement of the heads across the disk. For this purpose, one must reserve one side of one platter for navigational purposes. The voice coil moves the read/write head to its best guess about the correct position on the hard drive. The read/write heads then use the *map* on the platter side reserved for navigational purposes to determine its true position and make any necessary adjustments. This explains why, when reading a hard drive specification list, one will find an odd number of heads—one head is used for positioning all the others and thus is not available for data storage.

Another advantage is the use of the hard drive's controller to automatically park the heads when power to the disk is discontinued. It is meaningless to *park* a voice coil drive.

NOTE
***Parking* a drive is meaningless in today's PCs.**

GEOMETRY

If you wish to work with hard drives, you must be familiar with hard drive *geometry*, which is the internal electronic organization of the hard drive. Have you ever seen a cassette tape? If you look at the actual brown Mylar tape, you will not see anything. However, you know something is on the tape, correct? It's the magnetized lines on the tape that define the music, correct? We could say that the physical placement of those lines of magnetism is the tape's *geometry*.

The geometry determines where the data is stored on the hard drive. Just like the cassette tape analogy, if you were to open up the hard drive, you would not be able to see the geometry. The geometry for a particular hard drive is described with five special numerical values: *HEADS, CYLINDERS, SECTORS/TRACK, WRITE PRECOMP,* and *LANDING ZONE*. We will describe what each value means.

All hard drives have geometry. You must know these five numbers if you want to install or reinstall a hard drive!

Heads

Heads are the total number of sides of all the platters used to store data. If a hard drive has four platters, it has eight heads (see Figure 8.3).

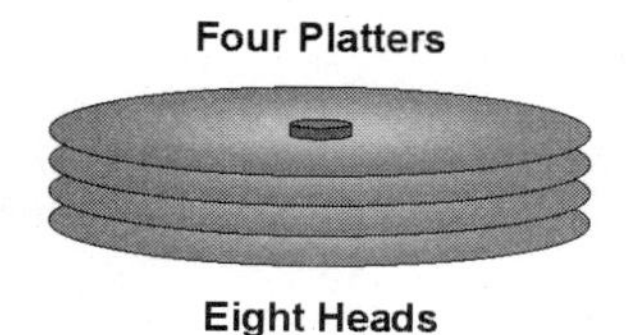

Figure 8.3 Heads.

Based on this description of heads, one would think that hard drives always have an even number of heads, right? Wrong! Most hard drives reserve a head or two for their own use. Therefore, a hard drive might have an even or odd number of heads.

Cylinders

Take a Campbell's soup can and open both ends of it. Run it in the dishwasher to get rid of the label and any leftover soup. When that can comes out of the dishwasher, it is no longer a soup can but a geometric shape called a cylinder.

Now take that soup can and sharpen one end until it can pass through the hardest metal. Place the can concentrically over the hard drive and push it through the drive. The can goes in one side and out the other of each platter. Each circle transcribed by the can is where data is stored on the drive and is called a *track* (see Figure 8.4).

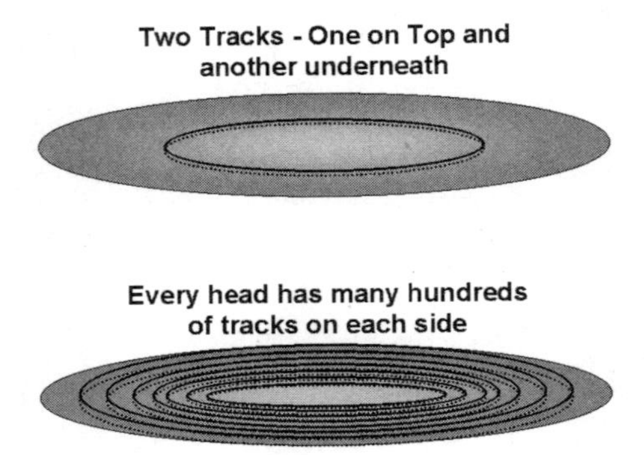

Figure 8.4 Tracks.

There are hundreds of tracks on each platter. Interestingly enough, tracks themselves are not directly part of the drive geometry. What we are interested in is ALL of the tracks of the same diameter, going all of the way through the drive. That IS a geometry, and it is called a *cylinder*. One cylinder is the set of all tracks of the same diameter on every head of the drive (see Figure 8.5).

Figure 8.5 Cylinder.

There's more than one cylinder! Go get yourself about a thousand more cans, each having a different diameter, and push them through the hard drive, too. Each of these is also one cylinder.

Sectors/Track

Imagine cutting the hard drive like a birthday cake, slicing all of the tracks into tens of thousands of small arcs. Each arc is called a *sector,* and each sector stores 512 bytes of data (see Figure 8.6). A sector is the smallest division of a hard drive. In hard drive geometry, we consider sectors by how many fit on each track. A typical value for a modern EIDE hard drive is 63 sectors per track (sectors/track).

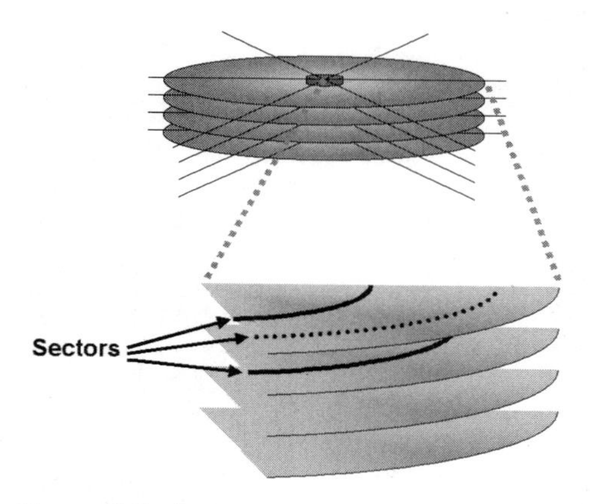

Figure 8.6 Sectors.

Write Precompensation Cylinder

When data gets packed too closely together, you get a slight shifting of the magnetism on the drive. In the cylinders that are closest to the center of the drive, this can be a real problem. To handle this, an older drive would write data a little further apart once it got to a particular cylinder. This cylinder was called the *Write Precomp* cylinder, and the PC had to know which one it was. This process is now handled internally by the drive; the PC no longer needs to know.

NOTE

The Write Precomp is obsolete.

Landing Zone

On older hard drives with stepper motors, the *Landing Zone* value designated an unused cylinder as a *parking place* for the read/write head. It was important to park the heads on drives with stepper motors to avoid accidental damage when moving hard drives. There are special parking programs that are designed to park these older drives. Today's drives are all voice-coil drives, which park themselves whenever they're not accessing data. The parking programs are simply ignored by voice-coil drives. As a result, the Landing Zone is no longer a necessary geometry.

NOTE
The Landing Zone is obsolete.

TALKING THE TALK

No one says things like, "What are your Cylinders, Heads and Sectors per track?" when discussing geometry on a hard drive. We just say "What's the CHS?" or "What is the geometry?" Also watch for abbreviations. A geometry like landing zone can be shortened to Lzone, LZ, Park, or just about anything. Use common sense and you'll be able to figure it out.

Why Geometry?

The Cylinders, Heads, and Sectors/Track are very important. When you buy a hard drive, it has these three values printed on the drive. The system will need these numbers when the drive is installed. Plus, the capacity of a hard drive is defined by the geometry. Just multiply the Cylinders × Heads × Sectors/Track to get the number of sectors. Because every sector stores 512 bytes, we just multiply the number of sectors times 512 to get the capacity of a drive. For example, suppose you buy a hard drive with the following geometry:

1024 Cylinders

32 Heads

63 Sectors/Track

The capacity of the drive is: 1024 × 32 × 63 = 2,064,384 sectors × 512 bytes/sector = 1.056 Billion bytes. A drive with 1024 Cylinders, 32 Heads, and 63 Sectors/Track is a 1.056-Billion byte drive.

This is NOT a 1.056-GIGABYTE drive! Read on.

You've got to be careful with capacities. When we talk about capacities, we use the units of megabytes (1,048,576) and Gigs (1,073,741,824). When a hard drive maker sells you a drive, they use the units of millions (1,000,000) and billions (1,000,000,000). This unit difference makes people think that there is something wrong with the drive or that they have been *ripped off*. For example, suppose you buy a 2.1 *Gig* hard drive. If you look on the label, the hard drive maker says the capacity is 2100MB. That is 2100 million bytes, not megabytes! The manufacturer isn't lying; you're just reading it wrong! Anyway, you install the drive and discover that the total capacity is shown as 1.96 gigabytes. It's as if you just lost 140 megabytes! No, it's just different units. Fortunately, Windows 95 reports both, as shown in Figure 8.7.

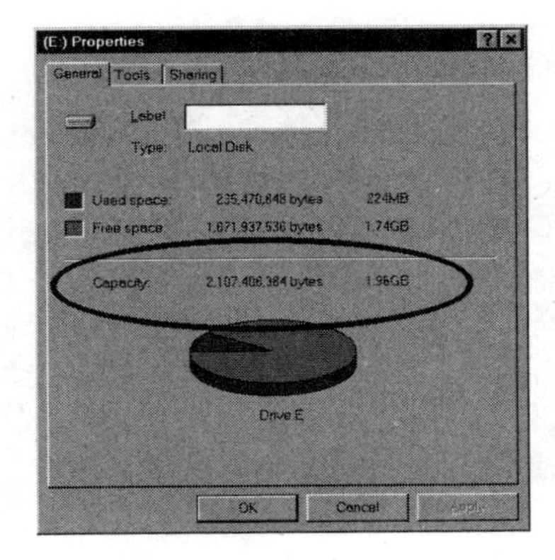

Figure 8.7 Win95 showing hard drive properties.

IDE/EIDE

Since the early 1990s, the primary type of hard drive available is the IDE drive type. The *Integrated Drive Electronics* (IDE) standard uses the BIOS on the system ROM. Western Digital and Compaq developed the 40-pin IDE ISA pinout specification, and put this specification before the ANSI standards committees. The committees then put out the *Common Access Method* (CAM) *AT* interface in March of 1989. To be exact, the term *IDE* is incorrect. The official name for these drives is *ATA* drives. ATA stands for AT Attachment. Even though the proper name is ATA, we all just say IDE. In 1990, Western Digital forwarded a series of improvements to the IDE standard called *Enhanced IDE* (EIDE). Virtually all of today's hard drives and computers are EIDE. We will first discuss EIDE drives, and then take a short look back at IDE so that we can understand the differences.

> **NOTE**
> **A lot of people use the term IDE when they mean EIDE.**

PHYSICAL CONNECTIONS

EIDE drives are connected to the computer via a 40-pin cable and a controller. Figure 8.8 is a picture of the *business end* of an IDE drive, showing the connectors for the controller and the power cable.

Figure 8.8 IDE drive connectors.

The controller is support circuitry that acts as the intermediary between the hard drive and the external data bus. There are usually two controllers in a system. Each controller can handle up to two hard drives, which limits the PC to a maximum of four drives. The controllers are usually on the motherboard (*onboard* controllers) and manifest themselves as nothing more than two 40-pin male connectors. Older machines may have the controllers on a card that is snapped into the motherboard. Here are some examples of EIDE controllers—both on cards and the more common onboard controller (see Figure 8.9).

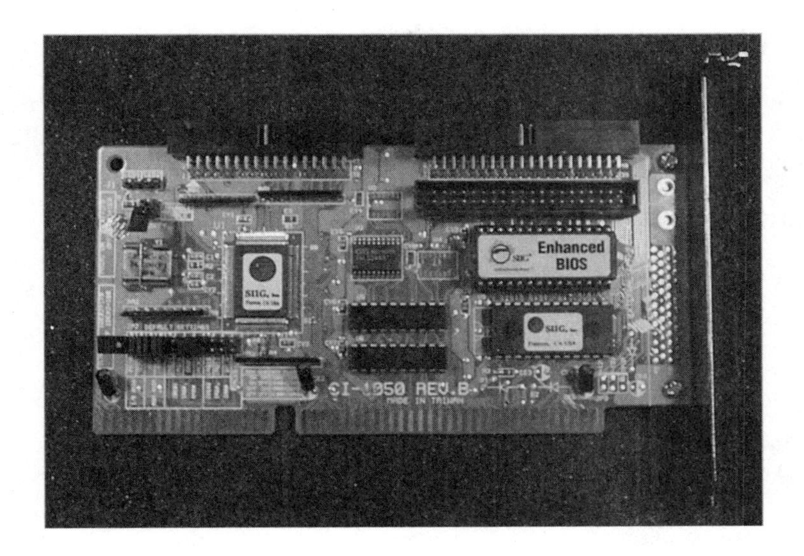

Figure 8.9 Typical EIDE controllers.

Although each controller is equal, one of the two controllers is the one that the computer looks for when the system boots up. This controller is called the *primary controller*. The other controller is called the *secondary controller*. If you're only going to use one controller, it must be the primary one. The motherboard manual shows which controller is which. Manufacturers often also stamp *IDE1* and *IDE2* on the motherboard itself, denoting primary and secondary controllers, as in the previous figure.

CABLING EIDE DRIVES

EIDE drives are connected to the controllers via a simple 40-pin cable. There are no twists, although you may occasionally see a cable that has a split. A single cable can connect up to two hard drives (see Figure 8.10).

Figure 8.10 IDE cable.

Because there can be up to two drives connected to one controller via a single cable, we need some way to identify each drive on the cable. The EIDE standard identifies the two different drives as *Master* and *Slave*. Moving jumpers on each hard drive perform these settings. If you have only one hard drive, you set the drive's jumpers to Master. If you have two drives, you set one to Master and the other to Slave.

Figure 8.11 is a close-up of an EIDE hard drive showing the jumpers.

At first glance, you may notice that there isn't any pretty text saying MASTER or SLAVE, is there? So how do you know how to properly set the jumpers? The easiest way is to simply read the front of the drive; most drives have a nice diagram that explains how to properly set the jumpers. Let's look at the front of one of these drives, shown in Figure 8.12, and see how to set the drive to Master or Slave.

You should be aware of two important areas here. First, notice that there are a lot of jumpers that you don't use. This is normal on most hard drives. These other jumpers are used for diagnostics at the manufactuing plant or for special settings in other kinds of devices that use hard drives. Ignore them. They have no bearing in the PC world. Many hard drives have a third setting called *1 Drive* or *Standalone*. Think of it as the *Master of None* setting. If a single drive has only Master and Slave settings, set it to Master.

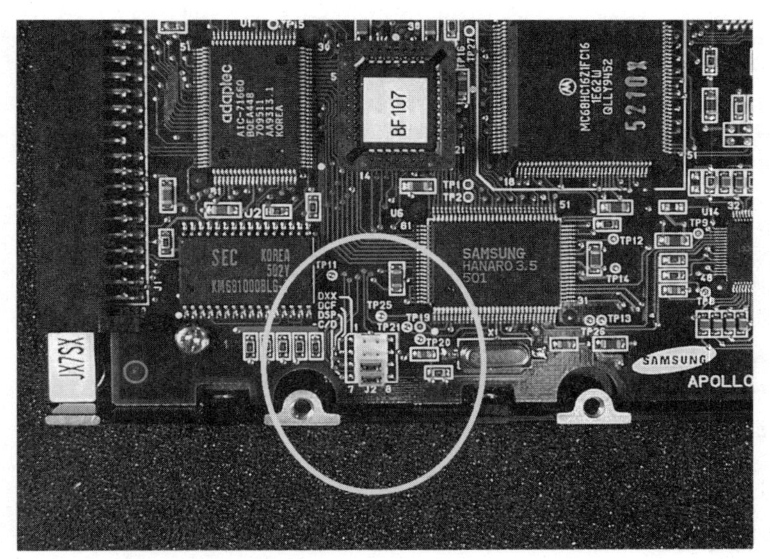

Figure 8.11 Typical master/slave jumpers.

Figure 8.12 Drive label showing master/slave settings.

How to Get Jumper Information

If you don't have a label on the drive that tells you how to set the jumpers, you have many options. First, look for the drive maker's Web site. Every drive manufacturer has every drive jumper setting on the Web—although it may take a while to get the information you are looking for. You can go to the Total Seminars Web site for handy links. Second, try phoning the hard drive maker directly. Unlike many other PC parts manufacturers, hard drive producers tend to stay in business for a longer period of time and have great technical support. For really fast information, your third choice is a powerful tool called the Microhouse Technical Library.

The Microhouse Technical Library is an exhaustive compilation of data on every hard drive ever made. It is constantly updated and is distributed on CD-ROM. It will tell you everything you need to know about any hard drive. Figure 8.13 is a sample screen:

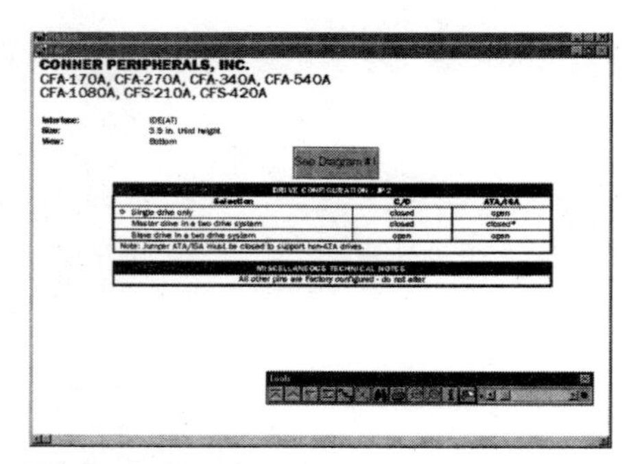

Figure 8.13 Microhouse Technical Library.

Figure 8.14 shows a continuation of the same drive, showing the jumper settings.

Figure 8.14 Microhouse Technical Library.

The Microhouse Technical Library also has info on motherboards, I/O cards, and network cards. It's a great tool that can be found at most software stores.

Plugging It In

It doesn't matter where the Master or Slave drive is installed on the cable, just make sure you have the jumpers set properly, or the computer won't be able to access the drives. Hard drive cables also have a colored stripe that corresponds to the number one pin on the connectors, just like on floppy drives. Failure to plug in the drive properly will also prevent the PC from recognizing the drive.

If you incorrectly set the Master/Slave jumpers or cable the hard drives, you won't break anything, but it just won't work.

There are only three ways you can install a hard drive to one controller, as shown in Figure 8.15.

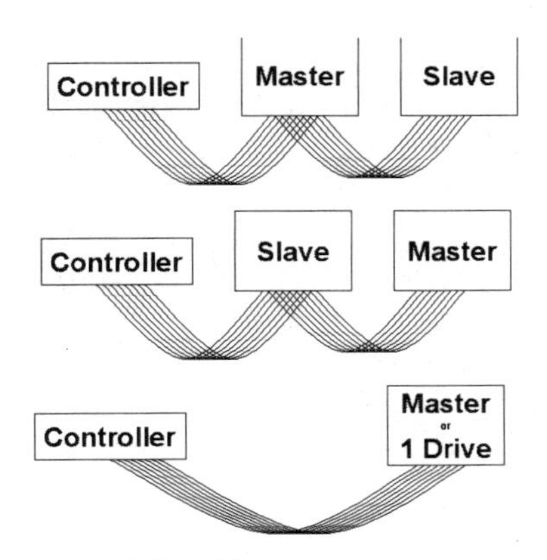

Figure 8.15 The three ways to connect to one controller.

CMOS

After physically installing the hard drive, the geometry of the hard drive must be entered into the CMOS through the CMOS setup program. Without this information, the hard drive will not work. Before IDE drives, you used to have to take the numbers from the drive and type in each value of Cylinders, Heads, Sectors/Track, Landing Zone, and Write Precomp. IDE/EIDE drives can be queried through software and they will simply tell the CMOS the correct settings. Look at the hard drive configuration information in a typical CMOS—in this case, a CMOS from an older AWARD BIOS (see Figure 8.16).

```
                    ROM PCI/ISA BIOS (2A69HQ1A)
                      STANDARD CMOS SETUP
                      AWARD SOFTWARE, INC.

 Date (mm:dd:yy) : Mon, Sep  8 1997
 Time (hh:mm:ss) : 16 : 13 : 59

 HARD DISKS              CYLS   HEAD  PRECOMP  LANDZ  SECTOR

 Drive C : None            0      0       0       0      0
 Drive D : None            0      0       0       0      0


 Drive A : 1.44M, 3.5 in.
 Drive B : None                          Base Memory:     0K
                                     Extended Memory:     0K
 Video   : EGA/VGA                      Other Memory:   512K
 Halt On : All Errors                  ---------------------
                                        Total Memory:   512K

ESC : Quit              ↑ ↓ → ←   : Select Item     PU/PD/+/- : Modify
F1  : Help              (Shift)F2 : Change Color
```

Figure 8.16 Award standard CMOS data-entry screen.

Note that there are settings for only two drives. In the days before EIDE, PCs could only use two drives. Why only two drives? Remember that the original CMOS in the first 286 could only store 64 bytes of data. The original IBM engineers allocated only enough space for two sets of drive information so the standard only allowed two drives. Besides, who would ever need more than two hard drives? Right?

Today's CMOSs are designed to handle up to four hard drives. The days of typing in values are long gone. In fact, you can simply set the *Type* to AUTO, and the system will set up the hard drive's CMOS settings for you. Setting up the drive in CMOS is very easy on today's PCs. However, there are a few concepts here that need to be explained, starting with hard drive *types*.

Hard Drive Types

The number of Heads, Cylinders, Sectors/Track, Write Precomp, and Landing Zone determine how the hard drive controller accesses the physical hard drive. Each number must be correct if the hard drive is to function properly. When IBM created the first CMOS on the 286 AT, they believed that the five different geometry numbers would be too complicated for the normal user to configure (see Table 8.1). For simplicity, IBM established 15 preset combinations of hard drive geometries. They called these preset combinations *hard drive types*. So, instead of worrying about five different variables, the user simply entered in a hard drive type into the CMOS.

Table 8.1 The Original Hard Drive Table for the IBM AT

Drive Type	Capacity (Meg)	Cylinders	Heads	Sectors	Write Precomp	Landing Zone
1	10	306	4	17	128	305
2	20	615	4	17	300	615
3	30	615	6	17	300	615
4	62	940	8	17	512	940
5	46	940	6	17	512	940
6	20	615	4	17	None	615
7	30	462	8	17	256	511
8	30	733	5	17	None	733
9	112	900	15	17	None	901
10	20	820	3	17	None	820
11	35	855	5	17	None	855
12	49	855	7	17	None	855
13	20	306	8	17	128	319
14	42	733	7	17	None	733
15		Reserved				

This worked well initially, but a problem arose. Note the capacity of the original 15 hard drive types. They are small. So, if a manufacturer came up with a new, larger hard drive type, the list would have to be expanded. At first, IBM did exactly that and eventually expanded the list to thirty-seven different types.

BIOS designers soon realized that adding to the list every time a manufacturer created a new hard drive geometry was not practical. IBM simply stopped using drives that required unique geometries (see ESDI drives) and stopped adding drive types. The other BIOS makers continued to add types until they got to around 45 different types. At that time, AMI created a new *USER* type. With a USER type, instead of selecting a special type, the user entered in the five geometry values manually, giving great flexibility to hard drive installation (see Table 8.2).

The flexibility of *user type* also allows us to make mistakes when we define the geometry of the hard drive. IDE/EIDE drives, for example, are very forgiving if you put incorrect information into the CMOS setup. If you install a 1020 megabyte hard drive and set up the CMOS to make it a 200 megabyte hard drive, that 1020 megabyte drive will become a perfectly good 200 megabyte hard drive! If you then reset the CMOS back to the proper settings to make the drive 1020 megabyte again, you'll lose all the data on your drive! Be careful and always keep a backup copy of your CMOS info, as described in the motherboard chapter. The concept of hard drive types is no longer critical. On today's systems, just set the hard drive type to AUTO or use the IDE AUTODETECT function.

Table 8.2 The IBM Drive Geometry Table

Type	Capacity	Cylinders	Heads	Sectors	Write Precomp	Landing Zone
1	10	306	4	17	128	305
2	20	615	4	17	300	615
3	31	615	6	17	300	615
4	62	940	8	17	512	940
5	47	940	6	17	512	940
6	20	615	4	17	None	615
7	31	462	8	17	256	511
8	30	733	5	17	None	733
9	112	900	15	17	None	901
10	20	820	3	17	None	820
11	36	855	5	17	None	855
12	50	855	7	17	None	855

continues

Table 8.2 Continued

Type	Capacity	Cylinders	Heads	Sectors	Write Precomp	Landing Zone
13	20	306	8	17	128	319
14	43	733	7	17	None	733
15					Reserved	
16	20	612	4	17	0	663
17	41	977	5	17	300	977
18	29	697	5	17	None	697
19	60	1024	7	17	512	1023
20	40	965	5	17	None	965
21	80	965	10	17	None	965
22	65	733	7	26	None	733
23	101	845	7	35	None	845
24	31	612	4	26	None	612
25	104	1024	8	26	None	1024

Type	Capacity	Cylinders	Heads	Sectors	Write Precomp	Landing Zone
26	65	1024	5	26	None	1024
27	42	1024	5	17	None	1024
28	102	855	7	35	None	855
29	100	776	8	33	None	776
30	149	1250	7	35	None	1250
31	149	303	16	63	None	303
32	322	1224	15	36	None	1224
33	322	656	16	63	None	656
34	645	1632	15	54	None	1632
35	644	1309	16	63	None	1309
36	633	1632	15	53	None	1632
37	304	1224	15	34	None	1224
38	304	619	16	63	None	619
39	109	960	9	26	None	960

continues

Table 8.2 Continued

Type	Capacity	Cylinders	Heads	Sectors	Write Precomp	Landing Zone
40	191	816	15	32	None	816
41	153	1249	7	36	None	1249
42	153	312	16	63	None	312
43	140	1024	8	35	None	1024
44	150	1224	7	36	None	1224
45	116	1314	7	26	None	1314
46	116	237	16	63	None	237
47		User Type				

Autodetection

Before roughly 1994, you had to use the hard drive type to install a hard drive. This manual installation process was always a bit of a problem. You had to have the proper CHS values—you might type them in wrong—and had to store these values in case your CMOS was accidentally erased. Today, all PCs can have the CMOS properly setup by using Autodetection. All IDE/EIDE drives have their CHS values stored inside of them. Autodetection simply means to tell the CMOS to ask the drive for those stored values and automatically update the CMOS. There are two common ways to perform Autodetection. First, most CMOSs have a hard drive type called AUTO. By setting the hard drive type to AUTO, the CMOS will automatically update itself every time the computer is started. Figure 8.17 shows a typical modern CMOS with the Primary Master and Slave hard drive types set to AUTO.

```
                 ROM PCI/ISA BIOS (2A69HQ1A)
                   STANDARD CMOS SETUP
                   AWARD SOFTWARE, INC.

  Date (mm:dd:yy) : Mon, Sep  8 1997
  Time (hh:mm:ss) : 16 : 13 : 59

  HARD DISKS         TYPE   SIZE  CYLS HEAD PRECOMP LANDZ SECTOR  MODE
  Primary Master   : Auto      0     0    0       0     0      0  AUTO
  Primary Slave    : Auto      0     0    0       0     0      0  AUTO
  Secondary Master : None      0     0    0       0     0      0 ------
  Secondary Slave  : None      0     0    0       0     0      0 ------

  Drive A : 1.44M, 3.5 in.
  Drive B : None                            Base Memory:      0K
                                        Extended Memory:      0K
  Video   : EGA/VGA                        Other Memory:    512K
  Halt On : All Errors
                                           Total Memory:    512K

ESC : Quit               ↑ ↓ → ←    : Select Item     PU/PD/+/- : Modify
F1  : Help               (Shift)F2  : Change Color
```

Figure 8.17 AUTO configuration.

The second and slightly older way to do Autodetection is through the IDE Autodetection option. This is a separate option that is usually accessed from the main CMOS screen, as in Figure 8.18.

```
ROM PCI/ISA BIOS (2A69HQ1A)
CMOS SETUP UTILITY
AWARD SOFTWARE, INC.

STANDARD CMOS SETUP            INTEGRATED PERIPHERALS
BIOS FEATURES SETUP            SUPERVISOR PASSWORD
CHIPSET FEATURES SETUP         USER PASSWORD
POWER MANAGEMENT SETUP         IDE HDD AUTO DETECTION
PNP/PCI CONFIGURATION          HDD LOW LEVEL FORMAT
LOAD BIOS DEFAULTS             SAVE & EXIT SETUP
LOAD SETUP DEFAULTS            EXIT WITHOUT SAVING

Esc : Quit                     ↑ ↓ → ←    : Select Item
F10 : Save & Exit Setup        (Shift)F2  : Change Color
```

Figure 8.18 Autodetect selection.

After selecting the Autodetection option, most CMOSs will look for any hard drive installed on the system. Let's take a look at a typical Autodetect in Figure 8.19.

```
ROM PCI/ISA BIOS (2A59CE1Q)
CMOS SETUP UTILITY
AWARD SOFTWARE, INC.

HARD DISKS        TYPE  SIZE   CYLS HEAD PRECOMP LANDZ SECTOR  MODE
Primary Master    :

     Select Primary Master    Option (N=Skip) : N

     OPTIONS     SIZE   CYLS HEAD PRECOMP LANDZ SECTOR  MODE
      2(Y)       1282    621   64       0  2483     63  LBA
      1          1282   2484   16   65535  2483     63  NORMAL
      3          1282   1242   32   65535  2483     63  LARGE

  Note: Some OSes (like SCO-UNIX) must use "NORMAL" for installation
                           ESC : Skip
```

Figure 8.19 Successfully finding a drive with Autodetect.

O.K., wait a minute! This CMOS has found a Master drive on the primary controller (a Primary Master), but it shows you three different CHS settings—what gives? Well, to explain what you are seeing, we're going to have to take a tangent into one big aspect of EIDE drives: LBA and ECHS.

LBA/ECHS

IBM created the BIOS to support hard drives many years before IDE drives were invented. This BIOS was first shown in the IBM *AT* 286 computer. When IDE was being developed, the creators wanted IDE to be run from the same AT BIOS command set. By providing this capability, you can use the same CMOS and BIOS routines to talk to a much more advanced drive.

Unfortunately, the BIOS routines for the original AT command set only allowed a hard drive size up to 528 million bytes (MB)/504 megabytes. Cylinders were limited to 1024, Heads to 16, and Sectors/Track to 63.

1024 Cylinders × 16 Heads × 63 Sectors/Track × 512 bytes/sector = 528MB/504Meg.

NOTE
Only when discussing hard drive capacity as listed by a manufacturer do we use the abbreviation "MB" to mean "millionbytes." In all other aspects of computing, MB means "megabyte."

For years, this limit was no problem until hard drives began to approach the 504Meg barrier, and it became clear that we needed a way to get past 504Meg. One of the differences between an IDE and an EIDE drive is that EIDE drives can be larger than 504Meg via one of two different, competing methods known as LBA and ECHS. LBA was developed by Western Digital, and ECHS was developed by Seagate. Because they are virtually identical in function, we will discuss both simultaneously. Basically, LBA/ECHS is the hard drive *lying* to the computer about its geometry. It is really nothing more than an advanced type of sector translation. Let's take a moment to understand sector translation.

Sector Translation

Long before hard drives approached the 504-megabyte limit, the 1024 Cylinders, 16 Heads, and 63 Sectors/Track limits caused hard drive makers fits. The big problem was the Heads. Remember, every two heads was another PLATTER, another physical disk that you had to squeeze into a hard drive. If you wanted a hard drive with the maximum number of 16 Heads, you had to have a hard drive with eight physical platters inside the drive! Nobody wanted that many heads: it made the drives too high, it took more power to spin up the drive and more parts cost more money. There was no problem to make a hard drive that had FEWER Heads and MORE Cylinders, but the stupid 1024/16/63 limit got in the way.

Plus, there's a tremendous amount of wastage with sectors. The sectors toward the inside of the drive are much shorter than the sectors on the outside. The sectors on the outside don't need to be that long, but with the current geometry setup, the hard drive makers have no choice. A hard drive could store a lot more information if it could be made with more sectors/track on the outside tracks (see Figure 8.20).

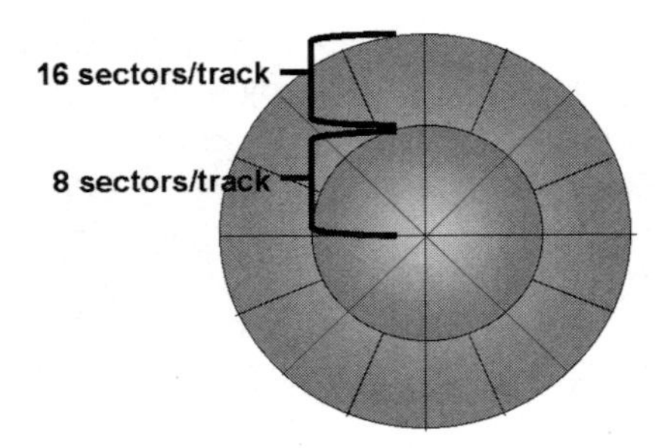

Figure 8.20 Multiple sectors/track.

The IDE specification was designed to have two geometries. First is the Physical Geometry, which is the real layout of the CHS inside the drive. The second geometry is the Logical Geometry, which is what the drive tells the CMOS. In other words, the IDE drive lies to the CMOS, thus allowing the physical drive to be no longer limited to the artificial limits of the BIOS. When data is being transferred to and from the drive, the on-board circuitry of the drive "translates" the logical geometry to the physical geometry. Thus, we call this function Sector translation.

Sector translation in Enhanced IDE and ECHS allows the drive to break the 504 megabyte limit by lying about the physical geometry of the drive. The following chart lists the physical and logical geometry of a Western Digital WD2160, a 2.1-gigabyte hard drive.

Physical		Logical	
Cylinders	16384	Cylinders	1024
Heads	4	Heads	64
Sectors/Track	63	Sectors/Track	63
Total Capacity	2016 Meg	Total Capacity	2016 Meg

Sector translation never changes the capacity of the drive—it only changes the geometry to stay within the BIOS limits. But wait! The WD2160 can have 64 logical heads? Here's where the magic comes in. The WD2160 is capable of Logical Block Addressing (LBA). Now, assuming that the BIOS is also capable of LBA, here's what happens. When the computer boots up, the BIOS queries the drive(s) to see if they can perform LBA. If they say yes, the BIOS and the drive work together to change slightly the way they talk to each other. They can do this without conflicting with the original AT BIOS commands by taking advantage of unused commands to add the capability to use up to 256 heads.

Enhanced CHS (ECHS) is nothing more than a competitor to Western Digital's LBA. It works the same way, but comes up with different values than LBA. With LBA/ECHS, you can have 1024 Cylinders, 256 Heads, and 63 Sectors/Track for a maximum size of 8.4 gigabytes.

In order for you to have drives larger than 504 megabytes, you must have a hard drive that has LBA/ECHs and a BIOS that has support for LBA/ECHS. If you have an EIDE drive larger than 504 megabytes, you can be sure that the drive supports LBA and ECHS. Virtually all BIOS support LBA and ECHS. Just run the Autodetect utility. If the BIOS doesn't support LBA, all EIDE drives come with an installation utility such as On Track's Disk Manager software that will provide its own LBA support.

Whew! That was a lot of information! But we can now go back to the IDE Autodetect screen and understand why we have three different choices (see Figure 8.21).

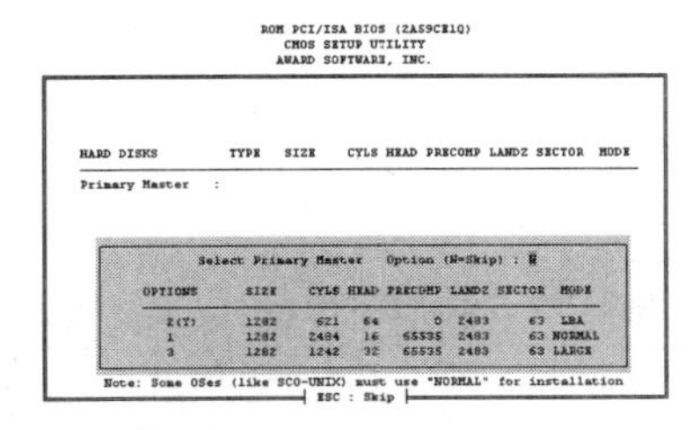

Figure 8.21 Autodetection revisited.

The three choices are LBA, NORMAL, and LARGE. LBA means that the drive is capable of LBA. This is the most common setting we use when setting up a drive. NORMAL is the physical geometry. We only use the NORMAL setting for operating systems that don't use the BIOS, like Novell NetWare and UNIX. Normal is never used otherwise. LARGE shows that the drive is capable of ECHS. If you want, you can also set the drive to ECHS. (WIN95 and Windows NT both use LBA and ECHS.)

I stay away from ECHS. It's not that there is anything wrong with it—it works perfectly. The problem is if I ever want to move the hard drive to another system, that other system will also have to support ECHS. If it doesn't, I can install the drive under LBA but *I will lose all the data on the drive.* Because all BIOSs support LBA, I never have to worry about moving the drive. Stick to LBA.

Autodetection has one other feature that makes it indispensable. When a drive doesn't work, the biggest question, especially during installation is: *Did I plug it in correctly?* With Autodetection, the answer is simple: If the Autodetection doesn't see the drives, there is usually something wrong with the connectivity of the hardware (i.e., cabling, jumpers, an enabled controller).

PIO Modes

ATA drives transfer data to and from the hard drive and memory via standardized protocols called *Programmable Input/Output* (PIO) modes. Although the ATA drives could originally transfer data from the hard drive to RAM at a maximum rate of roughly 3.3 Meg/s, this speed was very quickly bumped up to 5.2 Meg/s and then up to 8.3 Meg/s. The *Small Forms Factor* (SFF) Standards Committee defined these as PIO mode, 0, PIO mode 1, and PIO mode 2, respectively. In the ATA world, all drives can use PIO mode 0, 1, or 2.

The SFF committee released a follow-up to the ATA standard that defined some new data throughput speeds. First, there were two new PIO speeds, called PIO 3 and PIO 4, respectively (see Table 8.3).

Table 8.3 PIO Speeds

PIO Mode	Cycle Time (ns)	Transfer Rate (MB/s)
0	600	3.3
1	383	5.2
2	240	8.3
3	180	11.1
4	120	16.6

In order to get the best performance out of your hard drive, you must set the proper PIO mode for the drive.

Setting the PIO mode requires answering three questions:

1. What is the fastest mode the hard drive supports?
2. What is the fastest mode the controller supports?
3. What is the fastest mode the BIOS or device driver will support?

The fastest PIO mode you can set is limited by the weakest link. For example, if you have a hard drive capable of PIO mode 4, a controller capable of mode 2, and a BIOS capable of mode 4, the best you will get is mode 2 (see Figure 8.22). You should never try to use a mode faster than what is recommended by the drive manufacturer. Although the faster mode will not damage your drive, it will most certainly damage your data.

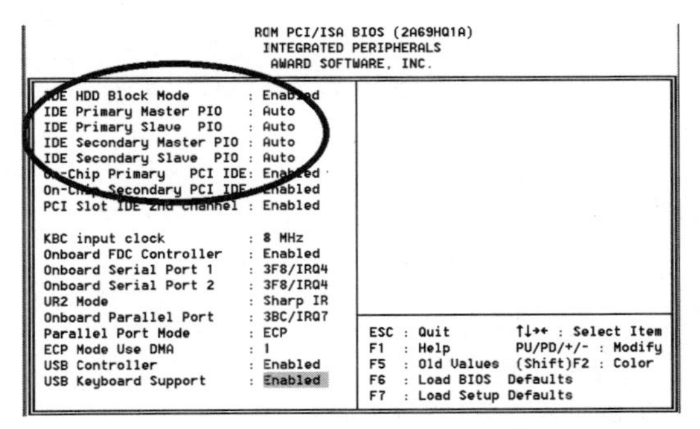

Figure 8.22 PIO mode settings in CMOS with onboard controller.

To make it simple, most modern PCs will talk to the hard drive at boot and automatically set the proper PIO modes. It's easy to determine whether the PC can perform this autonegotiation. Go into the CMOS and look for something that says *PIO*, usually under Advanced or Integrated Peripherals screens:

If the system has an option called AUTO, take it. The AUTO setting will query the drive for its top PIO mode and automatically set it up for you.

Sadly, many older PCs out there still use older-style hard drive controller cards. In this case, there's a little more work required. We need to manually set the controller to the highest PIO mode that the hard drive can handle.

First, determine the highest PIO mode for the drive. There are no settings on the drive to set PIO modes. The hard drive's top PIO mode is preset. If the PIO mode isn't stated on the hard drive, call the manufacturer . . . or guess. People don't like to see the word *guess* in print—it makes them uneasy. It shouldn't. The hard drive will lock up if the controller is too fast—then just move the controller to a slower mode. Most drives greater than 1Gig, or made after 1995, support mode 4.

Second, determine the fastest speed your controller can handle. All hard drives can at least support PIO mode 2. Therefore, the question is usually PIO mode 2, 3, or 4. If you're using an old ISA card, PIO mode 2 is the best you can achieve (see Figure 8.23). The two fastest PIO modes, 3 and 4, must be run from either a VL-BUS or a PCI controller. Many cards set their PIO mode by setting the cycle time and not the PIO mode.

Figure 8.23 PIO settings on a typical controller card.

Controllers that are capable of PIO mode 3 and 4 use a hardware flow control called *IO ReaDY* (IORDY), also known as IOCHRDY (see Figure 8.24). This setting allows the drive to slow down the data transfer as the head moves across the disk. If your drive does not support IORDY and you attempt to use your new EIDE controller and its software to force your elderly hard drive into PIO mode 3 or 4, data can be corrupted on the drive. So if a hard drive can't do PIO 3 or 4, don't try to force it. On older controllers, the

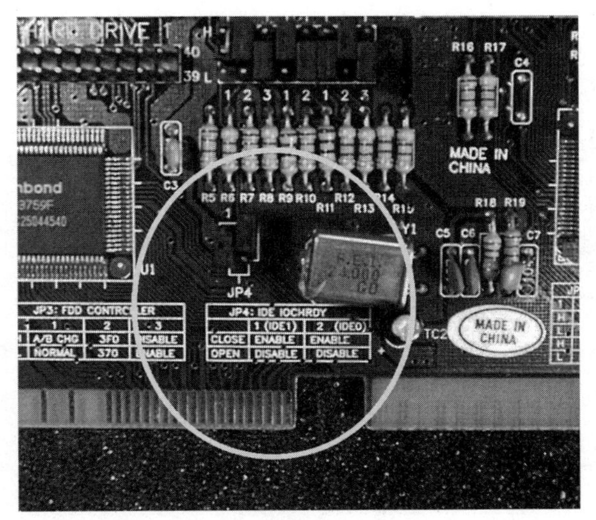

Figure 8.24 I/O CHRDY settings on typical controller.

IOCHRDY is usually a separate jumper setting that must set properly. Always enable IOCHRDY on older controllers.

DMA MODES

Direct Memory Access (DMA) is a data-transfer method that is very different from a PIO mode. This method bypasses the CPU and transfers data directly into memory, leaving the CPU free to run programs. Most devices other than hard drives will use the slow DMA controller on the ISA bus to accomplish these data transfers. Hard drives use instead a much faster bus-mastering controller that takes over the expansion bus and bypasses the built-in DMA controller. Bus-mastered DMA data transfers can be either 16 bits (single word) or 32 bits (double word) wide. The transfer width depends upon the data bus (ISA, EISA, PCI, VLB) being used. Any type of DMA data transfer for ATA hard drives is extremely rare. The transfer rates for the various DMA modes are shown in Table 8.4.

Table 8.4 DMA Speeds

DMA Mode Single Word (16-bit)	Cycle Time (ns)	Transfer Rate (MB/s)
0	960	2.1
1	480	4.2
2	240	8.3
DMA Mode Double Word (32-bit)	**Cycle Time (ns)**	**Transfer Rate (MB/s)**
0	480	4.2
1	150	13.3
2	120	16.6
"Ultra DMA"	60	33.3

Unlike PIO modes, most systems require special drivers to take advantage of DMA modes. A PC can use either DMA or PIO; not both. Fortunately, DMA drivers *turn off* PIO when they are used.

DMA is faster than PIO modes. However, a PC would have to be worked very hard in terms of data transfers to see a significant improvement. Most desktop PCs won't even notice the difference.

Drive-Naming Conventions

If only one hard drive has been installed, it must be configured as Primary Master. If another drive is installed, it must be installed as Primary Slave or Secondary Master. Unfortunately, many older CMOS configurations, like the examples here, use the terms C: and D:. Say to yourself, *The Master drive is C:; the Slave drive is D:.* This is an issue on older systems whose BIOS support only two drives (see Figure 8.25).

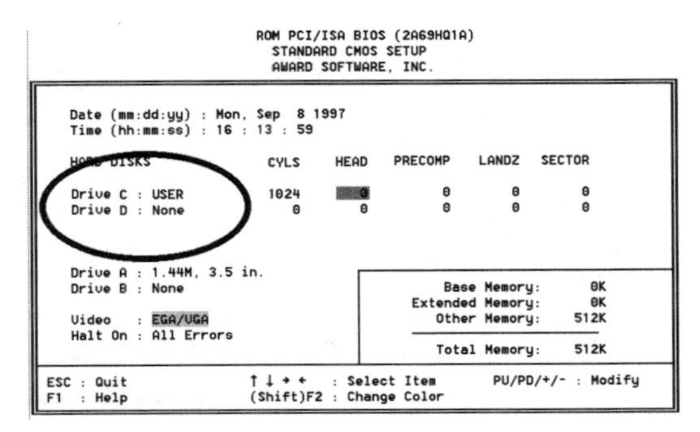

Figure 8.25 AWARD BIOS showing master as C: and slave as D.

LOW-LEVEL FORMATTING

Once the CMOS has been updated with the hard drive geometry, a program must be run to tell the controller to read that CMOS information and organize the hard drive. This is known as a low-level format. A low-level format performs three simultaneous functions: first, it creates and organizes the sectors, making them ready to accept data. Second, it sets the proper interleave. Third, it establishes the boot sector.

The problem with sector translation is in the low-level format: all low-level formatters use the CMOS values to perform their low-level format. But if the CMOS values aren't the true geometries, they try to make the drive think that its logical geometry is its actual geometry—this could be bad. If you attempt to low-level format a modern (post-1993) IDE drive, the drive would simply ignore the low-level format, the program would run and report a successful low-level format, but actually nothing would happen. However, most early (pre-1993) IDE drives would be destroyed!

NOTE

Low-level formatting is only done on pre-IDE drives! All IDE/EIDE drives are low-level formatted at the factory!

Although low-level formatting is basically obsolete, it warrants discussion because many concepts and terms of low-level formatting are still being used today. Let's take a moment to understand low-level formatting.

Sector Organization

In the earlier discussion of geometry, we stated that each sector contained 512 usable bytes of data. That's 512 bytes of *data*. However, there are actually 574 bytes per sector for RLL; the additional bytes are reserved for organization of the 512 usable bytes of data. Let's look at the structure of a sector (we'll use an RLL sector because RLL is all that's used anymore, and the differences between RLL and MFM are unimportant to repair techs); see Table 8.5.

Table 8.5 Sector structure.

Area of sector (bytes)	Size	Function
SYNC	10	Allows drive electronics time to respond
IDAM	2	Warns of approach of sector ID
ID	4	Gives the sector number
ECC	4	Checks the first three values
GAP 2	5	Dead space for ECC calculation time
SYNC	11	Dead space for resync with hard drive electronics
DAM	2	Warns of approach of data area
DATA	512	Data area
ECC	4	Checks the data area
GAP 3	20	Signals end of sector

Every hard drive comes from the factory with bad spots on the platters that are unacceptable for the placement of data. As the sectors are being created, the low-level format will attempt to skip over the bad spots. Sometimes, it is impossible to skip over a spot so the sector is marked as *bad* in the ID field.

Interleave

The second major aspect of low-level formatting is called *interleave*. To understand interleave, remember that when a file is being retrieved from a hard drive, it doesn't magically move from the hard drive to RAM in one step. Files are chopped up into 512 chunks in sectors, so that file retrieval is usually a matter of accessing many sectors in succession. Data retrieved from (or saved to) a hard drive must pass through a buffer on the hard drive controller. For writing data, the buffer is used to store data until the hard drive can save it. For reading, the buffer is used to store data until RAM needs it. This creates a problem with ST506 drives. If sectors are immediately next to each other, often the hard drive can't keep up with the spinning of the platters. As a result, if data was missed on a sector, you have to wait until the drive rotates back around before the data can be accessed.

To eliminate this waste, sectors can be numbered every other sector, every third sector, or even every eighth sector! That way, the controller's buffer can be ready for the data, and there is no waiting for the drive to spin back around to catch the next sector.

A drive can be anything from 1–to–1 interleave up to as high as an 8–to–1 interleave. The interleave is determined by the program that performs the low-level format. The interleave will not only be different between different models of drive, it can often be different between two drives of the exact same model. The interleave can be entered manually during the low-level format, or the low-level format itself can determine the best interleave automatically. It is always best to let the program determine the best interleave.

Again, THERE IS NO LOW-LEVEL FORMATTING ON IDE DRIVES! All IDE drives use a special type of low-level formatting called *embedded servo*. This type of low-level formatting can only be done by the manufacturer—so you can't. Once the CMOS is set up on an IDE drive, you go straight to partitioning.

There are programs out today that supposedly allow the low-level formatting of IDE drives. These programs simply mark sectors good or bad in the hard drive's own internal error map (do not confuse this with the high-level format marking of bad clusters in the FAT!). These programs can be useful and later, as we discuss hard drive repair, we will look at them. However, these programs are not true low-level formatters; they are *bad-sector mappers*.

Many CMOSs have a *Hard Drive Utility* option that allows users to low-level format their drives. These utilities are for ST506 drives exclusively! NEVER USE THEM ON IDE or EIDE DRIVES! YOU COULD DESTROY THEM!

The Old Stuff

Although EIDE hard drives dominate the PC world, other hard drive technologies have had their moments in the sun, most notably the ST506 and ESDI. The ST506, developed in 1980 by Seagate, allowed two drives in a system, which were designated Master and Slave by a set of jumpers or DIPP switches on the drives. The original ST506 had a 5 megabyte capacity and cost a whopping $3000.

ST506

Hard drives were not part of the original PC concept. PCs were to use one, or possibly two, floppy drives for permanent storage. Hard drives were the realm of mainframe and minicomputers; the normal PC user would never need the *massive* storage of 5 to 10 megabytes of the first hard drives. As a result, the earliest hard drives (and their interfaces) were proprietary. There was no common cabling or command set. Until ST506.

The ST506/412 interface was developed by Seagate Technologies around 1980 and originally appeared with the 5 MB ST506 drive. The ST506, with a capacity of 5MB and average access time on the order of 100ms, had a price tag of around $3000. A year later, Seagate offered a 10MB drive with the ST412 interface; this was the hard drive first offered in the IBM PC XT. Because the ST506/412 was the only hard drive available for the IBM PC, it was the first to be supported by the ROM BIOS chip on the motherboard, starting with IBM PC AT.

The term *ST506* was poorly used. In common usage, ST506 referred to all hard drives that used the ST506 or compatible controller, and not simply to the ST506 itself. The name ST506 came to designate an entire class of hard drives. Another common misleading term was *Winchester*. Winchesters were a popular brand of ST506 controllers, but many used the term *Winchester* to mean *ST506*. Although incorrect, its widespread common use was accepted

CABLING ST506 DRIVES

In the ST506 days, you could have no more than two hard drives in a computer. Whenever we installed ST506 hard drives into the computer, there had to be a hardware setting on each drive (see Figure 8.26). If you had just one hard drive in a computer, it was known as HARD DRIVE 0 or the MASTER DRIVE. If you installed a second hard drive in a computer, it was known as HARD DRIVE 1 or the SLAVE DRIVE. All hard drives had jumpers or DIPP switches to allow you to set them as DRIVE 0/MASTER or DRIVE 1/SLAVE.

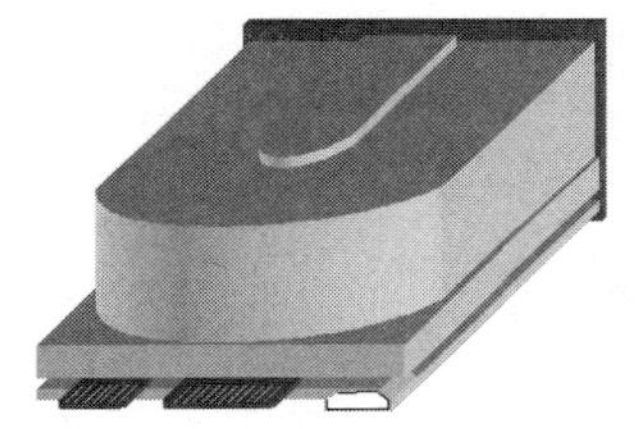

Figure 8.26 ST-506 drive.

The cabling scheme for the ST506/412 was composed of two cables for a one-drive installation or three cables for a two-drive installation (see Figure 8.27). These cables consisted of one 34-connector control cable that was daisy-chained for a dual-drive configuration, and a 20-connector data cable for each drive.

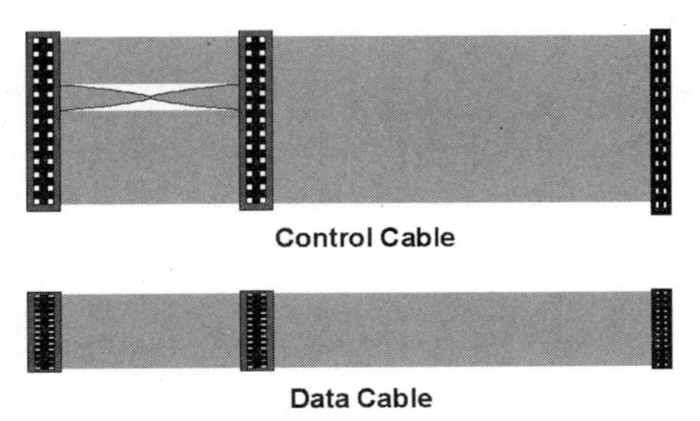

Figure 8.27 T-506 cables.

Although ST506 drives had *drive select* jumpers that determined which drive was 0 and which was 1, these jumpers were rarely used. Instead, the 34-wire control cable usually had a twist in it for line 25 through 29; this twist determined which hard drive was hard drive 0 and which was hard drive 1. If a ST506 was installed into the end connection, it was hard drive 0. If an ST506 drive was installed in the middle connection, the drive was drive 1. There were some rare ST506 controller cables that had NO TWIST. Because these cables had no twist, the jumper on the first drive had to be set to indicate drive select 0; if there was a second drive on the cable in the middle connector, it had its jumper set to drive select 1 (see Figure 8.28).

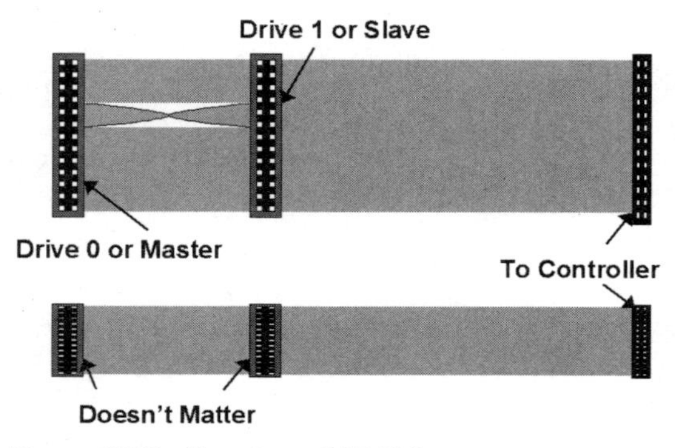

Figure 8.28 Function of ST-506 connectors.

In addition to a proper jumper setting on the hard drive, there was also another selectable device on the ST-506 hard drive called the *terminating resistor*. This resistor served to provide the proper electrical termination on the cable to prevent electrical signal noise and data degradation, and also served to provide proper electrical impedance for the interface card. As shipped, the drives came with the terminating resistor installed; if you were installing a drive as a second drive on a system, you had to be sure to remove the terminating resistor on the second drive.

Whenever you are installing any type of ribbon cable, be sure that the colored stripe points to the number one pin on the connector. This is true for all ribbon cables, not just hard drives!

ESDI

The *Enhanced Small Device Interface* (ESDI) was introduced in 1983 by the Maxtor Corporation, which led a consortium of other developers in adopting ESDI as the interface to succeed the under-powered ST506/412 design.

The biggest change called for by ESDI vs. the ST506/412 was the incorporation of most of the controller functions directly onto the hard drive, which served to improve data-transfer speeds greatly. Although the theoretical maximum transfer speed of an ESDI drive approached 25 Mbps (millions of bits per second), most drives could only sustain between 10 and 15 Mbps.

Some ESDI controllers offered enhanced command sets that supported auto-sensing of the drive's geometry by the motherboard ROM BIOS setup. In other cases, it was necessary to manually enter the data into the drive table. Although the ST506/412 interface supported 17 to 26 sectors per track, ESDI supported 32 sectors per track in most cases, although as many as 80 sectors per track was possible. ESDI also supported an interleave of 1–to–1, which resulted in an even greater transfer rate.

The installation of ESDI drives was almost identical to the installation of ST-506 drives. The cabling, drive select jumper, and terminating resistor were all configured in the same manner as the ST506/412. The CMOS hard drive type was almost always set to type 1 (the ESDI drive would convert that geometry to something it could use). There was still the need to low-level format most ESDI drives, although some didn't need to be low-level formatted. If you had an ESDI drive that didn't need to be low-level formatted, the formatter would not allow you to perform the low-level format. Partitioning and high-level formatting were identical to ST506. ESDI had one major disadvantage: it was extremely expensive. The high cost of ESDI drives made them obsolete by the early 90s (see Figure 8.29).

Figure 8.29 ST506 and ESDI are dead.

CHAPTER 9

SCSI

In this chapter we will:

- Understand the concept and motivation for SCSI
- Display SCSI chains, IDs, and terminations
- Show the different flavors of SCSI
- See basic SCSI repair techniques

What is SCSI?

Shugart systems introduced *Small Computer Systems Interface* (SCSI) in 1979 as a system-independent means of mass storage. SCSI can be best described as a *mini-network* inside your PC. Any type of peripheral can be built as a SCSI device. Common SCSI devices include Hard Drives, tape backup units, removable hard drives, scanners, CD-ROMs, printers, and lots more!

Since its introduction, SCSI has developed different *flavors*. Some of these flavors are industry standards such as SCSI-1, SCSI-2, and Wide SCSI. Other flavors are manufacturer-specific standards (i.e., somebody like Western Digital is trying to push something new, but the industry has not yet adopted it) with names like *Ultra SCSI*.

Using SCSI-2 as a basis, this chapter will address the basic issues involved in implementing SCSI in the PC. After we have a solid understanding of SCSI-2, we'll go into all the other types of SCSI and understand the differences between them.

SCSI manifests itself through a SCSI *chain,* which is a series of SCSI devices working together through a *host adapter.* The host adapter is the device that attaches the SCSI chain to the PC. Figure 9.1 shows a typical PCI host adapter.

Figure 9.1 SCSI host adapter.

Note that there are three connections on this card. The first connector, at the left of the figure, is for devices on the outside (external) of the PC. The second and third connectors are at the top of the figure. These connectors are for inside (internal) SCSI connections. All SCSI chains are connected to the PC through the host adapter. Note that this particular host adapter is PCI. However, there are also ISA, EISA and V-LB SCSI host adapters.

SCSI CHAINS

All SCSI devices can be divided into two groups: internal and external. External devices are stand-alone devices that are hooked to the external connector of the host adapter. Internal SCSI devices are installed inside the PC and are connected to the host adapter through the internal connector.

All internal devices are connected to the host adapter and each other with a 50-pin ribbon cable, which looks similar to a 40-pin IDE cable. Multiple internal devices can be connected together by using a cable with enough connectors. Figure 9.2, for example, shows a cable that can take up to three SCSI devices, including the host adapter.

Use caution when installing SCSI devices. IDE devices, if they are plugged in wrong, just do not work. SCSI devices, when plugged in incorrectly (i.e., cable backwards), can be damaged! Be careful to install them properly the first time!

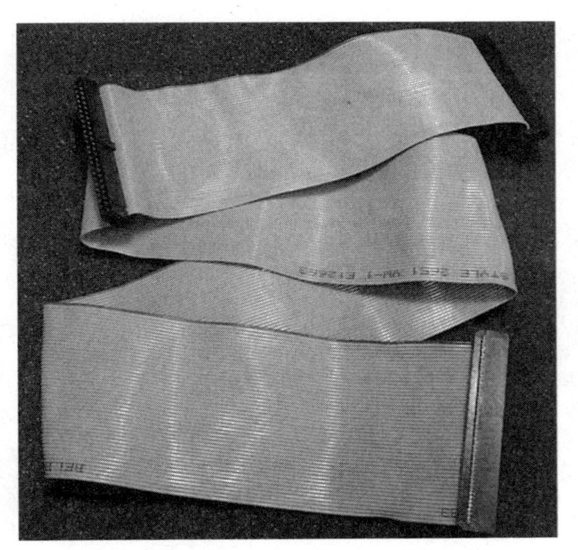

Figure 9.2 SCSI Cable with three connections

External SCSI devices are connected to the host adapter through the host adapter's special SCSI external connection. Some cheap host adapters do not have external connections—you cannot put external devices on them. Most external devices have two connections in the back, which allow you to daisy-chain multiple external devices together.

A SCSI *chain* refers to all the devices attached to a single host adapter. SCSI chains can have all internal devices, all external devices, or a combination of internal and external devices (see Figures 9.3 and 9.4). The maximum number of devices you can have on a SCSI chain, including the host adapter, is *eight*.

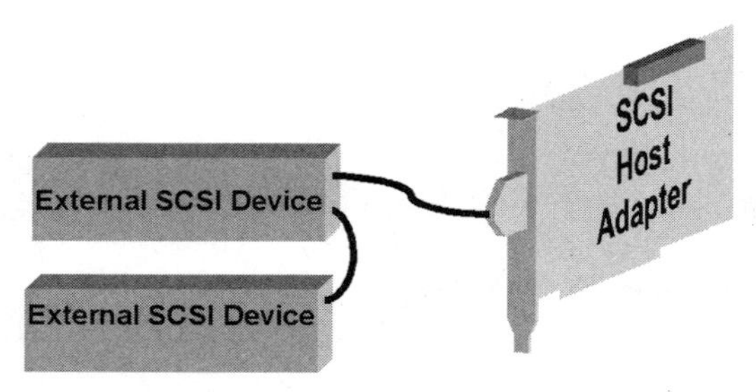

Figure 9.3 SCSI chain with two external devices.

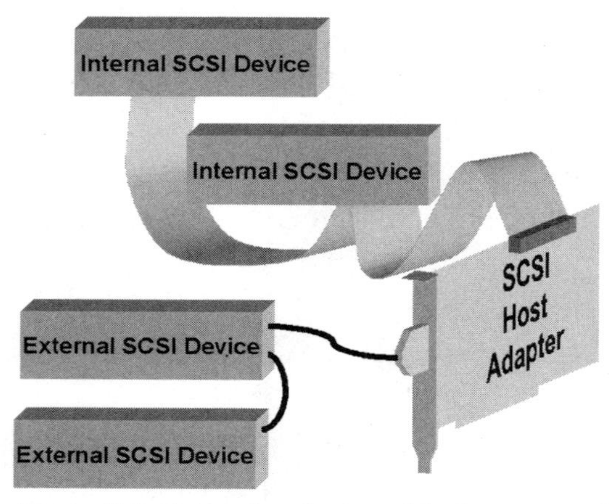

Figure 9.4 Internal and external devices on one SCSI chain.

SCSI IDS

The individual components of a SCSI chain each require a unique identifier—the ID number. The values for ID numbers range from 0 to 7. SCSI ID numbers are similar to many other hardware settings in a PC—no two devices can share the same ID number. A SCSI device can have any SCSI ID, as long as no two devices share the same ID.

There are some conventions on SCSI IDs. Typically, most people set the host adapter to SCSI ID 7. Although you can change this, there is nothing to gain by deviating from such a well-established tradition. Note that there is no order for the use of SCSI IDs. It does not matter which device gets which number. You can skip numbers. Any SCSI device can have any SCSI ID (see Figure 9.5).

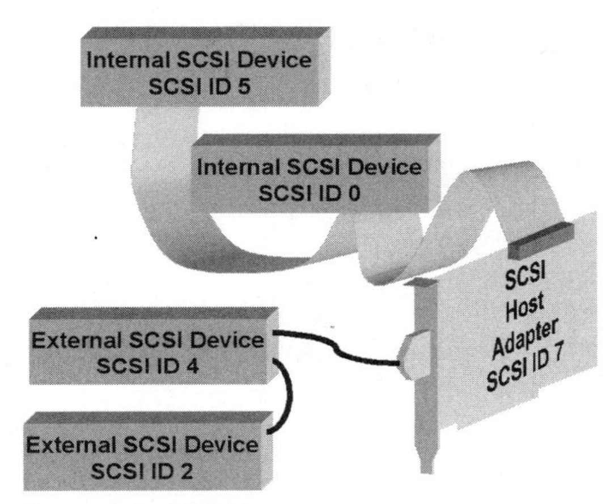

Figure 9.5 SCSI IDs.

Setting a SCSI ID for a particular device is usually done by either jumpers or switches on the SCSI device itself. All internal SCSI hard drives, for example, use jumpers to set their SCSI IDs.

Figure 9.6 shows a typical jumper setup for a SCSI hard drive. Note that the numbers are binary. Closing jumper 1, for example, would get ID 1. To get ID 3, you would need to close both jumpers 1 and 2.

Figure 9.6 SCSI hard drive jumper settings.

There is one exception to setting SCSI IDs. If you want a SCSI drive to be drive `C:>` (required if you want to boot DOS off this drive), you must set that drive to the SCSI ID specified by the host adapter as the *bootable* SCSI ID. Most manufacturers of host adapters use SCSI ID 0, although a few older adapters often require SCSI ID 6. Read the host adapter information or guess; you will not break anything if you are wrong. Booting SCSI drives is discussed later in this chapter.

Not all SCSI devices are designed to be set to every SCSI ID. For example, this ZIP drive can only be set to SCSI ID 5 or 6 (see Figure 9.7). Work around it!

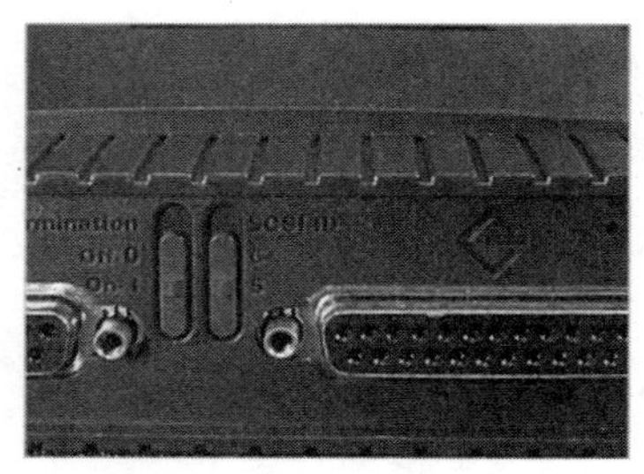

Figure 9.7 SCSI ZIP drive.

LOGICAL UNIT NUMBERS (LUN)

SCSI also supports more than one device per ID through the use of *Logical Unit Numbers* (LUNs) to provide a unique identifier for up to seven sub-units per ID number. These are used primarily in hard drive arrays, which create one large logical drive out of several smaller physical drives. LUNs are in the realm of network servers running NetWare, Windows NT, or UNIX. They require highly specialized software to run. With the previous exceptions, LUNs are to be ignored.

TERMINATION

Whenever you send a signal down a wire, some of that signal will reflect back up the wire, creating an echo of the signal. This echo causes tremendous confusion and must be stopped. *Termination* simply means to put something on the ends of the wire to prevent this echo. Terminators are usually *pull-down* resistors and can manifest themselves in many different ways. On most of the devices within a PC, the appropriate termination is built in. On other devices, including SCSI chains and some network cables, termination must be set during installation.

A SCSI chain consists of a number of devices linked by a cable. This cable must be terminated on the ends. In a SCSI chain, the ends of the cables are the devices into which they are plugged. Therefore, in a SCSI chain, whatever devices are on the ends of the chain must be *terminated*. Devices that are *not* on the ends must *not* be terminated. Because any SCSI device might be on the end of a chain, all SCSI devices usually have the capability to be terminated.

Figure 9.8 shows which devices must be terminated in a system with a variety of SCSI devices—internal, external, and internal and external. Note that the rule of termination applies: you must terminate *only* the ends of the SCSI chain.

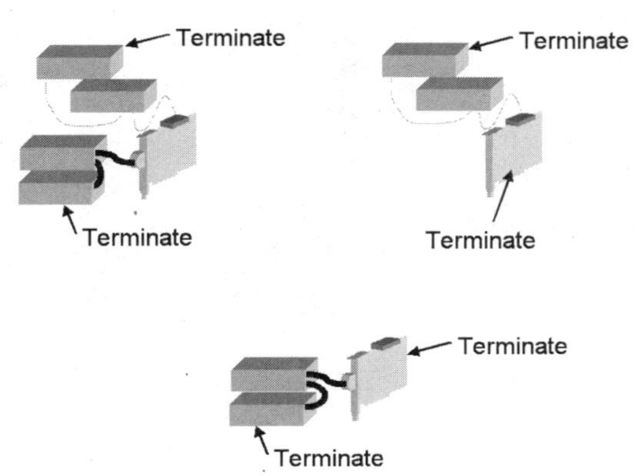

Figure 9.8 Location of the terminated devices.

There are a large number of ways to set the termination. Figure 9.9 shows a hard drive that is terminated by setting a jumper.

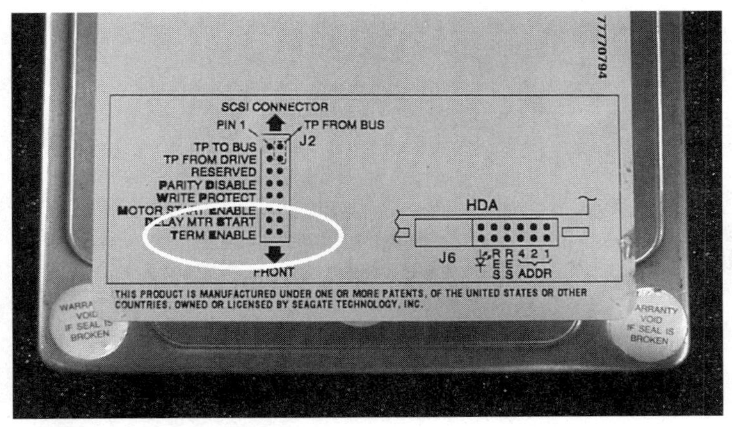

Figure 9.9 Setting termination.

The hard drive in Figure 9.10 has terminating resistors that are inserted for termination. They must be removed to un-terminate the adapter.

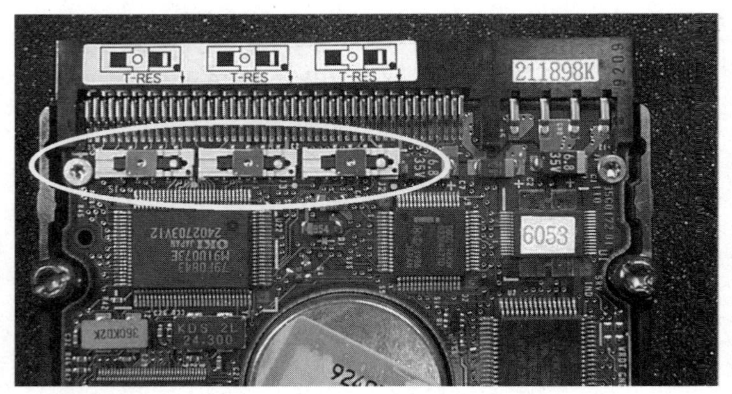

Figure 9.10 Hard drive with removable terminating resistors.

The ZIP drive in Figure 9.11 has a slide for termination.

Figure 9.11 Zip drive termination.

The advanced host adapter's termination in Figure 9.12 is set through software—here is a screen snapshot showing how termination is set through software:

The ancient hard drive in Figure 9.13 is not capable of terminating itself. It needs a separate terminator piece added for termination.

Some devices will detect that they are on the end of the SCSI chain and will automatically terminate themselves.

Be careful when you are terminating! Improper termination can cause damage to SCSI hard drives! Unlike setting SCSI IDs, termination can be a little tricky. But before we can discuss the different types of termination options, we must take some time to understand the different types of SCSI.

```
          Adaptec AHA-2940/AHA-2940W SCSISelect(TM) Utility v1.11

              AHA-2940/AHA-2q4ow at Bus:Device 00:12h
                            CONFIGURATION

SCSI Bus Tnterface Definitions
 Host Adapter SCSI ID . . . . . . . . . . . . . . . . . . . . . . 7
 SCSI Parity Checking . . . . . . . . . . . . . . . . . . . . . . Enabled
 Host Adapter SCSI Termination  . . . . . . . . . . . . . . . . . Enabled

Additional Options
 SCSI Device Configuration  . . . . . . . . . . . . . . . .Press <Enter>
 Advanced Configuration Options . . . . . . . . . . . . . .Press <Enter>

            <F6>    Reset to Host Adapter Defaults

   Arrow keys to move cursor, <Enter> to select option, <Esc> to exit
```

Figure 9.12 Software termination setting.

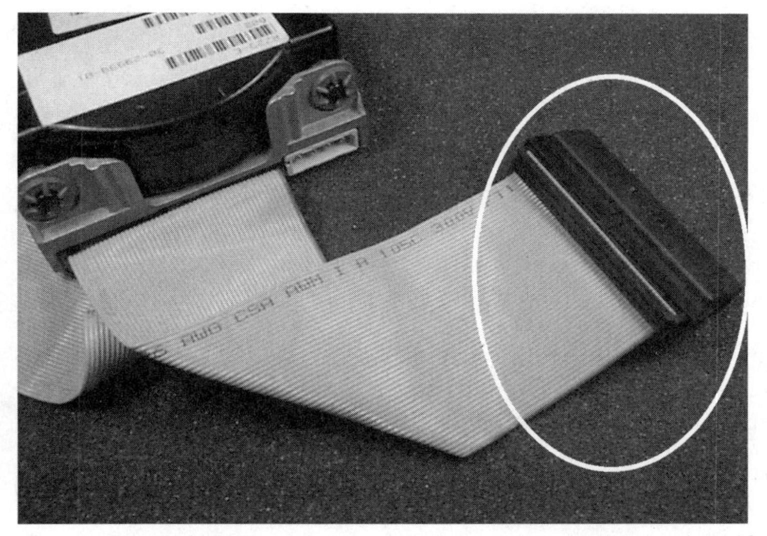

Figure 9.13 Old SCSI hard drive requires separate termination on the cable.

SCSI Flavors

Way back in 1979, Shugart Associates began work on an interface that would handle data transfers between devices, regardless of the type of device. This interface would work at the logical or operating system level instead of at the device level, creating a stable interface in a world faced with rapid device development. This new interface was called the *Shugart Associates System Interface* or SASI, which was the precursor to SCSI. During 1980–1981, various committees from Shugart and NCR met and developed a draft proposal to present to ANSI. In April of 1982, the Accredited Standards Committee X3T9.2 met and drafted a formal proposal for the *Small Computer System Interface*, which would be based on SASI. Between 1982 and 1986, the SCSI standard expanded to include more than just hard drives. In June of 1986, the first formal set of standards defining SCSI was approved by ANSI as document ANSI X3.131-1986. This standard was known as SCSI-1.

SCSI-1

SCSI-1 defined an 8-bit, 5MHz bus capable of supporting up to eight SCSI devices. The SCSI-1 standard was very fuzzy when describing many aspects of SCSI. As a result, many manufacturers of SCSI devices had different opinions about how to implement those standards (see Figure 9.14). Therefore, SCSI-1 was really more of an opinion than a standard. In 1986, SCSI began to appear on IBM-compatible PC machines, and everybody and their sister made a proprietary SCSI device. The key word here is *proprietary*. (Proprietary means that the device is supported only by the company that produced, designed, manufactured, and sold it). SCSI was being used in PCs for stand-alone devices such as hard drives, and each device came with its own host adapter. Makers of SCSI devices had no interest in chaining their particular device with anyone else's—primarily because they assumed (for the most part correctly) that their device was the only SCSI device in the PC. Each SCSI device had its own command set and no two command sets were the same. Trying to get one vendor's SCSI hard drive to work with another vendor's SCSI adapter card was often impossible.

SCSI-1 devices transferred data only through an 8-bit parallel path, but did support up to seven devices on the chain. For most PCs that used SCSI-1 devices, the 8-bit pathway was not much of a bottleneck. Although the devices themselves were not capable of high-speed data transfers, neither were the common 80286-based machines of the time. The SCSI-1 devices seemed fast in comparison. Plus, the only common hard drive interface competition was the ST-506 controller. 8-bit SCSI was far faster!

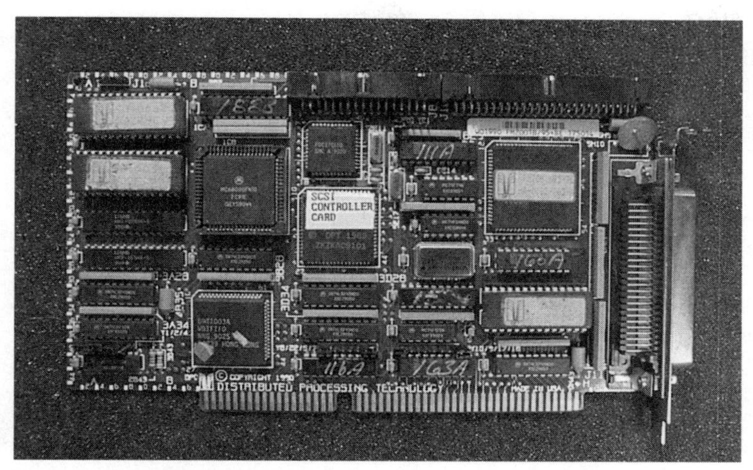

Figure 9.14 Early SCSI-1 adapter.

SCSI-2

By the time the SCSI-1 standard was adopted, a number of improvements in the SCSI standard were being adopted by manufacturers. As a result, the SCSI standards committee was put to work creating a new SCSI standard. Their work lasted from July 1986 to February 1989, when they sent their formal proposal (ASC X3T9.2) for SCSI-2 to ANSI. A formal adoption of SCSI-2 was not reached until July 1990.

The SCSI-2 standard was quite detailed and addressed a large number of issues within SCSI. One of the more important parts of the SCSI-2 standard was the definition of 18 commands that have to be supported by any device labeled as SCSI-2-compliant. This set of commands, called the *Common Command Set* (CCS) made hooking up devices from various manufacturers less of a nightmare. The CCS also introduced commands to address other devices besides hard drives—including CD-ROM drives, tape drives, and scanners, among others (see ASPI).

SCSI-2 also defined the types of connectors to be used. Before SCSI-2, there was no true standard for SCSI connectors, although a few types became de facto standards. The new SCSI-2 connectors ensured that any two SCSI-2-compliant devices would be able to connect. SCSI-2 also more closely defined terminations.

The areas that create the most confusion with SCSI-2 are the width and speed of the data bus. SCSI-2 defined two optional 16-bit and

32-bit busses called *wide* SCSI, and a new optional 10MHz speed called *fast* SCSI. SCSI-2 devices could now be 8-bit (narrow), 16-bit (wide) or 32-bit (wide); or they could be 5MHz (slow, standard) or 10MHz (fast). Therefore, there are now six *sub-flavors* of SCSI-2 (see Table 9.1). (We'll add SCSI-1 for comparison.)

Table 9.1 Standard SCSI vs. Fast SCSI

SCSI Type/ Bit width	5 MHz (Standard)	10 MHz (FAST)
SCSI-1: 8-bit	5 MB/s	NA
SCSI-2: 8-bit	5 MB/s	10 MB/s
SCSI-2: 16-bit (Wide)	10 MB/s	20 MB/s
SCSI-2: 32-bit (Wide)	20 MB/s	40 MB/s

Even though SCSI-2 defined a 32-bit SCSI bus, it was almost completely ignored by the industry due to high cost and lack of need for such a wide bus. In reality, when someone says *wide* SCSI, they are talking about 16-bit wide.

Fast SCSI-2 transfers data in FAST SYNCHRONOUS mode, meaning that the SCSI device being talked to (the *Target*) does not have to acknowledge (*Ack*) every individual request (*Req*) for data from the host adapter (the *Initiator)*. This allows for a doubling of transfer speed from approximately 5M/s to 10M/s. However, experience has shown that external fast SCSI devices will rarely provide *fast* performance unless the cable provides proper shielding and electrical impedance or load. Cables that do provide proper shielding and load are generally a bit more expensive, but are required to achieve true *fast* performance.

SCSI-1 devices were all *single ended.* A single ended device is one that communicates through only one wire per bit of information. This one wire is measured or referenced against the common ground provided by the metal chassis and in turn by the power supply of the system. Noise is usually spread through either the electrical power cables or the data cable, and is called *common-mode noise.* A single ended device is vulnerable to common-mode noise because it has no way of telling the difference between valid data and noise. When noise invades the data stream, the devices must re-send the data. The amount of noise generated grows dramatically over the length of the SCSI cable, creating significant limitations to the total length of the SCSI chain, up to only about six meters, depending on the type of SCSI.

To allow much longer SCSI chains, SCSI-2 offers an optional solution with *differential ended* devices. These devices employ two wires per bit of data—one wire for data and one for the inverse of this data. The inverse signal now takes the place of the ground wire in the single-ended cable. By taking the difference of the two signals, the device is able to reject the common-mode noise in the data stream. This allows for much longer SCSI chains—up to 25 meters.

There is no obvious difference between single ended and differential SCSI devices. The connectors and cabling look identical between the two types. This is a bit of a problem because under no circumstances should you try to connect single ended and differential ended devices on the same SCSI chain. At the very least, you will probably fry the single ended device, and if the differential ended device lacks a security circuit to detect your mistake, you will probably smoke it as well.

Don't panic! Although differential SCSI devices exist, they are rare. Single ended SCSI still reigns. The makers of differential SCSI know the danger and will clearly label their devices to show that they are differential.

There is a new type of differential SCSI that is becoming quite popular: *Low-Voltage Differential* SCSI (LVD). LVD uses less power and is compatible with existing single ended SCSI. LVD devices can sense the type of SCSI and then work accordingly. If you plug an LVD device into a single ended chain, it will act as a single ended device. If you plug an LVD device into LVD, it will run as LVD. LVD SCSI chains can be up to 12 meters in length. The safety, ease-of-use, and low cost of LVD is making it a technology that is becoming quite popular in higher-end PCs and servers.

Beyond SCSI-2

SCSI technology has not stood still since the adoption of SCSI-2. Manufacturers have developed significant improvements in SCSI-2, particularly in increased speeds and easier configuration. As there is yet no standard to reflect these improvements, we currently live in a hodge-podge of confusing, proprietary terms to show these improvements. We hear terms like *Ultra*, *Ultra-Wide*, *Ultra2*, and *SCSI-3*. Let's take a minute to understand these terms.

There is no standard beyond SCSI-2. The SCSI committees are working on a new standard called *SCSI-3* that will hopefully be adopted soon. The SCSI-3 standard is actually a group of standards, each defining a certain aspect of an improvement over SCSI-2. Any SCSI device that takes advantage of any of these options will be able to call itself SCSI-3. Many SCSI devices already do some SCSI-3 functions; as a result, there are already quite a few SCSI devices available that call themselves *SCSI-3*. A more accurate term might be *Upcoming SCSI-3*.

One of the more popular aspects of SCSI-3, and one that has already been widely adopted, is the capability for wide SCSI to control up to 16 devices on one chain. Each device gets a number from 0 to 15, as opposed to just 0 through 7. This capability is often erroneously thought to be part of SCSI-2, because wide, 16-device control came out very quickly after the adoption of the SCSI-2 standard.

The term *Ultra* or FAST-20 is used by many SCSI component manufacturers to define a high-speed 20MHz bus speed. *Ultra2* or FAST-40 defines 40MHz and *Ultra3* or FAST-80 defines an 80MHz bus speed. There is still narrow and wide SCSI (look at the differences in Table 9.2).

Table 9.2 Narrow SCSI vs. Wide SCSI

SCSI Type/Bit width	8-bit (narrow)	16-bit (wide)
Ultra SCSI (FAST20)	20 MB/s	40 MB/s
Ultra2 SCSI (FAST40)	40 MB/s	80 MB/s
Ultra3 SCSI (FAST80)	80 MB/s	160 MB/s

Ultra SCSI is not a true ANSI standard. It has been broadly accepted by all manufacturers, however, and is therefore a de facto standard. Not all of these Ultra speeds are yet available—for example, Ultra3 is not yet being produced. All speeds of Ultra SCSI will be incorporated into the SCSI-3 standard.

The upcoming SCSI-3 standard will also include optional *hot swap* capabilities. To hot swap means to be able to unplug a drive from the SCSI chain without rebooting/resetting the chain. Hot swap is extremely helpful in laptops and in servers. Hot swapping is already becoming popular for high-end SCSI drives.

The last and most interesting function under the SCSI-3 standard is serial SCSI. SCSI as we know it is a parallel interface. The SCSI bus consists of 8 or 16 parallel wires passing data. Serial SCSI means to transfer SCSI commands over a single wire—classic serial communications. There are three main types of serial SCSI cabling (see Table 9.3): IEEE 1394 (Firewire), Fiber channel, and *Serial Storage Architecture* (SSA). These new cabling systems are vying for predominance in the SCSI market, with fiber channel currently seeming to be the winner (although IEEE 1394 is also quite popular). SSA is not as widely used. These cabling systems offer long cable runs, hot swapping, and low cost, which may make them quite popular. Serial cabling systems will also allow many more devices on one chain. Currently, they are most commonly seen in servers and some laptops.

Table 9.3 Upcoming cabling standards

Cabling	Speed	Number Devices	Max bus length
SSA	Up to 80 MB/s	128	25 Meters
IEEE 1394	Up to 50 MB/s	63	72 Meters
Fiber Channel	Up to 400 MB/s	126	10 Kilometers

The SCSI-3 standards, or at least some of them, are now in the final stages of adoption.

Bus Mastering

Whenever we scan an image or seek a sector on a hard drive on a non-SCSI (e.g., IDE) system, we utilize the CPU to transfer data for as long as it takes to complete the operation. SCSI allows devices to perform these functions independently by providing a way for devices to disconnect through the SCSI bus. This allows other devices an opportunity to perform their tasks faster, with less waiting. When backing up a hard drive to a tape drive in the typical non-SCSI PC, the CPU requests data from the hard drive, loads the data into its registers, and then writes the information out to the tape drive where the data is finally stored. During this entire process, which can last for hours, the CPU must still try to handle your requests to run MS OFFICE.

With a SCSI-equipped PC, however, the process is more efficient. The tape drive (SCSI) and the hard drive (SCSI) will usually communicate through the same host adapter. In this case, the host adapter will remain in the circuit only long enough to arbitrate the connection between the hard drive and the tape unit. Once the data transfer is established, the host adapter will drop off and let the hard drive and tape unit communicate directly to each other while the backup is running. Once the backup is finished or if the user must interrupt the operation, the drives will re-establish their presence on the SCSI chain. The great beauty of this lies in the lack of CPU and expansion bus utilization. Once the connection is made, the two devices are for all intents and purposes no longer on the PC and are not consuming any system resources.

The downside to bus mastering devices is that they can seriously confuse a disk-caching program such as DOS' SMARTDRV. Bus mastering SCSI can change the address of data that may also be held in the cache, resulting in the disk cache causing really horrible corruption to your drive. Whenever you install a new SCSI device to a PC, check the status of your SMARTDRV. At a `C: >` prompt, type:

```
SMARTDRV /S
```

You will see the following:

```
Microsoft SMARTDrive Disk Cache version 5.0
Copyright 1991,1993 Microsoft Corp.

Room for 256 elements of 8,192 bytes each
There have been 44 cache hits
and 15 cache misses

Cache size: 2,097,152 bytes
Cache size while running Windows: 2,097,152 bytes

Disk Caching Status
drive  read cache  write cache  buffering
_______________________________________________
A:          yes          no           no
C:          yes          yes           -
D:          yes          yes          yes
Write behind data will be committed before command prompt
returns.

For help, type "Smartdrv /?"
```

Under buffering, if you see either a – or a *yes*, you need to add the following line to the `CONFIG.SYS` file:

```
DEVICE=C:\DOS\SMARTDRV.EXE /DOUBLE_BUFFER
```

This will allow the disk cache to translate the addresses of the cached data on bus mastered drives. This is only an issue with DOS disk caches! The Windows 3.X VCACHE and Windows 95/98 disk caches work perfectly with bus mastering SCSI.

SCSI Cabling & Connectors

First, there is no such thing as one official SCSI-1, SCSI-2, or Ultra-SCSI type cable. Although certain cables are designed for certain types of SCSI, there is a significant degree of overlap. The cable you need is based on whether the device is internal or external, what types of connectors are available, and the type of SCSI that you are using.

The most common type of SCSI cable is the type *A* cable (see Figure 9.15). This cable has 50 wires and is used for 8-bit data transfers in both the SCSI-1 and SCSI-2 standards. These are used for 8-bit fast SCSI-2 as well.

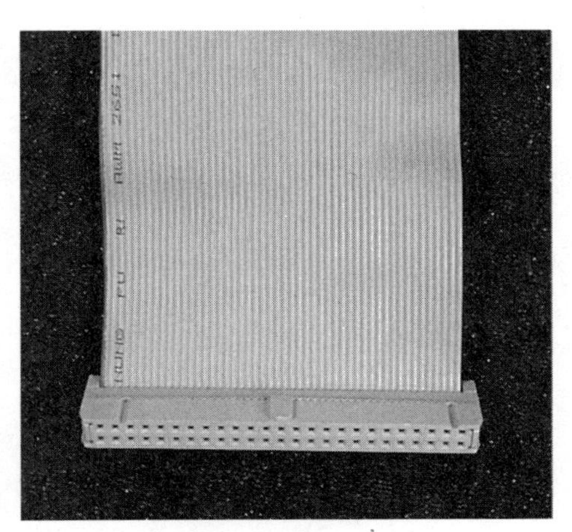

Figure 9.15 SCSI *A* cable.

In the earliest days of SCSI-2, 16-bit data transfers required another cable: the *B* cable. It had 68 wires and was used in parallel with the 50-wire *A* cable. Because the industry was so underwhelmed at the dual-cable concept, the *B* cable quietly and quickly disappeared, to be replaced by the *P* cable (see Figure 9.16). Like its predecessor, this cable also has 68 wires; unlike the *B* cable, the *P* cable is used alone.

Figure 9.16 SCSI *P* cable.

Cable/Bus Lengths

There are strict limits about the length of the SCSI cable/Bus. When we say the cable/Bus, we mean the total distance from one terminator to the other. There are basically five lengths:

SCSI-1 and SCSI-2 (5 MHz) Single-Ended: 6 meters

SCSI-2 and up (10 MHz), Single-Ended, up to 3 devices: 3 meters

SCSI-2 and up (10 MHz), Single-Ended, more than 3 devices: 1.5 meters

High-voltage differential SCSI bus: 25 meters

Low-voltage differential SCSI bus: 12 meters

TYPES OF EXTERNAL CONNECTORS

All External connectors are female on the devices.

50-pin Centronics: Obsolete SCSI-1 (see Figure 9.17)

50-pin HD *D*-type: SCSI-2 (see Figure 9.18)

68-pin HD *D*-type: Wide SCSI-2 (see Figure 9.19)

25-pin standard *D*-type (looks identical to parallel): SCSI-2, most commonly used on Macintosh (see Figure 9.20).

Figure 9.17 50-pin Centronics.

Figure 9.18 50-pin HD *D*-type—SCSI-2.

Figure 9.19 68-pin HD *D*-type—Wide SCSI-2.

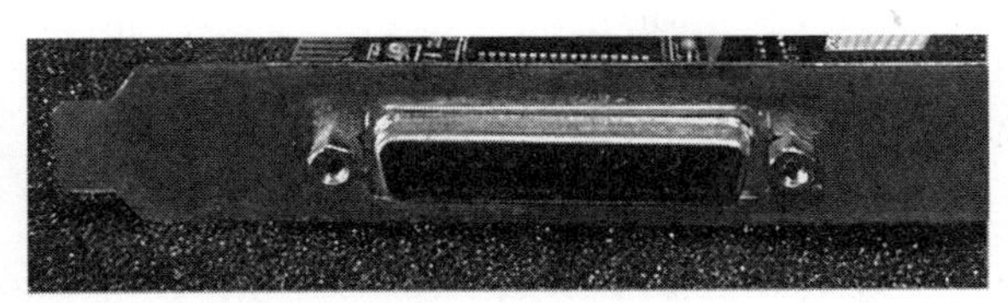

Figure 9.20 25-pin standard *D*-type.

ASPI

Everything within your computer must have *Basic Input/Output Services* (BIOS). BIOS is nothing more than the software that allows the CPU to talk to the rest of the hardware. It can be hardwired into the motherboard (the system BIOS), it can be hardwired into the device (e.g., a ROM chip built into a video card) or it can be a device driver loaded off of the hard drive. The BIOS for SCSI devices can come from any of these sources.

If all of your SCSI devices are hard drives, the ROM chip on the SCSI host adapter provides all of the BIOS needed. A program on the ROM chip runs during the boot process, detecting the SCSI hard drives and initializing the BIOS needed to communicate with them. Unfortunately, SCSI devices can be just about anything, not just hard drives. Although the SCSI scan program will detect devices other than hard drives, it does not know how to talk to them. The ROM chips on SCSI host adapters, with rare exceptions, only know how to talk to hard drives. We will need another source for our BIOS. We will need to load device drivers for our other SCSI devices.

Unfortunately, not all device drivers play well together. Device driver incompatibility plagued early SCSI devices. Sometimes, two device drivers simply could not be made to work together. Machines would lock up; reboot spontaneously; or simply give bizarre, seemingly unrelated errors because of bad device drivers. To solve this problem, a new standard evolved: *Advanced SCSI Programmers Interface* (ASPI).

ASPI mandates a standard way to write BIOS/device drivers for SCSI devices. The beauty of ASPI is that we can install a standardized set of device drivers for all of our SCSI devices. Because they are all ASPI drivers, we can have some confidence that the drivers for our SCSI-removable media drive and our SCSI scanner will work well together. Note, however, that there have been several *flavors* of ASPI. Adaptec's EZ SCSI is an excellent example.

With Adaptec's EZ SCSI, the host adapter requires its own device driver. Additional devices require additional EZ SCSI device drivers. However, some devices can share a single device's drivers. For example, the EZ SCSI driver `ASPIDSK.SYS` supports both removable media drives (e.g., Iomega's ZIP drive) and traditional SCSI hard drives (if the ROM chip on the host adapter has been disabled). The capability to use a single device driver for more than one device makes ASPI products such as EZ SCSI extremely attractive from a memory-management perspective.

Windows 95 has a complete copy of protected mode ASPI drivers built-in. With Windows 95, as long as the physical connections are all correct, an ASPI-compliant device will automatically be recognized by the system.

SHOULD YOU DISABLE THE ROM CHIP?

If you are using ASPI drivers to support SCSI devices and you have an IDE drive to boot from, consider disabling the SCSI host adapter's ROM BIOS. A typical SCSI BIOS takes up about 16K of reserved memory. The EZ SCSI ASPI drivers needed to support SCSI hard drives take up about 15K (9K for the host adapter driver and 6K for the `ASPIDSK.SYS` driver). Although there is only a 1K difference, remember that the same `ASPIDSK.SYS` driver can also support removable media drives such as Iomega's ZIP drive. If you know the device drivers can handle both, why not disable the SCSI ROM BIOS and let the ASPI drivers handle both devices? If all of your SCSI devices are hard drives, there is no real advantage either way. But if you are using ASPI drivers to support your hard drives, disabling the ROM chip frees up 16K of UMB space in the reserved area.

Remember that you will still need to boot from an IDE drive. Those device drivers have to be stored somewhere other than the boot drive. If you already have an IDE drive in the system, the primary DOS partition on it will already be your drive `C:>`. Because Windows95 and DOS both require that they be booted off of either `A:>` or `C:>`, it will already be your bootable drive. (See Enhanced IDE for a more detailed description of drive-letter assignments under DOS and Windows 95.)

PCI Systems and the ROM BIOS

A special case arises in a minority of PCI systems that have BIOS support for SCSI hard drives. Some systems provide an NCR chipset, which will support a bootable SCSI drive without loading an ASPI device driver or having an active host adapter BIOS. Of course, ASPI drivers would still be required for devices other than hard drives.

SCSI Performance

Which can move more cars more quickly: a 10-lane freeway or a four-lane city street? That sums up the effect of the expansion bus on SCSI performance.

SCSI is a bus mastering device. That is, it takes control of the expansion bus to transfer data from one device into memory or from one device to another device that is not on the SCSI host adapter. This is marvelous because it frees up the CPU to do more important things, like refresh our screen saver.

Unfortunately, if you plug a SCSI host adapter into an ISA slot, the best transfer speed you can obtain is approximately 5 MB/s. Before you panic, remember that the most advertised hard drive speeds are actually for burst mode between the on-board disk cache and the host adapter, not internally to the hard drive itself. Most hard drives can only sustain a transfer of between 2.5–5.5 MB/s.

But if you really want to see things fly, you will need to consider an adapter for either the EISA, the VLB, or the PCI busses. These busses can support transfers at up to 33 MB/s. Be aware that some PCI motherboards are available with NCR SCSI Device Management System support in the motherboard BIOS. This means you might be able to purchase a slightly cheaper host adapter that does not contain an on-board BIOS. This will allow you to install support for your SCSI devices directly from the motherboard. (But you will still need to load an ASPI driver for the other SCSI devices!)

Compatibility among Flavors of SCSI

Although it might seem unlikely that the various flavors of SCSI would be able to communicate through the same host adapter, that is exactly the case. Each device communicates at the maximum speed supported by that device.

Compatibility with IDE and Other Standards

The most important point to remember when it comes to compatibility is that it works. You can mix IDE and SCSI. However, if you have an IDE drive present on your system, it will be the boot drive. All IDE drives installed in the system BIOS will be assigned logical drive letters first.

There are a few permutations to this scenario and this is because of EIDE. Briefly, EIDE allows support for up to four hard drives: two on the primary 40-pin IDE connection and two on the secondary connection. Device driver support for at least the two primary hard drives will be present in the ROM BIOS. Support for the two secondary drives can be present in the ROM BIOS. You may need a device driver in `CONFIG.SYS` to enable access to the secondary port hard drives.

This will combine to give us at least two possible outcomes: 1) With BIOS support for the secondary IDE connection, the IDE drives will get drive letters before any SCSI drives. 2) If the system BIOS only provides support for the primary IDE port, use of the secondary chain requires a device driver.

With BIOS support for only the primary IDE port and a device driver required for the secondary port as well as the device driver, (resident either in an onboard BIOS or a program file, for the SCSI drives) the assigned drive letters will vary, according to the device driver load order in `CONFIG.SYS`.

Repair/Troubleshooting

SCSI problems can be reduced to certain categories. These categories overlap and not all categories apply to every problem.

POWER AND CONNECTIVITY

In any PC repair scenario, confirm connectivity and power before going any further. Nothing will work if the devices do not have power and if they cannot access the external data bus and the address bus. Fortunately, most SCSI host adapters provide an excellent utility for determining whether or not the devices are properly powered and connected: the SCSI Scan. As the host adapter initializes (provided that the host adapter's BIOS is active), a list of all of the devices detected by the host adapter will be displayed on the screen. If one or more of your devices fails to appear, power and/or connectivity are the most likely problems. If the devices are not properly hooked up, they will not respond to the *identify yourself* commands sent out by the host adapter.

Power

What kinds of power problems could prevent a device from showing up? Usually nothing more exotic than forgetting to plug it in. Make sure that both internal and external devices have power. Most SCSI devices, especially external ones, require power in order to provide termination, and all of them require power for operation.

Connectivity

Make sure that the devices are properly installed. Is the termination set properly (one terminator at each end of the chain and none in between)? Does each device have its own unique SCSI ID? Are the cables seated correctly and firmly? To double-check settings for termination and SCSI IDs, documentation will usually be needed.

BOOT FIRMWARE

If you do not see a SCSI scan during the boot process and before you see `Starting DOS` or `Starting Windows 95`, check to make sure that the ROM BIOS on the host adapter has not been disabled. In addition, other CMOS and SCSI ROM BIOS settings can cause problems. Is the ROM chip on the SCSI host adapter enabled or disabled? What IRQ, DMA, and I/O address is the card using? If you see an `HDD controller failure` or `HDD failure` message, is the CMOS set up to look for an IDE drive that is not present in the system?

MEMORY CHIPS

Problems with memory chips will usually cause problems with all of the devices in a PC, not just the SCSI devices. Diagnose problems carefully. Does the symptom, whatever it happens to be, crop up only when using SCSI devices or does it happen consistently with every device?

STORAGE

SCSI hard drives can have the same types of problems as any other hard drive. If you are using DOS/Windows 95, the partitions and FAT file system are no different than with IDE drives. In fact, except for the SCSI interface itself, IDE and SCSI drives are virtually identical. For the most part, the same repair and maintenance techniques apply. At a bare minimum, SCANDISK and DEFRAG should be run on a regular basis. For any error that ends in `Abort, Retry, Fail` or `Abort, Retry, Fail, Ignore`, use a program such as Norton's Disk Doctor or its equivalent. Use the `SYS` command and the `FDISK /MBR` command for boot problems. Treat hard drive errors the same way you treat IDE hard drive errors.

I/O

IRQ, DMA, and I/O address problems usually manifest themselves fairly quickly. Remember that if any of the IRQ, DMA, or I/O address settings are stored in a CMOS or EEPROM chip, power surges can reset them to their default settings. SCSI host adapters often store their settings in EEPROM chips. Do not assume that just because the user has not changed any settings, they have not changed. Many SCSI host adapters default to IRQ 3, which would cause an IRQ lockup with any device using COM 2 (often a modem or mouse).

Proper documentation of these settings for all of your devices is the best way to avoid problems. Without existing documentation, create your own. Use the F8 key to step through CONFIG.SYS and AUTOEXEC.BAT, one line at a time. Many device drivers report their settings as they load. Look at jumper settings. Use a PDI card or Discovery card to check for IRQ and DMA usage.

DEVICE DRIVERS

Do you have SCSI devices other than hard drives? They will require a device driver. Remember that some device drivers do not work well together. How do you determine if you have a conflict between two device drivers? Try loading only the device drivers for the SCSI devices. Does the symptom still occur? If not, then another device driver is causing the problem. Use the F8 key to determine which one. Once you know which device drivers are incompatible, you have several options. Look in the manuals or readme files of both devices. Your problem might be a known one with a known solution. If the device driver is an executable, try running it with the /? option, which will usually show you a variety of command-line switches for the device driver (e.g., MOUSE.EXE /?). Try a variety of switches and see if any of them solve the problem. If not, attempt to find an updated driver for one or both of the devices. If none of those solutions fix the problem, you may be forced to choose between the devices or go to a multiple boot configuration.

MEMORY MANAGEMENT

Remember that SCSI host adapters typically have their own ROM chips. Do not forget to put the appropriate X= statements in your EMM386.EXE line in CONFIG.SYS, and place the appropriate EMMEXCLUDE= statement in your SYSTEM.INI file. A forgotten exclude statement often explains those *every now and then I lock up* problems.

Cost/Benefit

SCSI is great for:

- file servers
- workstations (both graphical and audio)
- multi-tasking systems
- any system moving large amounts of data among peripheral devices

- any system with a large number of peripherals
- any system requiring fault tolerance (mostly fileservers)

Because the initial cost of SCSI is higher and the devices themselves are also more expensive, there are some questions to be answered to determine the need for SCSI:

1) Is this a graphics/CAD workstation?
2) Is this a network fileserver?
3) Is this a standalone machine frequently running multi-tasking applications?

If the answer is yes to any of these questions, it will probably be worth the money to invest in a SCSI-based expansion bus.

There are two reasons for this. First, a data-intensive application such as CAD/CAM design software or any other data-intensive application will benefit by the increased data throughput available with SCSI devices, especially hard drives and scanners. Second, SCSI is what is called a bus-mastering device. In a multi-tasking environment, this leaves the CPU free to handle more important things such as your game of Solitaire or updating the Excel spreadsheet.

For systems supporting a data-intensive peripheral such as a full page 24-bit color scanner or a 4 GB digital audiotape backup drive, a Bernoulli removable media disk drive, or multiple CD-ROM drives, SCSI is the best solution.

SCSI VS. EIDE

SCSI hard drives no longer hold as large an advantage over IDE devices as they once did. For many years, SCSI hard drives were the only large hard drives available. Now, EIDE drives are available that are pushing into the sizes that once belonged only to SCSI drives. Data throughput for EIDE has also increased to be as fast as 33.3MB/s. Although SCSI might support a transfer rate of up to 20MB/s, remember this: except for the chipset on the disk controller card, the IDE and SCSI hard drives are made the same way—the limitation in data transfer speeds comes from the hard drive assembly, not necessarily from the data bus. SCSI, with the potential for up to seven hard drives, also made sense if the machine needed a large number of hard drives. Now that Enhanced IDE can support up to four devices, including CD-ROMs and other mass-storage devices, the SCSI advantage in the number of devices allowed has also shrunk.

Although SCSI's advantages in some areas are not as pronounced as they once were, it still possesses a number of advantages that justify its higher cost. The bus-mastering capability of SCSI devices make it ideal for data-intensive operations such as disk mirroring (see RAID, following). In addition, for external devices that are not hard drives, SCSI remains the high-performance interface of choice.

RAID

A way to ensure constant access to critical data is through the use of disk arrays. Because the SCSI bus uses a bus mastering DMA transfer, this echo process does not impose additional overhead to the CPU. If, for example, IDE were to be used in this way, the system would run visibly slower because IDE drives use *Programmed Input/Output* (PIO) transfer modes that require CPU intervention.

RAID 0 provides the option to combine two or more disks into one big logical drive through a process called *striping*. This process divides the data into 32-KB blocks, which are then divided between the two disks. This can lead to better performance because the mechanical access times are reduced.

RAID 1 is also called disk mirroring. Disk mirroring provides a computer with instant on-line backups by echoing data writes to a second hard disk through a common host adapter. If the primary hard drive fails, the system will automatically transfer all reads and writes to the second drive. This transfer is transparent to the user and provides an excellent means of ensuring minimal downtime for mission-critical applications. Disk mirroring will typically slow down system performance because all disks must acknowledge write operations.

RAID 2 provides a greater degree of error detection by dedicating a drive for error correction information. RAID 2 also requires ECC error correction on all drives.

RAID 3 and 4 use at least two data drives and a dedicated ECC data drive. Again, data is striped between the drives with RAID 4, using larger data blocks or stripes, showing a slight performance gain over RAID 3. Neither option is the best because for every write operation, the ECC data must be written to the dedicated ECC drive.

RAID 5 is the better choice among the RAID options because it distributes the ECC data among all of the drives. This also has the side benefit of reducing ECC data redundancy to 25 percent.

RAID 6 is RAID 5 with the added capability of asynchronous and cached data transmission. RAID 6 is the last official level in the

RAID specification, so any vendor advertising additional levels is probably pushing a proprietary RAID implementation.

Other Storage Options

Probably the oldest and most familiar storage device, at least to us old-timers, is the Bernoulli disk. Bernoulli disks get their name from the Bernoulli effect, which states that between a fixed metal plate (the read write head) and a rotating flexible medium (the disk surface), a highly compressed air-cushion will develop. This cushion will maintain a very small distance between the head and the disk, as long as the disk is rotating, or the airflow between the head and the disk is uninterrupted. When the drive is shut down or the airflow is disrupted, the head will jump *away* from the disk surface. This is contrary to what we expect from a hard drive, where the opposite is true and where we get the traumatic term *head crash*. Bernoulli disks are a semi-flexible removable storage medium, ranging from as small as 20MB to 150MB on a disk.

Recently, the hot topic in removable storage are the Iomega ZIP and JAZ drives. The ZIP drive is 100MB in size, with access times not much slower than conventional non-removable hard drives. The JAZ drive also uses removable media, but holds either 540MB, 1GB, or 2GB.

Additional Facts from Adaptec Technical Support Line

- Any Adaptec host adapter ending in the number *2* has a floppy controller.
- Some host adapters, such as the Adaptec AHA-274xAT and the AHA-274xW, can support more than seven SCSI devices.
- When using a SCSI hard drive as the boot device, always set its ID to 0.
- The floppy controller on the SCSI adapter will have a DMA and IRQ conflict with any other floppy controller present in the computer.
- The on-board BIOS should be disabled if the adapter will not be supporting any hard drives.
- There is a possibility that a hard drive set up on one manufacturer's SCSI adapter will not be seen with the same parameters

when moved to another adapter and will require re-partitioning and re-formatting.

- On a system with only a SCSI hard drive, the error message `HDD controller failure` indicates an improper CMOS setting for the SCSI drive. SCSI drives should be set to either *not installed* or SCSI.
- Some host adapters allow boot up from a removable media drive. (AHA-2740/2W)
- Terminationcan be one of three flavors, depending on the type of SCSI chain:
  - Passive
  - Active
  - Forced Perfect Termination

Passive termination resembles a holdover from the dinosaur days of the ST-506. The termination is nothing more than a network of resistors. The resistors are usually small, black, and shiny—resembling very skinny black caterpillars. This type of termination is typically found only on plain old ordinary narrow *8-bit* SCSI devices.

For the quicker Fast/Wide SCSI we have to maintain a tighter tolerance on the voltage and impedance of the SCSI chain. To do this we must use active termination, which uses voltage regulators instead of resistors.

Forced Perfect Termination (FPT) also maintains the correct voltage level on the bus, but does so to a finer tolerance by using diodes. These diodes function like the resistors in the passive termination, with one exception: a diode has a lower resistance in one direction or orientation, than it does in the other. This is called polarity. The higher resistance in one direction helps to block current flow backward along the data cable much better than a plain resistor.

CHAPTER 10

Video

In this chapter we will:

- Understand the different components that make video work
- Explain refresh rates and the effect on monitors
- Clarify the concept of resolution
- Show basic monitor fixes

Video—Complex Choices

When the first IBM PC arrived, your choice of monitors was simple. You could choose which color—green or amber text—that was it. Today, our choices are not so simple. We need to decipher such things as dot pitch, resolution, convergence, refresh, interlaced vs. non-interlaced, multi-synch, pixels, color depth, and energy-saving features. And what about repairing a broken monitor?

This chapter will explain the basics of how video cards and monitors work. We will talk about what can be repaired and what requires a more specialized expertise to address. Make no mistake—the interior of a monitor might appear to be similar to the interior of a PC because of the printed circuit boards and related components. But that is precisely where the similarity ends. No PC has voltages exceeding 15,000–30,000 volts, but most monitors do. So let's get one thing perfectly clear: *Opening up a working monitor can be deadly!*

Even when power has been disconnected, certain components will retain a substantial voltage for an extended period of time. You can inadvertently short one of these components and fry yourself. Plus, monitors emit x-ray radiation. So there are certain aspects of monitor repair that we don't do, but we will show you how to address *safely* those problems that you can fix.

Video consists of two devices that work as a team to get a picture in front of you: the *video card,* often called the *display adapter,* and the *monitor* (see Figure 10.1). The video card is sort of like two devices on one card. One device takes commands from the computer and updates its own on-board RAM. The other device scans the RAM and sends the data to the monitor.

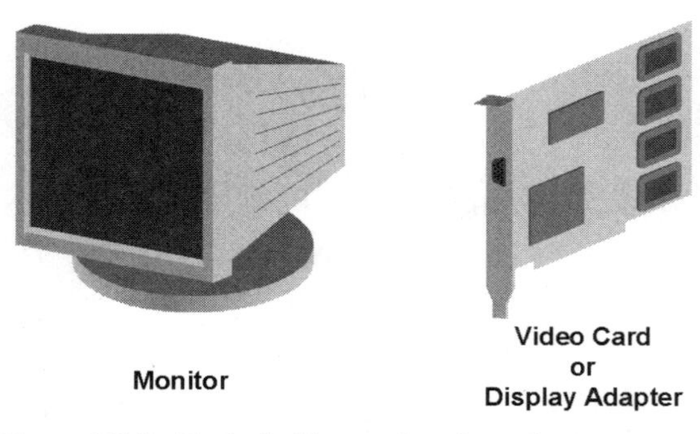

Figure 10.1 Typical video card and monitor.

Separate these two devices for a moment and look at them individually. Having done that, we will bring them back together as a team and understand the many nuances that make video so challenging.

Video Monitor Components

Before we can understand monitors, we need to take a moment to understand certain common elements of the monitor itself.

CRT

All monitors have a main vacuum tube called a *Cathode Ray Tube*, or CRT. One end of this tube is a very slender cylinder that contains three electron guns (see Figure 10.2). The fatter, wide end of the CRT is the display screen with a phosphor coating. When power is applied to one or more of the *electron guns*, a stream of electrons shoots outward toward the display end of the CRT (see Figure 10.3). Along the way, this stream is subjected to magnetic fields generated by a ring of electromagnets called a *yoke* that control the point of impact of the electron beam. When the phosphor coating is struck by an electron beam, it releases its energy as visible light. A picture of the electron guns and magnetic yoke assembly is shown as follows.

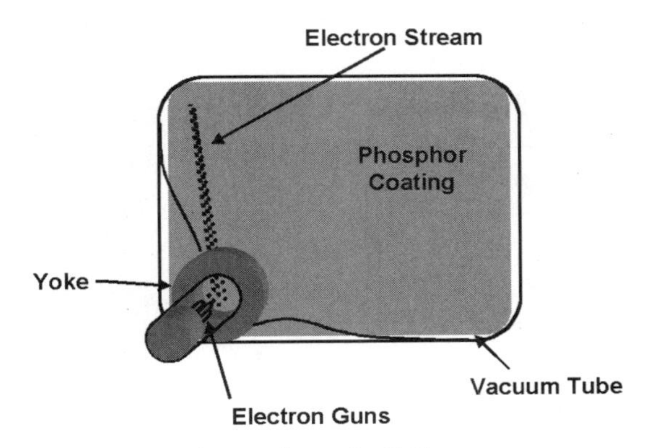

Figure 10.2 Electron beam in CRT.

Figure 10.3 Components of an electron gun.

This phosphorous energy release happens very quickly—too quickly for the human eye/brain connection to see. Fortunately for us, the phosphors on the display screen have a quality called *persistence*. Persistence defines how long the phosphors continue to glow after being struck by the electron beam. Too much persistence, and the image is smeary; too little, and the image appears to flicker (a lot).

REFRESH RATES

Video data is displayed on the monitor as the electron guns make a series of horizontal sweeps across the display, energizing the appropriate areas of the phosphorous coating. The sweeps start at the upper left-hand corner of the monitor and move across and down to the lower right-hand corner. The screen is *painted* only in one direction, and then the electron gun turns off as it retraces across the screen, ready for the next sweep (see Figure 10.4). These sweeps are called *raster lines*.

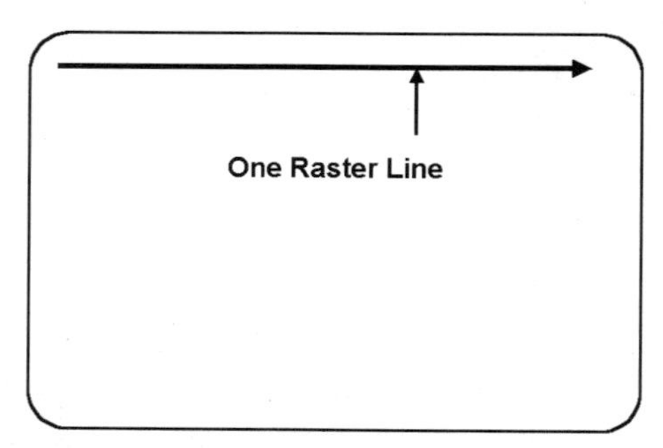

Figure 10.4 Screen traces on monitor.

The speed at which the electron beam runs across the screen is known as the *Horizontal Refresh Rate* (HRR) (see Figure 10.5).

The monitor draws a number of lines across the screen, eventually covering the screen with glowing phosphors. The number of lines is not fixed, unlike television screens, which all have a fixed number of lines. After the guns reach the lower-right corner of the screen, they are all turned off and pointed back to the upper-left hand part of the monitor. The amount of time that it takes to draw the entire screen and get the electron gun back up to the upper-left hand corner is called the *Vertical Refresh Rate* (VRR) (see Figure 10.6).

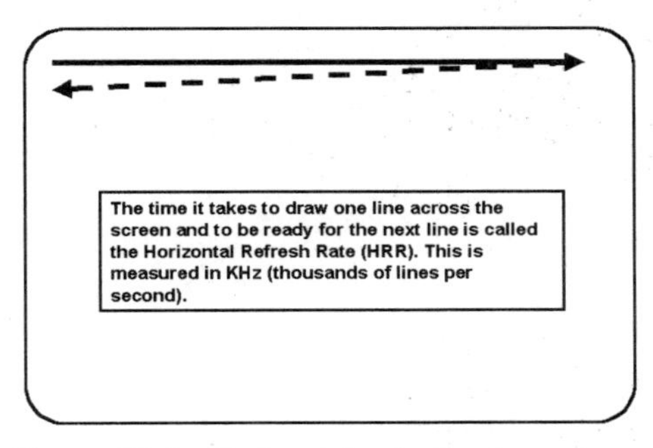

Figure 10.5 Horizontal refresh rate.

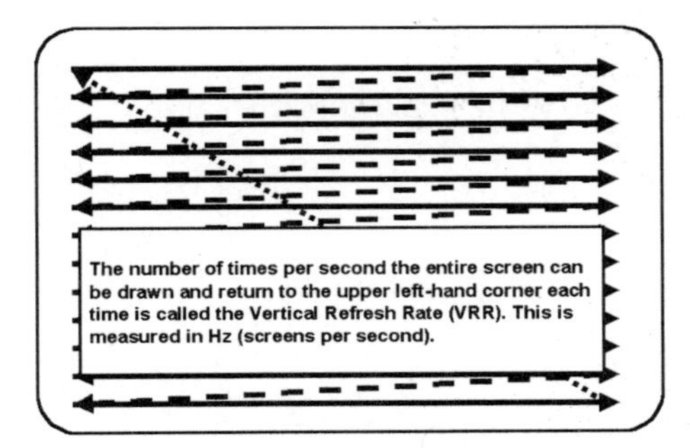

Figure 10.6 Vertical refresh rate.

The action of the beam across the phosphors is called *sweeping*. The number of times per second the electron beam sweeps across the phosphors is called the *refresh* rate. Too low a refresh rate results in a noticeable flicker, which can cause eyestrain and headaches for the user. Setting a refresh rate too high can cause a definite distortion of the screen image, and can damage or destroy the circuitry of the monitor. Up until the mid-1980s, monitors were limited to a fixed number of refresh rates, which had to be changed manually by the user. Around 1986, NEC introduced the first monitor to support automatic selection of multiple refresh rates. This type of monitor is called a *multiple frequency* monitor. NEC coined the term *multi-sync* (see multiple frequency) to describe its line of multiple frequency monitors. Multi-sync now means any monitor that can handle multiple refresh rates. Virtually all monitors used on PCs today are multi-sync.

RESOLUTION

Most monitors have dots of phosphorous or some other light sensitive compound that will glow red, green or blue when an electron gun sweeps over them. Each dot is called a *phosphor* (see Figure 10.7). These phosphors are evenly distributed across the front of the monitor.

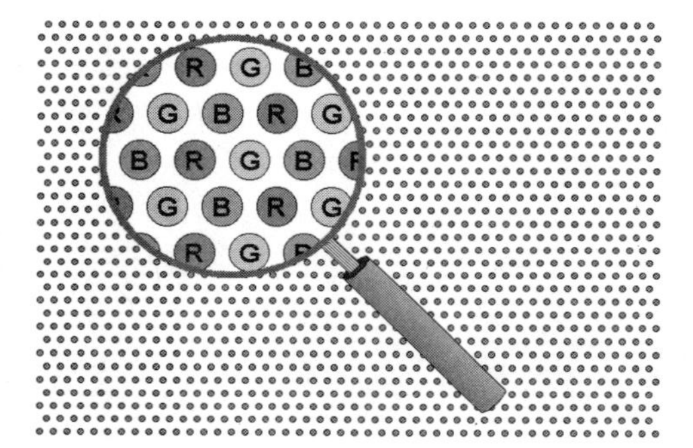

Figure 10.7 Graphic of phosphors.

The CRT has three electron guns: one to hit the red phosphors, one for the blue phosphors, and the last for the green phosphors. It is important to understand that the electron guns do not fire colored light—they only fire electrons at different intensities that then make the phosphors glow. The higher the intensity, the brighter the color. Directly behind the phosphors is the *shadow mask* (see Figure 10.8). The shadow mask is a screen that allows the proper electron gun to light only the proper phosphors. This prevents, for example, the red electron beam from *bleeding over* and lighting neighboring blue and green dots.

The electron guns sweep across the phosphors as a group, turning rapidly on and off as they move across the screen. When the group reaches the end of the screen, it moves to the next line. What is critical to understand here is that the combination of turning the guns on and off and moving them to new lines, creates a *mosaic* that is the image we see on the screen. The *number of times* the guns turn on and off, combined with the *number of lines* drawn on the screen determine the number of mosaic pieces used to create the image. These individual *tiles* are called *pixels,* from the term *picture elements*. You can't hold a pixel in your hand—the pixel is just the area of phosphors that is lit at one instant when the group of guns is turned on. The size of pixels can change, depending on the number of times the group of guns is turned on and off, and the number of lines drawn.

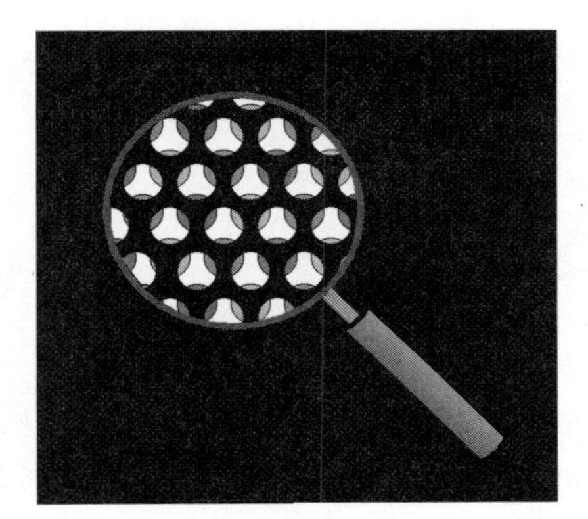

Figure 10.8 Shadow Mask.

Monitor resolution is always shown as (number of pixels across)×(number of pixels vertically). A resolution of 640×480 indicates a horizontal resolution of 640 pixels and a vertical resolution of 480 pixels. If we multiply the values together we can see how many pixels will be on each screen: 640×480 = 307,200 pixels/screen. An example of resolution affecting the pixel size is shown in Figure 10.9.

Some common resolutions are 640×480, 800×600, 1024×768, 1280×1024, and 1600×1200. Notice that these resolutions match a 4-to-3 ratio. Most monitors are shaped like television screens with a 4-to-3 width to height size. So most resolutions are designed to match—or at least be close to—that shape. They don't have to have a 4-to-3 resolution ratio. It would be trivial to make a monitor with any ratio and have a resolution ratio to match it.

The last important issue is to determine the maximum possible resolution for a monitor. In other words, how small can we make one pixel? Well, the answer lies in the phosphors. A pixel must be made up of at least one red, one green, and one blue phosphor to make any color, right? So the smallest possible pixel will be one group of red, green, and blue phosphors. This group is called a *triad* (see Figure 10.10).

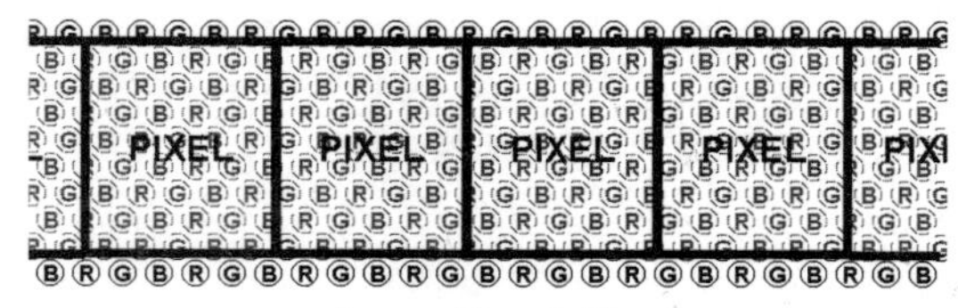

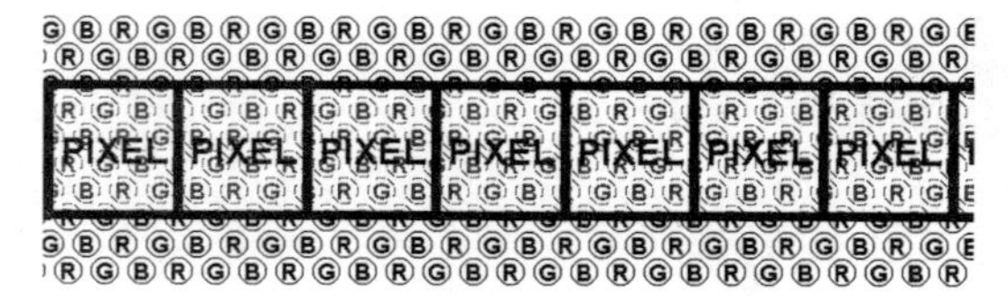

Figure 10.9 Resolution vs. pixel size.

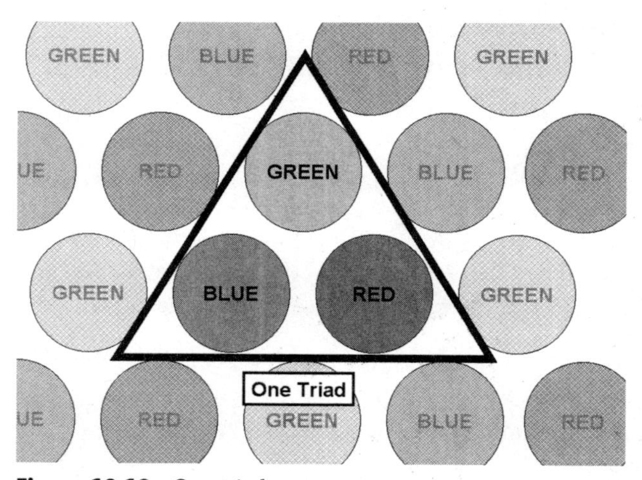

Figure 10.10 One triad.

To review:

Each discrete dot of phosphorus is called a *phosphor*.

Each triangle of three phosphors (one red, one green, one blue) is called a *triad*.

Each group of dots that is distinctly painted as the electron beam sweeps across the screen is called a *pixel.* Higher resolutions sweep a narrower beam with more pixels per row, lower resolutions sweep a wider beam with fewer pixels per row.

As shown previously, the *Horizontal Refresh Rate* (HRR) defines the speed at which the monitor can draw one line on the screen, while the *Vertical Refresh Rate* (VRR) defines how many times per second the entire screen is redrawn. These values relate to the number of vertical resolution lines as follows:

NOTE
HRR = (VRR)×(# of lines)

or

(# of lines) = (HRR) / (VRR)

Given the HRR and VRR, we can determine the maximum number of lines of resolution that a monitor can support.

Example #1: at a HRR of 31.5 KHz (KHz = kilohertz = thousands of cycles/second) and a VRR of 72Hz, what would be the maximum number of lines on the screen? (Could we support 640×480?)

Answer: Take 31.5KHz and divide it by 72Hz. 31,500/72 = 437 lines. So no, with a HRR of only 31.5KHz, we would either have to reduce the resolution, or reduce the VRR and put up with increased screen flicker

By reducing the VRR to 60Hz, our formula would be 31,500/60 = 525 lines. Now our monitor could support 640x480 resolution.

Example #2: Alternately, we could increase the HRR from 31.5 KHz to a value that would allow 480 lines at a VRR of 72 Hz. If we used a HRR of 37.9 KHz and divided it by 72, we would have a maximum line value of 526, which would allow us to use 640×480 resolution.

DOT PITCH

The resolution of a monitor is defined by the maximum amount of detail that the monitor can render. This resolution is ultimately limited by the dot pitch of the monitor. The dot pitch defines the diagonal distance between phosphorous dots of the same color and is measured in millimeters (millimetres if you are European). Because a lower dot pitch means more dots on the screen, a lower number will usually produce a sharper, more defined image (see Figure 10.11). Dot pitch works in tandem with the maximum number of lines that the monitor can support to determine the greatest working resolution of the monitor. It might be possible to place an image at 1600×1200 on a 15-inch monitor with a dot pitch of .31mm, but it would not be very readable.

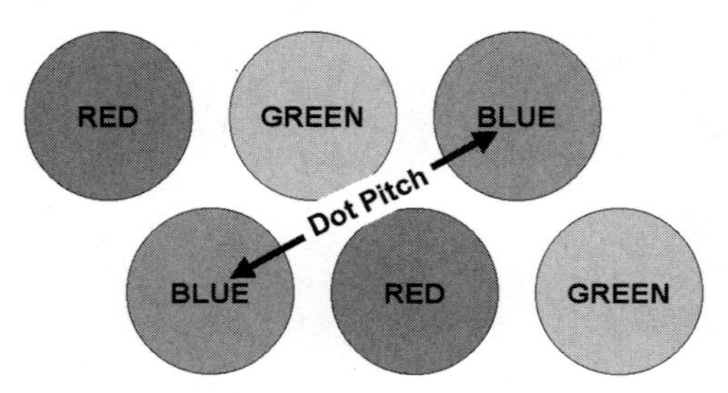

Figure 10.11 Measuring dot pitch.

The dot pitch can range from as high as .39mm to as low as .25mm. For most Windows-based applications on a 15-inch monitor, .31mm is the maximum usable pitch. For most CAD/CAM applications, the maximum pitch is around .26–.28mm. Note: when comparing advertised prices, make a note of the monitors' dot pitch in the ad. Watch out for monitors, usually the lowest-priced ones, that have an unacceptably high .39mm dot pitch. By comparison, a mid-price television has a dot pitch around .35mm.

INTERLACING

To keep costs down, some low-end monitors produce interlaced images. This means that the monitor will sweep or refresh alternate lines of pixels on the display. In other words, it takes two sweeps through the screen to make one image (see Figure 10.12). In the first pass, the monitor covers all the odd lines; on the next pass, the evens are covered. Interlacing allows a low-end monitor to support faster refresh rates by giving it twice as much time to make a screen. But interlacing depends on the ability of the eye and brain to combine the two separate sets of lines into one stable image. Interlacing is another quick way to eyestrain and headaches and is to be avoided.

Figure 10.12 Interlacing.

BANDWIDTH

Bandwidth is given in *megahertz* (MHz) and is the maximum number of times the electron gun can be turned on and off—in essence, how fast the monitor can put an image on the screen. Megahertz is millions of cycles per second and is used because the number of on and off cycles is so large. A typical value for a high-resolution 17-inch color monitor would be around 100MHz. This means that the electron beam can be turned on and off 100 million times per second.

The value for a monitor's bandwidth will determine the maximum vertical refresh rate, as follows:

> **NOTE**
> **Max. VRR = (Band width) / (pixels per page)**

For example:

What is the maximum VRR that a 17-inch monitor with bandwidth of 100MHz and a resolution of 1024×768 can support?

Answer:

Max. VRR = (100,000,000) / (1024 * 768) = 127 Hz

If the video card can go that high.

At a resolution of 1200×1024 the vertical refresh would be

100,000,000/(1200 * 1024) = 81 Hz

If we had a monitor with a bandwidth of only 75MHz, the maximum VRR at a 1200x1024 resolution would be only 61Hz.

POWER CONSERVATION

Approximately one-half of the power required to run a desktop PC is consumed by the monitor. Monitors that meet *the Video Electronics Standards Association* (VESA) specification for *Display Power-Management Signaling* (DPMS) can reduce monitor power consumption by roughly 75 percent. This is accomplished by reducing or eliminating the signals sent by the video card to the monitor during idle periods. By eliminating these pulses, the monitor will essentially be catnapping. The advantages over simply shutting the monitor off completely are apparent in the time it takes to restore the display. A typical monitor consumes in the neighborhood of 100 watts. During a catnap or power down mode, the energy consumption is reduced to below 25 watts, while allowing the screen to return to use in less than 10 seconds. Full shutoff is accomplished by eliminating all clocking pulses to the monitor. Although this reduces power consumption to below 15 watts, it will require anywhere from 15 to 30 seconds to restore a usable display.

The table on the facing page shows the various DPMS options.

Turning off the monitor with the power switch is the most basic form of power management. The downside to this is the wear and tear on the CRT. The CRT is the most expensive component of a monitor and one of the most damaging things to a CRT is to turn it on and off frequently. When using a non-DPMS monitor or video card, it is best to turn a monitor on once during the day, and then turn it off only when you are finished for the day. This on-off cycle must be balanced against the life of the CRT display phosphors. The typical monitor will lose about half its original brightness after roughly 10,000–15,000 hours of display time. Leaving the monitor on all the time will bring a noticeable decrease in brightness in just over a year (8,766 hours). The only way around this would be to enable the DPMS features of the monitor or take care to turn off the monitor.

Some monitors employ a form of power management known as screen blanking. Once the video signal from the video card ceases or the video cable comes loose, the monitor will go into suspend mode. Technically speaking, this is not a DPMS mode, but it still reduces wear on the CRT while saving power. Before panicking over a *dead* display, make sure the cable is secure on both ends.

Monitor Status	Horz Signal	Vert Signal	Display State	DPMS Requirement	Power Savings	Recovery Time
On	Pulses	Pulses	Active	Mandatory	None	N/A
Stand-By	No Pulses	Pulses	Inactive	Optional	Fair	Short
Suspend	Pulses	No Pulses	Inactive	Mandatory	Good	Long
Off	No Pulses	No Pulses	Inactive	Mandatory	Excellent	Longest

ADJUSTING THE IMAGE

Monitor adjustments will range from the simplest (brightness and contrast) to the more sophisticated (pin cushioning and trapezoidal adjustments). For anything more than a simple gross adjustment of image appearance, it will be necessary to have a program to produce an image suitable for calibrating the monitor.

An example of a calibration image is shown in Figure 10.13.

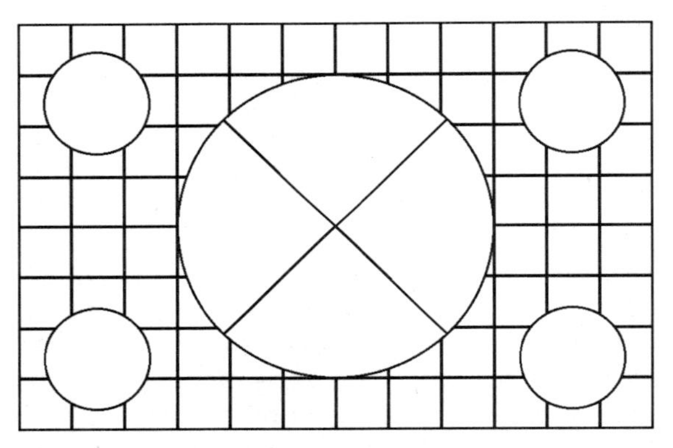

Figure 10.13 Example of aspect ratio calibration screen.

This particular image would be used to adjust the aspect ratio of the display. An image with an improper aspect would display the circles as ovals and the squares as rectangles. Usually the only adjustment possible for the user is the height and width controls on the exterior of the monitor. Additional finer adjustments require a trip inside the monitor.

As shipped, most monitors do not produce an image out to the limits of the screen because of poor convergence at the outer display edges. *Convergence* defines how closely the three colors can converge at a single point on the display. At the point of convergence, the three colors will combine to form a single white dot. With misconvergence, there will be a noticeable halo of one or more colors around the outside of the white point (see Figure 10.14). The farther away from the center of the screen, the more likely the chance for misconvergence. Low-end monitors are especially susceptible to this problem. Although adjusting the convergence of a monitor is not difficult, it does require getting inside the monitor case and having a copy of the schematic showing the location of the variable resistors to adjust. For this reason, it is a good idea to leave this adjustment to a trained specialist.

Figure 10.14 Example of misconvergence.

Today's monitors will have a large number of adjustments (see Figure 10.15). These adjustments can be individual knobs or in this case, an *Up, Down, Minus,* and *Plus,* which manipulate this pop-up menu on the screen. The effect of each control is obvious and straightforward, and with the possible exception of the Keystone and Pincushion controls, will be found on almost all 15-inch color monitors today. Many 15-inch and virtually all 17-inch monitors will offer the Pincushion and Keystone adjustments. These two adjustments are often necessary when using higher resolutions combined with higher refresh rates. A higher refresh rate can tend to pinch an image in the middle. These two controls work in tandem to allow the user to *square up* the image properly.

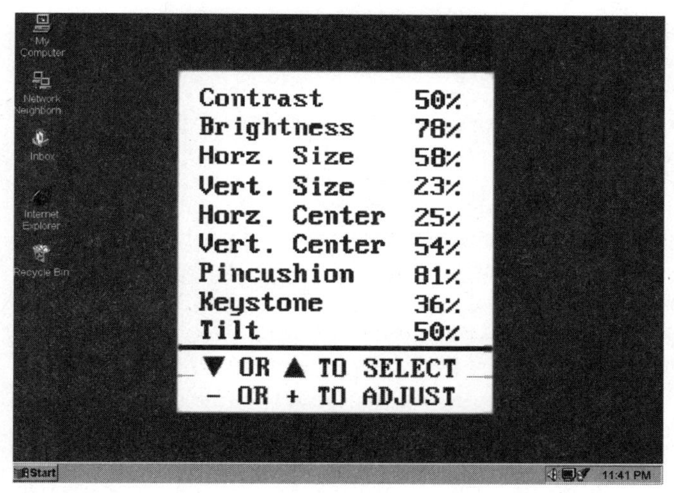

Figure 10.15 Common user controls on pop-up menu.

One other feature of 17-inch and larger monitors is the *Degaussing* button. When the degaussing circuit is used, an alternating current is sent through a coil of wire surrounding the CRT, and this current generates an alternating magnetic field. The purpose of this field is to demagnetize the *shadow mask*. Over time, the shadow mask can pick up a weak magnetic charge and interfere with the focus of the electron beams. Degaussing will randomize this magnetic charge and keep the colors purer and the dots more precisely defined.

Troubleshooting Monitors

First, keep your monitor clean. An occasional cleaning with a clean cloth and anti-static spray will do wonders for keeping down dust. Because of the inherent dangers of the high frequency/high voltage power required by monitors and because proper adjustment requires specialized training, this section will concentrate on giving the support person the information necessary to decide whether or not a trouble call is warranted. Virtually no monitor manufacturers will make schematics of their monitors available to the public because of liability issues regarding possible electrocution.

To simplify troubleshooting, look at the process as two separate things: external adjustments and internal adjustments.

EXTERNAL ADJUSTMENTS

The external controls were shown previously in the chapter. These controls provide the user the opportunity to fine-tune the on-screen image for brightness and contrast. Some monitors allow fine-tuning of image size and position. More sophisticated monitors allow fine-tuning of the geometric proportions to keep the image square.

INTERNAL ADJUSTMENTS

These controls are sometimes accessible without having to open the monitor. If this is the case, the only thing to worry about is causing a bigger problem by tweaking the wrong control. Generally, the accessible controls are related to the focus of the on-screen image and the overall picture brightness. If the image seems a little blurry, it may be possible to adjust the focus with this control. The brightness control might also provide a way to increase image brightness if the front panel brightness control is already set to maximum.

Controls that require removal of the monitor case to make adjustments include those for convergence, gain for each of the color guns, and sometimes the focus control. Before proceeding further, Figure 10.16.

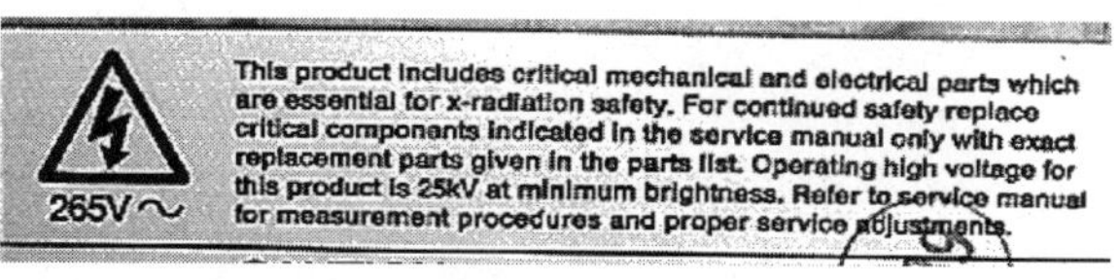

Figure 10.16 Hey! That's 25,000 volts! BE CAREFUL!

A technician with either informal or formal training in component level repair can usually figure out which controls do what. Balance the cost of repairing the monitor against the cost of death or serious/life changing injury. Is it worth it? Finally, before making adjustments to the display image, especially with the internal controls, give the monitor at least 15 to 30 minutes warm-up time. This is necessary for both the components on the printed circuit boards and for the CRT itself. The high voltage anode on the CRT is shown in Figure 10.17 in relation to the yoke.

Figure 10.17 High voltage anode.

COMMON PROBLEMS

- Ghosting, streaking, and/or fuzzy vertical edges: check the cable connections and the cable itself.
- One color is missing: check cables, if present check user controls for that color. If the color adjustment is already maxed out, the monitor will require internal service.
- Brightness: as monitors age, they lose brightness. If the user adjustable control is maxed out, the monitor will require internal adjustment. This is a good argument for power-management functions. *Don't* leave the monitor on with a picture on it, as this will reduce monitor life significantly. *Do* use the power management options in Windows or your BIOS setup, or use the power switch.
- Focus adjustments may be external but are usually on the inside somewhere close to the flyback transformer. This is the transformer that provides the high voltages to the CRT. Leave it alone. A typical flyback transformer is shown in Figure 10.18.

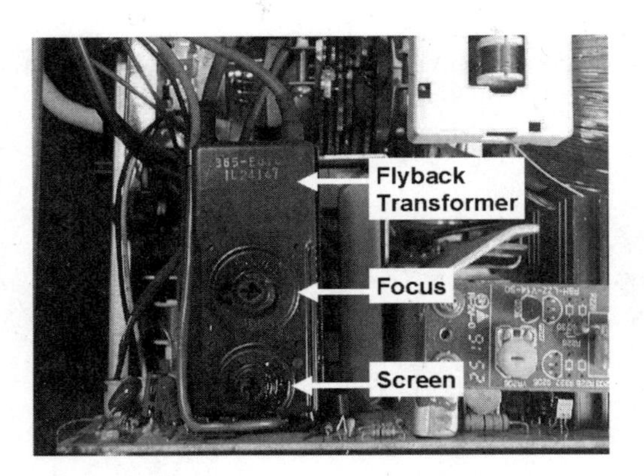

Figure 10.18 Typical flyback transformer and controls.

- Hissing or sparking sounds are often indicative of an insulation rupture on the flyback transformer. This sound is usually accompanied by the smell of ozone. If all this is Greek to you, the monitor definitely needs a qualified technician. Having replaced a flyback transformer once myself, I can say it is not worth the hassle, and potential loss of life or limb.

- There are big color blotches on the display. Easy and cheap. Find the degaussing button. Use it. If the monitor doesn't have a degaussing button, you can purchase a special tool called a degaussing coil at any electronics store.
- Bird-like chirping sounds that occur at regular intervals usually indicate a problem with the power supply.
- You got a good deal on a used 17-inch monitor, but the display is kind of dark, even though you have the brightness turned up all the way. This points to a dying CRT. So, how about a CRT replacement? Forget it. Even if the monitor was free ,it just ain't worth it because a replacement tube runs in the hundreds of dollars. Nobody ever sold a monitor because it was too bright and too sharp. Save your money and buy a new monitor.
- The monitor displays only a single vertical line. Probably a problem between the main circuit board and the yoke. Or a blown yoke coil. Definitely a service call.
- The monitor displays only a single horizontal line. Just like the previous—take it in.
- A single white dot means the high voltage flyback transformer is most likely shot. Take it in.

A few last do's and don'ts:
Do keep the screen clean.

Do keep the cables tightened.

Do use quality cabling.

Do use power-management features, if available.

Don't block the ventilation slots on the monitor.

Don't use a refresh rate higher than recommended by the manufacturer.

Don't leave the monitor on all the time, even with a screen saver.

Don't place magnetic objects such as unshielded speakers close to the monitor (this can cause color problems at best and could permanently magnetize the shadow mask at worst.)

Be careful about disposing of a dead monitor. Many local governments have laws regarding their safe disposal. Be sure to check with your local waste-disposal entity or your company to verify proper disposal methods.

Video Cards

The video card, or display adapter (see Figure 10.19), is the brain of the PC's video. The video card is composed of two major pieces: the video RAM and the video processor circuitry. The video RAM is where the video image is stored. On the first video cards, this RAM was just good ol' DRAM, just like the RAM on the motherboard. The video-processing circuitry takes the information on the video RAM and shoots it out to the monitor.

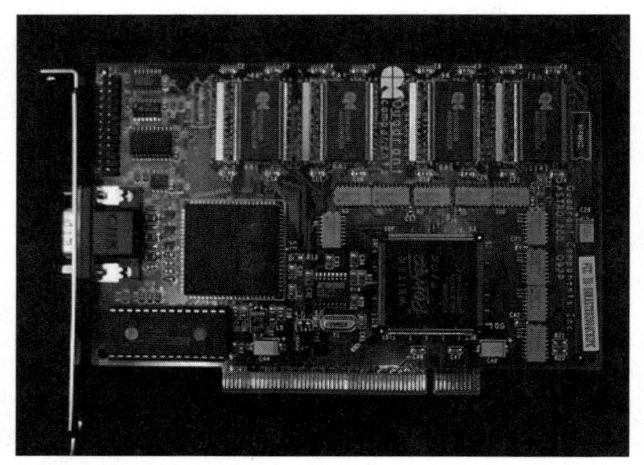

Figure 10.19 Typical video card.

The trick to understanding video cards is to appreciate the beginnings and the evolution of video. Video output to computers has been around long before PCs were created. At the time PCs became popular, video was exclusively text-based. By text, we mean that the only image that the video card could place on the monitor was one of the 256 ASCII characters. These characters were made up of patterns of pixels and these patterns were stored in the system BIOS. When a program wanted to make a character, it talked to DOS or to the BIOS, which then stored the image of that character in the video memory. The character then appeared on the screen.

The beauty of text video cards was that they were simple to use and cheap to make. The simplicity was based on the fact that there were only 256 characters. There were no color choices (we called it monochrome text), although you could choose to make the character bright, dim, normal, underlined, or blinking. It was easy to position the characters because there was space on the screen for only 80 characters per line and 24 lines (see Figure 10.20).

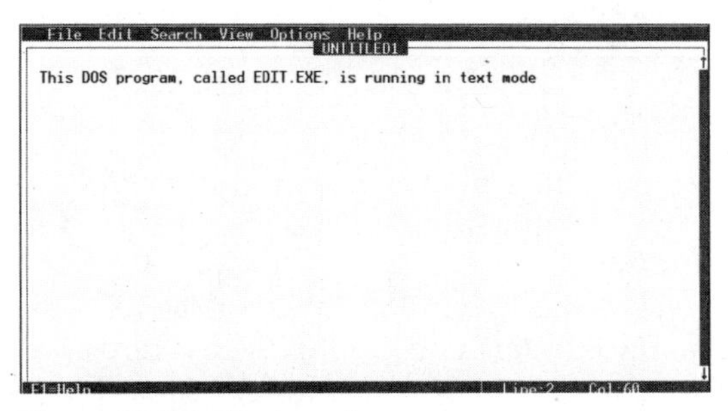

Figure 10.20 Text mode.

There was a time long, long ago when RAM was very expensive. Video card makers were interested in using the absolute least amount of RAM possible. Making a monochrome text video card was a great way to keep down RAM costs. Let's consider this for a minute. First, the video RAM is where the contents of the screen are located. You need enough video RAM to hold all of the necessary information for a completely full screen. Each ASCII character takes eight bits (by definition), so a monitor with 80 characters/line and 24 lines will need the following:

80 characters/line×24 lines = 1920 characters

1920 characters×8 bits/character = 15360 bits or 1920 bytes

The video card would need fewer than 2000 bytes of memory. That's not much, even in 1981, when the PC was first coming out. Now, be warned that we're glossing over a few things, such as where you store the information about underline, blinking, and so on. But the bottom line is that the tiny amounts of RAM needed kept monochrome text video cards cheap.

Very early on in the life of PCs, a new type of video card, called a *graphics video card,* was invented. A graphics card was quite similar to the text card, but while the text card was limited to the 256 ASCII characters, with a graphics video card a program could turn on or off any pixel on the screen. This is still monochrome, but now programs can access any individual pixel, allowing much more creative control of the screen. Of course, this took more video RAM. The first graphics cards ran at 320×200 pixels. We need one bit for each pixel (on or off), so:

320×200 = 64000 bits or 8000 bytes

A lot more than text, but still a pretty low amount of RAM. As resolutions increased, the amount of video RAM needed to store this information also increased.

Once monochrome video was invented, it was a relatively easy step to move into color for both text and graphics video cards. The only question was how to store color information for each character (text cards) or pixel (graphics cards). This was easy: just set aside a few more bits for each pixel or character. So now the question is, *How many bits do we set aside?* Well, that would depend on how many colors you wish to have—the first color graphic video cards were limited to only four colors and set aside only a few bits per pixel. Basically, the number of colors desired determines the number of colors. For example, if you wanted four colors, you need 2^2 = four bits per pixel. Then we could do something like this:

00 = black

01 = cyan (blue)

10 = magenta (reddish pink)

11 = white

So, if you set aside two bits, you could get four colors. If you want 16 colors, for example, you would set aside four bits, which would make 16 different combinations. There are no common color depths for text beyond 16 colors, so let's start thinking in terms of graphics mode and pixels. To get 256 colors, each pixel would have to be represented with eight bits. In PCs, the number of colors is always a power of 2: 4, 16, 256, 64K, etc. Notice that as more colors are added, more video RAM is needed to store this information. Here are the most common color depths and the number of bits necessary to store the color information per pixel:

2 colors = 1 bit (mono)

4 colors = 2 bits

16 colors = 4 bits

256 colors = 8 bits

64K colors = 16 bits

16MB colors = 24 bits

Most techs won't say things like, "I have a card that can show 16 megabytes of colors." Instead, we say "I have a 24-bit card." Talk in terms of bits, not colors. It is assumed that you know the number of colors for any color depth.

MODES

Based on what we know so far, it would seem as if there were four different types of video cards: monochrome text, color text, monochrome graphics, and color graphics. Now, any PC may want to do more than one of these. You may want to start with a text mode, and then switch into color graphics. What are you going to do, keep two video cards in the PC, and then switch the cable? Of course not. Instead, one video card can be all of these video cards in one. A modern video card can act as more than one type of card—it can output text or graphics, mono or color, as needed. Each different level of operation is called a *mode*. IBM and then the *Video Electronics Standard Association* (VESA) defined specific, uniform video modes for video cards. These video modes are given a hex value. For example, video mode 06h is defined as monochrome graphics at 640×200 pixels.

MDA

The first video card ever produced with the IBM PC was the text-only *Monochrome Display Adapter* (MDA). An MDA is perfectly fine for DOS-based word-processing and spreadsheet programs. The MDA has a 9-pin female socket and is found only in the most ancient of PCs and landfills.

CGA

The IBM PC offered the first-generation color monitor. The *Color Graphics Adapter* (CGA) card supports colors, but it does so at a price: resolution. A four-color screen offered only 320×200 resolution. It was possible to support 640×200 resolution, but the number of colors available dropped to only 2. Like its less gifted older brother, it also uses a 9-pin male connector.

EGA

The *Enhanced Graphics Adapter* (EGA) was introduced in late 1984 as an improvement on the CGA standard. It could support a resolution of up to 640×350 @ 16 colors in text mode or 640×200 @ 2 colors in graphics mode. Unfortunately, there were often problems with programs not working properly with an EGA card because the EGA standard was not fully backward-compatible with CGA and MDA. EGA used a 9-pin adapter with a distinct DIP switch visible from the outside.

PGA

The *Professional Graphics Adapter* (PGA) card was part of a package developed by IBM. Costing over $4000 and taking three ISA slots when fully configured, this system offered 3-D rotation and 60 frames/second animation. It was aimed at the engineering and scientific communities, but was dropped by IBM with the introduction of VGA in 1987.

VGA

With the introduction of the PS/2, IBM introduced the *Video Graphics Array* (VGA) standard. This new standard offered 16 colors at a resolution of 640×480 pixels. One of the ways that VGA was able to offer more colors was by using an analog video signal instead of a digital one, as was the case prior to the VGA standard. A digital signal is either all on or all off. By using an analog signal, the VGA standard is able to provide 64 distinct levels for each color, giving us 64^3 or 262,144 possible colors, although only 16 or 256 can be seen at a time. For most purposes, 640×480 @ 16 colors defines VGA mode. This is typically the display resolution and color depth referred to on many software packages as a minimum display requirement.

SVGA

For years, *Super Video Graphics Array* (SVGA) was a lot like SCSI-1 —more opinion than an established standard. Any video card maker who made a video card that could display greater than 640×480 @ 16 colors called itself SGVA. Typically, the minimum requirement for SVGA compatibility is 640×480 @ 256 colors. For many years, the lack of an SVGA standard created serious confusion. One manifestation of this confusion was the emergence of non-standard modes; in essence, extensions to the VGA modes. Each video card maker would define their own modes, even for identical resolution/color depths.

The Video Electronic Standards Association has established standards for SVGA resolutions, color depth, and video signal timings. Super VGA cards that follow the VESA standard are labeled VESA-compliant. All video cards are VESA-compliant today.

Resolution, Color Depth and Memory Requirements

To determine the amount of video memory required at a given resolution and color depth, multiply the resolution (800 * 600) by the number of bytes of color depth. From the RAM chapter, we know that memory on a PC is always in *byte*-sized units. Color depth on a 24-bit video card is referred to in bits. We know this to be 3 bytes. So our equation would now read 800 * 600 * 3 for the memory requirement in bytes. To convert this to megabytes, divide the result by 1,048,576, as follows:

800 * 600 = 480,000 pixels per screen

480,000 * 3 = 1,440,000 bits of memory per screen

1,440,000/1,048,576 = 1.373MB/screen

This means that a video card with only 1MB of RAM cannot support a resolution higher than 640×480 @ 16 million colors. Memory requirements for various resolutions and color depths are shown in Table 10.1. The amount of memory is given in megabytes because this is the usual increment for video memory.

Table 10.1 RAM requirements for various resolutions/color depths

Resolution	16 Colors	256 Colors	64K Colors	16.7M Colors
640×480	0.15MB	0.29MB	0.59MB	0.88MB
800×600	0.23MB	0.46MB	0.92MB	1.37MB
1024×768	0.38MB	0.75MB	1.5MB	2.25MB
1200×1024	0.63MB	1.25MB	2.5MB	3.75MB
1600×1200	0.92MB	1.83MB	3.66MB	5.49MB

Using more color depth slows down video functions. We've heard this time after time, ever since Windows 3.0 came out: use 16 or 256 colors; true color (24 bit) will slow you down to a crawl. In order to move data from the video card to the display, we have to go through the video cards' memory chips and the expansion bus. These things can only move so fast. VL-Bus and PCI both are limited to 32-bit transfers at roughly 33MHz, yielding a maximum bandwidth of 132MB/s. It sounds like a lot until you start using higher resolutions, high color depths, and higher refresh rates.

For example, take a typical display at 800 × 600 with a fairly low refresh of 70Hz. The 70Hz means the display screen is being redrawn 70 times per *second*. If we are using a reasonable color depth of 256 colors, which is 8-bit (2^8 =2 56), we can multiply all these values together to see how much data per second will have to be sent to the display:

800 * 600 * 1byte * 70 = 33.6MB/s

If we use the same example at 16 million (24-bit) colors, the figure jumps to 100.8MB/s.

The obvious desire for even higher bandwidth than that available with PCI has been answered by Intel's new *Advanced Graphics Port* (AGP). AGP is derived from the 66MHz, 32-bit PCI 2.1 specification and is currently the fastest video available. AGP is a single special port, similar to a PCI slot that is dedicated only for video. You will never see a motherboard with two AGP ports. AGP has a mind-boggling top speed of 533MB/s. AGP has taken the video world by storm. Although most systems still don't really need the speed of AGP, they benefit by AGP's support for the slew of powerful games that are so popular in PCs.

Video Memory

Video memory is critical for the operation of the PC. It is probably the hardest working electronics on the PC, constantly being updated to reflect every change that takes place on the screen. The original video RAM was plain old DRAM, just like the DRAM on the motherboard. Unfortunately, DRAM has some significant limitations. As a result, there are a number of other types of RAM that have been developed specifically for video.

Memory produces two bottlenecks for data: access speed and data throughput. Typical low cost ($50–$100) video cards commonly use DRAM for data storage. The speed of DRAM is limited by two things. One of these is the need to refresh DRAM memory approximately 18.5 times per second. During these refresh periods, the memory bits are unavailable to read. The other slowdown is the access/response time of DRAM. Even the fastest commonly available DRAM at 50ns is too slow for the higher resolutions and color depths found on larger monitors. Data throughput is limited by both the type of expansion card (i.e., ISA, PCI, AGP), and the wiring between the DRAM and the video processor. The data lines are used both for writing data to the video port and receiving data from the CPU.

Video card manufacturers defeat these two bottlenecks by re-engineering the display adapters to provide better throughput and by using specialized RAM to increase speed. Better video cards have their video display memory reorganized from the typical 32-bit wide structure to 64, 128, or even 192 bits wide. This would not be of much benefit if it weren't for the fact that most video display cards are really coprocessor boards. Most of the graphics horsepower is generated on the card by the video processor chip. The main system simply provides the input data to the processor on the video card. By making the memory bus on the video card as much as 6 times wider than the standard 32-bit pathway (i.e. 192 bits), data can be manipulated and then sent to the monitor much more quickly.

The first specialized video RAM option is dual port memory or *Video RAM* (VRAM). VRAM allows data to be written to video memory from the main system over the standard 8 data lines in parallel, and provide a serial data line for data to the video port. Although faster, VRAM is more expensive. But economies of scale have lowered its price to where it is quite common.

Windows RAM (WRAM) is another dual-ported RAM that has seen success in video cards. WRAM is slightly faster than VRAM and costs about the same. The downside to WRAM is that it has not been as widely manufactured as some of the other specialized video RAMs.

Synchronous Graphics RAM (SGRAM) is the most popular specialized video RAM available. SGRAM is like SDRAM in that it is synchronized to the system clock. SGRAM is extremely fast and is capable of supporting video for the next few years—a veritable lifetime in the PC world!

While specialized video RAMs offer substantial improvements in video speeds, they are also not needed in the majority of office applications because the need for high data throughput is typically found only with high resolutions at high color depths. For graphics work and games, however, specialized RAM can make a world of difference.

WHEN VIDEO CARDS GO BAD

Fortunately, video cards rarely break. The majority of problems in video can be attributed to improper drivers, poor connections, or bad monitors. Unfortunately, when they do, invariably the only option is to throw them away. One area in which repairs can sometimes take place is with the video RAM. On the rare occasion where the video card is the problem, the usual culprit is the video RAM. Many video cards today have video RAM that is mounted in sockets, as opposed to being soldered directly to the video card. The reason video cards come with sockets is to allow one video card to be sold with varying amounts of RAM. However, sockets also allow the video RAM to be replaced when needed.

The trick is to recognize the classic signs of bad video RAM. The first is fixed speckles or spots on the screen. These spots can be any color, but are usually black. The important point to note here is that the speckles don't move; they are fixed in one location, although they may turn on-and-off a few times an hour. The second symptom is funny colors in Windows. We're not talking about a bad Windows color scheme here! This looks like a monitor covered with a colored film. The color is almost always complex. It won't be blue or red, but rather a bluish-green with maybe a little purple type of color. If you get this *filmy* look, boot the PC with VGA drivers (Safe Mode in Windows 95/98). If the filmy look is still there, the RAM is bad.

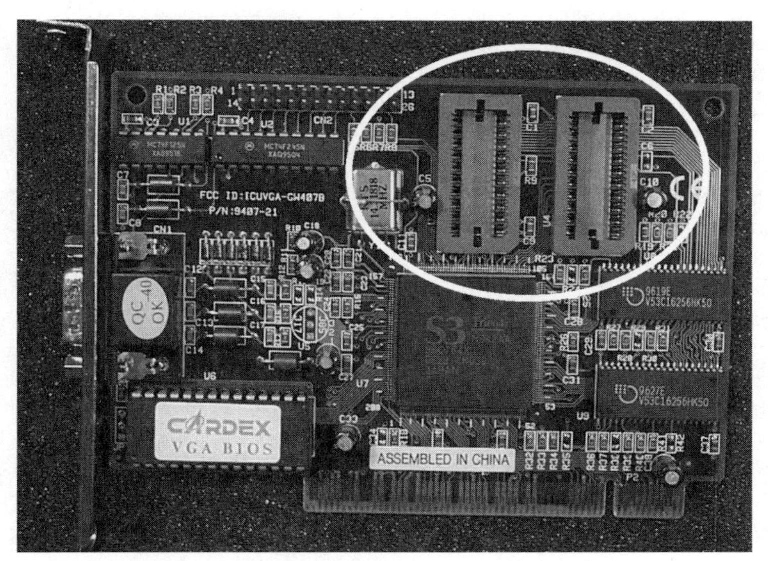

Figure 10.21 Replaceable video RAM.

Finally, and the most common symptom of this uncommon problem is what I call *screen decay*. Have you ever seen a movie where the film inside the projector suddenly melts? It usually starts with a small hole in the film and then quickly spreads throughout the film. Bad video RAM can cause this screen decay look. This is most common on video cards that have been upgraded and haven't been properly inserted into the sockets. The machine runs fine for a moment or two until the cards heat up, disconnecting the improperly inserted RAM.

CHAPTER 11

Printers

In this chapter we will:

- Understand the different types of printers used today
- Take a detailed tour through laser printers
- Observe and repair basic printer errors

Despite all of the talk about the *paperless office*, printers continue to be a vital part of the typical PC system. In many cases, the PC is used exclusively for the purpose of producing paper documents, but many people simply prefer dealing with *hard copy*. Programmers cater to this preference by using metaphors such as page, workbook, and binder in their applications. The A+ certification strongly stresses the area of printing and expects a high degree of technical knowledge of the function, components, maintenance, and repair of all types of printers.

Impact Printers

Impact printers leave an image on paper by physically striking an inked ribbon against the surface of the paper. Daisy wheel printers (essentially an electric typewriter attached to the PC instead of directly to a keyboard) and dot matrix printers are the two prominent examples of impact printers. Once the dominant printing technology, impact printers have largely disappeared from store shelves because of their inability to combine high quality and flexibility at a low cost. They still retain a niche market for two reasons: they have a large installed base and they can be used for multi-part forms because they actually strike the paper. Impact printers tend to be relatively slow and noisy, but when speed, flexibility, and print quality are not critical, they provide acceptable results. PCs used for printing multi-part forms such as *Point of Sale* (POS) machines that need to print receipts with multiple copies) represent the major market for new impact printers, although many older dot matrix and daisy wheel printers remain in use.

Daisy wheel printers, while producing an acceptable quality of text, lack flexibility: you only get the single font on the daisy wheel and only in one size. Daisy wheel printers are completely obsolete today, although they are still employed in some situations in which only a single font is needed or for multi-part forms.

Dot matrix printers offer far more flexibility than daisy wheel printers, although the quality of their character printing tends to be inferior to daisy wheel printers. Dot matrix printers use an array of pins to strike an inked printer ribbon and produce images on paper (see Figure 11.1). Using either 9 or 24 pins, dot matrix printers treat each page as a picture broken up into a raster image. The BIOS for the printer (either built into the printer or a *printer driver*) interprets the raster image in the same way that a monitor does, *painting* the image as individual *dots*. Naturally, the more pins the higher the resolution.

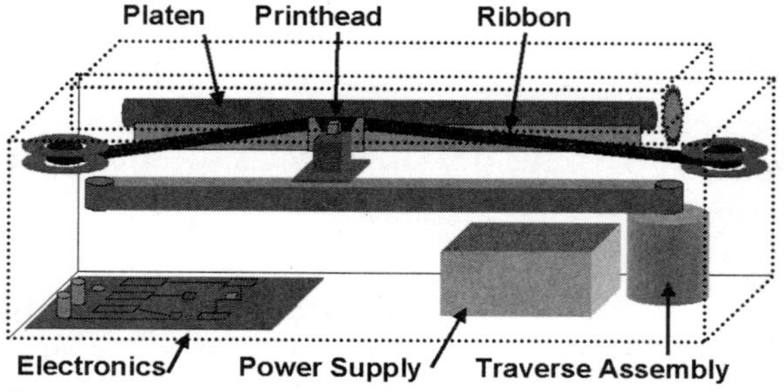

Figure 11.1 Internal of a dot-matrix printer.

TROUBLESHOOTING DOT MATRIX PRINTER PROBLEMS

One downside to dot matrix is the need for ongoing maintenance. Keep the platen (the roller or plate upon which the pins impact) and the printhead (see Figure 11.2) clean with denatured alcohol. Be sure to lubricate gears and pulleys based on the manufacturer's specifications. However, never lubricate the printhead as the lubricant will smear and stain the paper.

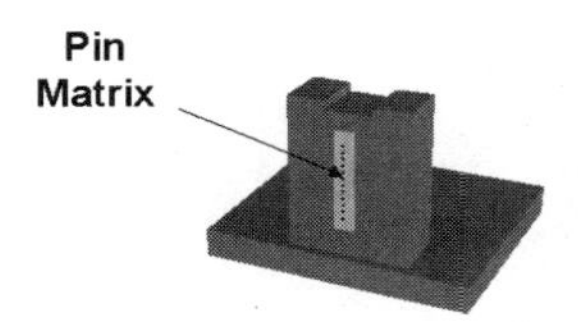

Figure 11.2 Detail of a dot-matrix printhead.

White Bars on Text

White bars going through the text point to a dirty or damaged printhead. Try cleaning the printhead with a little denatured alcohol. If the problem persists, replace the printhead. Printheads for most printers are readily available from the manufacturer.

Chopped Text

If the characters look chopped off at the top or bottom, the printhead probably needs to be adjusted. Refer to the manufacturer's instructions for proper adjustment.

Pepper Look

If the paper is covered with dots and small smudges (*pepper look*), the platen is dirty. Clean the platen with a soft cloth or a cloth with a *very* thin layer of oil. Spraying WD-40 in the vicinity of the cloth will do.

Faded Image

If the image is faded and you know the ribbon is good, try adjusting the printhead closer to the platen.

Light to Dark

If the image on one side fades to the other side of the paper, the platen is out of adjustment. Platens are generally difficult to adjust so send it to the local warranty center. The 30–50 bucks you spend is far cheaper than the frustration of trying to do it yourself.

Ink Jet Printers

Ink jet printers work by ejecting ink through tiny tubes (see Figure 11.3). The ink is ejected through the tubes by heating ink with tiny resistors or plates that are at one end of each tube. These resistors literally boil the ink, creating a tiny air bubble that ejects a droplet of ink onto the paper, thus creating portions of the image.

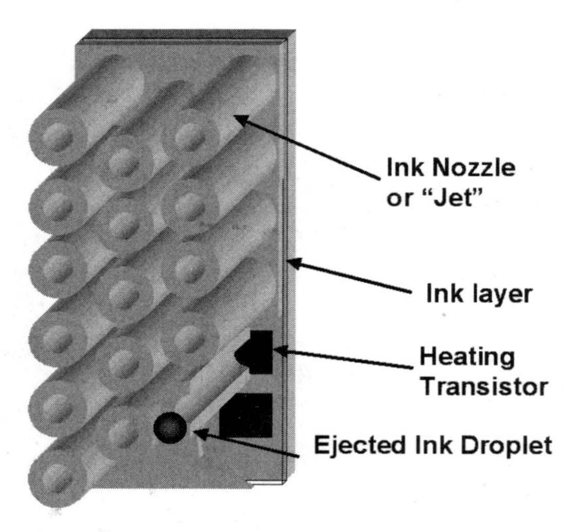

Figure 11.3 Detail of ink jet.

Ink jet printers are relatively simple devices, consisting of the printhead mechanism, support electronics, a transfer mechanism to move the prinhead back and forth, and a paper feed component to drag, move, and eject paper.

The ink inside the jets of ink jet printers has a tendency to dry out when not used for a relatively short time. To counter this problem, all inkjet printers move the printhead to a special position that keeps the ink from drying. This area has many names, usually called the *park, cleaning,* or *maintenance* area (see Figure 11.4).

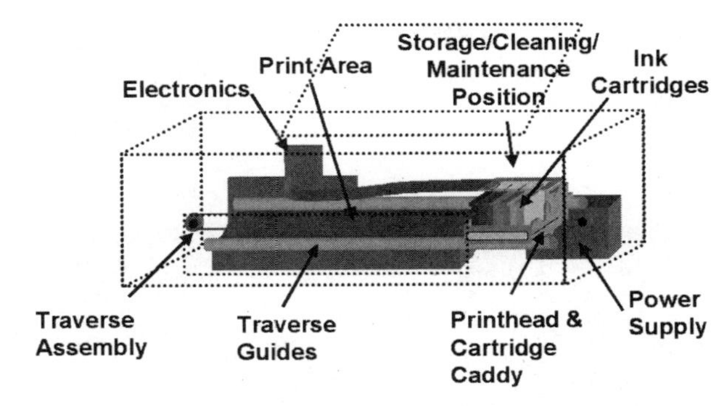

Figure 11.4 Internal of an ink jet printer.

Laser Printers

Laser printers (see Figure 11.5) have become the printer of choice in most applications. They produce high quality and high speed printing of both text and graphics. Although more expensive than ink jet or impact printers, their prices have steadily declined in recent years.

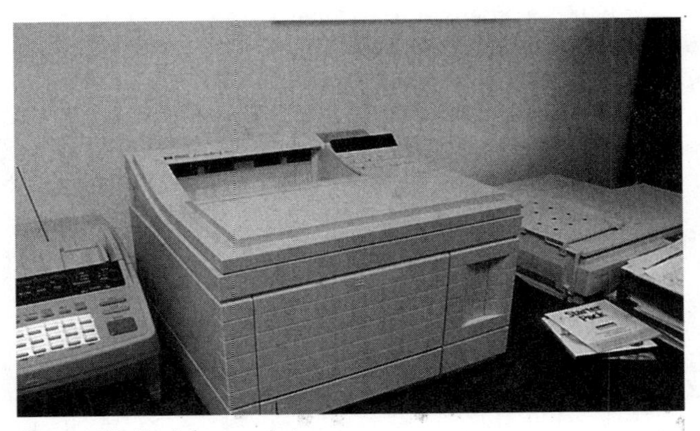

Figure 11.5 A laser printer.

Laser printers rely on the photoconductive properties of certain organic compounds. Photoconductive means that when exposed to light, particles of these compounds will conduct electricity. Laser printers use lasers as a light source because of their precision.

PARTS

In order to reduce maintenance costs, many of the laser jet parts, including those that suffer the most wear and tear, have been incorporated into the toner cartridge (see Figure 11.6).

Figure 11.6 Laser printer toner cartridge.

Although this makes replacement of individual parts nearly impossible, it greatly reduces the need for replacement; those parts that are most likely to break are replaced every time you replace the toner cartridge. Unlike ink jet printers, the relatively higher cost of laser printers makes their repair a common and popular option. There are a number of companies that sell laser printer parts. My personal favorite is The Printer Works. They are a large mail-order outfit with salesmen who are quite knowledgeable. Like an auto parts store, they can often help you determine the problem and sell you the part. Their number is 800-225-6116.

The Photosensitive Drum

The photosensitive drum (see Figure 11.7) is an aluminum cylinder coated with particles of photosensitive compounds. The drum itself is grounded to the power supply, but the coating is not. When light hits these particles, whatever electrical charge they may have had drains out through the grounded cylinder. The drum, usually contained in the toner cartridge, can be wiped clean if it becomes dirty. However, *EXTREME CAUTION SHOULD BE EXERCISED!!* If the drum becomes scratched, the scratch will appear on every page printed from that point on. The only repair in the event of a scratch is to replace the toner cartridge.

Figure 11.7 Toner cartridge with photosensitive drum exposed.

Erase Lamp

The erase lamp exposes the entire surface of the photosensitive drum with light, making the photosensitive coating conductive. Any electrical charge present in the particles bleeds away into the grounded drum, leaving the surface particles electrically neutral.

Primary Corona

The primary corona wire, located close to the photosensitive drum, never touches the drum. When charged with an extremely high voltage, an electric field (or corona) forms, allowing voltage to pass to the drum and charge the photosensitive particles on its surface. The *primary grid* regulates the transfer of voltage, ensuring that the surface of the drum receives a uniform negative voltage of between –600V and –1000V.

Laser

The laser acts as the writing mechanism of the printer. Any particle on the drum struck by the laser becomes conductive, allowing its charge to be drained away into the grounded core of the drum. The entire surface of the drum has a uniform negative charge of between –600V and –1000V following its charging by the primary corona wire. When particles are struck by the laser, they are discharged and left with a –100 volt negative charge. Using the laser, we can *write* an image onto the drum. Note that the laser writes a positive image to the drum.

Toner

The toner in a laser printer is a fine powder made up of plastic particles bonded to iron particles. The *toner cylinder* charges the toner with a negative charge of between –200V and –500V. Because that charge falls between the original uniform negative charge of the photosensitive drum (–600V and –1000V) and the charge of the particles on the drum's surface hit by the laser (–100V), particles of toner are attracted to the areas of the photosensitive drum that have been hit by the laser (i.e., areas that have a *relatively* positive charge with reference to the toner particles).

Transfer Corona

In order to transfer the image from the photosensitive drum to the paper, the paper must be given a charge that will attract the toner particles off of the drum and onto the paper. The transfer corona applies a positive charge to the paper, drawing the negatively charged toner particles to the paper. The paper, with its positive charge, is also attracted to the negatively charged drum. In order to prevent the paper from wrapping around the drum, a *static charge eliminator* removes the charge from the paper.

Fuser

The toner is merely resting on top of the paper after the static charge eliminator has removed the paper's static charge. The toner must be permanently attached to the paper to make the image permanent. Two rollers, a pressure roller and a heated roller, are used to fuse the toner to the paper. The pressure roller presses against the bottom of the page while the heated roller presses down on the top of the page, melting the toner into the paper. The heated roller has a non-stick coating such as Teflon to prevent the toner from sticking to the heated roller.

THE PRINTING PROCESS: THE PHYSICAL SIDE

Clean the Drum

The printing process begins with the physical and electrical cleaning of the photosensitive drum. Between the printing of each page, the drum must be returned to a clean, fresh condition. All residual toner left over from printing the previous page must be removed, usually by scraping the surface of the drum with a rubber cleaning blade. If the residual particles remain on the drum, they will appear as random black spots and streaks on the next page. The physical cleaning mechanism either deposits the residual toner in a debris cavity or recycles it by returning it to the toner supply in the toner cartridge. The physical cleaning must be done carefully. Damage to the drum will cause a permanent mark to be printed on every page printed after the damage occurs.

The printer must also be electrically cleaned (see Figure 11.8). One or more erase lamps bombard the surface of the drum with the appropriate wavelengths of light, causing the surface particles to completely discharge into the grounded drum. After the cleaning process, the drum should be completely free of toner and have a neutral charge.

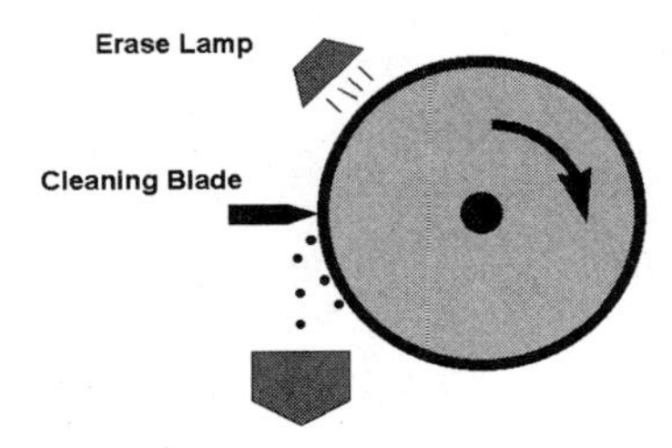

Figure 11.8 Cleaning and erasing the drum.

Charge the Drum

To make the drum receptive to new images, it must be charged (see Figure 11.9). Using the corona wire, we apply a uniform negative charge to the entire surface of the drum (usually between –600V and –1000V).

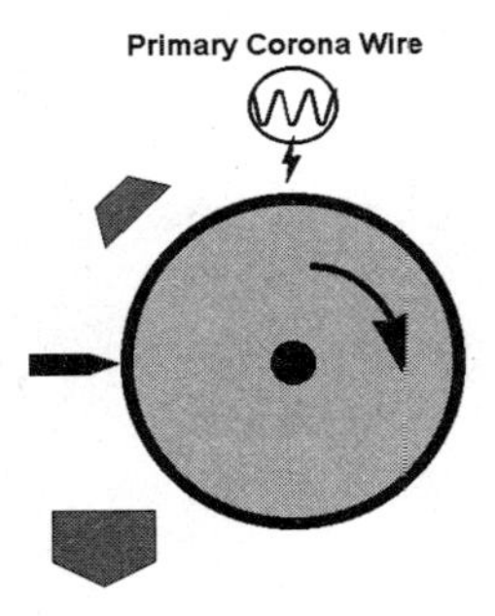

Figure 11.9 Charging the drum with a uniform negative charge.

Write the Image

The laser is used to write a positive image on the surface of the drum (see Figure 11.10). Every particle on the drum hit by the laser will release most of its negative charge into the drum. Those particles with a lesser negative charge will be relatively positive to the toner particles and will attract them.

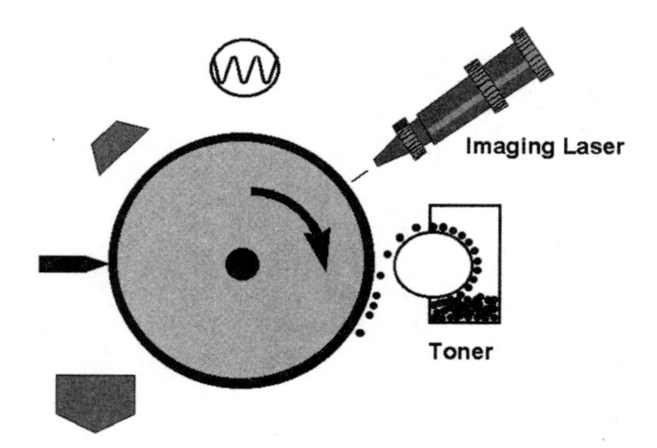

Figure 11.10 Writing the image.

Transfer the Image

The printer must transfer the image from the drum onto the paper. Using the transfer corona, we charge the paper with a positive charge. Once the paper has a positive charge, the negatively charge toner particles leap from the drum to the paper (see Figure 11.11). The paper's positive charge is removed by the static charge eliminator. Once the charge has been removed, the particles are merely resting on the paper. They must still be permanently affixed to the paper.

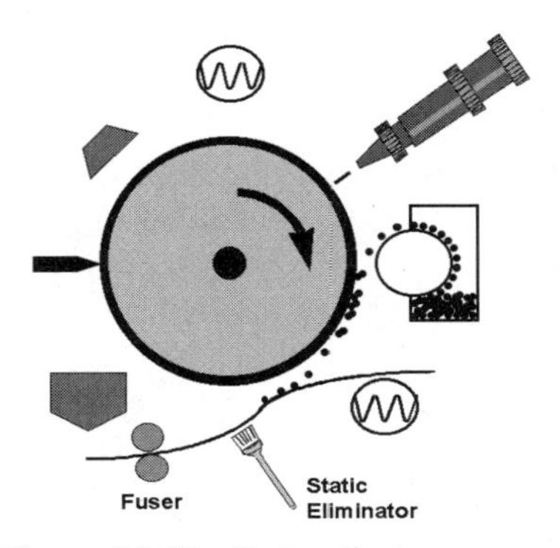

Figure 11.11 Fusing the image.

Fix the Image

The particles must be fused to the paper. They have been attracted to the paper because of the positive charge given to the paper by the transfer corona, but if the process stopped there the toner particles would fall off the page as soon as the page was lifted. The toner particles are mostly composed of plastic, so they can be melted to the page. Two rollers, the heated roller coated in a nonstick material and the pressure roller, melt the toner to the paper, permanently affixing it. The final printed copy is then ejected from the printer, and the process begins again with the physical and electrical cleaning of the printer.

NOTE

The heated roller produces enough heat to melt some types of plastic media, particularly overhead transparency materials. NEVER use transparencies in a laser printer unless they are specifically designed for use in laser printers. Use of non-approved materials can seriously damage your laser printer and void your warranty.

AND NOW: THE REST OF THE LASER PRINTER

Although the majority of the printing activity takes place within the toner cartridge, there are many other parts of the laser printer that are hard at work outside the cartridge (see Figure 11.12). In order to appreciate these *other* components and their functions, we need to take a look at a regular print job and the many steps that are necessary to make the page appear on the paper.

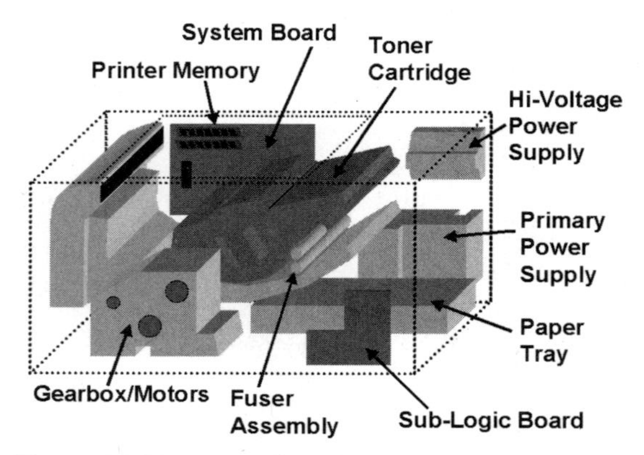

Figure 11.12 Internal of a laser printer.

Power Supplies

All laser printers are distinguished by at least two separate power supplies. The first power supply is called the *Primary power supply*, or sometimes just the *Power supply*. This power supply, that might also be more than one power supply, provides power to the motors that move the paper, the system electronics, the laser, and the transfer corona. The High Voltage power supply usually only provides power to the Primary Corona. The extremely high voltage of the High Voltage power supply makes it one of the most dangerous devices in the world of PCs! It is imperative to always TURN OFF a laser printer before you open it up—other than inserting a new toner cartridge!

Turning Gears

A laser printer has many mechanical functions. First, the paper must be picked up, printed upon, and kicked out of the printer. Second, the photosensitive roller must be turned and the laser, or a mirror, must be moved from left to right. Third, the toner must be evenly distributed and the fuser assembly needs to squish the toner into the paper. All of these functions are served by complex gear systems. In most laser printers, these gear systems are invariably packed together in discrete units, generically called Gear Packs or Gearboxes. Most laser printers will have two or three gearboxes that are relatively easy to remove in the rare case in which one of them fails. Most gearboxes will also have their own motor or solenoid to move the gears.

Fusing

The fuser assembly is almost always separate from the toner cartridge. It is usually quite easy to locate, as it will be close to the bottom of the toner cartridge and will usually have two rollers to fuse the toner. Sometimes the fuser is enclosed and difficult to recognize, given that the rollers are hidden from view. Think about the data path of the paper and the fact that the fusing will take place as the final step of printing to help you determine the location of the fuser. In some laser printers, the transfer corona also is outside the toner cartridge. This is identified by a thin wire, which is usually protected by other thin wires. The transfer corona is a particularly troublesome part as it is prone to building up dirt and must be cleaned; yet it is also quite fragile. Most printers with exposed transfer coronas will provide a special tool to clean the transfer corona.

System Board

Every laser printer will contain at least one electronic board. On this board is the main processor, the printer's ROM and RAM used to store the image before it is printed. Of particular importance is the printer RAM. One big problem with laser printers is when the printer doesn't have enough RAM to store the image before it prints, creating a Memory Overflow situation. Also, some printers will store other information in the RAM, including fonts or special commands. Adding RAM is usually a very simple job (just snapping in a SIMMs stick or two), but getting the *right* RAM is important. Call the printer manufacturer and ask the type of RAM they need. Although most printer companies will sell you their expensive RAM, most printers can use generic DRAM like the kind you use in your PC. Many printers will divide these functions among two or three boards dispersed around the PC. The printer may also have a ROM chip and/or a special slot to install a ROM chip. This is usually for special functions such as Postscript or special fonts.

Ozone Filter

The coronas inside the laser printer generate ozone (O_3). Although not harmful to humans, the high concentrations of ozone will cause damage to printer components. To counter this problem, most laser printers have a special ozone filter that needs to be replaced periodically.

Sensors and Switches

Every laser printer has a large number of sensors and switches that are spread throughout the machine. The sensors are used to detect a broad range of functions such as jammed paper, empty paper trays, or low toner. Many of these sensors are really tiny switches that detect open doors, etc. Most of the time, these sensors/ switches work reliably. Yet occasionally, they can become dirty or broken, sending a false signal to the printer. Simple inspection is usually sufficient to determine if the problem is real or just the result of a faulty sensor/switch.

THE PRINTING PROCESS: THE ELECTRONIC SIDE

Now that we are comfortable with the many parts of the laser printer and their basic functions, let's delve into some of the *electronic* functions of laser printing.

Raster Images

Although impact printers transfer the data to the printer one character or one line at a time, laser printers transfer entire pages to the printer. Laser printers send a raster image of the page representing what the final product should look like. A raster image is merely a pattern of dots. Laser printers use the same technique as video cards to produce images; they use a device—the laser in a laser printer or the electron gun in a *Cathode Ray Tube* (CRT)—to *paint* a raster image (on the photosensitive drum in a laser printer or on the phosphor coating on the inside of a CRT in a monitor). Because laser printers have to *paint* the entire surface of the photosensitive drum before they can begin to transfer the image to paper, they have to process the image one page at a time.

Laser printers use a chip called *the Raster Image Processor* (RIP) to translate the raster image sent to the printer into commands to the laser. The RIP needs memory (RAM) in order to store the data that it must process. A laser printer must have enough memory to process the entire page. Some images printed that require high resolutions require more memory. Insufficient memory to process the image will usually be indicated by a *MEM OVERFLOW* or memory overflow error. The solution to a memory overflow error is simply to add more RAM to the laser printer.

Do not assume that every error with the word *memory* in it can be fixed by simply adding more RAM to the printer. Just as adding more RAM chips will not solve conventional memory problems, adding more RAM will not solve every memory problem on laser printers. For example, on a HP LaserJet the message *21 ERROR* indicates that *the printer is unable to process very complex data fast enough for the print engine.* This indicates that the data is simply too complex for the RIP to handle. Adding more memory would NOT solve this problem; it would only make your wallet lighter. The only answer in that case is to reduce the complexity of the page image (i.e., fewer fonts, less formatting, reduced graphics resolution, etc.).

Resolution

Laser printers can print at different resolutions, just as monitors can display different resolutions. The maximum resolution that a laser printer can handle is determined by its physical characteristics. Laser printer resolution is expressed in *Dots per Inch* (DPI). Common resolutions are 300 dpi × 300 dpi or 600 dpi × 600 dpi. The first number, the horizontal resolution, is determined by how fine a focus can be achieved by the laser. The second number is determined by the smallest increment by which the EP drum can be turned. Higher resolutions produce higher quality, but keep in mind that higher resolutions also require more memory. In some instances, complex images can only be printed at lower resolutions because of their high memory demands. Even when printing at 300 dpi, laser printers produce far better quality than dot matrix printers because of *Resolution Enhancement Technology* (RET) (see Figure 11.13).

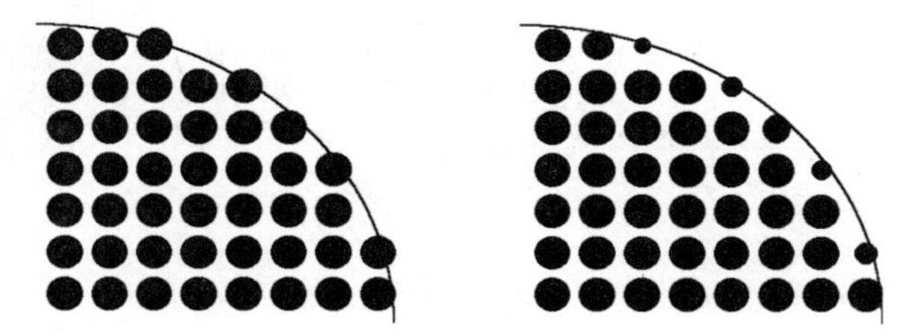

Figure 11.13 RET fills in gaps with smaller dots in order to smooth out jagged characters.

Resolution Enhancement Technology (RET)

Laser printers achieve high quality printing, not merely by printing at high resolutions, but also by employing RET. Resolution enhancement technology allows the printer to insert smaller dots among the characters, smoothing out the jagged curves that are typical of printers that do not use RET.

PRINTER LANGUAGES

American Standard Code for Information Interchange (ASCII)

We usually think of ASCII as nothing more than a standard set of characters, the basic alphabet in upper and lower case with a few strange symbols thrown in. ASCII actually contains a variety of control codes for transferring data, some of which can be used to control printers. For example, ASCII code 10 (or 0A in hex) means *Line Feed* and ASCII code 12 (0C) means *Form Feed*. These commands have been standard since before the creation of IBM PCs, and all printers respond to them. If they did not, the Print Screen key would not work with every printer. Being highly standardized has advantages, but the control codes are extremely limited. To utilize high-end graphics and a wide variety of fonts, more advanced languages are required.

Hewlett-Packard Printer Control Language (PCL)

Hewlett Packard developed PCL as a more advanced printer language. PCL features a greatly expanded set of printer commands. HP designed PCL with text based output in mind. It does not support advanced graphical functions, although some graphics are possible. The most recent version of PCL, PCL5, features scaleable fonts and additional line-drawing commands. However, unlike Postscript (see following section), PCL is dependent on the hardware. It is not a true page description language in the sense that it uses a series of commands to define the characters on the page; these commands must be supported by the individual printer and do not define the page as a single raster image. PCL5 is limited to 300 and 600 dpi laser printers and is not suitable for high-resolution graphics.

Postscript

Adobe systems developed Postscript *Page Description Language* (PDL) in the early 1980s as a device-independent printer language capable of high-resolution graphics and scalable fonts. Postscript interpreters are embedded in the printing device. Because the Postscript language is understood by the printers at a hardware level, Postscript printers print faster (the majority of the image processing is done by the printer and not the CPU) and Postscript files are extremely portable. They can be created on one machine or platform and reliably printed out on another machine or platform (including high-end typesetters, etc.).

Table 11.1 HP Laser Printer Power Requirements

Product Model (voltage)	Printer Peak (Amps)	Peak Duration (ms)	Fuser Lamp *ON* time(s)	Fuser Lamp On/Off cycle times(s)	Printing Amps/ watts	Standby Amps/ watts
33440A (115)	20	10	2.0	8.2	7.6/170	.77/170
33440AB (220)	10	10	2.0	6.0	3.4/850	.42/170
33447A (115)	28	10	2.0	7.5	8.0/870	.78/170
33447AB (220)	13	10	2.0	6.1	4.0/890	.48/170
33471A (115)	15.5	10	1.5	6.3	4.8/550	.36/90
33471AB (220)	7.1	10	1.4	5.7	2.5/500	.20/90
33449A (115)	20	10	2.0	8.2	7.6/870	.77/170
33449AB (220)	10	10	2.0	6.0	3.4/850	.42/170
33459A (115)	28	10	2.0	7.5	8.0/870	.78/170
33459AB (220)	13	10	2.0	6.1	4.0/890	.48/170
33481A (115)	15.5	10	1.5	6.3	5.0/574	.36/44
33481AB (220)	7.1	10	1.4	5.7	2.3/507	.20/44
33491A (115)	21	10	2.0	6.9	9.4/1100	2.0/240
33491AB 92200	11	10	2.0	6.9	4.5/1100	1.0/240

ELECTRICITY

Power Requirements

Laser printers draw considerably more power than other kinds of printers. When installing a laser printer, make sure that your circuit has adequate power to handle the printer's peak requirements. A common symptom of this is the dimming of office lights periodically while using the printer, indicating that the current wiring is not sufficient for the printer and everything else running on the same circuit. Certain functions of the printer, such as powering the erase lamp and heating up the fusing roller, require relatively large amounts of power. Refer to the printer documentation for the peak power requirements of your particular model of printer or refer to the chart on page 365. In addition, the power requirements are usually listed on the back of the printer.

Switch Boxes

If you want to use multiple printers hooked into the same parallel port, you have to use a switch box. Laser printers should never be used with mechanical switch boxes. Mechanical switch boxes create power surges that can damage your printer. If you must use a switch box, use a box that switches between printers electronically and has built in surge protection.

Reverse Power Up

Both laser printers and PCs require more power during their initial power up than later (the POST on a PC and the Warm Up on a laser printer). Hewlett Packard recommends a *reverse power up*. Turn on the laser printer first and allow it to finish its warm up before turning on the PC. This avoids having two devices drawing their peak loads simultaneously.

MAINTENANCE AND TROUBLESHOOTING LASER PRINTERS

Unlike PCs, laser printer maintenance and troubleshooting is a fairly well-established procedure

Keeping it Clean

Laser printers are quite robust as a rule. However, a good cleaning every time you replace the toner cartridge will help that printer last for many years. There are many cases of original HP LaserJet Is still running perfectly after 10 to 12 years of operation. The secret? They were kept immaculately clean.

There are generally only two items that get your laser printer dirty. First is excess toner. Toner is hard to see due to its black color but it will slowly coat the entire printer. Second is paper dust, sometimes called paper dander. This tends to build up where the paper is bent around rollers or where pickup rollers grab paper. Unlike toner, paper dust is easy to see and is usually a good test that a printer needs to be cleaned. Without being printer-specific, usually a thorough cleaning using a can of pressurized air to blow out the printer is the best cleaning you can do for that printer. It's best to do this outside or you may end up looking like one of those chimney sweeps from Mary Poppins! Unfortunately, specifics are difficult because every laser printer has its own unique cleaning method. However, one little area tends to be skipped in the cleaning instructions that come with your laser printer. Every laser printer has a number of rubber guide rollers through which the paper is run during the print process. These little rollers tend to pick up paper dust and dirt over time, making them slip and jam paper. They are easily cleaned with a little general-purpose cleaner such as Formula 409 or even just a little water. Also, remember to clean the corona wires, if specified by the manufacturer. Most of these wires are quite fragile and require a special tool or a delicate touch—or both!

If you're ready to get specific, get the printer's service manual. Almost every printer manufacturer sells these and they are the main tool for keeping a printer clean and running. Sadly, not all printer manufacturers provide these, but most do! Call The Printer Works for most service manuals. While you're at it, see whether the manufacturer has a Quick Reference Guide, which can be very handy for most printer problems.

Finally, be aware that Hewlett-Packard has maintenance kits for most of its laser printers. These are sets of replacement parts for the most commonly worn parts inside each particular type of HP LaserJet. Although not required for warranty, using these kits when prescribed by HP assures the ongoing reliability of your LaserJet.

Periodic Maintenance

Although keeping the printer clean is critical, every laser printer will have certain components that need to be periodically replaced. These parts vary between different models, but there are some that are commonly replaced. Here's a quick list of possible parts.

Ozone filter

Fuser assembly

Transfer corona

Paper guides/rollers

Thermal fuse (used to keep the fuser from overheating)

Of course, the ultimate source for determining the parts that need to be replaced (and when to replace them) is the printer manufacturer. Following the manufacturer's maintenance guideline will ensure years of trouble-free, dependable printing from your laser printer.

Ghosting

Ghost images sometimes appear at regular intervals on the printed page. This can be caused either because the EP drum has not fully discharged (and is picking up toner from a previous image) or because a previous image has used up so much toner that the supply of charged toner is either insufficient or has not been adequately charged.

Light Ghosting vs. Dark Ghosting

A variety of problems can cause both light and dark ghosting, but the most common source of light ghosting is *developer starvation*. If you ask a laser printer to print an extremely dark or complex image, it can use up so much toner that the toner cartridge cannot charge enough toner to print the next image. The proper solution is to use less toner (a.k.a. *don't do that anymore!*) by:

Lowering the resolution of the page (print at 300 dpi instead of 600 dpi)

Using a different pattern

Avoiding 50% gray scale and *dot on-dot off patterns*

Changing the layout so that gray scale patterns do not follow black areas

Making dark patterns lighter and light patterns darker

Printing in landscape orientation

Adjusting print density and *Resolution Enhancement Technology* (RET) settings

Printing a completely black page immediately prior to the page with the ghosting image, and as part of the same print job

Low temperature and low humidity can aggravate ghosting problems. Check your users' manual for environmental recommendations

Dark ghosting can sometimes be caused by a damaged EP drum. It may be fixed by replacing the toner cartridge. Light ghosting would *not* be solved in this way. Switching other components will not usually affect ghosting problems because they are a side affect of the entire process.

NOTE

Remember that most instances of light ghosting result from asking the printer to do too much: too complex an image, too dark an image, too high a resolution. Unfortunately, there are some problems that result from the limitations of the technology.

Vertical White Lines

Vertical white lines are usually caused by clogged toner that prevents the proper dispersion of toner on the drum. Try shaking the toner cartridge to dislodge the clog.

Blotchy Print

This is most commonly due to uneven dispersion of toner, especially if the toner is low. Try shaking the toner from side to side and try to print. Also be sure that the printer is level. Last, make sure the paper is not wet in spots. If the blotches are in a regular order, check the fusing rollers and the photosensitive drum to see if there are any foreign objects.

Spotty Print

If the spots are at regular intervals, the drum may be damaged or some toner may be stuck to the fuser rollers. Try wiping off the fuser rollers. Check the drum for damage. If the drum is damaged, get a new toner cartridge.

Emboss Effect

If your prints are getting an embossed effect (like putting a penny under a piece of paper and rubbing it with a lead pencil), there is almost certainly a foreign object on a roller. Use Formula 409 or regular water with a soft cloth to try to remove it. If the foreign object is on the photosensitive drum, you probably have to use a new cartridge.

Incomplete Characters

Incompletely printed characters on laser-printed transparencies can sometimes be corrected by adjusting the print density. Be extremely careful to use only materials approved for use in laser printers.

Creased Pages

Laser printers have up to 4 rollers. In addition to the heated and pressure rollers of the fusing assembly, there are rollers designed to move the paper from the source tray to the output tray. These rollers crease the paper in order to avoid curling that would cause paper jams in the printer. If the creases are noticeable, try using a different paper type. Cotton bond paper is usually more susceptible to noticeable creasing than other bonds. You might also try sending the output to the face-up tray, allowing you to avoid one roller. There is no hardware solution to this problem. It is simply a side effect of the process.

Warped, Overprinted, or Poorly Formed Characters

Poorly formed characters can indicate a problem either with the paper (or other media) or the hardware.

Media

Avoid paper that is too rough or too smooth. Paper that is too rough interferes with the fusing of characters and their initial definition. If the paper is too smooth (e.g., some coated papers), it may feed improperly, causing distorted or overwritten characters. Although you can purchase laser printer-specific paper, all laser printers will run acceptably on standard photocopy paper. Try to keep the paper from becoming too wet. Don't open a ream of paper until it is loaded into the printer. Always fan the paper before loading it into the printer, especially if the paper has been left out for more than just a few days.

Hardware

Most laser printers have a self-test function. This self-test shows whether the laser printer can properly develop an image, without anyone having to send a print command from the PC. The self-test is quite handy to answer those *Is it the printer or is it the computer?* Run the self-test to check for connectivity and configuration problems. Possible solutions:

Replace the toner cartridge, especially if you hear popping noises.

Check the cabling.

Replace the data cable, especially if there are bends, crimps, or objects resting on the cable.

If you have a Front Menu Panel, turn off Advanced Functions and High Speed Settings to determine whether the advanced functions are either not working properly or are not supported by your current software configuration (check your manuals for configuration information).

If you are using Windows 3.X, go into Control Panel, select Printers, and choose Connect. Change the port settings to `LPT1.DOS` and remove the X from the Fast Printing Direct to Port Box.

If these solutions do not work, the problem may not be user serviceable. Contact an authorized service center.

HP ERROR CODES

Because Hewlett Packard commands a huge portion of the laser printer market, a discussion of their common error codes is warranted. Other brands will use different codes, but the range of errors will be similar.

41.3 Error

Wrong size media in tray

Two pieces of paper picked up and fed at once

Incorrectly set up paper tray

To clear error message 41.3, hold down Shift key on printer control panel and press continue.

FC (TOP, LEFT, RIGHT)

The font cartridge was removed while the printer was online and the cartridge contained buffered print data. Replace the cartridge and press Continue.

FE FONT CART ERR

The font cartridge was removed while the printer was online. Turn printer on and off to clear message.

20 MEM OVERFLOW

Too much data sent. Simplify print job or add memory. HP no longer offers upgrade memory boards for HP LaserJet, LaserJet +, LaserJet 500, LaserJet series II, or LaserJet IID printers. Third-party parts may be available.

21 ERROR

The printer is unable to process very complex data fast enough for the print engine. This can be caused by multiple addressing of single pixels, too many different fonts or characters on a page, too many cursor-positioning requests per document, etc. Reduce the document's complexity by using fewer fonts and less formatting (bold, italics, shading, etc.), or by reducing the graphics resolution. Note: ADDING MEMORY WILL NOT SOLVE THE PROBLEM. It is a limitation of the print engine, usually the RIP (Raster Image Processor).

22 ERROR

Serial buffer overflow error, or, if you are running parallel, a bad cable or printer interface. If the error occurs on startup, the serial printer cable is probably plugged into a parallel port. If the error appears only after data is sent, then it is probably a bad or loose cable; or you are using an incompatible handshaking protocol, usually XON/XOFF or DTR. Make sure that the printer and the PC are both using the same protocol. (See the chapter on modems and communication protocols for more information on XON/XOFF and DTR).

40 ERROR

`Protocol error during the transfer of data from the PC to the printer.`

This error can have several causes, including:

Loose or damaged cable.

Loss of power to the computer while the printer is online.

Incompatible baud rate, parity, data bits, or stop bits settings.

On LaserJet III or IIID if the I/O is configured to serial and serial is set to 4RS-422 before a balun (matching transformer) is attached to the serial I/O on the printer and/or host system.

Solutions

For modular I/O cards, this means there was an abnormal connection break. Press If the problem continues to clear the error message.

Ensure that the printer and computer are configured for the same baud rate, typically 9600.

Do not turn the power to the computer on or off when the printer is powered on. If it persists, repair may be required.

41 ERROR— HP LaserJet IIP

Turn the printer off—data loss will occur.

Decrease the amount of paper in the MP tray or lower cassette, and do not refill until empty.

Can be caused by adding paper while a print job is in progress.

51 ERROR—Beam Detect Error

Press Continue and the printer will reprint the page.

If the error reoccurs, replace the toner cartridge.

If the printer has just been moved to a cold environment from a warm one, condensation may have formed inside the printer.

Allow the printer to stand for up to 6 hours until the condensation has dissipated.

50 Service Error or 50 Needs Service

Possible malfunction in fuser assembly.

Turn the printer off for 10–15 minutes.

If problem persists, seek service.

79 Service or 79.Xxx Service

Indicates an *unexpected firmware error.*

Turn the printer off and remove any font cartridges, personality cartridges, or memory expansion cards.

Turn printer back on.

79 01bb Error on HP LaserJet IIP+ Printer

If the software gives the option to enter in the amount of printer memory manually, make sure that it is set up properly.

These are only a small sample of the more common error codes! Get the printer's service manuals for a complete list of error codes!

All printers tend to generate a lot of trash. In today's environmentally sensitive world, there are many laws regarding the proper disposal of most printer components. Be sure to check with the local sanitation department or disposal-services company before throwing away any component. Of course, toner cartridges are never thrown away; in fact, there are companies that will PAY for used cartridges.

Parallel Communication

The parallel port was included in the original IBM PC as a faster alternative to serial communication. The IBM engineers considered serial communication, limited to one bit at a time, to be too slow for the *high-speed* devices of the day (e.g., dot matrix printers). Parallel is far faster than serial. Like so much of the technology used in the PC today, the standard parallel port (sometimes referred to as the Centronics standard) has been kept around for backward compatibility, despite several obvious weaknesses.

Speed has been the major concern with parallel ports. The speed of the standard parallel port has remained the same, despite speed improvements in almost every other part of the PC (the maximum data transfer rate of a standard parallel port is approximately 150 kilobytes/second). Standard parallel communication on the PC also relies heavily on software, eating up a considerable amount of CPU time that could be better used otherwise.

The second problem with the standard parallel port is that there is no standard. Although the phrase *Centronics standard* is widely used, there is no such animal. This lack of standardization remains a source of incompatibility problems for some parallel devices, although a very loose set of *standards* adopted by manufacturers has reduced the number of incompatible parallel devices on the market. This lack of standards also applies to the parallel cables. Because there are no standards for electromagnetic shielding on the cables, good parallel cables longer than 6 feet are rare.

A lack of true bi-directional capability has also become a problem. Although one-way communication for simple line printers and dot matrix printers was acceptable, parallel communication was becoming popular for a wide range of external devices that required two-way communication. Although there are ways to get two-way communication out of a standard parallel port (see Nibble Mode, following), the performance is not impressive. A new standard was needed.

IEEE 1284 STANDARD

The IEEE 1284 standard attempts to deal with both problems (poor performance and lack of standardization) while maintaining backward compatibility. In 1991, a group of printer manufacturers proposed to the *Institute of Electrical and Electronics Engineers* (IEEE) that a committee be formed to propose a standard for a backward-compatible, high-speed, bi-directional parallel port for the PC. The committee was the IEEE 1284 committee (hence the name of the standard).

The IEEE 1284 standard requires the following:

Support for all 5 modes of operation (Compatibility, Nibble Mode, Byte Mode, EPP, and ECP)

A standard method of negotiation for determining which modes are supported by both the host PC and by the peripheral device.

Standard physical interface (i.e., the cables and connectors).

Standard electrical interface (i.e., termination, impedance, etc.)

Because there is only one set of data wires, all data transfer modes included in the IEEE 1284 standard are half-duplex—data is transferred in only one direction at a time.

Compatibility Mode/Centronics Mode

The standard parallel port used in the original IBM PC is often referred to as a *Centronics* port. This connection normally manifests itself as a female DB25 (25-pin) connector on the PC and as a corresponding male connector on the cable.

Eight wires are used as grounds, 4 for control signals, 5 for status signals, and 8 for data signals going from the PC to the device. The control wires are used for control and handshaking signals going from the PC to the printer. The status wires are used for handshaking signals from the device to the PC, and for standardized signals from the printer to the PC such as *out of paper, busy,* and *offline*. Only 8 wires are used for transferring data, and that data only goes in one direction—from the PC to the peripheral device. All of the IEEE 1284 transfer modes use this 25-pin cable for backward compatibility reasons, although other types of connections are included in the standard.

The advantage of *Centronics* mode is backward compatibility, but its disadvantages are clear. Data passes in only one direction, from the PC to the peripheral device (a.k.a. *forward direction only*). In addition, the CPU must constantly poll the status wires for error messages and handshaking signals, using up significant amounts of CPU clock cycles. Standard/*Centronics* mode transfers are limited to approximately 150 kilobytes per second.

Some manufacturers have included an enhanced form of *Centronics* mode that is not a part of the IEEE 1284 standard. Referred to as *Fast Centronics* or *Parallel Port FIFO Mode,* devices that support this alternative mode add a hardwired *First In First Out* (FIFO) buffer to the parallel port. Once the data reaches the buffer, the software that had been handling the data transfer assumes that the data has reached the printer and relinquishes control of the CPU to other programs. Once the data is in the buffer, any further handshaking is then handled by it. The buffer emulates the handshaking normally done by the software, allowing *Fast Centronics* mode to work with legacy peripheral devices that operate on the *Centronics* standard. Using this non-standard mode, some systems can achieve data transfer rates of up to 500 kilobytes per second, a significant improvement. Remember that IEEE 1284 does *not* require support for this *Fast Centronics* mode. However, for use with legacy devices (e.g., older dot matrix and laser printers) that do not support the ECP or EPP modes, a *Fast Centronics* parallel port will actually provide superior performance to an IEEE 1284 parallel port that does not support it. If possible, look for parallel ports that support both *Fast Centronics* and the IEEE 1284 standard.

Nibble Mode

Nibble mode is the simplest way to transfer data in *reverse direction* from the peripheral device to the PC. Nibble mode requires no special hardware and can normally be used with any "standard" parallel port (i.e., it does not require an IEEE 1284 parallel port). All parallel ports have five status wires that are designed to send signals from the peripheral to the PC. Using four of these wires at a time, we can transfer a byte (8 bits) of data in two pieces, one nibble (4 bits) at time. Nibble mode is even more software-intensive than compatibility/*Centronics* mode, eating up many CPU clock cycles. This intensive use of CPU time, when combined with the limitation of transferring data one nibble at a time, limits nibble mode data transfers to approximately 50 kilobytes per second. However, nibble mode will work on any PC parallel port, and when used in concert with compatibility/*Centronics* mode, allows for a very limited form of *bi-directional* communication using any parallel port.

Byte Mode/Enhanced Bi-Directional Port

Although a combination of compatible/*Centronics* and nibble mode transfers can produce two-way communications, the resulting speed is not very satisfactory. As higher performance external peripherals came to market, a more powerful means of two-way parallel communication was needed. A number of manufacturers (including IBM with the PS/2 parallel port) began to add a new data transfer mode to their parallel ports—byte mode. Byte mode allows reverse direction (peripheral to PC) parallel communication that uses all eight data wires. To accomplish this, extra hardware is added that handles the negotiation between the PC and the peripheral (remember, the original standard only allowed the data wires to be used for forward communication, from the PC to the peripheral). By using byte mode in conjunction with *Centronics* mode, two-way communication that uses eight bits in each direction became possible. With byte mode, two-way communication can achieve speeds approaching the speed of the one-way *Centronics* data transfers, approximately 150 kilobytes per second. Parallel ports capable of byte mode transfers are sometimes referred to as *enhanced bi-directional ports*. This terminology has led to some confusion between these early bi-directional ports and the more advanced parallel ports. The enhanced bi-directional port is far less capable, but is often supported on parallel ports and devices that do not support the entire IEEE 1284 standard.

EPP (Enhanced Parallel Port)

For peripherals that require constant two-way communication with the PC, the *Enhanced Parallel Port* (EPP) protocol offers high-speed, two-way data transfers with relatively little software overhead. Handshaking and synchronization between the peripheral device and the PC are handled by hardware. By removing the CPU from the handshaking process, an EPP port allows the CPU to transfer data to and from the port with a single command, saving a significant number of clock cycles.

However, unlike ECP ports (see following), the EPP protocol calls for a close *coupling* between the program running the parallel port and the peripheral device, meaning that the program can monitor and control the flow of data at all times. This allows the program to change the direction of the communication easily, making EPP the ideal protocol for devices that frequently change from input to output and back again (e.g. external hard drives, tape backup units, etc.).

Because control of the handshaking and synchronization process is dependent on the hardware, manufacturers have considerable flexibility with regard to performance enhancements. As long as the device, whether the port or a peripheral, responds properly to the standardized EPP signals, manufacturers are free to implement any performance improvements they wish without violating the EPP standard. The end result is that data transfers using the EPP protocol can approach the speed of the ISA bus, transferring between 500 kilobytes and 2 megabytes per second.

The Enhanced Parallel Port was developed before the creation of the IEEE 1284 committee. As a result, the early EPP protocol has a minor difference from the version adopted by the IEEE 1284 committee. Because of this difference, IEEE 1284 EPP parallel ports can fail to recognize that a pre-IEEE 1284 device is not ready to receive or send data. In that case, the device may fail to work properly. However, IEEE 1284 peripherals work just fine with the pre-IEEE 1284 parallel ports. These pre-IEEE 1284 ports and devices are sometimes referred to as EPP 1.7 devices, referring to an earlier proposed standard.

ECP (Extended Capability Port)

Microsoft and Hewlett-Packard proposed the Extended Capability Port protocol as a response to the need for high-performance parallel communication for printers and scanners. ECP data transfers are loosely *coupled*, meaning that once the data transfer has begun, the software that initiated the transfer (e.g., a printer driver) cannot monitor the progress of the transfer. The software must wait for a signal that shows that the transfer has been completed. Even more than EPP, this reduces the number of clock cycles used by the transfer to a bare minimum. While it also reduces the amount of control that the software has over the process, not much control is needed. ECP is designed for operations that involve moving large chunks of data (i.e., a print job going out to a printer or an image coming in from a scanner). These types of data transfers do not require much monitoring.

ECP ports use a data-compression method called *Run Length Encoding* (RLE). With RLE, data can be compressed up to 64:1. This enhances performance significantly because printers and scanners deal with raster images that tend to compress well. For RLE to work, both the device and the parallel port must support it. Note that RLE compression is not actually part of the IEEE 1284 standard, but is instead part of Microsoft's standard for implementing the ECP protocol.

The ECP protocol works especially well for multifunction devices such as scanner/printer/fax machines because of a feature called channel addressing. Using a *Centronics* or nibble mode connection, if one device is busy the other parts of the integrated device are inaccessible. For example, with a scanner/printer/fax, you could not send a fax while a print job was being sent to the printer. The parallel cable was essentially a party line, and only one device could use it at a time. With channel addressing, you can specify the part of the integrated device with which you wish to talk. Without interrupting the print job, you can send a fax or even begin scanning a page (providing the device itself is capable of doing more than one thing at a time).

The ECP standard provides the same degree of flexibility to hardware manufacturers that EPP does. As long as the parallel port and devices respond to the standardized ECP commands, manufacturers can enhance performance any way that they wish. Because the data transfers that use ECP do not require manipulation of the data, many manufacturers have added special capabilities to the ports, often with DMA or through *Programmable Input/Output* (PIO). The capabilities of the port (or lack thereof) depend on the manufacturer.

Support for the Standard

Also remember that manufacturers do not always embrace the entire standard. On the peripheral side, this is not much of a problem. Some modes are more appropriate for some types of devices than for others. ECP excels at handling large blocks of data, making it ideal for printers and scanners, but not so attractive for devices such as external CD-ROMS. External devices that must frequently switch back and forth between read and write operations are better served by EPP, with its capability to change the direction of the data flow without additional handshaking and overhead. Many peripheral manufacturers will not support all five modes because it would be wasteful.

However, on the parallel port side, support for all five modes is vital. Because *Centronics* mode and nibble mode are controlled through software, any parallel port ever made for an IBM PC can do both. However, control for byte mode, ECP, and EPP resides in the hardware. Without the appropriate hardware support, expensive devices capable of high-speed communication must slow down to the speed of the parallel port.

Negotiation

The IEEE 1284 standard requires devices that operate in anything other than *Centronics* mode to respond to an identification command that determines which modes are supported both by the parallel port and by the peripheral. To ensure backward compatibility, a failure to respond to that command is interpreted as meaning the device is capable of only *Centronics* mode: forward only communication.

CONNECTIONS, CABLING, AND ELECTRICITY

Although no true standard existed, *standard parallel cable* has usually referred to a printer cable with a male DB25 connector on one end and a 36-pin *Centronics* connector on the other (see Figure 11.14). The shielding (or lack thereof) of the internal wiring and other electrical characteristics is largely undefined except by custom. In practice, these standard cables are acceptable for transferring data at 10 kilobytes per second and for distances under 6 feet, but would be dangerously unreliable for ECP or EPP operations.

Figure 11.14 36-pin Centronics connector.

While the specific electrical characteristics are not particularly important for individuals unless they wish to build their own cables from scratch, the mere existence of a standard is a tremendous boon to the consumer. All cables manufactured to the IEEE 1284 specifications are marked *IEEE Std 1284-1994 Compliant.* When using cables with that marking, you can be confident that the cable will support the high data throughput of ECP and EPP, and work reliably at lengths of up to 10 meters. Generally, the DB25 and 36 pin Champ connectors have been retained (see Figure 11.15).

Figure 11.15 DB25 connector.

IEEE 1284: Important Reminders

Fast Centronics is not a part of the IEEE 1284 standard, although it can be useful for legacy hardware.

Enhanced bi-directional port only means that the port is capable of byte mode. Do not confuse it with *Enhanced Parallel Port* (EPP).

IEEE 1284 devices that use EPP may not work with EPP parallel ports produced before the IEEE 1284 standard.

Just because a device supports some of the IEEE 1284 modes of operation does not mean that it complies with all aspects of the standard.

CHAPTER 12

Portable PCs

From the moment that PCs first began to appear in the early 1980s, there has been a tremendous desire to take a PC and move it from one location to another. The capability of a PC to hold and process data drove a strong market impetus to come up with a way to transform the static desktop PC into a mobile device designed to serve an increasingly mobile business environment. The upside to the mobile PC was the promise of increased efficiency and profitability. The downside to making a PC a mobile device was that the desktop PC, as envisioned by IBM, was an absolute nightmare to make mobile for a number of reasons (see Figure 12.1).

The biggest problem was power: the first desktop PCs were designed to run from standard 120-volt AC current with big switching power supplies to convert to multiple voltages of DC current. At least the low DC current demands of PCs made batteries, and therefore truly mobile PCs, possible. One interesting item is that there had been a push early on at IBM to go for higher voltages than 12 volts for some aspects of PCs. If that push had been successful, the mobile PC might have been substantially delayed. But even running at 12 volts or less, a first-generation PC with a hard drive could have quickly drained any of the smaller, inexpensive batteries of the early 1980s. The first generation of mobile computers got around the power problem quite elegantly—they didn't have batteries. If you wanted to move the PC, you turned it off, unplugged it, and lugged it (the first ones were heavy) to the next location, where you plugged it back in and turned it back on to start using it again. This was fine for a person moving from office to office, but what about the person working in a car, plane, or some other place where a power outlet wasn't available? Batteries, and the power they provided, quickly became very important for mobile computing. This demand for more power and for PC components that used less power has created an entire family of PC products that are functionally identical to their desktop equivalents, but use much less power. Low-power monitors, CPUs, chipsets, hard drives, and CD-ROMs are now the de facto standards on laptops. Many of these low-power components, or at least the technologies that make them low power, have made strong penetration back into the desktop market.

Figure 12.1 Getting a PC to *go mobile* was a daunting task.

The second big challenge was to ensure reliability. Desktop hard drives and floppy drives were never designed to be used in the back of a bouncing pickup truck or in a turbulent coach seat. Their read/write heads would bounce around, never properly accessing the data or worse, destroying it. This was countered by new methods of drive design that compensated for missed data and by providing methods to help to prevent the heads from crashing into the drive. These technologies eventually have become standard even on desktop PCs. In addition, there was a need to make the entire PC more robust. Many first-generation mobile PCs actually had small shock absorbers to help compensate for shocks and to make the PC generally more robust than its desktop equivalent.

The last challenge was functionality. Mobile PCs needed to be able to mimic the functions of their desktop brothers. This functionality ranges from the need to keep up with a mobile version of whatever *latest and greatest* device is on desktops, to the human factors of trying to make desktop devices smaller and lighter while still being functional to the average user.

A great example of the quandary is the mouse. Even though the first mobile PCs had the capability to use a mouse, the standard desktop rodent would hardly serve a businessman packed into the middle seat of a 737 or a busy duty nurse making his/her rounds in a ward. The demand for a mobile mouse spawned a series of new, innovative pointing devices, from trackballs to touchpads.

The challenges of power, reliability, and functionality continue to drive innovations in mobile computing. We continue to demand longer running, more reliable PCs while we expect the same convenience, firepower, and speed that we enjoy on our desktops. Unfortunately, the ability to conquer one challenge usually creates new problems elsewhere. As improvements in batteries and power management continue to increase, the availability of power and new demands for new devices continue to demand even more (see Figure 12.2). As new devices become available, new demands on reliability begin to surface. The cycle is unending.

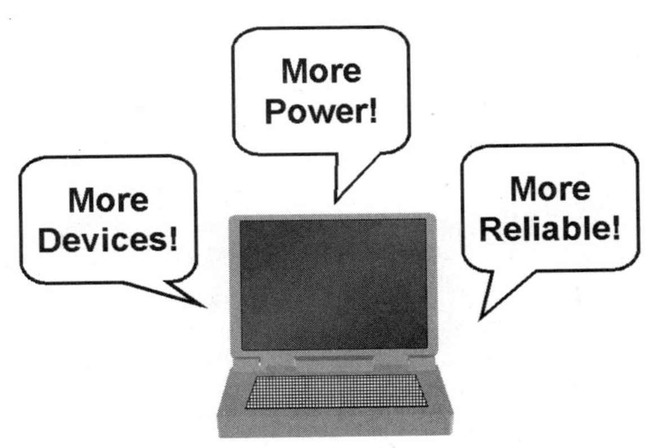

Figure 12.2 More, More, More!

History

Trying to point out the first mobile computer is guaranteed to produce fisticuffs between any two computer historians. Rather than start a fight, it may be easier to simply zero in on the first computers that were widely marketed and available to the public. This crown can arguably be given to the famous Osborne One from the late seventies. Although not truly a PC (it didn't use IBM's BIOS or have any interchangeable parts with the PC), the Osborne One (see Figure 12.3) defined a series of technologies that helped to define how the first generation of portable computers would look and operate. In particular, the Osborne defined the concept of *suitcase luggable*. The Osborne One was organized with a small screen, 5" floppy drives, and a keyboard that acted as a cover during transport.

Figure 12.3 The Osborne (Photo courtesy Tom Carlson, The Obsolete Computer Museum)

Due to its proprietary design, the Osborne cannot be officially listed as the first mobile PC clone. (Remember, only IBM can make a PC—everyone else makes clones. It's just that the term *PC* now envelops all IBM and IBM clones.) That moniker would have to be given to the mobile PCs developed by Compaq in the early eighties. Not only were these the first mobile PC clones, the Compaqs (see Figure 12.4) were the first PC clones of any type! Before Compaq, only IBM made PCs—it was Compaq that started the entire clone concept, and it was the Compaq mobiles that were the first clones. The Compaq portables were quickly followed by a succession of similar machines, including a genuine IBM luggable version.

Figure 12.4 The Compaq Portable (photo courtesy Tom Carlson, The Obsolete Computer Museum).

The luggables were all AC-powered, so there were no battery problems. They ran on 8086 CPUs or equivalent, and all ran the exact same DOS as their desktop cousins. Therefore, they could easily exchange data and programs with those machines. These mobile PC-compatible computers made a tremendous impact on many industries, substantially changing the way they did business. But of all the industries impacted by portable PCs, the public accounting business was probably the most significantly affected. First-generation luggables, combined with the early spreadsheet programs (i.e., Lotus 1-2-3), literally transformed the way the big—and not so big—accounting firms conducted their day-to-day business.

Public accounting firms like Coopers & Lybrand or Arthur Andersen are hired by companies to do their auditing. As any new CPA will tell you, the life of a young auditor is a highly mobile affair, which involves flying from one client's location to another, diving through records, and running around collecting financial information for the audit. The combination of luggables and spreadsheets was the perfect tool for this industry. Public accounting firms were definitely major purchasers of early mobile computers. They also gave rise to the ancient tech support joke: *What do you get when you cross an accountant with a spreadsheet? One helluva big spreadsheet!* Well, we thought it was funny back in the old days!

The first generation of suitcase-luggable PCs, although highly functional, were seriously limited (see Figure 12.5). First, they were very heavy. Some systems weighed in excess of 40 lbs. The high weight made a system's mobility a function of brawn more than convenience. Second, they had tiny screens due to the limited frontal area. Third, they were bulky. They needed to be placed on top of a stout platform in order to work safely. One would never even consider placing them on a flimsy table, cardboard box, or heaven forbid, a person's lap!

Figure 12.5 Luggable ain't Laptop!

Laptops

As the 286 CPUs began to dominate the desktop market, two separate technologies simultaneously came to fruition (or at least became cheap enough) that allowed PCs to become truly portable at last. First was the portable battery. Obviously, batteries have been around for quite a while, but regular batteries, like the *D* cells in a common flashlight, are unacceptable for usage in PCs. The problem was due to the voltage. Think about those *D* batteries in a flashlight for a moment. When a new set of batteries is placed into a flashlight, the light is quite bright. But over time, the batteries begin to wear down, and the light dims and eventually goes out (see Figure 12.6).

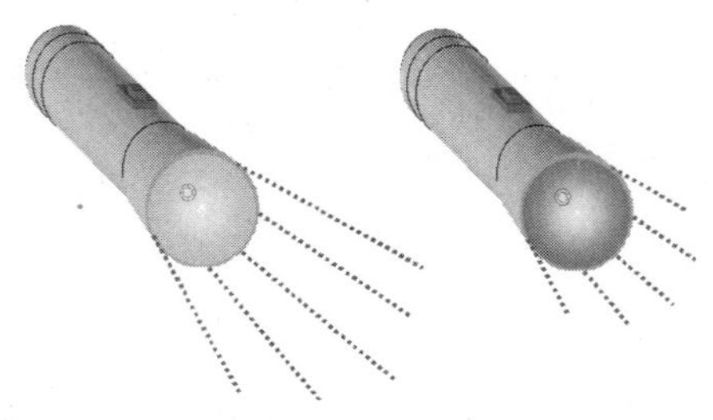

Figure 12.6 Flashlights can go dim.

The reason is simple. As the batteries begin to lose power, the voltage output of the batteries drops correspondingly. Although this voltage drop is no big deal with a flashlight, it is absolutely unacceptable for a computer. PCs need a continuous, steady voltage to operate properly, or they will lock up (see Figure 12.7).

If a PC voltage gets too low, they lock up

Figure 12.7 PCs need constant voltage.

The need for continuous voltage led to the invention of Nickel-Cadmium (Ni-Cd) batteries. Ni-Cd batteries were the first of a series of battery technologies that would provide the necessary constant voltage that the mobile PC needed to operate.

The second technology that allowed PCs to move from being luggable to truly mobile was *the Liquid-Crystal Display* (LCD). The CRT displays of the first generation mobile PCs were usually very small—they were usually no bigger than 4" to 6", measured diagonally. They couldn't be any larger because they wouldn't fit inside the luggable and the extra weight would make the already overweight portables even heavier. Clearly, there was a need for a lighter and larger display. The first common replacement for CRTs was called *Gas Plasma*. The Gas Plasma was a flat-panel display, as opposed to the elongated tube sticking out of the back of the typical CRT (see Figure 12.8). Gas Plasma panels were filled with a gas, usually neon or a similar gas, which would glow when exposed to an electrical charge. The monitor was covered with a grid of wires. By selecting the proper *X* and *Y* wire, a corresponding spot on the screen would glow. Gas Plasma displays were quite popular but they used large amounts of power and were limited to monochrome displays. Gas plasma displays were quite distinctive by their orange-red characters on a black background.

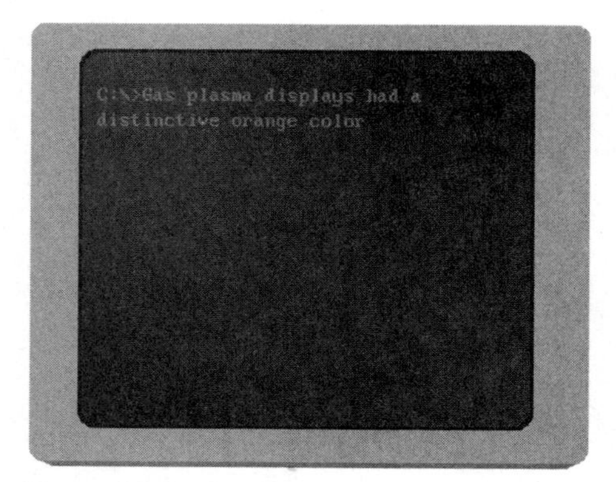

Figure 12.8 Gas Plasma display.

The Gas Plasma displays were quickly overshadowed by LCD displays. LCDs used a special fluid, a liquid crystal, to selectively allow the passage of light through the display. Unlike CRTs, LCDs don't emit light; they can only prevent light from passing through them. The liquid crystals most commonly used in PC displays have molecules that normally allow the passage of light. However, when they are exposed to an electrical charge, the molecules *line up* in a fashion that prevents light from passing through. Although LCDs had been around for some time and were heavily used in watches and calculators since the early seventies, the early LCDs were too slow to keep up with the constantly changing PC screens. This changed with a new technology called *Super Twist Nematic* (STN) that became the cornerstone of all LCD displays. The technology of LCDs continues to improve through today.

Zenith (some folks say it was Data General) was the first to combine the a Ni-Cd battery and LCD display with a mobile computer, thus massively reducing the overall size and taking a marginally mobile, heavy awkward device and turning it into the prototypical mobile device we know today (see Figure 12.9). These new mobile PCs could run anywhere due to their batteries and relatively low weight. In fact, the most common place for these new mobile PCs to operate was on the user's lap, hence coining the common name of *laptop*. The first laptops did away with the old suitcase concept and instead converted mobile PCs into the basic shape that is still used today: the clam-shell, keyboard-on-the-bottom and LCD screen-at-the-top design that is now considered *the shape* of all mobile PCs.

Figure 12.9 Zenith Laptops (photo courtesy Tom Carlson, The Obsolete Computer Museum).

As mobile computing, led by laptop PCs, continued to grow as an overall percentage of all PCs, users began to demand something even smaller and lighter. The problem with laptops was that they were still large enough to demand their own carrying case and even the lightest laptops still approached 15 lbs., making cross-town and cross-country trips still a rather daunting task for all but the most hearty laptop-hauling users. Now the dream was to reduce the size of the laptop so that it could fit in a briefcase. The laptop would have to reduce its size down to the size of a notebook, somewhere in the 8″ × 11″ range. Thus the term *notebook* was given to all mobile PCs in the new small size (see Figure 12.10).

Figure 12.10 Author's notebook.

Today's mobile PCs are still in the notebook size. It seems that the notebook size is just about the most optimal size for a mobile computer. Although the technology exists for much smaller PCs, human factors such as keyboard and display size keep the notebook form the standard today. Interestingly, mobile PCs may actually be getting larger instead of smaller. This is due to a number of reasons. First, the concept of throwing the PC in the briefcase hasn't really come to pass. Today's notebooks usually travel in their own specialized travel cases, so the idea of a little extra size no longer bothers most users. Second, the extra size is used to provide larger screens and keyboards—two areas that have always been too small for most people. Third, the extra size doesn't include significant extra weight, and it provides users with virtually all of the amenities and peripherals that they can get on their desktops—the Holy Grail of mobile computing.

Yet even since the earliest mobile computers, there has been a demand for very small, reduced-function PCs. These devices may or may not use the same operating systems as their desktop brethren, but they would be able to interface with them. These devices wouldn't have all of the firepower, but they would be able to handle the demands of on-the-go executive/sales types. These devices could at the very least store names, addresses, and phone numbers; track appointments and meetings; and provide to-do lists. Preferably, they could handle faxes, e-mail, and maybe even pagers and Internet access! Generically, these devices have been called *Palmtops* or *Personal Digital Assistants* (PDAs). PDAs are definitely niche players, but they have been around since the first of the mobile computers and continue to grow in popularity. Here's one of the first PDAs: the Poqet PC (see Figure 12.11). The Poqet had 640K RAM and an 8086 CPU. It ran DOS and all of the popular DOS programs of the day. It even had the first type of PC Card!

The goal of the PDA is to fit into a shirt or pants pocket, and to weigh as little as possible. With this in mind, PDAs over the years have made great strides in removing superfluous equipment (in particular, the keyboard). Many of today's PDAs use a combination of handwriting recognition combined with modified mouse functions, usually in the form of a pen-like stylus, to make a new type of input called pen-based computing. One example of a modern PDA is the popular Palm Pilot from 3COM (see Figure 12.12).

Figure 12.11 Poqet PC.

Figure 12.12 3COM Palm Pilot.

Let us take a moment to clear up some common misconceptions about names for the different mobile PC layouts. There are many layouts, from *suitcase* and *laptop*, to *notebook* and *palmtop*. The broad use of these terms implies that there are clear definitions for each layout. There are no such definitions—these are marketing terms that have moved into mainstream usage. As a result, many devices may fit more than one layout. For example, an extra-large notebook might just as easily be described as a small laptop. A more full-featured PDA might just as easily be considered by someone else as a small notebook. This overlap is perfectly acceptable.

Now that we understand the different layouts of mobile computing, it would be a good idea to delve into some of the technologies of mobile computing in detail. This will entail revisiting some previously discussed technologies such as batteries and LCDs, as well as a tour into a few that have not yet been covered. As these technologies are revealed, their history, growth, and current usage will be clarified so that any good tech can provide at least basic support for virtually any mobile PC.

Batteries

Of all the many technologies unique to mobile PCs, the usage, care, and troubleshooting of batteries is probably the most obvious, most frustrating, and yet most easily supported. The secret to understanding batteries is to understand the types of batteries used and appreciate each of their special needs/quirks. Once this is clear, the symptoms that point to battery problems are *usually* obvious and easily remedied. First of all, there are only three types of batteries commonly used in mobile PCs. They are *Nickel-Cadmium* (Ni-Cd), *Nickel-Metal Hydride* (Ni-MH) and *Lithium-Ion* (Li-Ion). Let's investigate each of these types.

NICKEL-CADMIUM

Ni-Cds (see Figure 12.13) were the first batteries commonly used in mobile PCs. As previously mentioned, PCs, unlike flashlights or Walkmans, must have a steady voltage. Before Ni-Cd, there wasn't a cheap battery technology that provided that necessary steady voltage. Ni-Cd, being the first of its type, was also full of little problems. Probably most irritating was a little thing called *battery memory*. This was the tendency for a Ni-Cd battery, which was repeatedly charged without being totally discharged, to lose a significant amount of its rechargeability. In essence, a battery that originally kept a laptop running for two hours would eventually keep that same laptop going for only 30 minutes or less. In order to prevent memory problems, a Ni-Cd battery should have been completely discharged before each recharging. Also, a Ni-Cd should not have been overcharged. Overcharging was sometimes difficult to determine because there was no way to verify when the battery was totally charged, unless one purchased an expensive charging machine (which none of us did). As a result, most Ni-Cd batteries lasted an extremely short time and were then replaced. It was unfortunate that so many people ignored this problem because the fixes allowed batteries to last three to four times longer. Another quick fix was to purchase a conditioning charger. These chargers would first totally discharge the Ni-Cd battery, and then provide a special *reverse* current that in a way *cleaned* internal parts of the Ni-Cd to allow it to recharge more often and to run longer on each recharge.

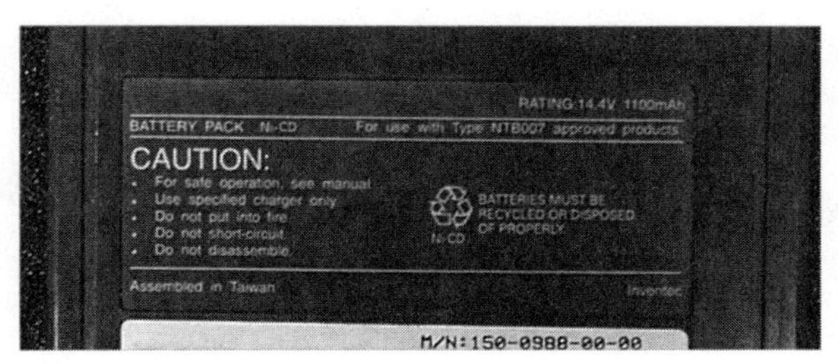

Figure 12.13 Ni-Cd battery.

Ni-Cd batteries would at best last for 1000 charges, although with poor treatment they would last far less. Ni-Cds were extremely susceptible to heat and would self-discharge over time if not used. Leaving a Ni-Cd in the car in the summer was the equivalent to throwing it in the garbage. But Ni-Cd batteries didn't stop causing trouble even after they died. The highly toxic metals inside the battery made it unacceptable simply to throw them in the trash. Ni-Cd batteries need to be disposed of via specialized disposal companies. This is very important! Even though Ni-Cd batteries aren't used in PCs very often anymore, many devices, such as cellular and cordless phones, still use Ni-Cds. Don't trash the environment by tossing Ni-Cds into a landfill. Turn them in to the closest special disposal site—most recycling centers are glad to take them. Also, many battery manufacturers/distributors will take them. The environment you help preserve just might be yours—or your kids'.

NICKEL METAL HYDRIDE

Ni-MH batteries were the next generation of mobile PC batteries and are still quite common today (see Figure 12.14). Basically, Ni-MH batteries are Ni-Cd batteries without most of the headaches. Ni-MH batteries aren't nearly as susceptible to memory problems, can take overcharging somewhat better, take more recharging, and last longer between recharges. Like a Ni-Cd, Ni-MH batteries are still susceptible to heat, but at least they are considered non-toxic to the environment. It's still a good idea to do a special disposal. It's usually better to recharge a Ni-MH with shallow re-charges as opposed to the complete discharge/recharge of Ni-Cd. Ni-MH batteries are a popular replacement for Ni-Cd systems.

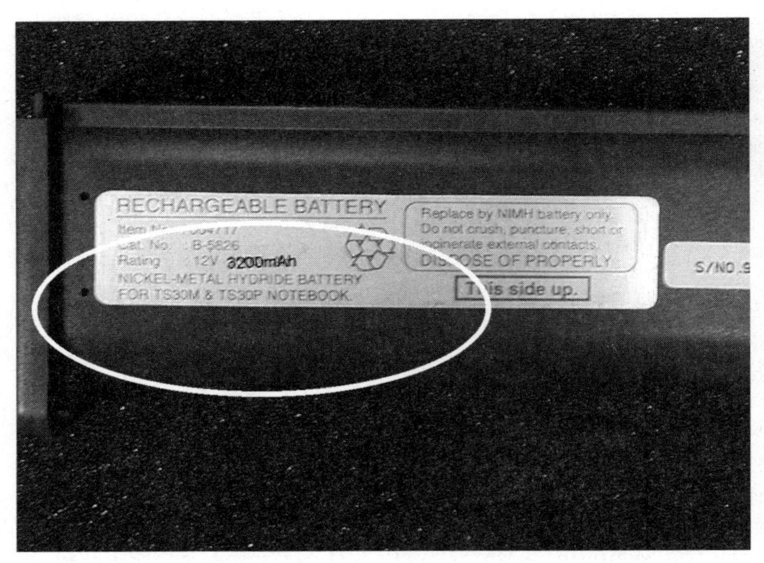

Figure 12.14 Ni-MH battery.

LITHIUM ION

The most common battery used today is the Lithium-Ion (see Figure 12.15). Lithium-Ion batteries are completely immune to memory problems, are very powerful, and last at least twice as long as a comparable Ni-MH battery on one charge. Sadly, they can't handle as many charges as Ni-MH, but today's users are usually more than glad to give up total battery life span for longer periods between charges. Lithium-Ion batteries simply can't be overcharged—they will explode—so all Lithium-Ion batteries sold with PCs have a built-in circuitry to prevent accidental overcharging. Therefore, Lithium-Ion batteries are also completely immune to overcharging. Lithium batteries can only be used on systems designed to use them. They can't be used as replacement batteries.

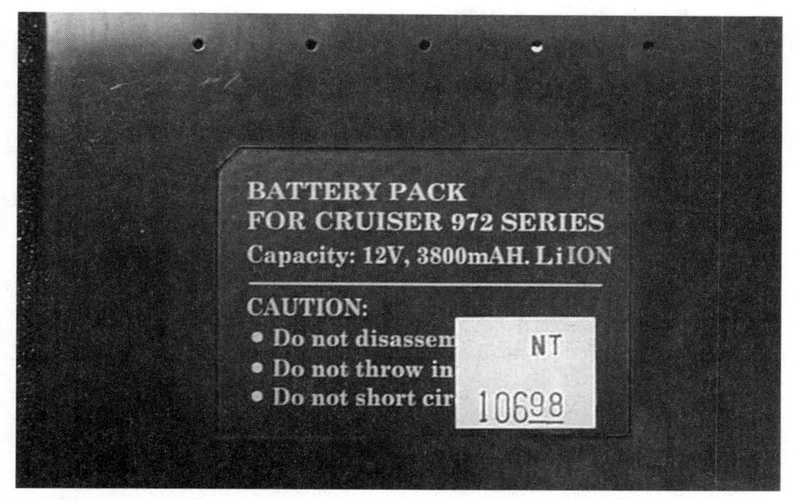

Figure 12.15 Li-Ion battery.

SMART BATTERIES

In an attempt to provide better maintenance for laptop batteries, manufacturers have developed a new type of battery called the smart battery. Just now becoming known, the smart battery is able to tell the computer when it needs to be charged, conditioned, or replaced.

In general, keep in mind the following. First, always store batteries in a cool place. Although a freezer is in concept an excellent storage place, moisture, metal racks, and food make it a bad idea. Second, condition Ni-Cd and Ni-MH batteries—they'll last longer. Third, keep battery contacts clean with a little alcohol or just a dry cloth. Fourth, never handle a battery that has ruptured/broken because the chemicals are very dangerous. Finally, always recycle old batteries.

LCD Displays

Although batteries can often cause angst for troubleshooting, LCD displays cause the most angst BEFORE the computer is purchased due to the high cost and broad selections. The cost of the LCD is usually 50 to 75 percent of the total cost of the laptop, so making sure that the proper LCD is purchased can be a huge money and job saver.

LCDs come in three basic styles: passive matrix, dual-scan passive matrix, and active matrix. Passive matrix screens use an X-Y axis of wires to charge the liquid crystal of the screen. The charged spots become dark or, in the case of a color screen, take on a certain color. These colors are painted dots on the face of the crystal matrix screen that are then lit up by the electricity in the crystals. Passive matrix screens produce decent resolution, but the screens tend to draw slowly and with some overlap or fuzziness. Dual-scan screens refresh two lines at a time and thus overcome some of the slowness of single-scan. Dual-scan passive matrix screens dominate the mid- to low end laptop market.

Active matrix screens use tiny transistors rather than an X-Y axis of lines, with each color dot controlled by its own transistor. Active matrix screens thus have faster refresh and much tighter color control than passive matrix or dual-scan passive matrix screens. Even though active matrix is much more expensive than passive or dual-scan, active matrix screens are the LCD of choice today.

Active matrix displays have many advantages over passive. First, they are brighter with better contrast. Second, they can handle far more colors. The passive's slow speed keeps it at a practical limit of no more than 256 colors (8-bit), while the latest active matrix displays can do up to 16.7 million (24-bit) color. Third, active matrix displays have a much wider viewing area. Where passive matrix is rarely more than 45 degrees, active is closer to 90–100 degrees (see Figure 12.16)—and improving!

Although the technology of LCD is vastly different from CRT, the daily support of LCD panels is quite similar to that of CRTs. LCD displays have a bandwidth, just like CRTs, although it is often referred as the *dot rate*. If you go past the dot rate, you create the same problems as pushing the refresh rate on a CRT. Fortunately, because the video is almost always a permanent part of the system, this is handled by the manufacturer of the PC. This leads to a bigger problem: video drivers on laptops. As discussed in the video chapter, it is common, even necessary, to constantly update video drivers and tweak CRT refresh rates on desktop systems. The opposite is true for laptops. Because laptop makers don't anticipate users replacing or tweaking their video drivers, many continue to place ancient, bizarre device drivers in their CONFIG.SYS, AUTOEXEC.BAT, SYSTEM.INI or WIN.INI files. Most of these drivers are simply to support DOS apps, but they can also be video refresh or screen re-mappers (to get rid of excess blank space on the monitor in different modes). When dealing with laptop video drivers, stick to the manufacturer's settings unless compelled to do otherwise.

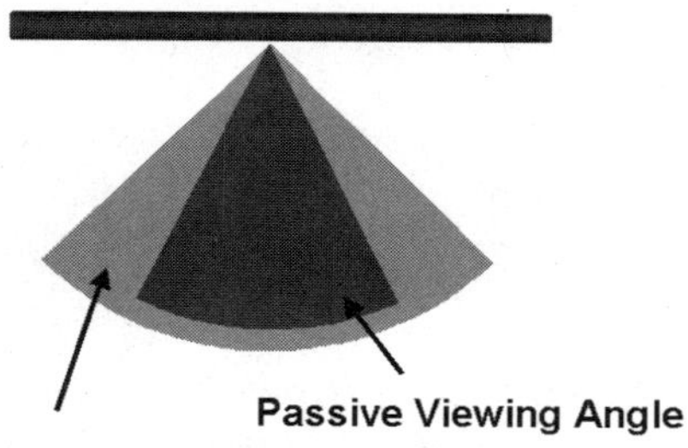

Figure 12.16 Viewing angle for active and passive matrix.

PC Cards

PC Cards, still commonly known by the older term of *Personal Computer Memory Card International Association* (PCMCIA) are as standard on today's mobile computers as the hard drive (see Figure 12.17). PC Cards are credit-card sized, hot-swappable devices that can, and do, perform virtually every PC function. Although originally visualized as a memory card, today there are PC Card hard drives, modems, network cards, soundcards, SCSI, and the list can continue indefinitely. PC Cards are easy to use, inexpensive, and convenient.

Unfortunately, it is this same convenience/ease of use that can make PC Cards a real challenge to configure or troubleshoot. Like so many other parts of the PC, the secret is to understand the individual components of PC Cards to allow one to recognize symptoms when they happen. The place to start with PC Cards is to recognize that there are three different physical sizes of PC Cards, as determined by the PCMCIA committee. They are called Type I, Type II, and Type III (see Table 12.1); and while PCMCIA doesn't require that certain sizes perform certain functions, most PC Cards follow their recommendations.

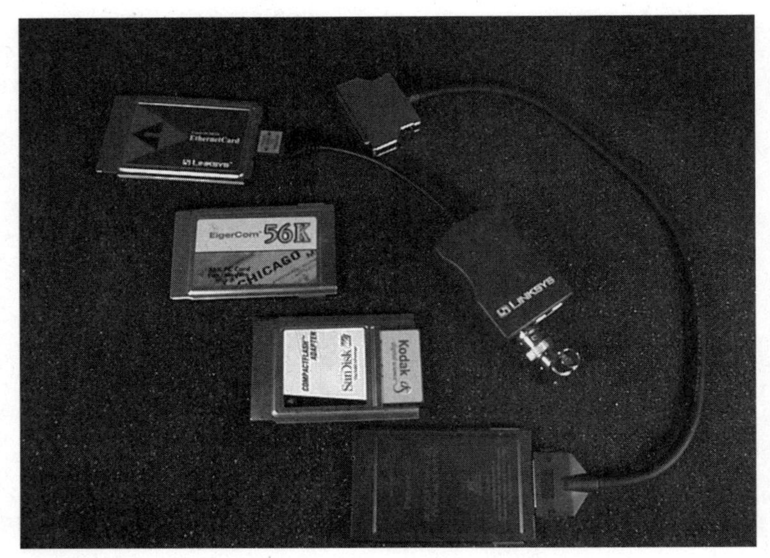

Figure 12.17 Assorted PC Cards.

Table 12.1

	Length	Width	Thickness	Recommended Use
Type I	85.6 mm	54.0 mm	3.3 mm	Flash Memory
Type II	"	"	5.0 mm	I/O (Modem, LAN, etc)
Type III	"	"	10.5 mm	Hard Drives

The only difference between these three types is the thickness of the card. All PC Cards share the same 68-pin interface, as long as the slot that accepts the card is high enough, any PC Card will work in that slot. Type II cards are by far the most common of PC Cards (see Figure 12.18). Therefore, most laptops will have two Type II slots, one above the other, to allow the computer to accept two Type I or II cards or one Type III card.

Figure 12.18 Two PC Cards in laptop.

The PCMCIA standard defines two levels of software drivers to support PC Cards. The first, lower level is known as *socket services*. Socket services are device drivers that are used to support the PC Card socket, allowing the system to detect when a PC Card has been inserted or removed, and providing the necessary I/O to the device. The second, higher level is known as *card services*. Card services recognize the function of the card and provides the specialized drivers necessary to make a particular PC Card work. When PC Cards first started to be used back in the days of DOS and Windows 3.X, Card and Socket services were manifested through device drivers in `CONFIG.SYS`, `AUTOEXEC.BAT`, and/or `SYSTEM.INI`. Here's a hypothetical example from an old laptop that only ran DOS.

```
DEVICE=C:\SERVICES\PCMCIA2.SYS /M=D000-DFFF /L
DEVICE=C:\SERVICES\TOSCS.SYS
```

The early days of PCMCIA put most of the responsibility for making PC Cards work in the hands of the individual laptop manufacturers. This meant that if you wanted to be sure a PC Card worked, you purchased the PC Card from the same place you got the laptop. This problem continued until Windows 95 and modern laptop chipsets arrived on the scene. In today's laptops, the socket services are standardized and are handled by the system BIOS. Windows 95 itself handles all card services and has a large pre-installed base of PC Card device drivers, although most PC Cards come with their own drivers (see Figure 12.19). The Windows 95 Card Services can be accessed via the PCMCIA option in the Control Panel.

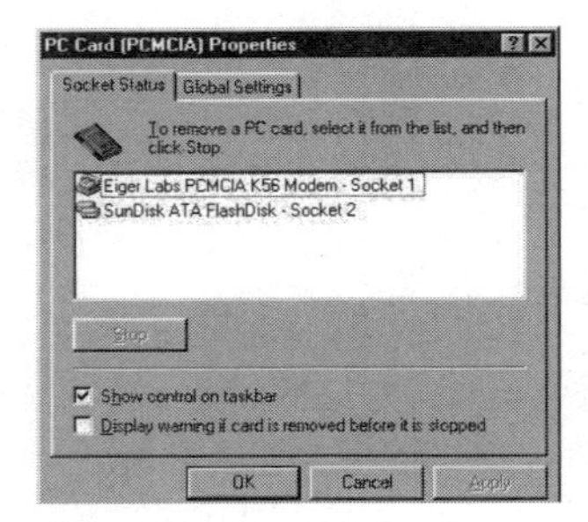

Figure 12.19 PC Card settings.

Many PC Card makers advertise a Type IV slot. This slot is not part of the PCMCIA standard and is used to describe any PC Card thicker than the Type III.

The newest type of PC Card is called Cardbus. Cardbus is nothing more than a special 32-bit PC Card type and special slot. Cardbus has some major advantages over regular PC Cards. First, it is 32-bit instead of the regular 16-bit PC card. Second, it can handle PCI bus mastering (Cardbus is really an extension of PCI). Last, it allows for single cards to have up to eight functions. Regular PC Cards can only have a maximum of two functions. An example of a two-function PC Card is a modem/network card. Well, don't be surprised when you can purchase a modem/network/ISDN/sound/SCSI card! A Cardbus PC Card is identical to a regular PC Card, using the same Types and having the exact same pinout. This allows regular PC Cards to work in a Cardbus slot. Unfortunately, a Cardbus card will not work in a regular PC Card socket. In fact, Cardbus uses 3.3-volt power instead of the regular 5-volt PC Card power, so a Cardbus card will have a special keying that won't allow you to plug it into a regular PC Card socket accidentally. Cardbus has become the PC Card of the future and is standard equipment on most new laptops. Finally, in order for Cardbus to operate, the laptop should be running Windows 95 OSR2 or later.

Power Management

There are a lot of different parts to the typical laptop and each part of that laptop uses power. The problem is that with early laptops, every one of these parts used power, whether the system needed that device or not. For example, the hard drive would continue to spin, whether or not it was being accessed; and the LCD panel would continue to display, even when the user walked away from the machine.

The optimal situation would be a system in which the user could instruct the PC to shut down unused devices selectively, preferably by defining an amount of time of inactivity, which if reached, would then shut down a particular device. Longer periods of inactivity would allow the entire system to shut even itself down, leaving critical information loaded in RAM, ready to restart if a *wake-up* event such as pressing a key or moving a mouse occurred. This system would have to be sensitive to potential hazards such as shutting down in the middle of writing to a drive, and could not add significantly to the cost of the PC. Clearly, a machine that could perform these functions would need specialized hardware, BIOS, and an operating system to allow proper operation. This process of cooperation between hardware, BIOS, and the OS to reduce power use is known generically as *power management.*

SMM

Intel began the process of power management with a series of new features built into the 386SX CPU. These new features allowed the CPU to slow down or stop its clock without erasing the register information, as well as a number of other features that dealt with power saving in peripherals. These collective features were called *System Management Mode* (SMM). From the humble beginnings of the 386SX, SMM slowly started to show up in (and is a now common addition to) all PC CPUs. Although a power-saving CPU was okay, the power management was relegated to little more than special *sleep* or *doze* buttons that would stop the CPU and all of the peripherals on the laptop. In order to really take advantage of SMM, the system required a specialized BIOS and OS to go with the SMM CPU. To this end, Intel forwarded the *Advanced Power Management* (APM) specification in 1992.

REQUIREMENTS FOR APM

APM requires four items in order to function fully. First is an SMM-capable CPU. Because virtually all CPUs are SMM-capable, this is easy. Second is an APM-compliant BIOS. This allows the CPU to send the necessary commands to shut off the peripherals when desired. Third are devices that will accept being shut off. These devices are usually called *Energy Star* devices to show their compliance with the EPA's Energy Star rating. To be an Energy Star device, the peripheral must have the capability to power down without actually turning off. Last, the system's OS must know how to request the shutting down of particular devices and the slowdown or stopping of the CPU's clock.

LEVELS OF APM

APM defines five different operating levels of power usage for a system. These levels are intentionally *fuzzy* to allow manufacturers considerable leeway in their use. The only real difference between them is the amount of time for each power usage level to return to normal usage. These levels are:

Full On

Everything in the system is running full power. No power management.

APM Enabled

The CPU and RAM are running full power. Power management is enabled. An unused device may or may not be shut down.

APM Standby

The CPU is stopped, RAM still stores all programs, and all peripherals are shut down, although configuration options are still stored. (In other words, to get back to APM Enabled, you won't have to re-initialize the devices.)

APM Suspend

Everything in the PC is shut down or in lowest power-consumption settings. Many systems use a special type of Suspend called *hibernation*, in which critical configuration information is written to the hard drive. Upon a wake-up event, the system is reinitialized and the data is read from the drive to return the system to the APM-enabled mode. Clearly, the recovery time from Suspend to Enabled will be much longer than the time from Standby to Enabled.

CONFIGURATION OF APM

APM BIOS can be configured via CMOS settings or through the OS (see Figure 12.20). Generally, OS settings will override CMOS settings. Even though the APM standards allow a great deal of flexibility, and therefore some confusion, between different implementations, there are certain settings that all CMOSs share. First is the capability to initialize power management, which allows the system to enter the APM Enabled mode. Many CMOSs will then give time frames for entering Standby and Suspend modes, as well as settings to determine which events take place in each of these modes. Finally, many CMOSs will give settings to determine wake-up events. An example is the capability of the system to monitor a modem or a particular IRQ.

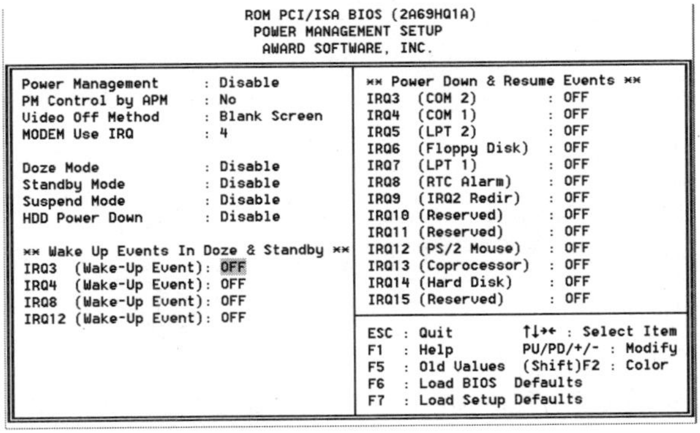

```
                        ROM PCI/ISA BIOS (2A69HQ1A)
                          POWER MANAGEMENT SETUP
                           AWARD SOFTWARE, INC.

Power Management      : Disable          ** Power Down & Resume Events **
PM Control by APM     : No               IRQ3  (COM 2)         : OFF
Video Off Method      : Blank Screen     IRQ4  (COM 1)         : OFF
MODEM Use IRQ         : 4                IRQ5  (LPT 2)         : OFF
                                         IRQ6  (Floppy Disk)   : OFF
Doze Mode             : Disable          IRQ7  (LPT 1)         : OFF
Standby Mode          : Disable          IRQ8  (RTC Alarm)     : OFF
Suspend Mode          : Disable          IRQ9  (IRQ2 Redir)    : OFF
HDD Power Down        : Disable          IRQ10 (Reserved)      : OFF
                                         IRQ11 (Reserved)      : OFF
** Wake Up Events In Doze & Standby **   IRQ12 (PS/2 Mouse)    : OFF
IRQ3  (Wake-Up Event): OFF               IRQ13 (Coprocessor)   : OFF
IRQ4  (Wake-Up Event): OFF               IRQ14 (Hard Disk)     : OFF
IRQ8  (Wake-Up Event): OFF               IRQ15 (Reserved)      : OFF
IRQ12 (Wake-Up Event): OFF
                                         ESC : Quit        ↑↓→← : Select Item
                                         F1  : Help        PU/PD/+/- : Modify
                                         F5  : Old Values  (Shift)F2 : Color
                                         F6  : Load BIOS  Defaults
                                         F7  : Load Setup Defaults
```

Figure 12.20 CMOS power settings.

Configuring the OS for power management has been a highly progressive process, dating from the early DOS-based systems, through Windows 3.X, and ending with the highly integrated functions of Windows 95/98.

In DOS, the only real tool was the POWER.EXE program. This program gave DOS the capability to handle power management and, depending on the version of POWER.EXE, was capable of a broad cross-section of settings for most APM functions. Interestingly, most users simply added POWER.EXE to the CONFIG.SYS and AUTOEXEC.BAT files and accepted the default settings. As Windows 3.X became more common, many laptop makers began to add special applications that would either add configurations to POWER.EXE or would add their own protected-mode APM tools. Either way, the lack of any standard interface made power management a rather interesting experience, requiring a significant degree of learning how each manufacturer manifested their opinion of power management!

APM in Windows 95 and later has greatly simplified the process of power management, primarily by creating a standard interface. Power management shows itself in two areas. First are the Monitor settings in the Control Panel (see Figure 12.21). These settings are also accessed by right-clicking on the Desktop. Because the monitor is one of the biggest power users, this is a great place to start the power-management configuration process.

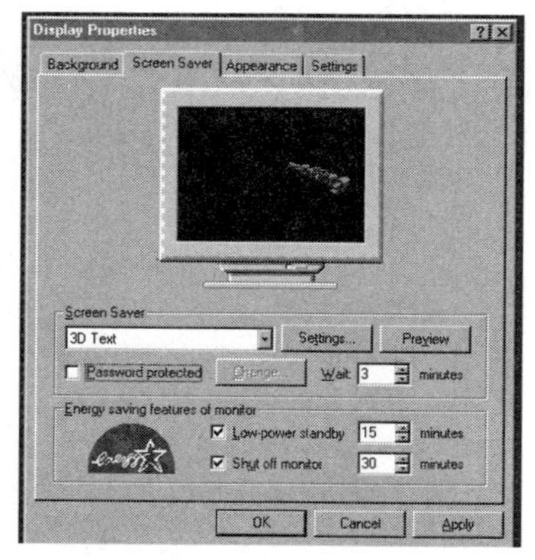

Figure 12.21 Monitor power settings.

Windows 95/98 hides the APM concept of Standby and Suspend, with the exception of adding the Suspend option to the Start button. Instead, Windows tries to give individual control for the big power eaters: monitors, PC Cards, and hard drives; and makes its own assumptions for everything else in the PC. These controls can be found in the Power section of the Control Panel (see Figure 12.22).

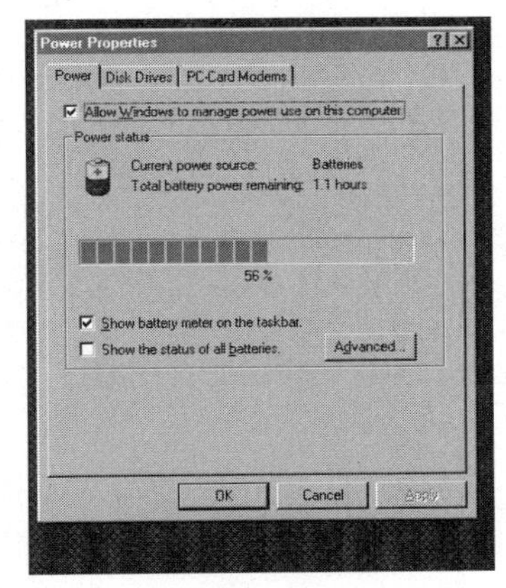

Figure 12.22 Power settings.

Index

Boldface folios denote illustrations.

8–bit ISA expansion bus, 206, **206**
16–bit ISA expansion bus, 207–208, **207**
32–bit drivers, 183
80xxx CPU family, 65–66, **68, 70**
386 protected mode CPU operation, 69, 71
486 CPU family, 75–81, 84–85
  overdrive CPUs for 486s, 88–89, 101
8042 keyboard controller chip, 165

access speed, DRAM, 141–142, **142,** 157
active vs. passive matrix LCDs, 398–399, **399**
Adaptec host adapters for SCSI drives, 316–317
adapters (*see* host adapters, SCSI; video cards (adapters) & monitors)
Add New Hardware Wizard, 183–184, **184**
address bus, 60–66, 164, **164**
  address space, reserved for BIOS, 168
  BIOS addressing, 168–169, **168**
  I/O addresses, 208–216
  interrupts (IRQ), 216–219
Advanced Graphics Port (AGP), 344–345
Advanced Power Management (APM), 404–407
Advanced SCSI Programmers Interface (ASPI), 308–309
Advanced Technology (AT) computers, 66
AMD CPUs, 4, **4,** 65–66, 97, **99,** 102
American Megatrends BIOS (AMIBIOS), 171–172, 175
arbitration, bus, 235
  SCSI, 303–304
ASCII code, 364
aspect ratio, video cards, adapters, monitors, 332
assumed hardware, IRQ and I/O assignment, 239
AT bus, 207, **207**
AT type motherboards, 194–197, **195**
AT-style keyboard connector, 30, **31**
ATX type motherboards, 194–197, **196, 197**
audio connectors, 26–27, **27**
Award Software BIOS, 171–172, 173–174

Baby AT type motherboards, 194
bad sectors, hard drives, 282
bandwidth, video cards, adapters, monitors, 329
banks of memory, 143–148, **144–147,** 152, 157–158
batteries, 71
  Advanced Power Management (APM), 404–407
  battery backup for CMOS, 177–179, **177, 178**
  battery memory, 394
  lithium ion batteries, 396–397, **397**
  Nickel Metal Hydride (Ni-MH), 396, **396**
  Nickel-Cadmium (Ni-Cd), 394–395, **395**
  numeric error codes, 190
  portable PCs, 383–384, 388, 389, 394–397
  smart batteries, 397
  storing batteries, 397
  System Management Mode (SMM), 403–404
battery memory, 394
beep codes from POST, 186–189
Bernoulli drives, 316
bi-directional communication/printing, 376
binary signals, CPUs, 49, 63–64
BIOS, 164–193
  Add New Hardware Wizard, 183–184, **184**

address bus and addressing, 168–169, **168**
Advanced SCSI Programmers Interface (ASPI), 308–309
American Megatrends (AMIBIOS), 171–172, 175
Award Software, 171–172, 173–174
battery backup for CMOS, 177–179, **177, 178**
beep codes from POST, 186–189
boot process, 192–193
Bring Your Own BIOS (BYOB), 180
CMOS, 169, 170–179
CMOS errors, lost CMOS, 175–176
CONFIG.SYS, 181–182
configuring CMOS, 170–175
core hardware, 169, 170
device drivers, 181–185
Device Manager, 183–184, **184**
Direct Memory Access (DMA), 226–229
drive letter assignment, 280, **281**
editing the CMOS, 172
Enhanced CHS (ECHS), hard drive, 272, 275–276
error messages (numeric & text) from POST, 189–191
flash ROM, 179–180, **179**
hard drives, 266, 308
I/O addresses, 208–216
interrupts (IRQ), 216–219
lines of programming code in typical BIOS, 167
Logical Block Addressing (LBA), hard drive, 272, 274–276
operating system, 193
option ROM, 180
Phoenix Technologies, 171–172, 174
POST cards, 191–192, **192**
Power On Self Test (POST), 185–192
printer settings, 350
Registry, Registry Editor (REGDIT), 183–184
saving CMOS settings, CMOSSAVE, 176
SCSI, 308, 312
Setup program to configure CMOS, 171–174
System BIOS ROM chip, 169
SYSTEM.INI, 182–183
updating BIOS, 179–180
video RAM, 338–340
Windows 95/98, device drivers, 183
bits and bytes of memory, 58–59
BNC type connectors, 26, **27**
boot process, 192–193
bootable drive, 193
bootable floppy disk, 245
bootable SCSI ID device, 293
operating system, 193
SCSI, 312
system disk, 193
bootable drive, 193
bootable SCSI ID device, 293
box or case for motherboard, 10–11, **11**, 198–199
branch prediction, CPUs, 106
brightness, video cards, adapters, monitors, 334, 336, 337
Bring Your Own BIOS (BYOB), 180
bubble memory, 69
buffers, printers, 376
burst mode, bus, 235–236, 238–239
bus mastering, 229, 235, 238
disk cache vs. bus mastering, 304–305
hard drives, 279
SCSI, 303–305, 310
byte mode, printers, 376–377

cables
A, B, and P wire cabling, SCSI, 305
CD-ROMs, 22, **23**
floppy drive cable, 15, **16,** 243–244, **243, 244,** 248
hard drive cables, 17–20, **18, 19,** 260–261, **260,** 290–291
laser printers, 370
length limits for SCSI cables, 306
printers, 380–381, **380, 381**
SCSI devices & hard drives, 290–291, 302–303, 305–307, **305–307**
ST506/412 hard drives & interfaces, 284–286, **285, 286**
cache
beep error codes, 186, 189
disk cache vs. bus mastering, 304–305
external (L2) cache, 80, **80**
internal (L1) cache, 79–80, **79**
onboard cache, 76–77, **77**
online L2 cache, CPUs, 102, 103

RAID 6, hard drives, 315
write-back vs. write-through cache, 80–81, **81**
calibration images, video cards, adapters, monitors, 332
capacities of floppy drives, 241–242
capacity of hard drives, 256–257, 273–276
card services, PC Cards, 401
Cardbus card, 402–403
Cathode Ray Tube (CRT)
laser printers, 362
video monitor, 321–322, 321
CD-ROMs, 20–23, **21–23,** 169
cables for CD-ROMs, 22, **23**
controllers, 22
IDE CD-ROMs, 22
power supplies connection, 22, **23**
SCSI CD-ROMs, 22
sound cards, 22
soundcard connection, 28, **29**
Central Processing Unit (CPU), 2–4, **3, 4,** 45–110, 163
80xxx CPU family, 65–66, **68, 70**
386 protected mode operation, 69, 71
486 CPU family, 75–81, **84–85**
address bus and BIOS, 168–169, **168**
address bus, 60–66
Advanced Technology (AT) computers, 66
AMD CPUs, 65–66, 97, **99**, 102
batteries, 71
beep error codes, 186
binary signals, 49, 63–64
BIOS, 164–193
branch prediction, 106
bus mastering, 229
cache
external (L2) cache, 80, **80**
internal (L1) cache, 79–80, **79**
onboard cache, 76–77, **77**
online L2 cache, 102, 103
chipsets, 229–230, **230**
clock circuits, 52–56, **57,** 81–83, 95–97, 106
clock doubling, 81–83, 95–97, 106
clock speed (in MHz), 4, 53–56, 81–83, 95–97, 106
codebook, 48, 50–51, **51,** 56, **57,** 166
commands, 51, 56
Complex Instruction Set Computing (CISC), 75
Cyrix CPUs, 65–66, 97, **99**
data registers, 50
daughter cards, 88–89
Direct Memory Access (DMA), 226–229
dual-pipelining, 90–93, **93**
dynamic processing, 102, 103
Dynamic RAM (DRAM), 77–79
external data bus, 47–49, **47,** 56–57, **57**
flip-flops, 79
general purpose registers, 50
high-order bits, 51
how they work, 45–46
I/O addresses, 208–216
inserting a CPU, 107, 109, **109**
instruction sets, 75, 166
Intel CPUs, 65–66
interrupts (IRQ), 216–219
jumpers and switches, 73–74, **74**
keyboard connection, 165
low-order bits, 51
machine language, 51
make and model numbers, 3–4, 45, 65–66
math coprocessors, 75–76
Memory Control Chip (MCC), 61, 78
memory, 58–59, **58, 59**
modes of operation, 66–71
motherboard connection, 7, **7,** 164
multimedia extension (MMX) Pentiums, 104–106
multiplier (*see* clock doubling)
orientation notch/index corner, 107, 109, **109**
overclocking a CPU, 54–56, 83
overdrive CPUs for 486s, 88–89, 101
overdrive CPUs for Pentium, 102
overheating of CPUs, 94
Pentium CPUs, 90–97, **90, 98**
Pentium II CPUs, 106–107, **107**
Pentium Pro (P6) CPU, 102–103, **102**
Pin Grid Array (PGA) type, 2
pipelines, 90–93, **92**
power-saving strategies, 71–75
P-ratings, 100
programs, 56–57

protected mode operation, 67, 69, 75
quad-pipelining, 102, 103
RAM connecting to CPU (*See* address bus)
Random Access Memory (RAM), 58–59, **58, 59**
read only memory (ROM), 166
real mode operation, 67, 69
Reduced Instruction Set Computing (RISC), 75, 97
registers, 49–51, **50,** 57
removal tool for CPUs, 86, **87**
running (executing) a program, 57
Single Edge Cartridge (SEC) type, 2
Slot 1 connection, SEC cartridges, 107
Socket 8 (online L2 cache), 103, **104**
socket types, Pentium, 100–101, **101**
split voltage CPUs, 106
Staggered Pin Grid Array (SPGA), 100
Static RAM (SRAM), 79
SX and DX Intel processors, 71
system crystal & clock speed, 54, **55,** 83, 204–205
System Management Mode (SMM), 71, 74–75
TTL logic circuits, 57
underclocking a CPU, 56
upgrading 386 CPUs, 89–90
upgrading 486 CPUs, 86
virtual 8086 mode, 69, 71, 75
virtual memory, 69, 71, 75
virtual registers, 69
Voltage Regulator Module (VRM), 95, **95**
voltage regulators, 73, **73**, 94–95, **95**
voltages, 72–74, 93–95, 106
wait states, 78, **78**
wires of address bus, 62–64, **64**
write-back vs. write-through cache, 80–81, **81**
Zero Insertion Force (ZIF) sockets, 86, **87, 88**

Centronics connectors, 25, **25,** 306, **307**
Centronics mode, printers, 375–376, 379
Centronics standard, printers, 374
chains, SCSI 290–291, **292**
channels in PCI bus, 240
checksum, beep error codes, 187, 189
chipsets, 229–230, **230**
clock circuits
beep error codes, 186, 188
CPUs, 52–56, **57,** 81–83, 95–97, 106
clock doubling, 81–83, 95–97, 106
clock speed, 4, 53–56, 81–83, 95–97, 106, 204–205
Complementary Metal Oxide Semiconductor (CMOS), 169, 170–179
Advanced Power Management (APM) configuration, 405, **405**
American Megatrends BIOS (AMIBIOS), 171–172, 175
autodetection of hard drive, 271–272, **271, 272,** 275–276, **275**
Award Software, 171–172, 173–174
battery backup for CMOS, 177–179, **177, 178**
beep error codes, 186, 187
boot process, 192–193
configuring CMOS, 170–175
drive letter assignment, 280, **281**
editing the CMOS, 172
Enhanced CHS (ECHS), hard drive, 272
floppy drive configuration, 244–245, **245,** 247
hard drives, 263–280, **264**
AUTO setting, 266, 271–272, **271, 272,** 275–276, **275**
I/O address assignment, 214
Logical Block Addressing (LBA), hard drive, 272
losing CMOS data, errors, 175–176
low-level formatting, 281–284
memory configuration, 160–161
parallel (LPT) port I/O and IRQ assignment, 224–225
Phoenix Technologies, 171–172, 174
Programmable I/O (PIO) modes, hard drive, 276–279, **277, 278**
saving CMOS settings, CMOSSAVE, 176
SCSI, 312–313
serial (COM) port I/O and IRQ assignment, 224–225

Setup program to configure CMOS, 171–174
video RAM, 338–340
codebook, CPUs, 48, 50–51, **51,** 56, **57**
color adapters, video cards, adapters, monitors, 340–341
color depth, video cards, adapters, monitors, 319, 343–346
Color Graphics Adapter (CGA), 342
COM ports (*see* serial ports)
commands, CPUs, 51, 56
common access method (CAM) AT interface, hard drives, 257
Common Command Set (CCS), SCSI, 299
compatibility mode, 375
Complex Instruction Set Computing (CISC), 75
computer components, 1–43
BIOS, 164–193
CD-ROMs, 20–23, **21–23,** 169
Central Processing Unit (CPU), 2–4, **3, 4,** 45–110, 163
CMOS devices, 169, 170–179
connectors, 24–27, **24–28**
cooling fan, 3, **3**
core hardware, 169, 170
documentation, 42
floppy drives, 14–17, **15–17,** 163, 169
hard drives, 17–20, **18–20,** 163, 169
joysticks, 36
jumpers and switches, 37–41, **37–41**
keyboards, 30–31, 163
modems, 34–35, **35**
motherboards, 6–12, 7–12, 163–201
mouse, 31–33, 163, 169
Network Interface Card (NIC), 30, **30**
on/off button, power switch, 123–125, **123, 124**
open architecture of PC design, 111–112
parallel ports, 35–36, **35, 36**
power requirements of typical components, 120
power supplies, 12–13, **13, 14,** 111–125, **112**
printers, 35–36
Random Access Memory (RAM), 4–5, **5, 6,** 127–162, 163, 169
serial ports, 31–33
soundcards, 28, 28, 29, 163, 169
tape drives, 169
tools for computer work, 2
video cards (adapters) & monitors, 29, **29,** 163
CONFIG.SYS, 181–182
connectors, 24–27, **24–28,** 194
AT-style keyboard connector, 30, **31**
audio connectors, 26–27, **27**
BNC type connectors, 26, **27**
Centronics connectors, 25, **25,** 306, **307**
converters for power supplies, 119, **119**
DB type connectors, 24, **24**
DIN type connectors, 24, **25**
dongles, 33, **34**
D-type connectors, 306, **307**
floppy drives, 243–244, **243, 244,** 248
hard drives, 258–260, **258,** 276
joystick, 36, **37**
keyboard, 30, **31**
laser printers, 370
mini-audio connectors, 26–27, **27**
mini-connectors, 116–117, **116, 117**
mini-DIN type connectors, 24, **25**
modems, 34–35, **35**
Molex connectors, 115–116, **115, 116**
mouse, 33, **33**
Network Interface Card (NIC), 30, **30**
parallel ports, 35–36, **35, 36**
pins or contacts on connectors, 25
power supplies, 113–114, **113, 114,** 197, **198**
printers, 380–381, **380, 381**
PS/2 style mini-DIN keyboard connector, 30, **31**
RJ type connectors, 26, **26**
SCSI, 305–307, **305–307,** 311
serial port connectors, 32
soundcards, 28, **28, 29**
splitters for power supplies, 119, **119**
ST506/412 hard drives & interfaces, 284–286, **285, 286**

sub-mini connectors, 118–119, **118, 119**
video cards, 29, **29,** 337
wings on connectors, 25
contrast, video cards, adapters, monitors, 334
controller
CD-ROM, 22
floppy drive, 14, **15,** 32, 247–248
hard drive, 19, **19,** 32, 258–260, **259,** 263, 264, 278–279, **279**
IO Ready (IORDRY) controllers, 278–279, **279**
keyboard, 165
convergence, video cards, adapters, monitors, 319, 332–333, 333, 335
converters for power supplies, 119, **119**
cooling (*see* fans)
coprocessors, math coprocessors, 75–76
core hardware, 169, 170
corona, primary, laser printers, 355
corona, transfer, laser printers, 356, 367
crashes, SCSI, 316
cylinders, hard drives, 253–254, 254, 256, 264
Cyrix CPUs, 65–66, 97, **99**

data encoding, hard drives, 251
data registers, CPUs, 50
daughter cards, 88–89
DB type connectors, 24, **24**
DEFRAG as diagnostic, hard drives, 312
degaussing button, video cards, adapters, monitors, 334, 337
depth of memory, 129–131, **130**
device drivers, 181–185
32–bit drivers, 183
Add New Hardware Wizard, 183–184, **184**
Advanced SCSI Programmers Interface (ASPI), 308–309
CONFIG.SYS, 181–182
Device Manager, 183–184, **184**
Direct Memory Access (DMA), 226–229
EZ SCSI device drivers, 308, 309
hot swapping, 302
I/O addresses, 208–216
interrupts (IRQ), 216–219
parallel (LPT) port I/O and IRQ assignment, 219–226
Plug and Play (PnP), 203–204
printers, 350
Registry, Registry Editor (REGDIT), 183–184
ROM chip disabling, ASPI issues, 309
SCSI, 313
serial (COM) port I/O and IRQ assignment, 219–226
SYSTEM.INI, 182–183
Device Manager, 183–184, **184**
differential-ended (SCSI-2) devices, 300–301
DIN type connectors, 24, **25**
DIP switches, 37, **37**
Direct Memory Access (DMA)
beep error codes, 187, 188
bus mastering, 229
chipsets, 229–230, **230**
hard drives, 279–280
I/O address assignment, 214
limitations, 228
printers, 379
SCSI, 312–313
Display Power Management Signaling (DPMS), 330
documentation, 42
dot matrix printers, 350–351, **350**
dot pitch, video cards, adapters, monitors, 319, 327–328, **328**
dots per inch (dpi) measurement of resolution, 363
double words of memory, 59
drive letter assignment
floppy drives, 242–242
hard drives, 280, **281**
drum, laser printers, 354, **355**
D-type connectors, 306, **307**
Dual Inline Memory Modules (DIMMs), **5, 6,** 151–153, **151–153,** 160, **160**
Dual Inline Pin Packages (DIPP), 136–137, **136**
dual-pipelining, CPUs, 90–93, **93**
dynamic processing, CPUs, 102, 103
Dynamic RAM (DRAM), 77–79, 128–162, 128, 128
access speed, 141–142, **142,** 157
adding memory, 133–135, **134**
banks of memory, 143–148, **144–147,** 152, 157–158

depth of memory, 129–131, **130**
DIMM installation, 160, **160**
Dual Inline Modules (DIMMs), 151–153, **151–153,** 160, **160**
Dual Inline Pin Packages (DIPP), 136–137, **136**
Error Correction Code (ECC) DRAM, 156–157
Extended Data Out (EDO) DRAM, 154–155, **155**
Memory Controller Chip (MCC), 133
mixing DRAM packages, 153
multiple DRAM rows, 133–135
organization of DRAM, 128–131
packages for memory, 136–143, 148–153
Random Access Memory (RAM), 4–5, **5, 6,** 127–162, 163, 169
SIMM installation, 158–159, **159, 160**
Single Inline Memory Module (SIMM), 138–143, 138–143, 148–150, **149, 150,** 158–159, **159, 160**
Single Inline Pin Package (SIPP), 137–138, **137**
SO type DIMMs, 151, **151**
sticks of memory, 142–143
Synchronous DRAM (SDRAM), 155–156
true vs. TTL parity SIMMs, 150
width of memory, 129–131, **130**

EIDE hard drives, 310–311, 314–315
electron guns, video cards, adapters, monitors, 321, 324
embedded servo formatting for IDE drives, 283–284
energy saving features, 71–75, 319
Energy Star devices, 404
enhanced bi-directional port, printers, 376–377, 381
Enhanced CHS (ECHS), hard drive, 272, 275–276
Enhanced Graphics Adapter (EGA), 342
Enhanced ISA (EISA) bus, 232, 233, 232
Enhanced Parallel Port (EPP) protocol, printers, 377–378, 381
erase lamp, laser printers, 355
error codes
beep codes from POST, 186–189
error messages (numeric & text) from POST, 189–191
laser printers, Hewlett-Packard, 371–373
power supplies, 125
Error Correction Code (ECC) DRAM, hard drives, 156–157, 315
error messages (numeric & text) from POST, 189–191
ESDI hard drives, 286–287
expansion slots/cards/buses, 10, **10,** 12, **12,** 32, 194, 203–204, 205, 233, **233**
8–bit ISA expansion bus, 206, **206**
16–bit ISA expansion bus, 207–208, **207**
arbitration, 235
assumed hardware, 239
AT bus, 207, **207**
beep error codes, 186
burst mode, 235–236, 238–239
bus mastering, 229, 235, 238
cascaded IRQs, 222, **223,** 224
channels in PCI bus, 240
chipsets, 229–230, **230**
Direct Memory Access (DMA), 226–229
Enhanced ISA (EISA) bus, 232, **233**
expansion bus, 205, 233, **233**
external data bus, 204
I/O addresses, 208–216, 239
Industry Standard Architecture (ISA) buses, 207
interrupts (IRQ), 216–219, 222–224, 239
local bus, 233, **233**
Memory Controller Chip (MCC), 204
mezzanine bus, 238
Micro Channel Architecture (MCA) bus, 231–232, **231**
parallel (LPT) port I/O and IRQ assignment, 219–226
parasitic slots, 235
PC bus, 206, **206**
Peripheral Component Interconnect (PCI) bus, 236–240, **236, 237**
Plug and Play (PnP), 203–204
SCSI, 309–310

serial (COM) port I/O and IRQ assignment, 219–226
speed, 204–205
system bus, 205
system crystal & clock speed, 204–205
transitional motherboards, 237
VESA VL-bus, 233–236, **234, 235**
XT bus, 207
Extended Capability Port (ECP) protocol, printers, 378–379
Extended Data Out (EDO) DRAM, 154–155, **155**
external connectors on motherboard, 9, **9**
external data bus, 47–49, **47,** 56–57, **57,** 163–164, **164,** 204
EZ SCSI device drivers, 308, 309

fans
CPU, 3, **3**
dead fan, 122–123
power supplies, 13, **14**
fast Centronics mode, 375, 376
fast SCSI, 299–301
fiber channel cabling, SCSI, 302
File Allocation Tables (FAT), hard drives, 312
Firewire cabling, SCSI, 302
First In First Out (FIFO) buffer, printers, 376
flash ROM, 179–180, **179**
flavors of SCSI, 289, 297–303, 310
flip-flops, 79
floppy drives, 14–17, **15–17,** 59, 163, 169, 241–248
bootable floppy disk, 245
cable for floppy drive, 15, **16,** 243–244, **243, 244,** 248
capacities of floppy drives, 241–242
cleaning floppy drives, 246
CMOS configuration, 244–245, **245,** 247
connectors, 243–244, **243, 244,** 248
controller, 14, **15,** 32, 247–248
data errors on disks, 247
disk problems, 246
DMA assignment, 229
drive letter assignment, 242–242
I/O address assignment, 215
interrupt (IRQ) assignment, 218
mini-connectors, 116–117, **116, 117**
motherboard connection, 8, **8,** 14, 243, **243,** 248
numeric error codes, 190
power supplies connection, 17, **17,** 116–117, 118–119
replace vs. repair considerations, 248
size of floppy drive, 241, **242**
sub-mini connectors, 118–119, **118, 119**
Swap Floppy Drive setting, 244–245
troubleshooting, 246–248
flux reversals used in data encoding, hard drives, 251
flyback transformer, video cards, adapters, monitors, 336, **336**
flying height of heads, hard drives, 250
focus, video cards, adapters, monitors, 334, 335, 336
Forced Perfect Termination (FPT), SCSI, 317
form factors, motherboard, 194–197
formatting hard drives
embedded servo formatting for IDE drives, 283–284
low-level formatting, 281–284
fragmentation, hard drives, 312
Frequency Modulation (FM) data encoding, hard drives, 251
fuse, thermal fuse, laser printers, 368
fuser assembly, 356, 361, 367
fuses, power supplies, 122, **122**

gain, video cards, adapters, monitors, 335
gas plasma display, 389–390, **390**
gearboxes, Gear Packs, laser printers, 360
General Protection Fault (GPF), memory errors, 162
general purpose registers, CPUs, 50
geometry of hard drives, 252–257
gigabytes as measure of hard drive capacity, 17
Graphical Use Interface (GUI), 233–234
grounding, power supplies, 114, **115**

handheld computers (*see* portable PCs)
hard drives, 17–20, **18–20,** 59, 163, 169, 249–287, **250**
Adaptec host adapters for SCSI drives, 316–317
Advanced SCSI Programmers Interface (ASPI), 308–309
AUTO setting in CMOS, 266, 271–272, **271, 272,** 275–276, **275**
autodetection, 271–272, **271, 272,** 275–276, **275**
bad sectors, 282
Bernoulli drives, 316
BIOS, 266, 308
bus mastering, 279
cables for hard drives, 17–20, **18,** 19, 260–261, **260**, 290–291, 305–307
cables for ST506/412 hard drives, 284–286, **286**
cache, RAID 6, 315
capacity of hard drives, 256–257, 273–276
CMOS configuration, 263–280, **264**
Common Access Method (CAM) AT interface, 257
Common Command Set (CCS), 299
compatibility of SCSI, IDE, and other standards, 310–311
connection to motherboard, 258–260
connectors, 276, 305–307, **305–307**
controller, 19, **19,** 32, 258–269, **259,** 263, 264, 278–279, **279**
crashes, 316
cylinders, 253–255, **254,** 256, 264
data encoding, 251
DEFRAG as diagnostic, 312
DMA assignment, 279–280, 312–313
drive letter assignment, 280, **281**
EIDE hard drives, 258, 310–311, 314–315
embedded servo formatting for IDE drives, 283–284
Enhanced CHS (ECHS), 272, 275–276
Error Correction Code (ECC) DRAM, 315
ESDI hard drives, 286–287
fast SCSI, 299–301
File Allocation Tables (FAT), 312
flux reversals used in data encoding, 251
flying height of heads, 250
Forced Perfect Termination (FPT), 317
formatting, 281–284
fragmentation, 312
Frequency Modulation (FM) data encoding, 251
geometry of hard drives, 252–257
geometry table, IBM drives, 267–270
gigabytes as measure of hard drive capacity, 17
heads, 256, 253, **253,** 264
I/O address assignment, 214, 215, 312–313
IDE hard drives, 17–20, **18, 19,** 257
IDentifiers (IDs) for SCSI devices on chain, 292–294, **293**
interleave, 283–284
interrupt (IRQ) assignment, 218–219, 312–313
IO Ready (IORDRY) controllers, 278–279, **279**
JAZ drives, 316
jumpers and switches, 262–263, 285–286, 293, **293**
landing zone, 256, 264
length limits for SCSI cables, 306
Logical Block Addressing (LBA), 272, 274–276
logical geometry, 273
Logical Unit Numbers (LUNs), SCSI, 294
low-level formatting, 281–284
Low-Voltage Differential SCSI (LVD), 301
mapping, 252
master drives, 260, 263, 280, **281**
megabytes as measure of hard drive capacity, 17
Microhouse Technical Library, jumper information, 262, **262**
mirroring, disk mirroring, 315
Modified Frequency Modulation (MFM) data encoding, 251

motherboard connection, 8, **8,** 276
numeric error codes, 190
parking a drive, 252, 256
partitions, 312
physical geometry, 273
platters, 250
portable PCs, 384–385
power supplies connection, 20, **21**
primary controller, 259
Programmable I/O (PIO) modes, 276–279, **277, 278**, 315
RAID, 315
read/write heads, 250, **250,** 251–252
removable drives, 316
Run Length Limited (RLL) data encoding, 251
SASI interface, SCSI, 297–298
SCANDISK as diagnostic, 312
SCSI hard drives, 17–20, 289–317
SCSI-1, 298–299, **298**
SCSI-2, 299–301
SCSI-3, 301–303
secondary controller, 260
sector organization, 282
sector translation, 273–276
sectors, 255, **255,** 256, 264, 273–276, **274,** 282
slave drives, 260, 263, 280, **281**
ST506/412 hard drives & interfaces, 284–286, **285, 286**
standalone drives, 261
stepper motor, 251–252
striping, 315
terminating resistor, ST506 drives, 286
termination, 294–297, **295, 296, 297,** 317
timing bits, 251
tracks, 254, **254,** 255, 256, 264
types of hard drives, 264, 265–266
ultra SCSI, 301–303
ultra wide SCSI, 301–303
user type of hard drive, 266
voice coil motor, 252
wide SCSI, 299–301
Winchester hard drives, 284–286, **285, 286**
write precompensation, 255, 264
ZIP drives, 294, 294, 316
heads, hard drives, 253, **253,** 256, 264
hexadecimal notation, I/O addresses, 210–213, 215–216
hibernation mode, portable PCs, 404–405
high-order bits, CPUs, 51
Horizontal Refresh Rate (HRR), video cards, adapters, monitors, 322, **323,** 327
host adapters, SCSI, 290–291, **290,** 303, 310, 316–317
hot swapping, SCSI, 302

I/O addresses, 32, 208–216
assumed hardware, 239
hexadecimal notation, 210–213, 215–216
SCSI, 312–313
IDE CD-ROMs, 22
IDE hard drives, 17–20, **18, 19,** 257
IDentifiers (IDs) for SCSI devices on chain, 292–294, **293**
IEEE 1284 standard, printers, 374–375
impact printers, 349–351
indicator lights (front of computer), motherboard connection, 200–201
Industry Standard Architecture (ISA) buses, 207
ink jet printers, 352, **352, 353**
inserting a CPU, 107, 109, **109**
instruction sets, CPUs, 75
Intel CPUs, 4, **4,** 65–66
interlace, video cards, adapters, monitors, 319, 328, 329
interleave, hard drives, 283–284
intermittent failures, power supplies, 125
interrupts (IRQ), 32, 216–219
assumed hardware, 239
cascaded IRQs, 222, **223,** 224
chipsets, 229–230, **230**
I/O address assignment, 214
SCSI, 312–313
IO Ready (IORDRY) controllers, hard drives, 278–279, **279**

JAZ drives, 316
joystick
connectors, 36, **37**
I/O address assignment, 215
interrupt (IRQ) assignment, 218–219
motherboard connection, 9, **9**

jumpers and switches, 37–41, **37–41**
configuring a jumper or switch, 38
DIP switches, 37, **37**
graphic representation of jumper, 41, **41**
hard drives, 262–263
labeling of jumpers, 40
Microhouse Technical Library, jumper information, 262, **262**
on and off/open and closed 38, **39**
parked jumper, 40, **40**
SCSI, 293, **293**
shunt in jumper, 39
ST506/412 hard drives & interfaces, 285–286
voltage settings, 73–74, **74**

keyboard, 30–31, 163
8042 controller chip, 165
beep error codes, 186, 188
connectors, 30, **31**
CPU connection, 165
I/O address assignment, 214
interrupt (IRQ) assignment, 218
motherboard connection, 9, **9,** 11, **11,** 30, **31**
numeric error codes, 190
scan codes, 165–166
typematic setting, 166–167
keystone adjustment, video cards, adapters, monitors, 333

landing zone, hard drives, 256, 264
languages for printers, 364
laptops (*see* portable PCs)
laser circuits, laser printers, 355, 362
laser printers, 353–373, **353**
ASCII code, 364
blotchy, spotty print, 369
cables, 370
Cathode Ray Tube (CRT), 362
charging the drum in printing process, 357, **357**
cleaning the drum in printing process, 356–357, **357**
cleaning the printer, 366–367
configuration, 371
connections, 370
corona, primary, 355
corona, transfer, 356, 367
creased pages, 370
dots per inch (dpi) measurement of resolution, 363
emboss effect print, 369
erase lamp, 355
error codes, Hewlett-Packard, 371–373
fuse, thermal fuse, 368
fuser, 356
fuser assembly, 361, 367
fusing or fixing image in printing process, 359, **359**
gearboxes, Gear Packs, 360
ghosting of images, 368–369
incomplete characters, 369
languages for printers, 364
laser circuits, 355, 362
lines in print, 369
ozone filter, 361, 367
Page Description Language (PDL), Adobe, 364
paper for laser printers, 370
periodic maintenance, 367–368
photosensitive drum, 354, **355**
poorly formed characters, 370
Postscript, Adobe, 364
power supplies, 360, 365, 366
Printer Control Language (PCL), Hewlett-Packard, 364
printing process, 356–359, 362–363
RAM, 361, 362
Raster Image Processor (RIP), 362
replacing parts, 354
Resolution Enhancement Technology (RET), 363
resolution, 363, **363**
reverse power up, 366
rollers, 368
self-test functions, 370–371
sensors and switches, 362
shock hazard, 360
static charge eliminator, 356
switch boxes, 366
system board, 361
toner cartridge, 354, **354,** 356
transfer of image in printing process, 358
transparencies in laser printers, 359
troubleshooting & maintenance, 366–373
tuning gears, 360
writing image in printing process, 358, **358**
LBX type motherboards, 195–196, **196**

line in/line out, soundcard connection, 28
Liquid Crystal Display (LCD), 389, 398–399
lithium ion batteries, 396–397, **397**
local bus, 233, **233**
lock ups
  memory errors, 161, 162
  power supplies, 125
  SCSI, 313
Logical Block Addressing (LBA), 272, 274–276
logical geometry, hard drives, 273
Logical Unit Numbers (LUNs), SCSI, 294
low-level formatting, 281–284
low-order bits, CPUs, 51
Low-Voltage Differential SCSI (LVD), 301
LPT ports (*see* parallel ports)

machine language, CPUs, 51
make and model numbers of CPUs, 45, 65–66
mapping, hard drives, 252
master drives, hard drives, 260, 263, 280, **281**
math coprocessor, 75–76
  beep error codes, 188
  I/O address assignment, 214
megabytes as measure of hard drive capacity, 17
megabytes as measure of RAM, 4–5
memory (*see* Random Access Memory (RAM); Read Only Memory (ROM))
Memory Controller Chip (MCC), 61, 78, 133, 204
mezzanine bus, 238
MHz (*see* clock speed, CPU)
Micro Channel Architecture (MCA) bus, 231–232, **231**
Microhouse Technical Library, jumper information, 262, **262**
microphone, soundcard connection, 28
microprocessors (*see* Central Processing Unit (CPUs))
mini-audio connectors, 26–27, **27**
mini-connectors, 116–117, **116, 117**
mini-DIN type connectors, 24, **25**
mirroring, disk mirroring, hard drives, 315
modes of CPU operation, 66–71
Modified Frequency Modulation (MFM) data encoding, hard drives, 251
Molex connectors, 115–116, **115, 116**
Monochrome Display Adapter (MDA), video cards, adapters, monitors, 340, 341
motherboards, 6–12, **7–12,** 163–201
  address bus, 164, **164**
  AT type motherboards, 194–197, **195**
  ATX type motherboards, 194–197, **196, 197**
  Baby AT type motherboards, 194
  BIOS, 164–193
  boot process, 192–193
  box or case for motherboard, 10–11, **11,** 198–199
  cache, onboard cache, 76–77, **77**
  Central Processing Unit (CPU), 7, **7**
  chipsets, 229–230, 230
  clock doubling, 81–83, 95–97, 106
  CMOS memory configuration, 160–161, 160
  connectors, 194
  daughter cards, 88–89, 88
  expansion slots/cards/buses, 10, **10,** 12, **12,** 194
  external connectors, 9, **9**
  external data bus, 163–164, **164**
  floppy drive connection, 8, **8,** 14, 243, **243,** 248
  form factors, 194–197
  hard drive connections, 8, **8,** 258–260, 276
  I/O addresses, 208–216
  indicator lights (front of computer) connection, 200–201
  inserting a CPU, 107, 109, **109**
  installing a motherboard, 198–201
  installing memory chips, 157–161
  interrupts (IRQ), 216–219
  joystick connection, 9, **9**
  keyboard connection, 9, **9,** 11, **11,** 30, **31**
  LBX type motherboards, 195–196, **196**
  mouse connection, 9, **9**
  multiplier (*see* clock doubling)
  overdrive CPUs for 486s, 88–89, 101

overdrive CPUs for Pentium, 102
parallel port connection, 35–36, **35, 36**
ports, 197
power supplies connection, 8, **8,** 12, 12, 113–114, **113, 114,** 197, **198**
printer connection, 9, **9**
Random Access Memory (RAM), 7, **8**
Read Only Memory (ROM), 166
removal tool for CPUs, 86, **87**
replacing a motherboard, 198–201
screws for motherboard, 199–200
SCSI connections, 311
sockets on motherboard, 7
soldered components on motherboard, 9, **9**
standouts on motherboard, 199–200
traces or wires linking motherboard components, 9, **10**
transitional motherboards, 237
updating BIOS, 179–180
upgrading 386 CPUs, 89–90
upgrading 486 CPUs, 86
voltage of motherboards, 73, 93
Zero Insertion Force (ZIF) sockets, 86, **87, 88**
mouse, 31–33, 163, 169
connectors, 33, **33**
dongles, 33, **34**
motherboard connection, 9, **9**
portable PCs, 385
multimedia extension (MMX) Pentiums, 104–106
multiplier (*see* clock doubling)
multi-synch, video cards, adapters, monitors, 319, 323

negotiation, printers, 379
Network Interface Card (NIC), 30, **30,** 32
nibble mode, printers, 376
nibbles of memory, 59
Nickel Metal Hydride (Ni-MH) batteries, 396, **396**
Nickel-Cadmium (Ni-Cd) batteries, 394–395, **395**
notebooks (*see* portable PCs), 386
nut drivers, 2

on/off button, power switch, 123–125, **123, 124**
open architecture of PC design, 111–112
operating system, 193
option ROM BIOS, 180
orientation notch/index corner, CPUs, 107, 109, **109**
Out of Memory errors, 69
overclocking a CPU, 54–55, 83
overdrive CPUs for 486s, 88–89, 101
overdrive CPUs for Pentium, 102
overheating of CPUs, 94
ozone filter, laser printers, 361, 367

Page Description Language (PDL), Adobe, 364
page faults, memory errors, 161, 162
palettes of color, video cards, adapters, monitors, 340–341
palmtops (*see* portable PCs)
paper for laser printers, 370
parallel port FIFO mode, 375
parallel (LPT) ports, 35–36, **35, 36**
beep error codes, 188
I/O address assignment, 215, 219–226
interrupt (IRQ) assignment, 218, 219–226
LPT port, 219–226, 219
motherboard connection, 35–36, **35, 36**
printers, 374
physical (parallel) vs. I/O (LPT) ports, 221–226, **222**
parasitic slots, 235
parity, 135–136, 141, 142, 150, 161, 162
beep error codes, 189
true vs. TTL parity SIMMs, 150
parked jumper, 40, **40**
parking a drive, hard drives, 252, 256
partitions, hard drives, 312
PC bus, 206, **206**
PC Cards (PCMCIA), 399–403, **400**
card services, 401
Cardbus card, 402–403
settings, 402–403, **402**
socket services, 401
Pentium CPUs, 4, 90–97, **90, 98**
multimedia extension (MMX) Pentiums, 104–106
overdrive CPUs for Pentium, 102

Pentium II CPUs, 106–107, **107**
Slot 1 connection, SEC cartridges, 107
Socket 8 (online L2 cache), 103, **104**
split voltage CPUs, 106
Pentium Pro (P6) CPU, 102–103
Peripheral Component Interconnect (PCI) bus, 236–240, **236, 237**
persistence of vision, video cards, adapters, monitors, 322
Personal Digital Assistants (PDAs) (*see* portable PCs)
Phoenix Technologies BIOS, 171–172, 174
phosphor coatings, video cards, adapters, monitors, 321, 324, **324,** 326
photosensitive drum, laser printers, 354, **355**
physical geometry, hard drives, 273
Pin Grid Array (PGA) type CPUs, 2
pincushion, video cards, adapters, monitors, 333
pins or contacts on connectors, 25
pipelines, CPUs, 90–93, **92**
pixels, video cards, adapters, monitors, 319, 324–325, 327
platters, hard drives, 250
Plug and Play (PnP), 203–204
portable PCs, 383–407
active vs. passive matrix LCDs, 398–399, **399**
Advanced Power Management (APM), 404–407
batteries, 383–384, 388, 389, 394–397
battery memory, 394
Cardbus card, 402–403
development of portables, 386–387
functionality, 385
gas plasma display, 389–390, **390**
hard drives, 384–385
hibernation mode, 404–405
laptops, 388–394, **391**
Liquid Crystal Display (LCD), 389, 398–399
mouse, 385
notebooks, 391, **391**
palmtops, 392, **393**
PC Card settings, 402–403, **402**
PC Cards (PCMIA), 399–403, **400**
Personal Digital Assistants (PDAs), 392, **393**
power management, 403
power supplies, 383–384, 388, 389, 394–397, 403
reliability, 384–385
size reduction, 391
sleep or doze mode, 404
smart batteries, 397
standby mode, 404
Super Twist Nematic (STN) in LCD displays, 390
suspend mode, 404
System Management Mode (SMM), 403–404
ports (*see* parallel ports; serial ports)
POST cards, 191–192, **192**
Postscript, Adobe, 364
Power On Self Test (POST), 185–192
beep codes from POST, 186–189
error messages (numeric & text) from POST, 189–191
laser printers, 366
POST cards, 191–192, **192**
power supplies, 12–13, **13, 14,** 111–125, **112**
See also batteries
Advanced Power Management (APM), 404–407
battery backup for CMOS, 177–179, **177, 178**
CD-ROM connection, 22, **23**
CMOS errors, lost CMOS, 175, 176, 177–179
connectors, 197, **198**
converters, 119, **119**
cooling fans, 13, **14**
dead fan, 122–123
Display Power Management Signaling (DPMS), 330
energy saving monitors, 330–331
Energy Star devices, 404
error codes, 125
failure of power supplies, 120–123, 125
floppy drive connection, 17, **17,** 116–117, 118–119
fuses, 122, **122**
general use connectors, 13, **14**
grounding, 114, **115**
hard drive connections, 20, **21**
intermittent failures, 125
laser printers, 360, 365, 366

lock ups of system, 125
memory errors, 162
mini-connectors, 116–117, **116, 117**
Molex connectors, 115–116, **115, 116**
motherboard connection, 8, **8,** 12, **12,** 197, 13–114, **113, 114, 198**
peripheral connections, 115–120
portable PCs, 383–384, 388, 389, 394–397, 403
power requirements of typical components, 120
power-saving strategies, 71–75
printers, 380–381, **380, 381**
SCSI, 311
shock hazards, 125
size, 120
soft power, 197
splitters, 119, **119**
step-down transformer action, 112
sub-mini connectors, 118–119, **118, 119**
switches, 123–125, **123, 124**
rocker vs. plunger type, 124–125, **124**
System Management Mode (SMM)
CPUs, 71, 74–75
portable PCs, 403–404
video cards, adapters, monitors, 337
Voltage Regulator Module (VRM), 95, **95**
voltage regulators, 73, **73**, 94–95, **95**
voltage requirements, 112–113
voltage settings, jumpers and switches, 73–74, **74**
voltage testing, 120, **121,** 122
wattage, 120
power switch, 123–125, **123, 124**
P-ratings, CPUs, 100
Printer Control Language (PCL), Hewlett-Packard, 364
printers, 35–36, 349–381
See also laser printers
bi-directional communication/printing, 376
BIOS settings, 350
buffers, 376
byte mode, 376–377
cables, 380–381, **380, 381**
Centronics mode, 375–376, 379
Centronics standard, 374
compatibility mode, 375
connectors, 380–381, **380, 381**
DMA, 379
dot matrix printers, 350–351, 350
drivers, 350
enhanced bi-directional port, 376–377, 381
Enhanced Parallel Port (EPP) protocols, 377–378, 381
error codes, Hewlett-Packard, 371–373
Extended Capability Port (ECP) protocol, 378–379
fast Centronics mode, 375, 376
First In First Out (FIFO) buffer, 376
IEEE 1284 standard, 374–375, 374
IEEE Std 1284–1994 compliance, 380–381
impact printers, 349–351
ink jet printers, 352, **352, 353**
languages for printers, 364
laser printers, 353–373, **353**
motherboard connection, 9, **9**
negotiation, 379
nibble mode, 376
paper for laser printers, 370
parallel (LPT) port I/O and IRQ assignment, 219–226
parallel communication, 374
parallel port FIFO mode, 375
parallel ports, 35–36, **35, 36**
power supplies, 380–381, **380, 381**
Programmable I/O (PIO) mode, 379
Run Length Encoding (RLE), 378
troubleshooting, dot matrix, 351
Professional Graphics Adapter (PGA), 342
Programmable I/O (PIO) mode
hard drive, 276–279, **277, 278**, 315
printers, 379
programs, CPUs, 56–57
proprietary SCSI, 298
protected mode CPU operation, 67, 69, 75
PS/2 style mini-DIN keyboard connector, 30, 31, 30

QAPlus/FE, Diagsoft, memory diagnostic, 162

quad words or paragraphs of memory, 59
quad-pipelining, CPUs, 102, 103

RAID, hard drives, 315
Random Access Memory (RAM), 4–5, **5, 6,** 58–59, **58, 59,** 127–162, 163, 169
  access speed, 141–142, **142,** 157
  adding memory, 133–135, **134**, 157–161
  address bus, 60–66
  banks of memory, 143–148, 144–147, 152, 157–158
  beep error codes, 186, 187–188, 189
  bits and bytes of memory, 58–59
  bubble memory, 69
  cache, external (L2) cache, 80, **80**
  cache, internal (L1) cache, 79–80, **79**
  cache, onboard cache, 76–77, **77**
  cache, online L2 cache, CPUs, 102, 103
  CMOS configuration for memory, 160–161
  Dynamic RAM (DRAM), 77–79, 128–162, **128**
    access speed, 141–142, **142,** 157
    adding memory, 133–135, **134**
    banks of memory, 143–148, **144–147,** 152, 157–158
    depth and width of DRAM, 129–131, **130**
    DIMM installation, 160, **160**
    Error Correction Code (ECC) DRAM, 156–157
    Extended Data Out (EDO) DRAM, 154–155, **155**
    mixing DRAM packages, 153
    multiple DRAM rows, 133–135, **134**
    organization of DRAM, 128–131
    packages for memory, 136–143, 148–153
    SIMM installation, 158–159, **159, 160**
    Synchronous DRAM (SDRAM), 155–156
  depth of memory, 129–131, **130**
  diagnostics/testers, 162
  DIMM installation, 160, **160**
  Direct Memory Access (DMA), 226–229
  Dual Inline Memory Modules (DIMMs), **5, 6,** 151–153, **151–153,** 160, **160**
  Dual Inline Pin Packages (DIPP), 136–137, **136**
  Error Correction Code (ECC) DRAM, 156–157
  Extended Data Out (EDO) DRAM, 154–155, **155**
  flip-flops, 79
  General Protection Fault (GPF), 162
  HIMEM.SYS, 162
  installing memory chips, 157–161
  laser printers, 361, 362
  lock ups, 161, 162
  megabytes as measure of RAM, 4–5, 4
  Memory Control Chip (MCC), 61, 78, 133
  mixing DRAM packages, 153
  motherboard connection, 7, **8**
  organization of memory, 132–133, **132, 133**
  Out of Memory errors, 69
  packages for memory, 136–143, 148–153
  page faults, 161, 162
  parity, 135–136, 141, 142, 150, 161, 162
  power supplies, 162
  QAPlus/FE, Diagsoft, 162
  refresh, 79
  SIMM installation, 158–159, **159, 160**
  Single Inline Memory Module (SIMM), **5, 6,** 138–143, **138–143,** 148–150, **149, 150,** 158–159, **159, 160**
  Single Inline Pin Package (SIPP), 137–138, **137**
  SO type DIMMs, **5, 6,** 151, **151**
  Static RAM (SRAM), 79
  sticks of memory, 142–143
  storage devices (floppy/hard drives) vs. memory, 59
  swapfiles, 69
  Synchronous DRAM (SDRAM), 155–156
  synchronous graphics RAM (SGRAM), 346

Troubleshooter, Forefront, 162
troubleshooting RAM, 161–162
true parity SIMMs, 150
TTL parity SIMMs, 150
video RAM, 338–340, 343–346, **347**
virtual memory, 69, 71, 75
volatile RAM, 78
wait states, 78, **78**
width of memory, 129–131, **130**
Windows RAM (WRAM), 346
wires of address bus, 62–64, **64**
write-back vs. write-through cache, 80–81, **81**
Raster Image Processor (RIP), laser printers, 362
raster lines, video cards, adapters, monitors, 322, **322**
Read Only Memory (ROM), 166
address bus and BIOS, 168–169, **168**
beep error codes, 186
BIOS, 164–193
disabling ROM chip, ASPI issues, 309
flash ROM, 179–180, **179**
I/O addresses, 208–216
option ROM, 180
read/write heads, hard drives, 250, **250,** 251–252
real mode CPU operation, 67, 69
Reduced Instruction Set Computing (RISC), 75, 97
refresh, video cards, adapters, monitors, 319, 322–323, **323,** 327, 344
refresh, memory, 79
beep error codes, 187
registers
CPUs, 49–51, **50,** 57
virtual registers, 69
Registry, Registry Editor (REGDIT), 183–184
regulators, voltage regulators, 73, **73,** 94–95, **95**
removable hard drives, 316
removal tool for CPUs, 86, **87**
resolution
laser printers, 363, **363**
video cards, adapters, monitors, 319, 324–327, 343–346
Resolution Enhancement Technology (RET), laser printers, 363
RJ type connectors, 26, **26**
rollers, laser printers, 368
Run Length Encoding (RLE), printers, 378
Run Length Limited (RLL) data encoding, hard drives, 251
running (executing) a program, 57

SASI interface, SCSI, 297–298
saving CMOS settings, CMOSSAVE, 176
scan codes, keyboard, 165–166
SCANDISK as diagnostic, hard drives, 312
screwdrivers, 2
SCSI CD-ROMs, 22
SCSI hard drives, 17–20, 289–317
A, B, and P wire cabling, 305
Adaptec host adapters for SCSI drives, 316–317
adapters (*see* host adapters below)
Advanced SCSI Programmers Interface (ASPI), 308–309, 308
arbitration, 303–304
BIOS connection, 308, 312
boot process, 312
bootable SCSI ID device, 293
bus mastering, 303–305, 310
cables for SCSI hard drives, 290–291, 302–303, 305–307, **305–307**
cache, RAID 6, 315
Centronics connectors, 306, **307**
chains, 290–291, **292**
CMOS configuration, 312–313
Common Command Set (CCS), 299
compatibility of flavors, 310
compatibility with IDE and other standards, 310–311
connections to motherboard, 311
connectors, 305–307, **305–307,** 311
cost/benefit analysis, 313–314
DEFRAG as diagnostic, 312
device drivers, 313
differential-ended (SCSI-2) devices, 300–301
disk cache vs. bus mastering, 304–305
DMA, 312–313
D-type connectors, 306, **307**

EIDE compatibility, 310–311, 314–315
Error Correction Code (ECC) DRAM, 315
expansion bus, 309–310
fast SCSI, 299–301
fiber channel cabling, 302
File Allocation Tables (FAT), 312
Firewire cabling, 302
flavors of SCSI, 289, 297–303, 310
Forced Perfect Termination (FPT), 317
fragmentation, 312
hard drive, 303
host adapters, 290–291, 290, 303, 309–310, 316–317
hot swapping, 302
how it works, 289–290
I/O addresses, 312–313
IDentifiers (IDs) for SCSI devices on chain, 292–294, **293**
interrupts (IRQ), 312–313
jumper setting, 293, **293**
length limits for SCSI cables, 306
lock ups, 313
Logical Unit Numbers (LUNs), 294
Low-Voltage Differential SCSI (LVD), 301
memory problems, 312, 313
mirroring, disk mirroring, 315
partitions, 312
power supplies, 311
Programming Input/Output (PIO) modes, 315
proprietary SCSI, 298
RAID, 315
ROM chip disabling, ASPI issues, 309
SASI interface, 297–298
SCANDISK as diagnostic, 312
SCSI-1, 289, 298–299, **298**
SCSI-2, 289–290, 299–301
SCSI-3, 301–303
serial storage architecture (SSA), 302–303
single-ended (SCSI-1) devices, 300
striping, 315
tape drive, 303
termination, 294–297, **295, 296, 297,** 317
troubleshooting/repair, 311–313
ultra SCSI, 289, 301–303
ultra wide SCSI, 301–303
wide SCSI, 289, 299–301
ZIP drives, 294, **294**
SCSI-1, 289, 298–299, **298**
SCSI-2, 289–290, 299–301
SCSI-3, 301–303
sector translation, hard drives, 273–276
sectors, hard drives, 255, **255,** 256, 264, 273–276, **274,** 282
serial (COM) ports, 31–33
beep error codes, 188
COM port, 219–226
connectors, 32
dongles, 33, **34**
I/O address assignment, 215, 219–226
interrupt (IRQ) assignment, 218, 219–226
modems, 34–35, **35**
numeric error codes, 190
physical (serial) vs. I/O (COM) ports, 221–226, **222**
serial data, 32
Serial Storage Architecture (SSA), SCSI, 302–303
Setup program to configure CMOS, 171–174
shadow masks, video cards, adapters, monitors, 324, **325,** 334
shock hazard
laser printers, 360
video cards, adapters, monitors, 319–320, 335
Shugart Associates System Interface (SASI), 297–298
shunt in jumper, 39
Single Edge Cartridge (SEC) type CPUs, 2
Single Inline Memory Module (SIMM), **5, 6,** 138–143, **138–143**, 148–150, **149, 150,** 158–159, **159, 160**
Single Inline Pin Package (SIPP), 137–138, **137**
single-ended (SCSI-1) device, 300
slave drives, hard drives, 260, 263, 280, **281**
sleep or doze mode, portable PCs, 404
Slot 1 connection, SEC cartridges, CPUs, 107
smart batteries, 397
SMARTDRV, disk cache vs. bus mastering, 304–305

SO type DIMMs, **5, 6,** 151, **151**
Socket 8 (online L2 cache), 103, **104**
socket service, PC Cards, 401
soft power, 197
soldered components on motherboard, 9, **9**
soundcards, 28, **28, 29,** 32, 163, 169
  CD-ROM connection, 22, 28, **29**
  line in/line out connector, 28
  microphone connector, 28
  mini-audio connectors, 28
  speaker connector, 28
speaker, soundcard connection, 28
split voltage CPUs, 106
splitters for power supplies, 119, **119**
ST506/412 hard drives & interfaces, 284–286, **285, 286**
Staggered Pin Grid Array (SPGA) CPUs, 100
standalone drives, hard drives, 261
standby mode, portable PCs, 404
standouts on motherboard, 199–200
static charge eliminator, laser printers, 356
Static RAM (SRAM), 79
step-down transformer action, in power supplies, 112
stepper motor, hard drives, 251–252
sticks of memory, 142–143
storage devices (floppy/hard drives) vs. memory, 59
striping, hard drives, 315
sub-mini connectors, 118–119, **118, 119**
Super Twist Nematic (STN) in LCD displays, 390
Super VGA (SVGA), video cards, adapters, monitors, 343
suspend mode, portable PCs, 404
swapfiles, 69
sweep, video cards, adapters, monitors, 323, 328
switches (*see* jumpers and switches)
SX and DX Intel processors, 71
Synchronous DRAM (SDRAM), 155–156
Synchronous Graphics RAM (SGRAM), 346
System BIOS ROM chip (*see* BIOS)
system board, laser printers, 361
system bus, 205
system crystal & clock speed, 54, **55,** 83, 204–205
system disk, 193
System Management Mode (SMM)
  CPUs, 71, 74–75
  portable PCs, 403–404
SYSTEM.INI, 182–183

tape drive, 169, 303
telephone lines
  modems, 34–35, **35**
  RJ type connectors, 26, **26**
terminating resistor, ST506 drives, 286
termination
  Forced Perfect Termination (FPT), 317
  hard drives, 317
  SCSI, 294–297, **295, 296, 297**
timer
  beep error codes, 187
  I/O address assignment, 214
  interrupt (IRQ) assignment, 218
timing bits, hard drives, 251
toner, laser printers, 356
tools for computer work, 2
traces or wires linking motherboard components, 9, **10**
tracks, hard drives, 254, **254,** 255, 256, 264
transitional motherboards, 237
transparencies in laser printers, 359
triads of color, 325, **326**
Troubleshooter, Forefront, memory diagnostic, 162
true parity SIMMs, 150
TTL logic circuits, CPUs, 57
TTL parity SIMMs, 150
tuning gears, laser printers, 360
typematic setting, keyboard, 166–167
types of hard drives, 264, 265–266

ultra SCSI, 289, 301–303
ultra wide SCSI, 301–303
underclocking a CPU, 56
upgrades
  adding memory, 133–135, **134**
  CPU upgrades, 86, 89–90
user type of hard drive, 266

Vertical Refresh Rate (VRR), video cards, adapters, monitors, 322–323, **323,** 327
VESA specification, video cards, adapters, monitors, 341

VESA VL-bus, 233–236, **234, 235**
video cards (adapters) & monitors, 32, 29, **29,** 163, 319–347, **320**
  active vs. passive matrix LCDs, 398–399, **399**
  adjusting image, 332–334
  Advanced Graphics Port (AGP), 344–345
  Advanced Power Management (APM), 406–407, **406, 407**
  aspect ratio, 332
  bandwidth in MHz, 329
  beep error codes, 186, 188, 189
  brightness, 334, 336, 337
  calibration images, 332
  Cathode Ray Tube (CRT), 321–322, **321**
  chirping sounds, 337
  cleaning the monitor, 334, 337
  color adapters, 340–341
  color depth, 319, 343–346
  Color Graphics Adapter (CGA), 342
  color problems, 336, 337, 346–347
  connections, 337
  contrast, 334
  convergence, 319, 332–333, **333,** 335
  degaussing button, 334, 337
  Display Power Management Signaling (DPMS), 330
  disposing of old monitors, 337
  dot pitch, 319, 327–328, **328**
  electron guns, 321, 324
  energy saving features, 319, 330–331
  Enhanced Graphics Adapter (EGA), 342
  external controls/adjustments, 334
  flyback transformer, 336, **336**
  focus, 334, 335, 336
  fuzzy images, 336
  gain, 335
  gas plasma display, 389–390, **390**
  ghosting, 336
  Graphical Use Interface (GUI), 233–234
  hissing or sparking, 336
  Horizontal Refresh Rate (HRR), 322, **323,** 327
  I/O address assignment, 215
  interlace, 319, 328, 329
  internal controls/adjustments, 334
  keystone adjustment, 333
  Liquid Crystal Display (LCD), 389, 398–399
  memory requirements, 343–346
  modes of operation, 341
  Monochrome Display Adapter (MDA), 340, 341
  multi-synch, 319, 323
  palettes of color, 340–341
  persistence of vision, 322
  phosphor coatings, 321, 324, **324,** 326
  pincushion, 333
  pixels, 319, 324–325, 327
  power supplies, 337
  Professional Graphics Adapter (PGA), 342
  raster lines, 322, **322**
  refresh, 319, 322–323, **323,** 327, 344
  resolution, 319, 324–327, 343–346
  screen decay problem, 347
  shadow masks, 324, **325,** 334
  shock hazards, 319–320, 335
  single line across screen, 337
  single white dot on screen, 337
  streaky images, 336
  Super Twist Nematic (STN) in LCD displays, 390
  Super VGA (SVGA), 343
  sweep, 323, 328
  Synchronous Graphics RAM (SGRAM), 346
  triads of color, 325, **326**
  troubleshooting, 334–337, 346–347
  Vertical Refresh Rate (VRR), 327, 322–323, **323**
  VESA specification, 330, 341
  video cards, 338–343
  Video Graphics Array (VGA), 342
  video RAM, 338–340, 343–346, **347**
  Windows RAM (WRAM), 346
  yoke, 321
Video Graphics Array (VGA), 342
video RAM, 338–340, 343–346, **347**
  Synchronous Graphics RAM (SGRAM), 346
  Windows RAM (WRAM), 346
virtual 8086 CPU mode operation, 69, 71, 75
virtual memory, 69, 71, 75

virtual registers, 69
voice coil motor, hard drives, 252
volatile RAM, 78
Volt Ohm meter (VOM), 122
voltage of CPU/motherboard, 72–74, 93–95, 106
Voltage Regulator Module (VRM), 95, **95**
voltage regulators, **73,** 94–95, **95**
voltage testing, power supplies, 112, 120, **121,** 122

wait states, 78, **78**
wattage, power supplies, 120
wide SCSI, 289, 299–301
width of memory, 129–131, **130**
Winchester hard drives, 284–286, **285, 286**
Windows 95/98
  Add New Hardware Wizard, 183–184, **184**
  Device Manager, 183–184, **184**
  Registry, Registry Editor (REGDIT), 183–184
Windows RAM (WRAM), 346
wings on connectors, 25
wires of address bus, 62–64, **64**
words of memory, 59
wrenches, 2
write precompensation, hard drives, 255, 264
write-back vs. write-through cache, 80–81, **81**

XT bus, 207

yoke, video cards, adapters, monitors, 321

Zero Insertion Force (ZIF) sockets, 86, **87, 88**
ZIP drives, 294, **294,** 316
  termination, 295, **296**

About the Authors

Mike Meyers is the President of Total Seminars and the head keeper of the Total Seminars creative group. He is also the ultimate computer nerd. Mike is the author of McGraw Hill's *A+ Certification Exam Guide*.

Scott Jernigan wields a mighty red pen as Chief Technical Editor for Total Seminars. With an M.A. in Medieval History, Scott feels as much at home in the musty archives of London as he does in the warm CRT glow at Total Seminars' Houston HQ. After fleeing from a purely academic life, Scott has spent the last couple of years teaching computer hardware seminars around the United States, including stints at the FBI Academy and the United Nations, among others.

Total Seminars is a unique group of teachers, authors, and presenters, who all share one common trait: we love computers. *Total* has many venues that enable us to display that love of computers, including seminars, videos, CD-ROMs, and books, such as the one you are reading right now. We have trained thousands of people from every level including individuals as well as corporate, federal, state, and local government employees.